**Boundaries
of Analysis**

Photography by A.W. Koster

We would like to share with you the response of David Socolow, age 6, when it was explained to him that in the Tocks Island Dam controversy, those who wanted a dam wanted to control the river, and those who wanted no dam wanted the shad to remain able to swim upstream past the dam to spawn:

I think it would be better if two very very strong dad and mom shad were the dam. Then they could make babies when they wanted to and call another two to take their place while they're out. So that the people who don't care about the shad can have their control of the water, and the ones who do care about the shad can have the shad have babies.

Boundaries of Analysis

An Inquiry into the Tocks Island Dam Controversy

Edited by

Harold A. Feiveson
Frank W. Sinden
Robert H. Socolow
Center for Environmental Studies
Princeton University

Published for the American Academy of Arts and Sciences

Ballinger Publishing Company ● Cambridge, Massachusetts
A Subsidiary of J.B. Lippincott Company

Published for the American Academy of Arts and Sciences
a companion volume to *Boundaries of Analysis.*
Tribe, L. H., Schelling, C. S., Voss, J., eds.
*When Values Conflict: Essays on Environmental
Analysis, Discourse, and Decision.*

 This book is printed on recycled paper.

International Standard Book Number: 0-88410-430-3

Library of Congress Catalog Card Number: 76-3773

Printed in the United States of America

Library of Congress Cataloging in Publication Data

Main entry under title:

Boundaries of analysis.

The result of symposia organized by the American Academy of Arts and Sci-
ences. Its companion volume of essays is titled: When values conflict.
 Bibliography: p.
 Includes index.
 1. Water resources development—Environmental aspects—Delaware River
watershed—Addresses, essays, lectures. I. Feiveson, Harold A. II. Sinden,
Frank W. III. Socolow, Robert H. IV. Title: Tocks Island Dam controversy.
TC425.D3B68   333.9'102'0974825   76-3773
ISBN 0-88410-430-3

"This book was prepared with the support of National Science Foundation
Grant No. ESR 72-03540. However, any opinions, findings, conclusions or
recommendations expressed herein are those of the authors and do not necessarily reflect the views of NSF."

Contents

List of Tables

List of Figures

Acknowledgments

This volume of essays emerges from a brew concocted by Murray Gell-Mann more than four years ago, when he asked insistently, "What shall be the style of modern analytic work on environmental problems?" and proposed that theoreticians and practitioners of problem solving be brought together to address that question. John Voss and Corinne Schelling at the American Academy of Arts and Sciences, principal investigators of the research contract from the National Science Foundation, found creative ways of engaging disparate intellects in this activity. The American Academy hosted two symposia at which extraordinarily constructive discussion of the drafts of these essays took place. Raymond Bauer, Harvey Brooks, Robert Dorfman, Charles Frankel, Leo Marx, Harry Rowen, Irene Taviss Thomson, and Laurence Tribe made especially useful contributions to our efforts on these and related occasions.

Lawrence Tombaugh, the monitor of our program at the National Science Foundation, deserves our special thanks for his tact and his patience.

Many of the actors in the Tocks Island drama have taken the time to discuss their perceptions with us and to read our drafts. We especially appreciate the time lavished on our activity by John Burns, Gordon Dilley, Mina Haefele, Thomas O'Neill, Richard Sullivan, Tom Taber, Richard Tortoriello, and Brinton Whitall.

On numerous occasions we turned to our colleagues for advice. In particular, Bruce Ackerman, William Alonso, Smith Freeman, William Hall, George Pinder, Leonard Rodberg, Gary Simon, and Thomas Scanlon made numerous helpful suggestions in the course of a series of informal meetings and conversations over the past two years here at Princeton. Our research assistants, Lynn Anderson, Felicity Brock, Benjamin Eng, John Heintz, Joseph Serota, and Douglas Zaeh, were invaluable for their tenacity and sensitivity. Irvin Glassman and George Reynolds created a frame of reference at the Center for Environmental Studies within which our program could prosper, and Jean Wiggs, with Barbara Hawk and Kathy Shahay, presided skillfully and with remarkable good spirit over a long procession of drafts.

Foreword

This book has derived from a two-year research project sponsored by the National Science Foundation, "Research Needs Concerning the Incorporation of Human Values into Environmental Decision Making." The project was organized jointly by the American Academy of Arts and Sciences and by the Center for Environmental Studies at Princeton University through a subcontract from the American Academy.

Two sets of essays have emerged from the research project, one of which is the present collection. The Table of Contents of the companion set of essays, edited by Laurence Tribe, Corinne S. Schelling and John Voss is set forth here.

When Values Conflict: Essays on Environmental Analysis, Discourse, and Decision

CONTENTS

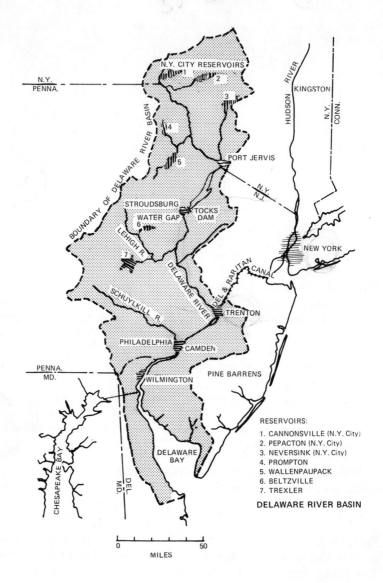

N.Y. CITY RESERVOIRS

N.Y.
PENNA.

1
2
3

HUDSON RIVER

KINGSTON

N.Y.
CONN.

BOUNDARY OF DELAWARE RIVER BASIN

4

5

PORT JERVIS

N.Y.
N.J.

STROUDSBURG
WATER GAP
TOCKS DAM

6

LEHIGH R.

7

NEW YORK

DEL. & RARITAN CANAL

SCHUYLKILL R.

DELAWARE RIVER

DEL. & RARITAN CANAL

TRENTON

PHILADELPHIA
CAMDEN

PENNA.
MD.

WILMINGTON

PINE BARRENS

CHESAPEAKE BAY

DELAWARE BAY

DEL.
MD.

RESERVOIRS:

1. CANNONSVILLE (N.Y. City)
2. PEPACTON (N.Y. City)
3. NEVERSINK (N.Y. City)
4. PROMPTON
5. WALLENPAUPACK
6. BELTZVILLE
7. TREXLER

DELAWARE RIVER BASIN

0   50
MILES

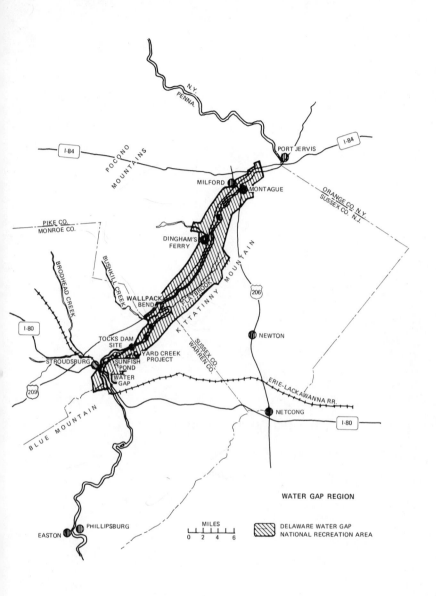

N.Y.
PENNA.

I-84

PORT JERVIS

I-84

POCONO

MOUNTAINS

MILFORD

MONTAGUE

ORANGE CO. N.Y.
SUSSEX CO. N.J.

PIKE CO.
MONROE CO.

DINGHAM'S
FERRY

BUSHKILL CREEK

BRODHEAD CREEK

WALLPACK
BEND

FLATBROOK

206

K I T T A T I N N Y   M O U N T A I N

I-80

NEWTON

TOCKS DAM
SITE

YARD CREEK
PROJECT

SUSSEX CO.
WARREN CO.

STROUDSBURG

SUNFISH
POND

WATER
GAP

ERIE-LACKAWANNA RR.

209

BLUE   MOUNTAIN

NETCONG

I-80

WATER GAP REGION

MILES
0 2 4 6

DELAWARE WATER GAP
NATIONAL RECREATION AREA

EASTON

PHILLIPSBURG

**Boundaries
of Analysis**

Introduction

This is a study of what happens to technical analyses in the real world of politics. The portion of the real world we have chosen for our governing illustration is the decade-old controversy over whether to construct a dam on the Delaware River at Tocks Island, five miles north of the Delaware Water Gap. This controversy is imbedded in a tangle of interconnected problems involving floods and droughts, energy, growth, congestion, recreation, and the uprooting of people and communities. Almost all the pieces of this tangle have been staked out and studied in some fashion or other. They have been measured and modeled by economists, scientists, and planners, by exuberant technologists, committed bureaucrats, and skeptical environmentalists; and the result of all this has been a weighty legacy of technical and economic analyses, along with a decade of political stalemate regarding the fate of the dam.

The Tocks Island Dam controversy affords us an opportunity not only to measure the influence of technical studies on the political process, but also, because of the long stalemate, to observe this influence across the environmental watershed of the past several years. The Tocks Island Dam project was planned and developed in the early 1960s with scarcely a murmur of dissent. Indeed, early on, the project was considered a model of water resource planning. It was one component of the path-breaking plan of the U.S. Army Corps of Engineers for the Delaware Basin, the first comprehensive survey of a river basin undertaken under the new water resource planning guidelines developed within the federal government during the 1950s; and it was a project ardently adopted by the newly formed Delaware River Basin Commission, the first federal-state river basin authority of its type ever established in the United States. The project design was not completed, however, until 1970, by which time there was in progress a subtle but striking revolution in the ways many Americans thought about their environment and about economic growth. The debate over the dam since that time has been largely a clash between the two sensibilities that lie on either side of that revolution.

The Tocks controversy has spanned still another, even more subtle, watershed, this one involving objective, systematic analysis. Both policy makers and analysts just a decade ago had high hopes that comprehensive planning, benefit-cost analysis, computer techniques, and other elements of systems analysis would contribute increasingly to the solution of social problems. These hopes by now have largely withered under the several disillusionments of the 1960s. Too often the search for objective, quantitative techniques and measures produced distortions in ways only dimly perceived by the analysts. The values that both the policy makers and the analysts most cared about were either concealed or altogether neglected in the ostensible search for objectivity. Analysts, hobbled by narrow conceptions of their disciplines and of the prerogatives of the institutions which employ them, operate in a world befogged by dogma.

These themes are indeed observable in the Tocks controversy. The technical and economic analyses did, to a substantial degree, mask the value conflicts at stake; they concealed the real political and human issues of who would win and who would lose were the Tocks Island Dam project undertaken; and they were infected by rigid categories of thought and divisions of bureaucratic responsibility. The essays in this volume are only in part about these shortcomings. Their more ambitious objective is to deal freshly with the environmental issues at stake in the Tocks Island controversy, especially by cutting across the old restrictive boundaries. Viewed as a whole, the essays try to ally systematic analysis with an explicit concern for the human values most strongly held by the protagonists of all persuasions in the struggle over the dam.

Together the essays here tell a reasonably complete and, we hope, coherent story of the Tocks Island controversy. The essays have been coordinated to minimize repetitiveness, but we have tried not to suppress their distinctive spirit and style. Although the authors have spent countless argumentative hours together, and have read and re-read each other's drafts, the reader will quickly discern the individual personalities of the authors and their noncongruent perceptions of the benefits and costs of the Tocks project. Despite these differences, however, our views as outsiders to the controversy are not nearly as sharply polarized as are those of the protagonists.

The Tocks Island controversy has been going on all around us. Our work place is less than twelve miles from Trenton (the site of the New Jersey government and the headquarters of the Delaware River Basin Commission) and half way between the New York Division and Philadelphia District offices of the U. S. Army Corps of Engineers. During the three years in which this book has been in the making, there has been time and occasion to get to know a number of the officials in these agencies rather well. They and many of the leading local environmentalists have read drafts of many of the chapters of this book, and the reader will find in several of the final versions here that our interactions with these men and women have become part of the narrative.

We must report how relatively little the interactions have altered the view of the dam any of the principals has held . . . or any of us has held. Those most hostile to the dam three years ago remain hostile; those most in tune to traditional arguments in favor of dam building remain skeptical that the current fashion for nonstructural alternatives is an adequate response to human frailty. To the extent that we had hoped that, by teaching the tools of the professionals to the nonprofessionals, our book would sharpen the issues and focus the discussion, we have occasionally been rewarded. To the extent that we had imagined that analyses could persuade, we have been humbled.

The ten essays are divided into five major groups. In Part One, "Failures of Discourse," by Robert Socolow, several of the major themes of the overall study are introduced through a portrayal of the limitations of the conceptual categories within which policy problems are structured and analyzed. This essay especially stresses the psychological and institutional barriers to more rational and direct communication that have marked the Tocks controversy and environmental discourse more generally.

Part Two tells the political and analytic history of the Tocks Island Dam project. The first essay in this section, "Historical Currents," by Michael Reich, provides a panoramic narrative history of the ancient and not so ancient attempts to control the Delaware River, from an antidam treaty between New Jersey and Pennsylvania in 1783, through two dramatic Supreme Court Cases in the 1930s and 1950s involving the allocation of Delaware River water, to the filing of the Tocks project's Environmental Impact Statement in 1971. The essay "Conflict and Irresolution" by Harold Feiveson brings into focus one main theme of our study: the impact of technical analysis on the political process. It does this through a detailed study of the Tocks Island Dam controversy over the past four years, during which time the conflict over the dam was at its fiercest and pitted embittered citizens against lordly Poobahs of Congress.

The essays in Part Three investigate the demands for water, flood control, and electric power in the Basin, and, in so doing, lay bare the work of the water resource professionals and the economists. The first essay of Part Three, "Benefits and Costs, Winners and Losers," by David Bradford and Harold Feiveson, provides a somewhat unconventional summary of the benefits and costs of the Tocks Island Dam project and of its beneficiaries and its victims. This essay also undertakes a critical examination of the ability of benefit-cost analysis to contend with real problems as complex as Tocks. Frank Sinden's essay, "The Water Cycle, Supply and Demand," makes clear that the comfortable categories of supply and demand typically used in analyses of water economics are in fact deeply and subtly misleading; and the essay attempts to set forth an alternative conceptualization of water supply. Using the new framework, the essay investigates alternative ways of guarding against severe droughts. The problem of too little water has its counterpart in the problem of too much water; Allan Krass's essay, "Floods and People" presents a tutorial on floods and the variety of structural and nonstructural measures one may adopt to combat them. The final essay of Part Three, "Electric Power on the Delaware," by Thomas Schrader and Robert Socolow illuminates some of the ways in which regulation of the consumptive use of water has influenced decisions about the siting of power plants; more broadly, it illustrates how the finiteness of a regional water supply can drive technology in new directions.

The two essays in Part Four address one of the most perplexing issues on the environmental agenda; the degree to which the science of ecology, especially in alliance with modern tools of computer-based mathematical modeling, can illuminate real environmental policy problems. Robert Cleary's "Mathematical Models" grapples with the perils and promises of the computer. While sharply critical of the ways in which mathematical models were wielded in the Tocks controversy, the essay is at essence optimistic. It argues that even complex ecological questions can be understood by intelligent and patient applications of computer technology and environmental science. The essay by Daniel Goodman, "Ecological Expertise," adopts a far more gloomy and skeptical stance, however. His essay warns that the foundations of ecology are weak and that they provide shaky support indeed for many of the most cherished hypotheses of environmental interest groups.

Part Five presents the final essay of the volume, "A New Park on the Delaware," by Frank Sinden. This essay is an attempt to integrate the conventionally disjoint activities of transportation and recreation planning. Its intent is to illustrate how analysis can cut into environmental problems in a novel manner.

It is a risk, in an undertaking like this one, to tell the reader more than he or she wants to know. The essays here give considerable detail about how the environmental policy process works and about such deceptively simple topics as water demand and supply, floods, droughts, benefit-cost analysis, mathematical modeling, recreation planning, and ecology. We have written for the reader who likes such detail; large blocks of several essays are tutorials, presuming no special background of the reader, taking little for granted. The more experienced reader, we dare hope, will not be bored by these tutorials; they are generally unconventional in their approach to subject matter which is ordinarily the property of in-groups.

We expect these essays to find their way into undergraduate and graduate courses at colleges and universities. In teaching an environmental seminar at Princeton for the past three years, two of us have been struck with how little detailed illustrative material is currently available. At the present stage of environmental studies, with its intrinsically interdisciplinary character, there is a clear need for detailed case studies that capture the richness of environmental decision making and document the contribution of economics and the scientific disciplines.

We believe this book will also interest audiences outside the universities—in particular, citizens on both sides of the environmental firing line. It has been our experience that environmental policy makers and activists of all persuasions welcome the chance to stand back from the fray for a few moments, to place their own work and their beliefs in a broader context. It is our hope that these essays will provide such an opportunity.

Princeton, April 1976

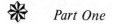 *Part One*

Failures of Discourse

Chapter 1

Failures of Discourse

Robert H. Socolow

1. ANALYSES ARE NOT ABOUT WHAT PEOPLE CARE ABOUT

Major environmental decisions have a way of getting stuck and staying stuck. The discussions about whether to under-take substantial transformations of natural areas—to bring about new power plants, dams, airports, pipelines, deep water ports—have several pathologies in common. A cluster of detailed technical analyses accompanies the formulation of the program and its initial rush onto the stage; the proponents of the project imply, and generally believe, that all one could reasonably have expected has been done, both to justify the program and to anticipate its pitfalls. As after a carefully planned transplant, the reaction of rejection is slow in coming but grows relentlessly. The analyses are shown to be incomplete, and new analyses starting from different premises are eventually produced by those who wish to stop the program. But, contrary to what one might naively expect, the existence of disparate analyses does not help appreciably to resolve the debate. Rarely are the antagonists proud of their analyses; more rarely still are they moved by the analyses of their opponents. The combatants on both

This essay also appears in the companion volume. *When Values Conflict: Essays on Environmental Analysis, Discourse, and Decision*, edited by Laurence H. Tribe, Corinne S. Schelling, and John Voss (Cambridge, Mass.: Ballinger, 1976). The occasional references here to the other essays in the two volumes do not begin to measure the size of the debt this essay owes to those I have joined in both volumes. I am particularly grateful to Laurence Tribe for deft and sensitive editing.

sides have been constrained by mandated rules of procedure as well as by the tactics of compromise. Understandably, the politicians in a position to determine the outcome conclude that their time is not well spent pondering the available analyses, even though they may commission still more of them.

The failure of technical studies to assist in the resolution of environmental controversies is part of a larger pattern of failures of discourse in problems that put major societal values at stake. Discussions of goals, of visions of the future, are enormously inhibited. Privately, goals will be talked about readily, as one discovers in even the most casual encounter with any of the participants. But the public debate is cloaked in a formality that excludes a large part of what people most care about.

Analyses are part of the formal debate. We should not be surprised to learn, therefore, that the disciplined analyses brought to bear on a current societal dispute hardly ever do justice to the values in conflict. Terribly little is asked of analysis, and analysts respond in a way that allows the potentialities of their disciplines to be undervalued. A recurrent theme in this and the companion volume is that disciplined analysis has enormous unused capability. My sense is that we need to look much more carefully at the reasons why this capability lies unused. There is a dynamic interaction between the demands made and the tools developed. It is not realistic to expect much refinement in tools to occur in the absence of a contemporaneous evolution in the rules of public discourse.

The land use debate I have most pondered, and the source of most of my generalizations, is the debate over whether to build a major rock-fill dam on the Delaware River at Tocks Island, thereby creating a 37-mile-long lake along the New Jersey-Pennsylvania border. The dam was proposed by the Corps of Engineers and was authorized by Congress in 1962. Although land has been acquired, and the National Park Service has arrived on the scene to administer the Delaware Water Gap National Recreation Area that is intended to surround the lake, construction has not yet begun. It may never begin. The likelihood of construction has diminished considerably during the period of our study (roughly, 1972 to 1975). However, there is a well known asymmetry: one can decide over and over not to build a dam; one only need decide *once* to begin construction, and there it is.

I happen to hope that the dam will not be built. Building the dam, it seems to me, would buttress an attitude of impudence toward our natural resources. Not building a dam, on the other hand, would stimulate the development of alternative technologies, intrinsically more respectful of nature, which are ever more urgently needed. Of all the arguments for and against the dam, this need to stimulate a reorientation of our technology is for me the single most compelling one. This essay, in part, seeks to imagine what a technology responsive to an environmental ethic would look like. The search for such a technology is one of the absent features of current analysis.

Others, who hope that the dam *will* be built, are persuaded by arguments with which current analysis is also unconcerned. There are some who sustain a vivid image of the havoc wrought by floods. They regard the rest of us as their wards, who need to be protected from our faulty memories. They are almost surely right in their assertion that if another flood were to strike the Delaware Valley during the remaining period of debate, those in favor of the dam would have a far easier time prevailing. They may be wrong, however, as to whether a program to limit flood damage ought to concentrate its construction on the river's main stem, instead of on its tributaries. I know of no serious analysis that captures the essence of this particular issue. Others in favor of the dam resonate to the argument that many poor people in the metropolitan areas not very distant from this project have needs deserving priority in federal programs; one of these needs—getting away—is better matched to lake recreation than to river recreation; the preferences of the environmentalists are those of people just a bit too comfortable with themselves and too self-centered.[a] This, too, is a position strongly held, politically salient, and not, to my knowledge, captured by a single piece of sustained analysis. One possible analysis along these lines would explore the institutional, economic, and social factors relevant to a comparison of recreation at Tocks Island Lake with recreation at improved urban facilities, including swimming pools.

There are a wide variety of reasons why those concerned with affecting the outcome of a major land use issue are not envisioning (or at least are not expressing) many of the concerns that in fact move them and many of the options that in fact are open to them. Given the fact that virtually all the participants are dissatisfied with the way discourse currently proceeds, it seems worthwhile to make a substantial effort to understand some of the underlying reasons for these failures of discourse and some of the possibilities for averting them.

[a]Robert Dorfman suggests, in his eloquent essay in the companion volume, that the argument that the dam will provide benefits to the least privileged members of society deserves special prominence in a heirarchy of arguments pro and con.

II. BLUNT TOOLS AND SKEWED DISCOURSE

A. Golden Rules

The decision about whether to build Tocks Island Dam is widely perceived to be a choice among alternative conceptions of the region's future and, at a deeper but still articulated level, among alternative conceptions of man's appropriate relationship to nature. The tools that might have assisted in clarifying what the possible futures entail include cost-benefit analysis, which has been designed to facilitate comparisons between programs offering differing streams of future costs and benefits. Working with these tools ought to lead to translations of dimly perceived preferences into relatively explicit strategies, and ought to reveal the incompatibility of some sets of aspirations and the compatibility of others.[b] Current practice, however, follows a series of golden rules—prescriptions and routines that the analyst perceives to be a means of simplifying the tangle of options (and of staying out of trouble), but that prevent the analyst from taking full advantage of the capabilities the tools provide.

The best conceivable use of the tools, to be sure, will leave serious problems unsolved. David Bradford and Harold Feiveson, in an essay on cost-benefit analysis in this volume, make the useful three-way distinction among "ideal," "best practicable," and "actual" cost-benefit analyses. The abuse of tools through overuse of golden rules creates a gulf between actual and best practicable analyses to which I return momentarily. But even best practicable cost-benefit analyses are going to have serious shortcomings, which discussions of ideal cost-benefit analysis have often underestimated. Discussions of the limitations of cost-benefit analysis nearly always emphasize uncertainties about the discount rate and contain caveats about the lack of sensitivity regarding who gets what. Only rarely do they call attention to the problem of drawing a boundary around the system being studied. As in idealized thermodynamics, the cost-benefit theory presupposes a system coupled with its surroundings in such a simple way that one can change the system without perceptibly affecting the surroundings. To do a sensible cost-benefit comparison of two alternative futures, one has to include in the "system" all the activities with which are associated large differences depending on which future is being considered.

If one is to compare a future with the Tocks Island Dam to one without it, even the dollar costs are such that one must include the incremental sewage treatment facilities required to coexist with a

---

[b]See Henry Rowen's essay in the companion volume for a particularly strong statement of the usefulness of analyses as means of discovery.

lake instead of a river, and the extra roads needed to bring the visitors to the recreation area, if lake-based recreation will indeed attract more visitors than river-based recreation. Both these costs, it turns out, are comparable to the cost of building the dam itself (several hundred million dollars). One may also have to include the uncompensated costs endured by the roughly 20,000 residents in the valley whom the reservoir project is displacing. But then what about including, on the other side of the balance sheet, the increases in property values expected if the dam is built? Does the series of new entries terminate, in the sense that one is finally considering effects (such as gross interregional migration?) that, even though large, are still effectively unchanged by the existence or nonexistence of the project? No analysis has convinced me that the series does terminate or converge in this sense.

Golden rules have been developed that shelter the practitioner of cost-benefit analysis from this uncertainty about boundaries. The analysis becomes stylized, like the folk art of an isolated village. Those costs and benefits which it is permissible to include in the analysis become codified, as do many of the procedures for evaluating their dollar magnitudes. The warping effect on discourse is substantial. It is hard not to introduce the project to a newcomer with: "The project has four intended benefits" (water supply, flood control, recreation, and electric power, in this instance).

The formal rules also carry weight in the detailed planning of a project. The Corps of Engineers continues to maintain that the "highest and best" use of the lake requires the provision of recreation facilities on its shores for 9.4 million visitors (actually, visitor-days) per year, in spite of the statement by two successive governors of New Jersey that they will approve the project only if the recreation facilities are scaled down to 40 percent of that figure. The Corps' persistence must be strongly affected by the way the analyses come out when the formal conventions are followed, for recreation comes to almost half the total annual benefits when the higher figure is used. Others in this volume comment on the extraordinary reduction in the problem's structure that occurs when the value of recreation is calculated by multiplying a fixed dollar value per visitor-day ($1.35) with a number of visitor-days per year, irrespective of who the visitors are, or how crowded the facilities are, or whether the same visitor spends several days or several visitors spend one day.[c] Here I wish to emphasize that these oddly formal rules do have real consequences—consequences such as extra roads being built

---

[c]The dollar values of alternative forms of recreation *are* distinguished; $1.35 is a weighted average of the forms of recreation Tocks will provide. See p. 136.

through open country to provide the access needed to keep the park populated.

The rules of procedure that govern the planning process have yet further impact in restricting the search for alternatives. One of the rules, for example, is that, at a given site, either a multipurpose project or a single-purpose project is to be undertaken—and that, once this choice is made, *multipurpose projects are not to be compared with packages of single-purpose projects addressing the same needs.* Invoking this golden rule, the principal government agencies (the Corps of Engineers and the Delaware River Basin Commission) can dismiss a proposal without analysis if it addresses just one of the four intended benefits—even if another, companion proposal addresses the other three. Environmental critics of the Tocks Island Dam have advocated the use of "high-flow skimming" to provide increments to water supply equivalent to those which the dam would produce. If one enlarged an existing reservoir (Round Valley) and perhaps built an additional small reservoir in a subsidiary valley, filling the reservoirs with Delaware water in high-flow months and emptying them in low-flow months, offstream storage would be achieved and the main stem of the Delaware would remain unblocked.[d] This suggestion, to be sure, does nothing about main stem flood control, but flood plain zoning does. The package needs to be placed alongside the Tocks project. Yet high-flow skimming has been dismissed with a single comment: "This is not a multipurpose project."[e]

When the routine procedures of a government agency are consistent with the perfunctory rejection of ideas emerging from outside its bureaucracy, "noise" is thereby built into the discourse between that agency and its critics. The environmentalist critics have pushed the idea of high-flow skimming harder (and with more success, per-

---

[d]The proposal was initially suggested by Smith Freeman, a scientist acting as an interested bystander. It was explored in greater detail in a study commissioned by the Environmental Defense Fund, *New Jersey Water Supply: Alternatives to Tocks Island Reservoir* (M. Disko Associates, W. Orange, N.J., October 1973).

[e]The rule operates in another instance that stacks the deck against packages of single-purpose projects. The water supply benefit is quantified as the dollar cost of the least expensive alternative way of providing an equivalent amount of water, and the cost of building this alternative is calculated using a higher discount rate than the discount rate for the multipurpose project. The grounds for using two different discount rates are that the Corps may not build the single purpose project it is evaluating, and any other builder would have to borrow money at a higher rate of interest. (The rates used are 3 1/8% for Corps projects and 4 1/2% for alternative projects.)

haps, than the idea deserves), because of the inability of the government agencies involved to look at it squarely.

B. Golden Numbers

Environmental discourse likewise manifests a powerful dependence on numbers. A number that may once have been an effusion of a tentative model evolves into an immutable constraint. Apparently, the need to have precision in the rules of the game is so desperate that administrators seize on numbers (in fact, get legislators to write them into laws) and then carefully forget where they came from. Then *no one* wants to reopen an argument that hinges on one of these golden numbers.

In the Tocks case, one such golden number is 3,000 cubic feet per second (cfs), the target minimum flow for the Delaware as it passes Trenton, New Jersey. During the drought years from 1963 to 1965, the flow at Trenton fell below that value for months. (The minimum recorded daily low flow was 1,240 cfs in July 1965). This happened largely because New York did not live up to an agreement with New Jersey and Pennsylvania, negotiated by a river master appointed by the Supreme Court,[f] to release water from its own reservoirs on the Delaware tributaries so as to sustain a flow of 1,525 cfs (another golden number) at Montague, New Jersey, a little over 100 miles upstream from Trenton. (Not surprisingly, nearby New York City—half of whose water comes from these reservoirs—had grounds to fear a water shortage in the same months.) The salt concentration in the river near Philadelphia increased as a result of this low flow. The Public Health Service standard for drinking water is 250 parts chloride per million parts of water (still another golden number). During the autumn of 1964, the line in the river where this concentration is found crept to within ten miles of the place (called the Torresdale intake) where Philadelphia takes its water supply out of the Delaware.[g]

Somewhere (no one appears to remember the details) it was de-

---

[f]Amended Decree of the Supreme Court of the United States Re Delaware River Diversion, 347 U.S. 995 (1954). The 1960s drought exceeded the drought of record (in the 1930s) on the basis of which the original agreements had been quantified.

[g]The Torresdale intake is at mile 110.53, and the mean daily 250 parts per million chloride line was found at approximately mile 101 on Nov. 20, 1964, according to Plate III-1 of *Water Resources Study for Power Systems: Delaware River Basin* (consultants' report prepared by Tippetts-Abbett-McCarthy-Stratton, March 1972). The salinity level falls rapidly with distance in that range of concentrations; it was only 40 ppm at Torresdale on that same (worst) day. The same chloride line at high water slack may have been a mile closer.

cided that "3,000 cfs at Trenton" would give everyone a proper margin of safety. And proposed reservoirs upstream from Trenton are now judged in significant part by their ability to provide enough "low-flow augmentation" to assure that 3,000 cfs at Trenton could be achieved if there were another drought like 1963–65. Without the Tocks Island Dam, under a contemporary rerun of the historic drought (but assuming that New York maintains its obligations and that reservoirs built since the drought are utilized), flows at Trenton that stay above 2,700 cfs could be achieved. But the missing 300 cfs, or 10 percent, causes genuine alarm. Even *one* percent values have policy content. Electric utilities are told to provide offstream storage of cooling water for their planned riverfront power plants, on the basis that the associated evaporative losses from cooling (about 30 cfs for a typical 1,000 megawatt electric generating plant with a cooling tower) threaten the 3,000 cfs guideline. A few government officials and utility executives wonder aloud where the "3,000 cfs" number came from, and what they are hoping for is the instatement of some lower number that experts will say is safe for Philadelphia (and for the wells of Camden, New Jersey, across the river).

But to hallow *any* minimum flow is to skew the discourse. Whenever a ground rule of discussion is that some standard or guideline is to be accepted as an on-off number, above which there is "safety" and below which there is "peril," two vital kinds of discourse become illegitimate: discussions of acceptable damage, and discussions of damage limitation.

C. Acceptable Damage

The apparent thrust of engineering is to protect man and his works from nature's assaults. Bridges are to survive the highest winds, buildings are to stay warm on the coldest days. Dams, especially, are perceived as symbols of security, as protectors from both floods and droughts. "When water is stored behind a dam, it is there when you need it, like money in the bank," an old-timer told me. A dam's aura of invincibility derives, no doubt, from its sheer bulk, its monumentality. Yet the image is a most incomplete one, for the reservoir, which comes along with every dam, is the exemplar of compromise. How high should the reservoir be filled? Too high and a surprise flood will not be contained, too low and the reserve supply will be absent in a drought. From which of the multiple outlets, at varying heights, should water be withdrawn in late summer (when the reservoir is thermally stratified and the deep, cold water is laden with decaying organic matter)? One answer emerges if the goal is to "enhance" the fish life downstream, another if the goal is to remove nutrients that contribute to the eutrophication of the lake; the two goals are unlikely to be perfectly compatible. The hallmark of engineering is the trade-off and the artful compromise.

But people prefer appearance to reality. There is rarely any clamor to make trade-offs explicit; it is enough for many that the compromises reached reflect professional judgment. Public discourse is thus dominated by solutions offered as risk free. Among his colleagues, an administrator for the Federal Aviation Administration responsible for equipping private airports with traffic control equipment can admit to having a target figure in his head for "acceptable annual fatalities from general aviations operations." And military officers get used to thinking in terms of acceptable losses of troops and materiel. But neither the mayor whose town abuts the airport nor the President preparing the battle plan can use such language with his constituency. The larger the issue of public accountability (as opposed to professional accountability alone) looms in an official's mind, the less willing he becomes even to formulate a problem in terms of acceptable risk. These·reflexes persist even when no lives are at stake: thus the desire to find a safe minimum flow so as not to think about tolerable levels of discomfort and dislocation.

Yet the usefulness of phrasing problems in terms of acceptable risk is probably nowhere so obvious as in problems that involve fitting man's activities into a highly variable natural background. This has been recognized explicitly in some of the air pollution legislation, where standards are typically written in the form: the concentration of pollutant X shall not exceed C_O more than N times each year. The most compelling reason for drawing up probabilistic standards of this sort is to recognize and bend with the variability of atmospheric phenomena; atmospheric inversions, for example, will occur occasionally, with little notice, and will produce a buildup of pollution levels. It may be unreasonable to have so much pollution control equipment in place that on the occasion of the worst inversion on record, the pollution concentration C_O is not exceeded. Put another way, it may be possible to win community acceptance of a C_O that is lower as long as an occasional escape is permitted. Mathematically, having C_O and N to play with instead of just C_O (with N set equal to zero) gives the legislator and the community more options in terms of environmental planning.

The regulation of water use seems not to have manifested the same subtlety of design. Pollution targets are almost invariably set at specific values, rarely even adjusted for the time of the year.[h] Minimum

[h]For a detailed discussion of the remarkable oversimplification of the structure of the pollution problem in the planning for the cleanup of the Delaware estuary, see Bruce Ackerman, Susan Rose Ackerman, James W. Sawyer, Jr., and Dale W. Henderson, *The Uncertain Search for Environmental Quality* (New York: Free Press, 1974).

river flows, as specified in rules and procedures without built-in escapes, determine the operation of reservoirs. New reservoirs are judged primarily in terms of their "safe yield." All these simplifications channel the imagination in similar ways. The safe yield of a reservoir is that rate of extraction of water from the reservoir which, under a recurrence of the most severe drought of record, could be sustained continuously. Usually the reservoir, at the extremum of the drought, lies nearly empty.[i] Attention is thus diverted from any consideration of riding with the punch, organizing one's affairs differently when the drought arrives, and leaving the reservoir with most of its water in it.[j]

From the standpoint of public health, there would seem to be no explanation for this distinction between air and water standards. The adverse health effects of air and water pollution are structurally similar; both involve no clear-cut level at which acute reactions ensue, no physiological warning that levels have become toxic, enormous variability among individuals (including certain groups that are especially susceptible), and uncertain synergisms. River flow is an even better example of stochastic (random) variability in nature than are the movements of cold and warm fronts of air. It is perplexing that environmental design reflecting this variability has not arisen. Perhaps the older traditions of water law and the concomitant self-images of the "water professionals" are historically inhibiting factors.

The water professionals make continual use of the stochastic concept of the N-year storm, or flood, or drought—one whose severity should be exceeded, on the average, just once in N years. The concept is most often used in situations where N is large (50 or 100 or more) and a decision is to be made about how high to build a levee or how strong to make a mooring buoy. The concept unfortunately happens to be on least secure scientific footing when N is large, because of the shortness and uncertainty of the available hydrological record and the significance of unaccountable changes in topography.[k] The concept is rarely used when N is small, say 10. It would be worth searching for a way of activating an interest in

[i] If a reservoir is constrained by rules of operation to retain some minimum water level, this is incorporated into the calculation of its yield.

[j] The dissonance between the recreation and water supply objectives of the Tocks reservoir has figured prominently in its political history. In those years when "drawdown" of the reservoir would be necessary, mudflats would be exposed at its periphery and the opportunities for recreation correspondingly impaired. The Council on Environmental Quality has called particular attention to this problem, and to the problem of eutrophication (see section III A), in its reviews of the project.

[k] This brief discussion of the variability of water flow is amplified and illustrated in Allan Krass's insightful tutorial on floods in this volume.

procedures where, say, one year in every ten (with the dates determined by nature), the planned interactions of man with river will be qualitatively different. If the river is ordinarily used for waste removal and for commercial fishing, for evaporative cooling and for drinking water, then, during the summer and autumn months of a once-in-ten year of unusual low flow, either the wastes will be removed in a different way (or will be more highly treated or stored) or the commercial fishing will be suspended; and either the power production upstream will be cut back (or another form of cooling used) or the drinking water will be taken from somewhere else.

If one is willing to confront the costs of occasional disruption, one is led quite naturally to modify the usual analyses of the optimal timing of construction of water supply projects. When a positive discount rate is used to relate intertemporal preferences, the result, necessarily, is that it pays to delay any project somewhat beyond the time when it would be needed under the (usual) assumption that the historic worst drought will certainly befall the region the very year that the project is completed.[1]

Once acceptable damage becomes a legitimate subject for discourse, much of the fabric of water resource planning must be rewoven. Projects are deferred with a nonzero probability of their arriving too late; reservoir management proceeds under the expectation that in low rainfall periods there will be some compromise between drawdown and curtailment of consumption; and consumption is scanned for its lower and higher priority components. The cumulative effect of such a reweaving will be to weaken the insulation of society from natural events. Acceptable damage is disruption of routine at times beyond our choosing: it means brown lawns, and fountains empty in droughts, closed highways and downed power lines in floods.

Nature modulating society: is this something we could ever get used to? The thrust of most of industrial society has been in the opposite direction: to reduce man's vulnerability to nature's excesses and, by extension, to reduce man's subordination to nature's variability. The starkest contrast in nature is *dead-alive*. Man has labored hard to be in control of that dichotomy to the largest extent possible; judging from the present concern with the treatment of the

---

[1]These ideas have been worked out quantitatively, with a highly simplified model of the variable hydrology, in a significant but unpublished Appendix to the Northeastern United States Water Supply Study of the Corps of Engineers, *Economic Analysis for Organization, Legal, and Public Finance Aspects of Regional Water Supply*, 1972. The appendix was prepared by the Institute of Public Administration, New York, N.Y., and, in particular, I believe, by Dr. Ruth Mack.

terminally ill, man may indeed be overdoing it. But there are lesser contrasts that industrial man has also felt it was his destiny to override, where it is even more certain that we are in sight of a boundary of reasonableness. *Light-dark:* The candle, the electric light, the night shift, the night ball game. *Cold-hot:* Clothing and housing, refrigeration, hothouse fruits and vegetables, air conditioning, heated patios in winter. *Wet-dry:* Boats, dikes, irrigation, umbrellas, humidifiers and dehumidifiers. One could go on—*grass-crabgrass*, overcome by herbicides, *grass-mud*, overcome by artificial turf (and plastic trees!). The shame of a city surprised by an early snowstorm, and of a town faced with a washed-out bridge—might that shame now have become excessive?

The vast majority of us are uncomfortable contemplating even the possibility of deliberately subjecting ourselves to the variability of nature. A representative of the Delaware River Basin Commission finds such a concept "not socially acceptable." Yet the possibility of *success* in insulating ourselves from nature is a horror it is time to confront. Have we indeed instructed the engineers to produce a technology such that no natural event, however rare, would require us to react? Did we really mean to do this?[m]

D. Damage Limitation

When discussion of acceptable damage comes more naturally to the planners, more inventive approaches to *damage limitation* can be expected to follow. In recent years, there has been a start in this direction, promoted in considerable measure by The National Environmental Policy Act of 1970 (NEPA), which requires the examination of "nonstructural alternatives" to all federally assisted construction programs. The nonstructural alternatives to dams as a means of flood control include floodplain zoning, carrot-and-stick flood damage insurance, and early warning systems. At least the first of these has figured prominently in the discourse in the State of New Jersey, whose legislature has passed a floodplain zoning act as a direct result of a chain of argument originating with the proposal for the Tocks Island Dam.

The nonstructural alternatives to dams as a way of extending water supplies include, above all, strategies to improve water conservation, including metering and charging for water in a way that discriminates between consumptive and nonconsumptive uses and between high- and low-flow periods. Efforts along these lines have begun recently at the Delaware River Basin Commission. Indeed, part

---

[m]For further discussion of the philosophical dimensions of this question, see the contending essays by Laurence Tribe and Charles Frankel in the companion volume.

of the water resources community regards the Tocks Island Dam as an old-fashioned project precisely because it fails, by and large, to incorporate the currently more fashionable nonstructural approach to the historic objectives of water management.

But damage limitation strategies are by no means limited to non-structural strategies. There are "engineering strategies" to minimize the damage of droughts and floods, which nonetheless may involve hardware in the cities instead of hardware in the wilderness. The new state buildings in downtown Trenton in the flood plain of the Delaware were built with their heating and cooling plants on higher floors so that flooding could be withstood. One damage limitation strategy for drought periods for Philadelphia might be to run a pipe upstream ten or even twenty miles, so that water could be taken from the Delaware in a region of lower salinity in the event of a severe drought; in normal times, the pipe would just lie there.[n] Another damage limitation strategy—one that would take much longer to implement and that might apply only to a new or rebuilt city—would be to maintain two parallel water systems, one for uses that require high quality water (drinking, cooking, bathing) and one for uses which can tolerate water of lower quality (many industrial uses, toilet flushing). In so doing, a city would substantially reduce the task of producing enough high quality water.[o] All these are "structural" or "engineering" solutions; conceivably, the system of parallel piping would be even more complex and costly than a system of dams and reservoirs. The difference, however, lies in the location at which the enterprise is carried out: engineering our urban complexes rather than our wilderness areas and landscapes. Those encouraging the search for nonstructural solutions are largely motivated by a desire to be more gentle to the natural environment; they should be reminded that one can often achieve the same end by a geographical transposition of the technological imagination.

If creative technology should one day return to the cities and there display an increased cybernetic emphasis, we will begin to raise our expectations of the machines around us. We will insist that they last longer, be easier to repair, and undergo a more satisfactory metamorphosis at the end of their lives. We will also learn to insist that our machines report to us more faithfully how they are functioning,

[n]The earliest reference I know that presents this idea is the *Report on the Utilization of the Waters of the Delaware River Basin* (Malcolm Pirnie Engineers—Albright and Friel, September 1950).

[o]An analogous approach to the likely energy problems of the next two decades would seek a means to supply priority users of electrical energy (hospital facilities, refrigerators, elevators) even in situations of substantial brownout or blackout. As a colleague of mine put it, "invest in switching equipment."

so that we know when to repair them or replace them. Finally—and perhaps this is more controversial—we will come to insist that our machines allow us to increase our sensual contact with our natural surroundings.

Of all the impacts of the "energy crisis" of the 1973–74 winter, the most lasting, I predict, will be its impact on architecture. The downtown office building of the 1960s already stands as a metaphor for the whole society's desire for enforced independence from the natural setting: temperature, humidity, air exchange, and lighting are all controlled mechanically, independent of season, wind speed, or whether one is on the north or south side of the building. Neither materials nor design change as the location is moved in latitude by thousands of miles. (In physicists' jargon, the building is invariant under ninety-degree rotations, displacements in space, and translations in time.) The notion of air conditioning a sealed office building on a mild day appears grotesque once one becomes aware that upstream from the power lines there are scarce resources whose extraction and conversion are necessarily accompanied by environmental damage. The office building of the near future will have openable windows, fewer lights and more switches, north-facing walls very different from south-facing walls (the latter having awnings or comparable "soleil briser" projections), and east-facing walls different from west-facing walls if either east or west is the direction of the prevailing wind. It may also have solar energy collectors and water collectors on the roof and windmills mounted on the vertical edges. Less symmetry, more deliberate hassle, more life.

I could be wrong. The technology of the near future may instead be designed to refine our sensibilities still further in the directions of change of the past several decades: toward personal security, toward isolating ourselves from our machines, and toward being able to do everything everywhere. Cities connected by cars on rails that arrive empty at your home and leave you at work before they pick up another passenger, heavy cars to make the ride smooth. (The Personalized Rapid Transit systems on the drawing boards are usually presumed to operate under such constraints.) Junking consumer products at the first sign of breakdown. Recreation of all kinds available at all places and all times: outdoor iceskating rinks in the Caribbean, heated swimming pools (heated *lakes*?) for winter swimming in the Adirondacks.

It seems more likely to me that we are in the early stages of an intellectual and cultural sea change. Images of saturation of wants go only part of the way toward explaining why the near future should not be predictable by a straightforward extrapolation of the recent past. For part of what is involved is the development of new wants and the rediscovery of ancient ones, a development that Laurence Tribe and Robert Dorfman call, in the companion volume, "groping upward." An important class of new wants that is already palpable expresses a desire for interaction with "the only earth we have." These wants will call into being still uninvented technologies, public policies, and styles of discourse appropriate for such a resource-respectful new world.

III. THE SPECIAL PROBLEMS OF ECOLOGY

Biological information can be relatively easily tracked by the observer of decision making, in part because it is less emotionally charged than political or economic information, so people will talk about it, and in part because it is still novel, so people tend to have clear impressions of what they know and where they've learned it. Accordingly, the study of how biological information is processed in the course of making decisions about the use of natural resources ought to give insight into how other kinds of information are processed as well. In three matters—eutrophication, shad, and oysters—ecology has played a prominent and visible role in decision making in the Tocks Island case.

A. Eutrophication of Tocks Island Lake

Tocks Island Lake, so named at the time of its conception, may turn out to have poor prospects for a healthy existence. Other reservoirs in the region regularly eutrophy in the late summer—that is, they develop pockets of foul smelling weeds along their shores. Rivers are intrinsically easier to take care of; they train themselves. The key quantitative parameter is the flushing time—the mean residence time for the water (and hence for any nutrients entrained in the water) from time of entry to time of exit. It is measured in *months* for a lake and in *days* for a river.

If the shoreline is coated with scum, the lake's value for recreation will be greatly impaired. This direct connection between biology and people has made the issue of eutrophication the pivot for large political motions. Eutrophication provides the opponents of a dam with the first argument that matches flood control in its capacity to embarrass: signs saying *Highway Flooded* with a dam unbuilt and signs saying *Beach Closed* with a dam built are both distressing images, and the politician instinctively shuns association with either of them. He cares about embarrassment a lot more than about the possible need to recompute the number of recreation visitor-days, but the two are linked.

The eutrophication issue has implicated the upstream bystander,

New York State, in a new way. The nutrients carried in the runoff from poultry farms and municipalities far above the dam site would be trapped in the lake, where they could contribute substantially to the stimulation of unwanted biological growth. The votes of New York's politicians, including its governor (a member of the Delaware River Basin Commission) are now cast more cautiously, for the expenses of controlling runoff are considerable. Ecology has shrunk the distances along the river, involving those over 100 miles upstream from the dam in the fate of those beside the dam and (as will be seen below) with the fate of those over 100 miles downstream from the dam as well.

But the reservoir may not eutrophy. Systematic measurements of the mineral content of the inflows into the Delaware and its tributaries are only just beginning, and it is not possible to make even an educated guess. In all the data available in 1973 there were just twenty measurements of phosphorus (the most critical nutrient) in the entire reach of the river where the lake would form. The extraordinary casualness about data acquisition is a significant phenomenon in its own right. It is especially mystifying in a setting where the same people who are casual about data are found commissioning a procession of technical reports on the subject of eutrophication. The earliest of these, the "McCormick Report," carries a lament at the sorry condition of the data and pleads that something be done before the next report is commissioned.[1] Thomas Cahill, two years after participating in the writing of the McCormick Report, found the "resistance by the responsible agencies" to undertaking programs of data acquisition in the field "stubborn, almost irrational."[2] In the past three years, the Corps of Engineers has spent its research funds on an elaborate computer model, *LAKECO,*[3] *and* on a study of how eutrophication, if it were to occur, could be cleaned up.[4]

With the introduction of *LAKECO,* the discourse about Tocks Island Lake may demonstrate new pathologies. Computer output has a way of paralyzing those who look at it, at least temporarily. The output of *LAKECO* takes the form of graphs of biological load in the lake versus month of the year, for various assumptions about inputs of nutrients; it appears to give the answers the political process needs. To the credit of the Corps and its contractor, *LAKECO* has been published with complete annotation, and the computer deck has been made available to interested bystanders. Nonetheless, there is no institutional mechanism to provide a critique of the report, which is full of patently unjustified assumptions. The model is an exercise, a milestone in a developing art. It has not yet carried more weight in the political process than it deserves, but it stands unchallenged, waiting to be believed.[P]

B. Shad

The shad, like many species of salmon and trout, is anadramous—that is, it spawns in fresh water and lives most of its life at sea. One of its spawning areas is above the site of the dam. The shad problem was recognized from the outset of the project, and has been dealt with in the traditional fashion: a fish ladder was included in the dam project. It was acknowledged that most of the shad trying to use the spawning area would not get there or that their offspring would not get back to the ocean. The ladder, however, was clearly better than nothing and was not very costly. The shad was acknowledged to be abundant elsewhere, to be subject to numerous other hazards (such as those encountered in navigating the stretch of water with low dissolved-oxygen content in the polluted Delaware estuary), and to be replaceable (at least from the fisherman's standpoint) if a program of stocking the lake behind the dam were undertaken.

To many builders of dams, fish ladders represent "going the extra step" to accommodate their environmentalist critics, and to placate the environmentalist in themselves. At some dams in the west, a visitors' gallery is installed from which the fish can be watched as they climb. Evidently, our fascination with their strength and determination overrides our dismay that we are putting them through such paces. Or perhaps debates ensue in the galleries—I should like to know—and consciousness is raised. To some ecologists, however, fish ladders represent kidding yourself. You see fish climb the ladder successfully, but you do not see them lost in the lake, or (even more likely) their offspring unable to find their way back downstream. Both migrations are keyed to fast-moving water.

How can such incompatible perspectives continue to coexist? Fish ladders appear to provide the means for resolving the conflict, for they usually double as devices for counting fish, keeping score each season. With so many fish-ladder-years of experience behind us, we must have some respectable quantitative information about how various ladders affect the numbers of fish arriving each year, sorted by species, by distance upriver, by month of the year. Or are ecologists

[P]Three of my colleagues on this research project, Robert Cleary, Daniel Goodman, and Douglas Zaeh, have been investigating *LAKECO* and its application to Tocks Island Lake, and their ideas are presented in two of the essays in this volume. It is possible that their critique of the model's hydrology and biology will check the usual tendency of models of this kind to carry unjustified weight. But such matters obviously should not be left to the chance attentions of a nearby research group.

unwilling to consider such data respectable? Ecologists are wary of quantitative indices of performance, for they are oriented to a world full of nonlinearities and thresholds. If the population climbing a fish ladder drops annually an average of 5 percent over several seasons, the ecologist will not agree that one could infer the number of years it would take for the population to drop to one-fourth, because a later drop could be abrupt. "No one knows the minimal oceanic population necessary for the survival of the species."[q] The ecologist thus spreads a pall of ominous uncertainty over the entire enterprise of environmental planning. Still, it is curious how little attempt is made to make the argument quantitative.[5]

C. Oysters

The fate of the Delaware Bay oyster is bound up with the dam much as is the shad's. A routine approach analogous to the fish ladder does not exist in this instance, however, and the discourse on oysters has accordingly been more inventive and more bizarre. The oyster beds, 150 miles downstream from the dam, are in a deteriorated condition relative to 50 years ago, and they are menaced by a predator known as the oyster drill. It is widely believed that the seasonal high flows of fresh water down the Delaware and into the Bay in April, May, and June are protecting the beds from further assault by the drill, because the oyster is able to tolerate less saline water than the oyster drill and hence gets rid of the drill during that season.

Except for one year in 60, the lake behind the dam is supposed to be full before the spring months of high flow begin. Thus the natural flows (except flood flows, defined as flows in excess of 70,000 cfs) are expected to pass through the dam undiminished each spring. Between the dam and the oysters, however, water is expected to be withdrawn for out-of-basin shipment. The continuity of out-of-basin diversion provided by the reservoir constitutes a major justification for the dam. This diversion can only continue during the spring months at the expense of the water flow to the oysters. Thus, advocates of oysters and advocates of out-of-basin regional growth are potential adversaries.[r]

[q]This was Lincoln Brower's response to an early draft of this essay.

[r]By the hydrologist's measure, the Tocks Island Dam, relative to its basin, is not big. To further even out the uneven flow would have required larger storage capacity, and the dam is *not* larger primarily to avoid either drowning or diking Port Jervis, 37 miles upstream. The construction of additional storage capacity on- or offstream should be expected if the goal continues to be to increase the "yield" (the minimum continuously deliverable flow) from the river valley; the yield is maximized only when the flow is completely evened out. Each future

No one who understands this conflict of interest appears willing to break the news to those who don't. Once, searching vainly for an analysis of this conflict, I was told by a minor Corps functionary, "Who can put a price on the life of a fish?" Yet, within the Corps, it is clear that the overconstrained character of the oyster problem is recognized. With quintessential American optimism, however, the Corps is trying to find a way to *improve* the oyster beds, a way to get them back to their state of 50 years ago, or even better. The Corps is hoping to find a way to do this through a procedure of timed releases of fresh water, all through the year.

The presupposition of such a study is that man can improve on nature. Among conservation groups, however, the oyster issue has had a completely different symbolism. The oyster's dependence on an annual pulse of fresh water is regarded as an *indicator* of the dependence of an entire estuarine ecosystem on that same annual pulse. The life cycles of myriad organisms are tied to these seasonal fluctuations, and even if another way could be found to protect the oysters from the drill (by chemical or biological control, for example), there would still be other kinds of damage in the estuary if the fresh water pulse were removed. The presupposition here is that man can only diminish the quality of the natural environment by his intervention—that "nature knows best." Although logically inadequate as a guide to problems such as pollution control, in which one intervention of man is designed to reduce the consequences of another, the presupposition is nonetheless a touchstone for a large number of "preservationist" attitudes, which contravene the prevailing interventionist attitudes of most foresters, fisheries managers, and other environmental scientists.

So, whither has policy evolved in this new Age of Ecology? The Corps of Engineers now explores the ecological consequences of its projects. The Fish and Wildlife Service of the U.S. Government intervenes on man's behalf whenever either commercial fishing (oysters) or sports fishing (shad) is threatened. The Corps, in response, reformulates the task of protecting a fishing resource into the task of enhancing it. The Corps consults with leading biologists. It is a new Corps, a more and differently responsive bureaucracy, and, far more than previously, there is a biological dimension to decision making.

The economists tear their hair. What happened to costs and benefits and to the market—to transfer payments to the oystermen, for example, if their beds are destroyed, or payments *by* the oystermen if the beds are improved? There is nothing intangible or fragile about

storage area will present the same trade-off problem: uneven flow for the oysters, steady withdrawal for man.

oystermen, so why should traditional methods of economic analysis suddenly be abandoned?[8]

The conservationists tear *their* hair. Their starting point is piety and self-doubt in the face of nature, and somehow it has gotten lost. To gain entry into the discourse, they talk about a cash crop; to avoid sounding softheaded, they fail to emphasize that, in their view, the "cash crop" is merely an indicator of the condition of a far more valuable ecosystem. The conservationists have separate languages for talking to one another, to politicians, and to their avowed opponents. Except when they talk to one another (and perhaps even then) they refrain all too often from articulating what really matters to them.

"Professionals," according to one definition, "don't back one another into corners." "I'd rather argue a point of procedure than a point of substance," another professional told me. Self-censorship is a tactic that keeps coalitions together and keeps opponents on speaking terms. But self-censorship, nonetheless, has considerable costs. Some of the costs are political. When a dialogue proceeds under false pretenses, its participants rapidly grow bitter; if after much effort you have scored a point, and your opponent acts as if the score is unchanged (because it really is), you want to quit. The Philadelphia office of the Corps now feels this way about the Environmental Defense Fund, and expresses a strong desire to keep its distance.

At another level, perhaps even more vital, the cost of the conservationist's failure to articulate what most troubles him is the loss of crucial information in the decision process. Many people outside the conservation groups assume that ecological insights are the property of conservationists and are up to them to introduce into the discourse. But what if they don't want to? Once, among conservationists planning strategy, I asked whether floods were beneficial to the life on the river banks. I was told to stop wasting everyone's time; the answer was obviously yes, there was a good movie that showed why,[6] and "this is not what one whispers in the governor's ear." Well, why *not* whisper this into the governor's ear? If the river banks will deteriorate, the governor should know it. If ecologists don't really know, but think they know how to find out, then the support of such research should get high priority.

The question, "Do ecologists really know anything useful?" is on many people's minds. The answer appears to be that, at the very

---

[8]To be sure, there are intangible values at stake in the survival of the villages whose local economies are entirely dependent on the oysters, villages with pride, tradition, and people having untransferable skills. Such costs are like the costs of burying under water some of the historic farming villages upstream from Tocks, costs that the present-day cost-benefit analysis appears not equipped to incorporate.

least, they can distinguish among what they know with assurance, what they have hunches about, and what "pop" concepts they see no evidence for whatever. As long as their knowledge is not systematically incorporated into environmental discourse, the United States can continue unfolding its environmental programs and then folding them up again, acting as if only distributive issues and not "real" consequences (duck hunters' votes and not ducks) are at stake. Do estuarine ecosystems become less productive or just different when dams are built? I have the impression that most ecologists believe they know the answer to that one—that indeed a lot *can* be said about how an estuary is damaged when it is simplified; if so, the information may be too important to be left to the conservation groups to introduce.[t]

The ecologists may not have welcome news (indeed, one of the first anthologies on ecology was called *The Subversive Science*), but they must be encouraged to speak, and they must be *questioned*. They have had something essential to say about DDT, and about predator control programs; in the process, we have all learned about food chains. By clarifying the importance of rhythms in nature, ecologists may cause us to rethink some of the practices that have grown up around the assumption that it is invariably to man's advantage to smooth out nature's peaks and valleys. To take a single example, the whole basis of the bartering between interests representing different river basins may be built on faulty ecological principles. The crux of this bartering is the concept that if you take water out of a basin when water is abundant, you must promise to return water to the basin (by releases from a reservoir) when water is scarce. (This is the sort of arrangement New York City has with New Jersey and Pennsylvania, as described in Section II B above.) The result, if the agreement is respected, is that river flow is evened out. But a river that flows evenly is not a natural river, however convenient it may be to man; plants and animals, in countless well-understood ways, are keyed to the seasonal flow engendered by melting snow. By various yardsticks, like species diversity or production of desired species, the evening of flow could be judged to have deteriorated the river. The repayment with low-flow augmentation could be judged to have negative value.[u]

Ecologists may have something even more disturbing to say about

[t]Daniel Goodman's essay in this volume carries the important message that the ecologists themselves do not entirely agree; *that* information seems especially resistant to dissemination at present.

[u]A system of values that elevates man's convenience is flawed in other ways, as Charles Frankel reminds us in his essay in the companion volume: the very enterprise of bringing some of nature's rhythms under deliberate control takes something important from our experience of the world.

the benefit nature derives from her most *extreme* variations, such as forest fires and floods, as opposed to her regular seasonal variations. If redwoods have depended on periodic forest fires to clear away the understory, and if mangroves have depended on floods to propagate to new locations, what is man to make of such information? The benefits of nature's excesses come as a surprise to those of us who grew up in a culture that emphasized that what was destructive in nature it was man's responsibility to tame (like his temper). The benefits of seasonal flow are less difficult to appreciate; after all, we have our own daily and monthly clocks built in.

IV. IF I LEARN TO LISTEN, YOU MAY LEARN TO CONVERSE

A. People Are Imagining Futures Very Different From One Another

- A man high in the Corps of Engineers says, "Either there is a problem with this valley or there isn't one." He means that the valley has many rivers and streams that with little notice can cause destruction and loss of life, more severe with each passing year because of the way land development increases the speed of storm runoff. He also means that the available water supply, if no further dams are built, is going to inhibit regional economic development; perhaps the permanent underground aquifers are already being depleted.

- A Park Service official shows his visitors a sloping cornfield upstream from the dam site and describes how it will become a site of "quality recreation" when the lake fills in: the site will become a beach (it has just the right slope) and, between it and the parking lots, there will be self-guided nature walks, ecology exhibits, shops where local craftsmen will display their works, and the oldest houses and barns of the region, transplanted to these places of highest frequency visitation so that the maximum number of people can become involved. "If the dam isn't built and there isn't a lake here to attract visitors," he argues, "the National Park Service has no business being here."

- A planner in a state agency says, "If we hadn't gotten the federal government into the area, the whole riverfront would have been overwhelmed by land developers, carving up the area for second homes. Until that far-off time when local zoning is effective, we have no choice but to get the federal government involved in restricting the area's development."

- A local mayor tells an inquiring commissioner that he doesn't see how his town can afford another ambulance to handle the accidents that the increased traffic on his roads will generate, and that a majority of his constituents oppose the dam because, with all those city people coming through, each will have to get a lock for his front door.[v]

• A Washington-based planner says, "The number of people who live in New Jersey and commute to work in New York City is too large already. If we don't build the dam, the regional economic and population growth will be slower, and the country will be the better for it. Some of the people who would otherwise have moved to New Jersey from the states in the middle of the country will stay there and some of the people who are leaving New York City will go on past New Jersey to live in those same states; otherwise, those states will soon be losing population."

• An ecologist worries that managing the water quality in the lake behind the dam will be a continual headache, and that asking for the lake to be suitable for recreation as well as water supply is compounding the problem, both because the visitors' activities add to the waste load entering the lake and because the visitors' activities require higher minimum water quality standards to be met.[w] He also comments, "The river is an organic unit, and now flows well over three hundred miles with hardly an obstruction. Plugging it up at mile 217 will alter the entire structure of interdependence of upstream and downstream life."

• A scoutmaster says, "The valley is perfect just as it is for getting boys and girls from suburbia into the woods for a weekend, where they don't see many people and can learn to take care of themselves. You can't find a better place for beginners to learn canoeing near here either."

• A conservationist says, "We've got to learn to accommodate to nature sometime; why not start here, while there is still some room to maneuver? If the dam is built, nuclear power plants will follow, plants now foreclosed because of the undependable flow in the dry season; that's just pushing your luck. If the dam isn't built, a lot of promising ideas about how we should accommodate to natural limits, like water metering and recycling, flood plain zoning, effluent fees for pollution discharge, energy conservation technologies, and staggered work weeks,[x]

[v]In a referendum in November 1972, in Warren County, New Jersey, which includes the dam site but little of the land that would be flooded, 9,218 people approved the construction of the dam and 14,864 opposed it.

[w]The Cannonsville Reservoir on the west branch of the Delaware is currently used for water supply and also develops "nuisance blooms of blue-green algae" in the summer. Recreation on the reservoir is not permitted.

[x]In the Corps calculation of recreation benefits, it is assumed that 32% of the annual visits to the National Recreation Area will occur on just fourteen days— summer Sundays. See the *Report on the Comprehensive Survey of the Water Resources of the Delaware River Basin*, Appendix W, "Recreation Needs and Appraisals," House Document 522, 87th Congress, 2nd Session (1962), p. W-18.

will get a more serious hearing. The better ideas will be sorted out from the worse ones while there is still little risk in experimentation."

- An esthete says, "You can see over twenty miles across the valley on a clear day, and there's hardly a work of man in sight. There's no other view of rolling hills anything like the one looking out over Wallpack Bend. And downstream, where each Christmas Washington's crossing is reenacted, you still see the river as it flowed in 1776 (though the bridge right at the spot does detract somewhat); even if only for its place in history, wouldn't the Delaware be a good river to leave unmanaged?"

Out of such conflict, what resolution? It is presumptuous to give blithe answers, but to offer no answers at all is irresponsible. I join several of the other authors in this volume in believing that, as a modest first step, it is worth trying to refine the ways in which the participants in such discourse are assisted by the available technical information. The basic methods of science, for all but a very few participants, are not themselves controversial. If some consensus can be achieved over matters of geophysics (hydrology in the Tocks case, meteorology in many other land use disputes), matters of biology, and, perhaps, matters of economics, then it is possible that a foundation for productively confronting ever more sensitive layers of the debate could be established. Even by itself, the exercise of ordering the existing disagreements according to a hierarchy of arguability may be salutory.

B. Models and Data Must Be Located in More Helpful Places

A moderate amount of science and an enormous amount of data usually pertain to a given policy decision related to natural resources. In the case of the Tocks Island Dam, historical flows of the Delaware at several gauging stations are available stretching back many decades. The historical record can be restated in stochastic form (giving the probability of recurrence of various degrees of flooding and drought, among other things) and can be "rerun" on a computer with any desired assumption about reservoir releases, out-of-basin shipments, consumptive losses, and so forth. The water professionals agree with one another to a very large extent concerning how their analytical tools should be used, and the approach they take is not particularly dependent on who the client is: anyone's preferred strategy for management of the river's water flows would be analyzed in essentially the same way. Not only are the data base and the analytical procedures common property resources; so too are the problems of uncertain and missing data, of extrapolation, and of oversimplification in modelling.

One might expect analysts occasionally to be encouraged to assume a neutral stance and to generate an array of results flowing from deliberately varied starting assumptions representative of several conflicting points of view. But this does not in fact happen. One reason, I believe, is that expertise is so widely presumed to be the captive of the adversaries. The model of the court of law is devastating: we have come to expect an insanity trial to produce a psychiatrist for the defense and a psychiatrist for the prosecution. Some environmental expert is presumed to be available who will come out with any answer for which a combatant is willing to pay. The analyst's results are presumed to be little more than the packaging of opinion and sentiment.

Although such attitudes are more often accurate than one might wish, they represent a significant exaggeration. And the costs of such attitudes are high indeed. Not only does a common ground among adversaries fail to be established, but, perhaps just as serious, a constituency for nurturing the data base and the analytic techniques fails to develop. No one in a position to do anything about it cares whether measurements are made or not. Yet almost inevitably, because new issues keep arising, critical data are missing. After years of consultants' reports pleading for the taking of data on the flow of nutrients into the river (as discussed in section III), such a program is still not underway, in spite of the fact (or perhaps because of the fact) that the politically most troublesome technical issue in the current Tocks debate—the likelihood of eutrophication of the reservoir behind the dam—largely depends for its resolution on the availability of such data.

The most unfortunate cost of excessively disparaging the technical tools is the discouragement of sustained efforts to generate alternatives. When a computer stores large blocks of historical flow data and a few elementary routing routines, it cries out to be played with. Questions of the "What If" variety, the seeds of all inventive proposals, are all but certain to germinate if such an invitation is accepted. Yet, today, the ground is not fertile. No one wants to hear. No one has such play as his work.

It is worth looking hard for ways to activate the better use of the relevant "hard science" in policy making. One obvious possibility would be to dissociate the experts from the historic adversaries, in at least a few institutions. Suppose that, in each major river basin, a facility could be established and nurtured which at the least would house the hydrological capability I have just described as well as, presumably, comparable demographic, social, economic, and ecological data banks and software. It is conceivable that, over time and abetted by the staff of such a facility (who would of course seek to justify their existence), the facility would find ways to be useful to a wide range of clients. At such a Center for the Delaware River Basin, the Greater New Jersey Chamber of Commerce, Trout Unlimited, the City of New York, the Environmental Defense Fund, all could come to refine their preferences.

The staff of such a facility would press for further data gathering and model development, and might logically take responsibility for this enterprise. But monitoring the modelers must also be accomplished somehow. There is a market in elaborate computer models today, and it resembles the market in dangerous toys; there is something a little unsavory about sellers and buyers alike.

The seller may have initially developed his model for a research problem to which it was relatively well suited, and the buyer may have begun with a policy problem an appropriate model could clarify. But bargains are struck when there is no match possible. Perhaps the necessary input data do not exist; perhaps the model has structural limitations (inadequate grid size, dimensionality, time dependence); perhaps the positivist character of the output is certain to blind the recipient to its defects. At an earlier time, before computers, it was harder to lose track of a model's uncertainties and imperfections. The water professionals resorted to physical analog models, scaled and distorted, equipped with faucets, wave generators, bottom rougheners, and other hardware. But today's numerical models are often not significantly better in fact at prediction, especially when they are run under a constraint of "modest cost." It is worth thinking about how to structure a center for modeling so that it has incentives to be candid about its models' shortcomings.

The structuring of improved environmental discourse poses other problems of institutional design that can only be touched on here: sources of financial support for the facility, the merits of embedding the facility within a university or national laboratory, its relation to existing facilities, and the confidentiality of both the data and the assistance rendered the clients. The facility should almost surely retain a "service" character (like the Library of Congress) rather than becoming itself the generator of policy. The best (most thorough, most inventive) analysis will usually be demanded only by those who have a stake in the outcome (whether bureaucratic, financial, or emotional), and it would surely be unwise (even if possible) to create a facility that becomes so smart that all the initiative passes to it.

Even those with no initial stake in the outcome can often be helpful: they ask usefully awkward questions. One would like to build in a role for them. I have twice been part of a group of such outsiders, and in each case we left behind us a considerable alteration in perceptions.[y]

In a 1969 summer study run by the National Academy of Sciences, a group of us worked quietly in California trying to understand the raging debate over whether a jetport should be built near the northern boundary of Everglades National Park, in Florida. The conservationists and the land developers flew across the country to talk to us. We discovered that both groups had a working hypothesis that if one was for something, the other ought to be against it. But, in fact, there was an outcome *both* had reason to fear, on different grounds, and so could unite to prevent: the drainage of the interior. The water flowing slowly southward through the inland region containing the jetport site not only prolonged the wet season in the Everglades, establishing critical rhythms for the entire ecosystem, but also played an essential role in protecting coastal fresh water supplies, so that coastal land development and inland drainage were incompatible over the long term. The developers, in particular, had not appreciated the scale of planning that limits to fresh water resources demanded. By emphasizing the opportunity costs of a future of unplanned regional development, our report (along with several others) led state and federal officials to reappraise the value of "undeveloped" land. A consequence of that reappraisal has been the creation by the federal government of the Big Cypress Swamp Water Conservation Area, a development which, at the time of our study two years before, had seemed unwise both to the conservationists and to the developers—extravagant to the former, an infringement on property rights to the latter. Another consequence has been the relocation of the jetport 30 miles to the northeast.[7]

A similar reappraisal of the value of undeveloped land occurred as a consequence of the 1970 National Academy of Sciences summer study of plans to extend Kennedy International Airport into Jamaica Bay. The attitude of public officials to the Bay as a recreational resource, other than for bird watching and nature study, was well expressed by the head of the New York City Department of Parks and Cultural Affairs when he said, "If you put your foot in that water, it will come out bones." Accepting the assumption that the objectives of an extensive program of water pollution control already underway would be fulfilled, our group emphasized a possible future

[y]Frank Sinden's intervention in the Tocks Island Dam debate, well represented by his two extraordinary essays in this volume, appears to be having an effect similar to those described in the two paragraphs below.

in which Jamaica Bay would be intensively used by the people of Brooklyn and Queens for water sports. By suggesting modifications of a plan for the extension of regional subways that would permit access to the Jamaica Bay shore, and by suggesting locations and estimating costs of shoreline beaches, we were able to help those involved in the future of the area to imagine new alternatives. A consequence of such altered perceptions has been the redesign of the Gateway National Recreation Area: it now includes the shore of Jamaica Bay, where previously the boundary had been drawn at the water's edge.

The moral of these two stories, for me, is that no group of analysts, however constituted, should ever imagine that their work—whether it focuses on the "science" of a dispute or its politics—can proceed apart from the debate, for it always becomes part of the debate. As Laurence Tribe observes in his essay, in the companion volume, "any analysis must become part of the process it has helped to shape." This is the classic conundrum of the observer and the observed embodied in Heisenberg's Uncertainty Principle, and it assures that the work of the analyst of land use disputes will have consequences—in the unfolding of that dispute and other disputes. I would rather commend to analysts the assumption that *everyone* is listening and will go on listening. Like Lord Keynes, I would expect that "madmen in authority, who hear voices in the air, are distilling their frenzy from some academic scribbler of a few years back. . . . Soon or late, it is ideas, not vested interests, which are dangerous for good or evil."[8]

C. What We Should Hear Before We Say the Discourse Is Good Enough

Once the quantitative analysis is so located that all interested parties are served, the discourse might just begin to sound quite different. I cannot imagine more than a fraction of the themes we might hear; but I would regard the appearance of straight talk about any of the following to be a signal that a transition had occurred.

1. **Bigshots.** The sheer size of Tocks is a source of excitement. For those who might build the dam, it is a challenge to their organizational and technical skills—a challenge that enlarges their perception of themselves. Correspondingly, the high stakes (the expenditure of about a billion dollars is in the cards for dam construction, new sewer facilities, and additional transportation access) spur on the activists in the conservation groups, who believe that only victories on issues like Tocks will ever get a fair hearing for their broader philosophical analysis of modern society.

Stopping a project this big will thrill a conservationist in a way not very different from the way building it will thrill a Corps engineer. It is debatable, under the circumstances, whether big projects get wiser consideration than little ones. Big projects may get a first-string team, so that there is less carelessness and foolishness, but they also engender momentum for its own sake—the drive for victory rather than compromise.

To like being a bigshot is pretty human. Yet it dampens the enthusiasm for taking seriously the packages of single-purpose projects, the half-dam and quarter-dam strategies, which (as discussed in section II) are often meritorious alternatives to the one big structure. Building a set of wing dams that jut partway across the river and create swimming areas in the slow-moving water behind them doesn't count for much today. A discourse grown sensitive to bigness will display creativity in the scoring and rewarding of intermediate accomplishments.

2. Little Guys. The local residents live with the uncertainty that the stalled discourse has brought. Most would prefer a decision either to build or not to build, relative to a decision to postpone deciding. This fact confounds the kind of analysis usually regarded as optimal: one that keeps the options open.

The Corps has been acquiring the land where the lake and the National Recreation Area are to go. Some of the people who have had to sell to the Corps are bitter about the procedures by which these sales have been accomplished, and they are persuasive when they argue that there are not enough built-in safeguards to protect them. Given the fact that much of the fuel for the opposition to the dam comes from these bitter residents, the current procedures for land acquisition are clearly suboptimal.

It used to be presumed that if people want to live on flood plains, the government should not stop or even dissuade them; a proper role for government was simply to assure that those living in flood plains were aware of the risks. Flood plain zoning generally goes much further, setting the government in systematic opposition to the determined risk taker. It may be that the characteristics of this silent confrontation could be usefully illuminated.

The urban poor in the inner cities of Newark, New York City, and Philadelphia who do not have cars will not be able to travel the 50 to 75 miles to the National Recreation Area, whether river based *or* lake based, if there is no public transportation. What subsidies, if any, would be required to provide such public transportation at prices these groups could afford? If subsidies of this sort prove to be necessary, those who make their approval of any particular form of the project conditional on its serving the needs of the urban poor ought to insist that the project incorporate such subsidies. There is a risk of self-deception if this problem remains unexamined.

The recreation area, politicians sense, will be used by different groups if it is built around a river or around a lake. What characteristics differentiate these two groups? A careful answer to this question would clarify the currently muddled perception of winners and losers.

3.   **Wilderness.**   Men can now move mountains, melt icecaps, turn rivers around. Their power to assault leads to competing images of nature as victim and nature as ward. In either case, nature is politicized.

Doing nothing has now become a judgment: the act of not implementing a technology to modify a natural phenomenon is politically and morally different from the act of leaving nature alone at a time of innocence. Apparently, Fidel Castro, following a devastating hurricane over Cuba, went on the radio to accuse the United States *not* of seeding the hurricane in a way that went awry, but of *failing* to seed the hurricane, knowing that it would hit his country.[z]

Suppose a decision is made not to build the dam, and the following year an immense crack develops in the Kittatiny Ridge, rocks begin to tumble into the valley, the river becomes plugged, and a lake builds up behind the plug. Does the Corps restore the navigable waterway?[aa] That the river should have standing in such a decision seems appropriate.[9] But if I were the guardian for the Delaware, I would be perplexed. I would not want my ward to drown Port Jervis

---

[z]I owe the story, as well as the basic thought in this paragraph, to Edith Brown Weiss.

[aa]The Corps of Engineers, in its Environmental Impact Statement, considered the possibility of taking the *dam* apart at a later time. The two relevant paragraphs are extraordinary enough to merit full quotation:

> With the exception of a large permanent rock face at the left abutment, occupation of the area by the project facilities does not in general constitute an irreversible or irretrievable commitment of resources.
>
> The major resource commitments are less enduring and of restorable character. In areas of local protection works the natural stream banks will be lost and replaced with flood walls and levees. The corridor of relocated U.S. 209 due to grade adjustments requiring cut and file represents an artificial land modification. These features could be removed and the area completely restored to its pre-project uses, should future generations find that such removal and restoration could serve some greater public economic or social good. The construction of the basic dam embankment although very massive does not preclude its alteration or removal. While truly a major undertaking, this change could be made for a compelling (and as yet unknown) future need.

and other human settlements on her banks. I would expect to see some abridgement of her prerogatives. Why should I assume that my river is a savage? Might not a river *like* the idea of being helpful to man? It is not obvious to me that the end result of an enlargement of rights must be an enlargement of selfishness.[ab]

The problem of rocks falling into the river was posed in a discussion between dam builders and dam stoppers at a university, a setting that permits some of the usual rules of discourse to be suspended. I look forward to the day when it is usual to have more open, more self-critical, even more playful discourse. I do not argue on grounds of efficiency alone; I rely on more than the enhanced potential for resolution of conflict. Such arguments from efficiency are not self-evident; if one knows one's neighbors better, one may want *less* to compromise with them. Improvements in discourse can be better justified in terms of higher ends than the instrumental one of "solving" the problem at hand. The new discourse would manifest a fuller expression of the diversity of preferences and emotional commitments of the participants. It would enhance the sensitivities of both participants and bystanders to the complex, tragicomic process of self-definition a culture goes through when it seeks to resolve any of its hard problems. It seems worth pursuing for its own sake.

NOTES

1. Jack McCormick and Associates, *An Appraisal of the Potential for Cultural Eutrophication of Tocks Island Lake*, U.S. Army Corps of Engineers, September 1971.

2. Thomas H. Cahill, "The Potential for Water Quality Problems in the Proposed Tocks Island Dam Reservoir," in G.E. Schindler and F.W. Sinden, eds., *The Tocks Island Dam, A Preliminary Review* (Save-the-Delaware-Coalition, 1973).

3. Water Resources Engineers, *LAKECO: A Model of a Reservoir* (December 1972), and *Ecologic Simulation—Tocks Island Lake* (February 1973).

4. Wapora, Inc., *Tocks Island Lake: Techniques for Water Quality Management* (1974).

5. For a qualitative description of the state of the art, and a glimpse at the magnitude of current effort, see G.J. Eicher, "Stream Biology and Electric Power," *Water Power* (June 1973): 211–218.

6. *The Flooding River*, by Lincoln Brower, made in 1972 and available from John Wiley & Sons, New York.

[ab] As Laurence Tribe argues in his essay in the companion volume, "recognizing rights in a previously rightless entity is entirely consistent with acknowledging circumstances in which such rights might be overridden. . . ." My point goes a bit further: it is that recognizing rights does not preclude imposing responsibilities.

7. See "The Everglades: Wilderness Versus Rampant Land Development in South Florida," in John Harte and Robert H. Socolow, *Patient Earth* (New York: Holt, Rinehart and Winston, 1971).

8. J.M. Keynes, *The General Theory of Employment, Interest and Money* (New York: Harcourt Brace and World, 1964 ed.), p. 383; originally published in 1936.

9. The seminal essay on this subject is Christopher D. Stone, "Should Trees Have Standing?—Toward Legal Rights for Natural Objects," *Southern California Law Review* 45 (2): 450–501. He was anticipated in some respects by Dr. Seuss (Theodor Seuss Geisel), *The Lorax* (New York: Random House, 1971).

✳ *Part Two*

People and Events

Despite its location on the fringe of megalopolis, the Delaware River is still relatively unspoiled for most of its 300-mile length and is still unobstructed by major dams. For almost two centuries it earned its freedom by serving as a highway for commerce, its status formalized in the Anti-Dam Treaty between New Jersey and Pennsylvania that remained in force from 1783 to 1953. Then, in 1955, long after commerce on the upper Delaware had disappeared, the Basin suffered the worst flood of record and within a decade after that it suffered the worst drought of record. For the first time in history a serious effort to dam up the main stem was launched. But as the project planning dragged on, delayed by the Vietnam War, a sharp change in the public's perception of major public works occurred. Opposition to the dam spread from those who would be forced from the valley to a much wider group with broad concerns about growth, and finally created a stormy battle.

Though the direct stimuli for the Tocks project were the flood and the drought, many threads in the controversy start far back in history. These threads are traced in the first essay of this section by Michael Reich. The controversy itself, together with its main characters, is described and analyzed by Harold Feiveson in the second essay.

Table 2-1. Time Line History of the Delaware River

Prediscovery period—Lenni Lenape Indians occupy Water Gap and upstream flood plain, which they call the "Minisink."

1609 — Henry Hudson discovers Delaware Bay.

1623 — Dutch West India Company takes formal possession of river.

1675 — Colonized area ceded to the British.

1742 — Thomas Penn forces the Delaware Indians to leave.

1783 — Pennsylvania and New Jersey sign the Anti-Dam Treaty to protect fishing and navigation.

1800 — Navigation by rafts and Durham boats is commercially important.

1832 — Parallel canals open, eventually driving Durham boats out of business; coal is important commodity.

Ca. 1850 — Railroads begin to compete with canals; Water Gap begins rise as fashionable resort.

1923 — New York, New Jersey, and Pennsylvania appoint commission to recommend a division of flow among the states.

1928 — New York starts legal steps to divert upper Basin water; New Jersey objects, case goes to Supreme Court.

Ca. 1930 — Water Gap resort declines

1931 — Drought; Supreme Court compromises: limits New York's diversion to 440 mgd; New York moves ahead with plans for upper Basin dams.

1934 — Corps of Engineers completes a Basinwide survey—publishes "308" report; recommends against federal control, proposes interstate agency.

1936 — Incodel formed.

1949 — (June) Driest June in 78 years; water shortage in New York City (upper Basin dams not yet built because of the Depression and war).

1950 — Pirnie Report recommends dam at Wallpack Bend, others in New York.

1952 — New York asks Supreme Court to increase New York's diversion to 800 mgd; New Jersey, Pennsylvania enter case.

1953 — New Jersey, Pennsylvania abrogate Anti-Dam Treaty of 1783.

1954 — Supreme Court accepts a compromise, but permits 800 mgd for New York.

1955 — (August) Largest flood of record occurs on Delaware.

(September) Congress asks Corps to recommend flood control measures.

1956 — (January) Corps holds hearings on flood damage.

1961 — (March) 700 acres of New Jersey park land including Sunfish Pond quietly traded to the utilities, who want it for pumped storage.

(September) DRBC is established by Congress.

(1961–1965) Worst drought of record.

1962 — Federal government funds the Delaware Estuary Comprehensive Study (DECS).

(August) Corps' comprehensive study submitted to Congress as House Document 522; study fills 11 volumes; Congress authorizes Corps' plan.

1964 — Public hearings on Tocks lead to first organization of opponents: Delaware Valley Conservation Association.

1965 — (July) DRBC exercises authority at climax of drought: allocates water between New York and lower Delaware; Yard's Creek Pumped Storage plant goes into operation.

1966 — DECS study appears, offers alternative pollution abatement programs; National Park Service Master Plan for recreation area around Tocks appears.
(Mother's Day) Newly formed Lenni Lenape League organizes first protest pilgrimage to Sunfish Pond.
(Fall) First local landowners notified of condemnation; class action suit to stop Tocks is filed (dismissed on a technicality by Supreme Court in 1968).

1967 — Justice William O. Douglas joins protest march to Sunfish Pond.

1968 — Utilities agree to compromise that leaves Sunfish Pond intact, will expand Yard's Creek instead.

1970 — (January) NEPA becomes law: requires Environmental Impact Statements on all federal projects; establishes CEQ.
(November) Corps submits eight-page Impact Statement on Tocks, ignites new public indignation.
(December) Save-the-Delaware Coalition is formed.

1971 — (October) Corps releases expanded Environmental Impact Statement along with McCormick Report.

1972 — (February) Russell Train, in letter to Army, says CEQ approval depends on solution of environmental problems, especially eutrophication problem raised by McCormick Report.
(September) Governor Cahill announces seven conditions that must be met for his approval of dam.

1974 — (February) Squatters evicted in sudden early morning raid. Adverse publicity for Corps.
(August) Congress authorizes one and one-half million dollar comprehensive study of Tocks under direction of Corps of Engineers.
(October) URS/Madigan-Praeger and Conklin & Rossant chosen to carry out study; "Study Management Team," including Corps, DRBC, and state government officials specify broad scope for study.

1975 — (July) With study finished, DRBC meets to consider Tocks. Three governors (N.J., N.Y., Del.) vote against proceeding with construction, one (Pa.) votes for; the federal representative abstains; in a second vote, a majority votes for continued land acquisition for a park.
(October) Corps in letter to Congress recommends deauthorization, but bills to deauthorize remain dormant.

Early Transport on the Delaware

※ *Chapter 2*

Historical Currents

Michael Reich

I. A DAM IS BORN

FLOODS BATTER THE NORTHEAST; 73 KILLED, DAMAGE IN BILLIONS; 4 STATES DECLARE EMERGENCIES

> —Front page headlines,
> *The New York Times*,
> August 20, 1955

East Stroudsburg, Pa. August 20, 1955—Chaos and benumbed shock overlie this area today in the wake of the worst flood in its history.

There are thirty bodies in one funeral home alone, and no one knows how much higher the figures will go. Some estimates are at least 100. Helicopter pilots this afternoon reported seeing at least nine bodies floating in the still wildly overflowing Delaware River.

The greatest concentrated tragedy was at Camp Davis, the summer colony of fourteen modest bungalows near Analomink, three mines northwest of here. More than forty persons, most of them women and children from New York and New Jersey, were vacationing at the camp.

The toll at Camp Davis was twelve persons known dead and nineteen missing. . . .

It was there that the normally placid Brodhead Creek flashed up twenty-five to thirty feet in fifteen minutes Thursday night.

The camp residents fled to a building on slightly higher ground. As they reached the attic, the structure collapsed hurling them into the turbulent water. . . .

—*The New York Times*,
Sunday, August 21, 1955

. . . the whole problem of flood control in the New England and Middle Atlantic States must now undergo searching examination. Obviously the whole existing system of dams and similar measures was grossly inadequate last week, and we paid heavily for that inadequacy. What measures need to be undertaken to prevent a repetition of this disaster? Our people look to and expect that our national, state and local government officials will answer this question and initiate promptly the needed remedial measures.

—*The New York Times*,
Editorial,
August 22, 1955

On August 11, 1955, the New York City Weather Bureau issued a hurricane alert, warning the area's residents to brace themselves for a disaster. Hurricane Connie, with over 150 mile-per-hour winds, was traveling up from the South Atlantic, and meteorologists feared that it might strike the densely populated urban area around New York. But on that Thursday afternoon, the path of Connie turned to the west and let loose its winds 500 miles south of New York on the Carolina coast. By the time she reached New York City on Friday, August 12, Connie's winds had slowed to a mere 75 miles per hour. A Weather Bureau spokesman declared, "It's as weak as a hurricane can be."

The third hurricane of the 1955 season, Connie packed more water than wind. The heaviest rains were on the coast, creating unexpected flooding problems for New York City. Between Thursday night and Saturday morning, 9.37 inches of rain fell on the city, cutting off electricity and telephone service to thousands of customers. The most disruptive incident was a two-hour halt for all trains to and from Grand Central Station. Connie continued to lose her punch as she moved northwest, and by the time she passed over the Great Lakes on Sunday (August 14) she was "just another rainstorm." By Monday, most of the damages in New York City had been cleaned up. For inland areas, Connie had been a mixture of blessings and sorrows. The rains saved many northeastern "drought-suffering farmers" from ruin and poured 18 billion gallons of water into four New York City reservoirs, filling them to 92 percent capacity compared with 74 percent one year earlier. But at the same time, Connie had left in her path 41 deaths.

While Connie disappeared over the Great Lakes, another hurricane named Diane was brewing in the West Indies. Early in the morning of Wednesday, August 17, Diane struck the North Carolina coast with 90 mph winds. The next day, the Weather Bureau announced that Diane had lost her force and the threat to New York City no longer existed. A Weather Bureau bulletin, which described Diane as a mere "storm" rather than a hurricane, noted that "the only serious danger now is from heavy rains and flooding." The same article in *The New York Times* remarked that Diane's rains "were much lighter than those that danced attendance to her big sister, Connie."[1] That Thursday, New York City relaxed "with Diane's passage into meteorological history" as the Washington Office of the Weather Bureau shifted its attention to a new low pressure area out at sea. News of Diane was completely absent from the front page on Friday, August 19, and the weather summary at the back of the *Times* spoke of the "remains of Diane."

It was one of those quirks of nature that revived Diane on Thursday night and transformed her into a "full-fledged flood-maker." Weather forecasters were all but ignoring Diane on Thursday as she dwindled to an apparently harmless low pressure area in central Pennsylvania. Then:

> ...her winds reduced to a comparative whisper,... [Diane] sucked in vast quantities of moisture-laden air from over the Atlantic and ... dumped the water by the ton in advance of her leisurely path.[2]

These new flood waters, unable to soak into grounds saturated one week earlier by Connie's rains, wreaked havoc throughout the Northeast. Pennsylvania, New Jersey, Connecticut, and Massachusetts were the worst damaged. Eight cities in Pennsylvania, including Scranton, the state's fourth largest, were without drinking water, power, or gas. And in New Jersey, four northwestern and central counties were declared disaster areas, as helicopters, scows, boats, and amphibious vehicles were mobilized to rescue those stranded in flooded and low-lying areas. Backup flood waters from tributaries washed away massive bridges spanning the Delaware River at Yardley, Phillipsburg, and Columbia.

Those areas struck most savagely by floods—and with the most tragic accounts of human suffering—were largely cut off on Friday, and it was not until Saturday, August 20, that the news became widely known. Some areas of East Stroudsburg, near the Delaware Water Gap, had been flooded to a depth of ten feet, and tributaries near the Gap alone counted 45 dead and 70 missing. The Camp Davis tragedy was the most concentrated source of suffering and death, but similar incidents of flash floods on tributaries left Hurricane Diane with the reputation of a killer. The August 1955 floods in the Delaware Valley surpassed previous records set in 1936 and 1903 rainstorms. Later tabulations counted 99 deaths in the Delaware River Basin—all on the Brodhead Creek—and damages totalling nearly one billion dollars. It was by far the worst flooding ever experienced in the Basin, and it was to have important and long-lasting impacts.

Although plans for the Tocks Island Dam and reservoir can be traced to the late 1920s, the stimulus to begin real planning arose out of the flood waters of Hurricanes Connie and Diane. The floods of August 1955 shocked the public, sparked state and federal governments to action, and gave the Corps impetus to reconstruct the Delaware River Basin water resources through a comprehensive plan. It is noteworthy that although the floods of 1955 formed the immediate catalyst for the chain of events that solidified the Tocks plans, all the deaths and a large amount of the damages in 1955 occurred on the Delaware tributaries, not the mainstream which would be protected by the Tocks Island Dam.[a]

Within one week after the rains stopped, the U.S. Army Corps of Engineers initiated a survey of the damaged areas to assess the need for flood control. Although beginning in the 1920s the Corps had conducted numerous investigations of possible dam sites in the Delaware River Basin, its reports had consistently concluded that the severity of floods in the Basin did not warrant federal expenditures for control measures. Dam construction on the Delaware had also been opposed by the Interstate Commission on the Delaware River Basin (Incodel), a body formed in 1936 by the Basin states to coordinate management of Basin water resources. Incodel consistently opposed federal participation in its watershed. The floods of 1955, with their overwhelming costs in property and human life, catalytically transformed this situation. Nature's intervention set in motion a planning process for comprehensive Basin development, which became the basis for the Tocks Island controversy.

In mid September of 1955, the Senate Public Works Committee issued a formal request to the Corps of Engineers to review prior reports on the Delaware, to determine the extent of flood damages, and to recommend those measures necessary to prevent similar disasters. As part of this survey the Corps held hearings in January 1956 in Philadelphia and in three of the cities struck by the floods— Stroudsburg, Port Jervis, and Trenton—in order to secure data on damages and to record local views on the proposed investigation and

[a]The role of the Tocks Island Dam in preventing floods is discussed in detail in essay 6 in this volume.

on preventive measures. These hearings marked a major turning point in the history of the Delaware River Basin management. Many of the local officials and politicians who testified called for federal and state cooperation to develop the Basin's water resources, while the Democratic administrations in New Jersey and Pennsylvania appealed for federal government aid and leadership.

Among the private groups that began to organize was the Delaware River Basin Research, Inc., whose proclaimed purpose was the furthering of public knowledge about water resources management. This group, later renamed the Water Research Foundation, was an active lobbying force for the Basin's industrial interests, and its members included representatives from various power companies, petroleum and chemical firms, consulting companies, etc. It subsequently received a $131,000 grant from the Ford Foundation and gave a contract to the Syracuse University Research Institute to analyze the legal, fiscal, and governmental problems involved in managing water resources on an interstate stream.

The Corps of Engineers, in the same period, was gearing up to develop a comprehensive regional plan. By April 1956 it was circulating copies of a preliminary procedural plan. And in December 1956, the Philadelphia Office of the Corps submitted its "Procedural Plan of Survey" to the Chief of Engineers for approval. The survey was divided into 24 separate components, many of which were prepared by federal and state agencies other than the Corps, including, for example, the Office of Business Economics, the National Park Service of the Department of Interior, and the Federal Power Commission. The Corps supervised the various studies, designed the comprehensive plan, and prepared the final report.

In June 1960, the eleven-volume survey was completed. The fundamental purpose of this massive attempt at rational multiple-purpose planning for the entire Basis was set out in the preface:

> Of prime importance is water; man can survive without food longer than without water. What is true of the individual is true of his civilization. History has proven that civilizations perish, dwindle, or migrate because of lack of water, which in most instances occurs when the demand exceeds the supply. This does not happen all at once, but is in nature a slow process; however, if the impending disaster is evaluated and provided for, the loss of growth and development can be prevented.

> Lest we forget—the water resources problems of the future loom large indeed. We must aim to provide for future generations. If we persist in conservative planning, our efforts will not fulfill our needs. We must plan broadly so that it is possible to achieve our goals.[3]

The Corps believed that the Basin's needs could not be denied. There were the natural disasters—the droughts and the floods—that had to be prevented and the ultimate shortage of supplies that had to be avoided. Congress had decreed that the Corps was responsible for averting further disasters in the Delaware River Basin. The Corps felt it had a mission; the comprehensive plan with its dams and reservoirs was its means.

In August 1962 the Delaware River Basin Report was submitted to Congress as House Document 522, and that fall it came before its Committees of Public Works. The hearings before the Flood Control Subcommittees were cursory and brief. Only representatives for the Corps of Engineers testified, and in the House Subcommittee, for example, the project was approved after less than twenty minutes of discussion. Once approved by the House and Senate Committees on Public Works, the entire eleven-volume Delaware River Basin Comprehensive Plan became part of the omnibus Flood Control Act of 1962. Congress, which was preparing to break for elections, subsequently passed the Act (Public Law 87-874) in a voice vote, and the Delaware River Basin Comprehensive Plan, along with nearly 200 other public works projects, became law.

The Corps' development plan for the Delaware watershed proposed eight major multiple purpose dam projects requiring both federal and nonfederal participation: at Prompton, Tocks Island, Bear Creek, Beltzville, Aquashicola, Trexler, Maiden Creek, and Blue Marsh (map, p. xiv, shows those in place in 1976). The keystone to the comprehensive plan was the Tocks Island Dam and Reservoir—the only project proposed for the main stem of the Delaware River and by far the largest and most expensive component of the Basin plan. Tocks Island lay in the middle of the river five miles above the Water Gap. The earth and rock-fill dam was to be 160 feet high, and would create a long, narrow lake, rarely exceeding 2,000 feet in width, extending 37 miles up the Delaware Valley from Tocks Island to Port Jervis. From its vantage at Tocks Island the dam would control a drainage area of almost 4,000 square miles, one-half the total Delaware Basin runoff above Trenton. The project's multiple purposes included water supply, recreation, flood control, and hydroelectric power. The total project cost was estimated in 1962 at $120 million. The dam not only overshadowed all other water development projects planned for the Delaware River Basin, but promised to be one of the largest dams in the East.

In 1965 Congress expanded the Tocks project through the creation of the Delaware Water Gap National Recreation Area (PL

89-158) centered on the proposed Tocks Island Dam and Reservoir. For this purpose, Congress approved $37 million for acquiring 48,000 acres of land around the reservoir area and $18 million for construction of recreation facilities. DWGNRA thereby became the first inland national recreation area authorized east of the Mississippi.

The Tocks project would have its major impact in Warren and Sussex Counties of New Jersey, and Monroe and Pike Counties of Pennsylvania. These counties might loosely be termed the "primary impact area." It is from this region, and particularly the "taking area" within it (in which private property has been purchased by the government) that opposition to the Tocks Island project originated. The more than 20,000 people living on the approximately 8,000 properties slated for acquisition were losing an irreplaceable natural resource. It was a few spokesmen for these people who galvanized much of the initial opposition to the dam. In doing so, they had to fight a momentum to dam the Delaware which had gathered over five decades.

II. THE DELAWARE OF THE PAST

Europeans first came to the Delaware River in the seventeenth century. Henry Hudson is credited with discovering the expansive bay in 1609 while searching for a route to the Indies, but instead of travelling up the waterway, he chose to continue north, eventually exploring the river which now bears his name. A few years later, a Dutch adventurer, Cornelius May, came to the same spot, giving his name to one of the outer capes. The river was named for Lord Delaware, and, in 1623, the Dutch West India Company took formal possession of the Delaware. Control over the river, whose broad waters and deep channel provided easy access far into the interior of the new country, changed hands several times in the next few decades, going from the Dutch to the Swedes to the British and back to the Dutch, until in 1675 the colonized area was ceded to the British.

Indians came to the Delaware River Valley long before white men, and tribes of the Lenni Lenape nation, who called the river "the great tidal water stream," inhabited the area near the Water Gap. They also gave the large level area north of the Gap the name of Minisink, meaning "the water is gone," and this led early western explorers of the region to speculate that the area once contained a large lake, which disappeared when the Gap was formed. In the early 1700s the Europeans began to establish missions among the Indians, and by mid century their houses were scattered throughout the Delaware, Lehigh, and Susquehanna Valleys. Although six or seven distinct tribes lived in the area, Europeans referred to all Indians with the same name, simply as the Delaware Indians.[4]

The first white settlers to the Minisink Valley were Dutch from New York, who traveled down from the north. The original attraction to the Minisink was copper. Dutch explorers who reached the Valley in 1657 by traveling up the Hudson to Kingston and then overland to the southwest were shown the valuable metal ore by Indians. They reported the discovery to their mother country, which was in need of the metal, and subsequently began a costly program to modernize Indian trails leading from Kingston to the area with copper deposits three miles above the Water Gap. This 104-mile stretch of road, the Old Mine Road, was the first road of any considerable length built in the United States. The trail is believed to have been completed as early as 1659, and in 1689 the first recorded white settler located in a valley one mile above what today is Port Jervis.

The road's construction opened up the area, and communities were established in the Minisink Valley for 40 miles or more on both sides of the river. Initially Minisink settlers traveled by the road to Kingston several times a year to sell their cider and wheat and to buy salt and other necessities, but once the more treacherous rapids were cleared in the river, most trade turned downstream and the road gradually fell into disuse.[5] Many of the homes established along the Old Mine Road during the 1700s still stand, and their threatened destruction by the Tocks project has been one of the deepest sources of bitterness and opposition to the project among the local inhabitants.

By the late 1700s the Delaware River had become one of the new nation's major interstate waterways. Its two main tributaries, the East Branch and the West Branch, rose in the western slopes of the Catskill Mountains of New York State, then joined together at Hancock, New York, to form the main stem, which wound its way to the southeast through rolling hills rich with timber. This portion of the river, from a few miles above Hancock to just below Port Jervis, served as the boundary between New York and Pennsylvania. The Delaware then met New Jersey at a point known as Tri-State Rock, where it turned 90 degrees to become the Pennsylvania–New Jersey line, and followed the Kittatinny Range of the Appalachian Mountains to the southwest. Fifty miles downstream from Port Jervis, the river cut sharply again, this time through the steep slopes of the Delaware Water Gap, flowing more leisurely to the south, past new factories at Trenton and Philadelphia, into the estuary of the Delaware Bay, and eventually into the Atlantic Ocean. Although the upper reaches of the river's 290 miles from Hancock to the Bay were sprinkled with rapids and riffles, the Delaware, in comparison with raging western rivers like the Columbia and the Colorado, was tame with age.

The records of an interstate court case in the 1930s concerning diversion of waters from the Delaware River Basin provide a rich source of firsthand accounts of early navigation on the river. From the testimonies of 80- and 90-year-old residents along the river, New Jersey hoped to prove, for its legal argument, that the Delaware was navigable. These old timers described the two major modes of transportation that existed around the turn of the nineteenth century: rafts, and arklike vessels known as Durham boats. The rafts were enormous; two of them lashed together, as they often were, extended 40 to 50 feet wide and 180 to 200 feet long. They usually carried timber and sometimes carried sawed cherry and beech board from the headwaters of the river in New York to the mills and markets in Trenton and Philadelphia. These rafts served an important transportation function, often ferrying passengers down stream, and gave rise to numerous hotels along the river's banks for the raftsmen. It was not uncommon for 20 to 25 rafts to tie up at a single mooring where the expert pilots and raftsmen were resting for the night. Rafting continued as a major business until the twentieth century when, due to deforestation, the lumber business began to decline. Rafts on the Delaware finally disappeared in the mid 1920s.

Durham boats, invented by Robert Durham in 1723, came into regular use on the Delaware in the mid eighteenth century and at their peak in the early 1800s, several hundred of these vessels plied the river, employing two or three thousand men. The boats were described as somewhat longer and narrower than canal boats, in a shape resembling a "weaver's shuttlecock." Empty boats were poled upstream close to shore, so that their operators could use overhanging limbs and brush to pull themselves along. On return trips they carried minerals, flour, stone, sand, and other materials needed in the industrial cities of Trenton and Philadelphia.

Use of Durham boats declined precipitously when the Lehigh Coal and Navigation Company's canal began operations in 1832 and the Delaware Division Canal opened two years later. The Lehigh Canal was 73 miles long and paralleled the Lehigh River from Easton to White Haven, Pennsylvania; the Delaware Division Canal paralleled the Delaware River on the Pennsylvania side for 60 miles between Easton and Bristol. These canals did away with the necessity to wait for high water to transport goods and eliminated the physical strains of fighting the current to go upstream and the dangers of maneuvering the rapids to go downstream. New towns were opened up for development and their industries began to flourish. The total tonnage of coal and other commodities hauled on canals reached its peak in 1855. Soon thereafter, with vast construction and rapid acceptance of railway transport, canals began to decline in use, and by 1901, both the Lehigh and Delaware Division Canals were losing money.[6]

Because of its importance to navigation, the protection and enhancement of the Delaware's channels began early. In 1783, in order to protect fishing and navigation interests, Pennsylvania and New Jersey signed an Anti-Dam Treaty, which prohibited the building of structures completely across the Delaware.[7] This Treaty was actually an interstate compact and provided that the river "in the whole length and breadth thereof, is and shall continue to be and remain a common highway, equally free and open to the use, benefit, and advantage of the said contracting parties."[8] Numerous acts based on the Treaty, concerning navigation and bridge construction, were passed in later years by both states. For 170 years this agreement not to obstruct the river was upheld, until it was abrogated in 1953 at a time when the two Delaware states were involved in an intense interstate controversy, to be discussed later.

The railroad brought other changes to the Delaware and its environs. In 1820 only a solitary hut stood at the Water Gap, but once the area was connected to Philadelphia and New York by rail, the number and size of resort establishments grew rapidly. By the turn of the century the riverfront at the Gap had become a fashionable resort area, offering bathing beaches, motor boats, canoes, and a chance to escape the summer heat of the cities for cool mountain air. And by 1930 the Gap could boast a choice among nearly twenty hotels.

Until the 1920s the main uses of the Delaware River were navigation and recreation, although the river also supported substantial sports and commercial fishing activities. But demands on the river were changing. In the late 1920s New York City experienced critical water supply problems which led it to propose and then procure out-of-Basin diversions from the Delaware watershed, against the violent objections of the downstream riparian states, New Jersey, Pennsylvania, and Delaware. The political history of this conflict over the Delaware's waters as it has unfolded since the 1920s well sets the stage for the more recent conflict over the Tocks Island Dam, for many of the salient political and technical issues that have marked the Tocks controversy have persisted in one form or other almost unabated for over half a century.

III. THE EARLY CONFLICTS

"There is a sobering finality in the construction of a river basin development, and it behooves us to be sure we are right before we go ahead."[b]

In the 1920s there emerged the first systematic plans to exploit the Delaware River for municipal and industrial water supply. Although many of these early plans became sources of interstate friction and were never realized, they did contribute greatly to structuring present-day development schemes. Three major themes characterized this early period, and indeed the entire period up to the floods of 1955, First, New York City increasingly turned to dams on the Delaware tributaries to "solve" its periodic shortages. From this policy originated many of the early conflicts. Second, there were recurrent problems in establishing an agency to manage Basin water resources and to deal with federal-interstate disagreements. Third, natural disasters, both floods and droughts, repeatedly tested the decision making process.

For most of the towns in what would later be defined as the Delaware Basin Service Area (reaching from the Delaware's northernmost headwaters past Kingston, New York, to Bridgeport, Connecticut, south past New York City, and including eastern Pennsylvania, northern Delaware, and the entire state of New Jersey) water supply problems in the early twentieth century had not reached a point where the allocation of Delaware waters was a major issue. Trenton, Camden, and Philadelphia were pumping water for municipal and industrical uses from the river and then returning it—as they continue to do today. But New York City, which had been obliged early on to reach beyond the ambient, brackish Hudson to the fresh waters of the Hudson-Mohawk Valley, was facing the prospect of a severe shortage. The Catskill water supply system, scheduled for completion in 1928, would add significantly to the Croton Reservoir system, and additional ground water supplies would boost the City's dependable yield to above one billion gallons per day. But the City's water needs were growing even more rapidly, and the Board of Water Supply thought it only prudent to begin an investigation of other sources.[9]

Five alternatives were proposed, and four were rejected. The remaining proposal—to divert for the first time the headwaters of the Delaware River—appeared most advantageous to the City. Although it would initially require high capital construction costs, it was not

[b]This is a quote from the President's Water Resources Policy Commission, *A Water Policy for the American People*, 1950.

subject to debt limits, and it minimized operating costs, which would have to come out of the City's annual budget. It also avoided the politically difficult tasks of plugging up New York City's decades-old leaky water mains or of imposing metering on industries and residents accustomed to low, flat rate water prices. The project would supply an estimated 600 million gallons per day (mgd) of pollution-free mountain water from five Delaware tributaries, with gravity funnelling the precious resource into a reservoir on Roundout Creek, a Hudson tributary on the eastern side of the Catskill mountains, and then down to the City. All in all, the idea of damming the head-waters of the Delaware rather than using the polluted Hudson or its tributaries was very attractive to City officials. But gaining approval for the new reservoirs was not as easy as these officials had hoped.

In addition to the expected opposition from local residents whose homes and farms were to be flooded by the reservoirs, New York had to contend with the interests and demands of the downstream states. Although earlier conflicts had erupted between New Jersey and Pennsylvania over the use of the river, the states had not devised a legal mechanism, other than the 1783 treaty, for managing the Delaware River Basin. New York's entry into the debate, however, motivated the legislatures of New York, New Jersey, and Pennsylvania to authorize, in 1923, the appointment of a commission to draft an interstate compact for dividing the river's flow between the three states.

As negotiations continued into 1926 without any agreement in sight, the New York City Board of Water Supply made an ominous announcement: according to its calculations, by 1935 the City's water consumption would equal the available supply. Finally, in 1928, flaunting opposition by the downstream states, New York initiated legal steps to divert the Delaware headwaters. New Jersey responded to New York's threat to reduce unilaterally the Delaware's flow by filing a bill of complaint with the United States Supreme Court in April 1929 to halt all out-of-Basin diversions proposed by New York. Pennsylvania jointed the suit as an intervenor to protect its commercial, industrial, and community interests within the watershed. The Court appointed a Special Master to hear the states' arguments and supporting oral testimony, and thus was born the Delaware Diversion case, which established many of the basic issues that were to persist to the present day.

New Jersey argued four main points: first, that New York's proposed diversion would obstruct a navigable interstate waterway without the legally required consent of Congress, the Secretary of

War and New Jersey; second, that the diversion would deprive riparian owners along the river of the "natural, unobstructed and undiminished" flow of its waters, thereby violating common law as adopted and applied in New York and New Jersey;[10] third, that the diversion would adversely affect its own plans to develop navigation, hydroelectric power, and sanitation facilities, as well as harming the estuary and its oysters, the shad, municipal water supplies, farming, and recreation; and fourth, that there was no necessity for the diversion, since New York possessed other possible sources and was wasting water by failing to extend its metering and by maintaining the same water rates for over 50 years. In sum, New Jersey claimed that the diversion would impose an irreparable damage on the state and its citizens and demanded an immediate injunction.

New York, in turn, claimed that the diversion would have no injurious effects. Instead, the state argued that the reservoir system would actually be beneficial by removing flood and "waste waters" from the river that would otherwise flow to the sea without benefiting anyone and often causing damages. According to New York's counsel, the dams would allow releases during the dry months of July, August, September, and October, and level the river's flows, thereby improving water quality. Finally, New York pointed out that the City had an imperative need for water supplies and that previous attempts to reach an agreement with New Jersey and Pennsylvania had been rebuffed.

After hearing months of expert testimony from hydraulic, water supply, and sanitary engineers, from geologists, biologists, and agricultural specialists, and from many lay witnesses, the Special Master, Charles N. Burch, filed his report on February 2, 1931. Burch ruled that "no state should have a monopoly of the stream,"[11] and that "a reasonable diversion by New York City should not be enjoined."[12] Burch then proceeded to propose an equitable formula for diversion that would resolve New York's water supply problems without imposing substantial damages on New Jersey. He reduced the amount of the diversion from 600 mgd to 440 mgd, and he instituted minimum flows of 1,535 cfs at Port Jervis and 3,400 cfs at Trenton.

The Special Master was not in a position to suggest and analyze inventive solutions radically different from the main arguments presented by the states. His primary responsibility was to balance the conflicting demands of the involved states, his primary task to sort out conflicting expert testimony—to look for "outstanding facts from which the lay mind can safely draw inferences."[13] He did this task well, examining the experts with great care and listening not only to the experts but as well attaching "considerable weight to the evidence of numerous lay witnesses who live on the banks of the river."[14]

Two years after New Jersey filed its complaint, Supreme Court Justice Oliver Wendell Holmes accepted the Special Master's Report and its conclusions, and in May 1931 he presented the Courts's opinion:

> A river is more than an amenity, it is a treasure. It offers a necessity of life that must be rationed among those who have power over it. New York has the physical power to cut off all the water within its jurisdiction. But clearly the exercise of such a power to the destruction of the interest of the lower States could not be tolerated. And on the other hand equally little could New Jersey be permitted to require New York to give up its power altogether in order that the river might come down to it undiminished. Both States have real and substantial interests in the River that must be reconciled as best they may be. The different traditions and practices in different parts of the country may lead to varying results but the effort is always to secure an equitable apportionment without quibbling over formulas.[15]

The Supreme Court's decision finally gave New York the official approval it needed for proceeding with plans to dam the headwaters of the Delaware and settled, though only temporarily, eight years of interstate bickering over water supply.

While the Court case was developing, another strand leading to the Tocks Island Dam began to unwind. In 1927 Congress passed a Rivers and Harbors Act, which embodied two new planning concepts: comprehensive management of Basin resources, and multiple purpose development. Section I of this Act, derived from House Document 308 (69th Congress, 1st Session), authorized the United States Army Corps of Engineers to conduct a series of Basinwide surveys of navigation, flood control, hydroelectric power, and irrigation needs to assess the feasibility of federal projects.

The survey of the Delaware conducted under this Act, known as the "308 Report," was important in two respects. First it contributed to transferring initiatives for Basinwide planning from the states to the Corps of Engineers, a trend that was further advanced by bitter political antagonisms generated during both the unsuccessful compact attempts of the 1920s and the ongoing Supreme Court case. Second, the broad investigation of the Delaware's needs contained in the 308 Report structured the future thinking of water resource planners. The Report identified all the "outstanding" power and water storage sites in the Basin (including Tocks Island) which marked the later plans; and many of the Report's analyses and recommendations in January 1934 have remained virtually unaltered during the following 40 years.

However, in 1934, the Corps concluded that there was no urgency for dam construction in the Basin. The 308 Report noted that although disastrous flooding had occurred in the Lehigh Valley on several occasions, the Delaware Valley had not experienced any major floods since 1903, and that flood was judged to have a periodicity of 150 to 300 years. The Corps stated categorically that "there is no record of any flood on the Delaware which attained the magnitude of a disaster or caused great loss of life or property." The report concluded:

> The localities subject to flooding are widely scattered and flood losses occur so seldom that it is improbable that local support could be gained for any general flood-control project. Such flood problems as exist are purely local in character and in the few instances, where any considerable expenditure for protection is justified, it could properly be met by local interests without any Federal Contribution.[16]

The Corps concluded that while the Delaware was an important potential source of water supply and power that would probably be used at a future date, rather than the federal government assuming responsibility for such developments within the Delaware watershed, future projects "should be coordinated, supervised, or controlled" by an interstate agency. With this, the Corps handed responsibility for managing the Delaware River Basin back to the states.

At first the states needed some outside encouragement and support in the new undertaking. The country was in the depths of the Depression, and Roosevelt was initiating a vast array of New Deal programs that concentrated governmental powers in Washington. By 1935, partly in reaction to centralization, a nationwide movement towards greater interstate ties began, with New Jersey, New York, and Pennsylvania becoming the first states to establish Commissions on Interstate Cooperation. Representatives from these commissions and several federal agencies formed the nucleus of a group which in 1936 established the Interstate Commission on the Delaware River Basin (Incodel) to coordinate regional management of the Basin.

Incodel was created, not by compact, as had been attempted in the 1920s, but as the product of parallel legislation in Pennsylvania, New Jersey, New York, and later Delaware. Its mode of operation, which required the approval of eight legislative houses before any concrete actions could be taken, made Incodel into a mere channel for agreement among the participating commissions and assured that it could not develop any measure of independence. Incodel also soon developed a strong antifederalist bias and solidly opposed federal intervention in Delaware River affairs. Partly for these reasons, in its early years Incodel shunned expensive plans that would require federal aid, and it focused almost entirely upon pollution control.

However, the policy began to shift after the war, especially in response to a severe drought that struck the Northeast in 1949. In the summer of that year, New Jersey and parts of New York experienced their driest June in the 78 years of weather records, and New York City water supplies dropped precipitously. The City turned to other available sources of water, squeezing an additional 50 million gallons a day from wells, ponds, and infiltration galleries tapped on Long Island and Staten Island, while officials implored residents to cut back on consumption. In mid October, due to light summer rainfalls and an upsurge in water consumption in the fall, City reservoirs registered only 50 percent capacity—the lowest level since their construction in 1916. Mayor Fred O'Dwyer called the situation "most serious," and in late December instituted a conservation program of "dry" Thursdays. On December 30, a spokesman announced that if consumption continued at the same rate, New York had only 71 days left before its water would be gone and only 44 days before pressure would fail.

One reason for New York's severe but brief water shortage in 1949 was that none of the reservoirs authorized by the 1931 Supreme Court case had been completed. Construction of two dams on Delaware tributaries (the Pepacton Reservoir on the East Branch and the Neversink Reservoir on the Neversink River) and of one dam on a Hudson tributary (the Rondout Reservoir on the Rondout Creek) had been postponed, first by the Depression and then by World War II. If, in 1949, New York had had this additional 440 mgd of Delaware waters (335 mgd from Pepacton and 105 from Neversink), the drought would not have caused such an extreme water shortage. The City responded to the crisis by announcing plans for a new reservoir at Cannonsville on the West Branch of the Delaware River, again choosing neither to develop the upper Hudson nor to attack more fundamental causes of the shortage such as the massive leaks in the City's water system and the lack of metering.

The crisis atmosphere produced by the intense drought and by the threatened diversion provided a major impetus to an Incodel proposal to survey the Delaware River Basin, and in the winter of 1949, at the height of the water shortage, the legislatures of New York,

Pennsylvania, and New Jersey appropriated funds to investigate possible development schemes. Incodel contracted two engineering firms—Malcolm Pirnie Engineers, and Albright and Friel, Inc.—to design an integrated plan to meet water needs in the Basin until the year 2000. Incodel received the consulting firms' final recommendations, known as the "Pirnie Report," in August 1950 and presented them to the state legislatures the following month. The Pirnie Report recommended a two-stage development of the Delaware River Basin, the first stage to include two dams on Delaware tributaries in New York and a main stem dam at Wallpack Bend, between the Water Gap and Port Jervis. (This dam would later be shifted a few miles downstream to the Tocks Island site due to unsatisfactory geologic conditions of the original location.) The eight-page report concluded with the recommendation that:

> ... immediate consideration be given to the establishment by compact of a Delaware River Water Commission, with appropriate representation from each of the proprietary states, to which would be delegated power to plan, finance, construct and operate the Stage 1 integrated water project, to sell water service capacity to political sub-divisions and other water supply agencies and to provide stream flow regulations which would benefit each of the proprietary states.[17]

By 1952, New York despaired that the recommendations of the Pirnie Report would soon be acted upon. Unable to expand its water supplies while demand continued to rise, New York City once again considered itself caught in a bind, and in April 1952 the City filed a petition with the Supreme Court to modify the 1931 decision to allow a 800 mgd diversion from the Delaware watershed. Within two months New York State, New Jersey, and Pennsylvania had all joined the suit, and in February 1953 the issue of allocating the waters of the Delaware was back before the nation's highest court.

The second court case was also heard by a Special Master. In this instance the Special Master emphasized the importance of the states' reaching an agreement, and by mid 1953 they had designed a compromise which was subsequently endorsed by the Court. New York was allocated the 800 mgd it requested in exchange for allocating to New Jersey a "free" 100 mgd without compensating releases. The Court instituted a slightly revised formula for New York's compensating releases known as the "Montague formula," and appointed a river master to supervise it. Pennsylvania in turn gained New Jersey's abrogation of the 1783 Anti-Dam Treaty and a promise by New

Jersey to condemn land for a dam site on the Delaware between the two states. The Supreme Court adopted the Special Master's report on June 4, 1954.

The horse trading that characterized the 1954 Court case maximized each state's benefits. Although many of the same issues were raised once again (the effects of dams and diversions on salinity control, recreation, and shad and oyster populations), they received less emphasis in 1954 than they had in 1931. This may have been due to a change in New Jersey's position. Abandoning its 1931 position of total opposition to main stem dams and out-of-Basin diversions, the state recognized that similar measures would be necessary to solve its own water supply problems in the not so distant future.

In the spring of 1955, the District Office of the Corps of Engineers in Philadelphia completed the review of the 308 Report, requested by the Senate Committee on Public Works five years earlier, to determine whether changes in conditions warranted modifications in that report's recommendations. The preliminary draft of their review concluded that conditions had not significantly changed and that federal expenditures in the River Basis were still unjustified. The timing was spooky. Soon after the draft was completed the double hurricanes struck the Northeast.

IV. THE INSTITUTIONAL RESPONSE: CREATING AN "EXPEDITER"

The massive floods of 1955 indelibly altered the political debate over the necessity of a main stem dam for the Delaware River. The natural disaster created a powerful demand for more effective flood control measures in the Basin and gave the Corps of Engineers its mandate to conduct a comprehensive survey. While the Corps proceeded with its investigation, the governors of the four Basin states and mayors of New York City and Philadelphia entered negotiations aimed at the design of a suitable interstate commission. Changing its name to the Delaware River Basin Advisory Committee (DRBAC), this group of politicians began organizing support for the enactment of a new interstate compact to assure implementation of the Corps Basin development plans.

The process by which the compact was designed significantly determined the particulars and the tone of the document. State government representatives, with minimal federal participation, assumed the major responsibility for drawing up the terms of the agreement. Drafters of the compact had as their goal the creation of a strong regional organization that would bind the federal government and the four states equally, and would have powers to develop and implement a comprehensive, multiple purpose river basin development program.

In September 1959, the Syracuse University report, which had been sponsored by the Water Research Foundation, was submitted; it bore the title "The Problem of Water-Resource Administration, with Special Reference to the Delaware River Basin." It was then passed to the Advisory Committee:

> The Syracuse researchers recommended initial establishment of a federal organization which could be phased into a federal-interstate organization at a later date. When the members of the Advisory Committee considered the recommendation, they decided that if a federal-interstate compact was the ultimate goal, it should be created initially. Thus, the committee decided to propose a federal-interstate compact organization which had not been tried in the past and for which there was no indication of federal support.[18]

The Advisory Committee made particular efforts to smooth those controversial issues that had snagged past proposals for the interstate-federal commission. The drafters resolved possible conflicts in the final draft as follows:

1. The Commission was given no jurisdiction over navigation.
2. The question of private versus public power development was left open.
3. The compact did not attempt to lay out a division of the Basin's water but left the allocation open to future negotiations.
4. No changes would be permitted in the Supreme Court's rulings for the 100-year term of the compact except by unanimous consent.
5. Philadelphia and New York City were not given voting rights but representatives were to be invited to advise the alternates from their respective states.
6. The federal government received the same one vote as did each of the four states.

After extensive consultations between the state oriented drafters and federal officials, the compact was approved by Congress, and on September 27, 1961, it was signed into law (PL 87-328) by President Kennedy. The compact endowed the new federal interstate commission, known as the Delaware River Basin Commission, with unique authority and centralized power in the Basin. Section 318 of the compact establishes that:

> No project having a substantial effect on the water resources of the Basin shall hereafter be undertaken by any person, corporation or governmental authority unless it shall have been first submitted to and approved by the commission.

The DRBC also was accorded jurisdiction over out-of-Basin diversions, subject to the 1954 Supreme Court decision, as well as flood plain zoning. But the Commission's primary objective, according to Section 3.1, was the implementation of development plans in the Basin:

> Purpose and Policy. The commission shall develop and effectuate plans, policies and projects relating to the water resources of the Basin. It shall adopt and promote uniform and coordinated policies for water conservation, control, use and management in the basin. It shall encourage the planning, development and financing of water resources projects according to such plans and policies.

Pursuant to this end, soon after its creation the DRBC adopted most elements of the Corps' Delaware River Basin Report and comprehensive plan. The Corps' plans became the DRBC's commitment.

Passage of the Delaware River Basin Compact of 1961 and the Flood Control Act of 1962, which contained the comprehensive Basin development plan of HD 522, ushered the Delaware Valley and the country into a new era of water resources management. The DRBC reflected a unique concept of interstate-federal cooperation in the field of Basinwide planning and management. It has since been characterized as "one of the most sophisticated forms of 'cooperative federalism' yet attempted—the epitome of the American effort to obtain the advantages of decentralized decision making while simultaneously avoiding the perils of provincialism."[19]

As the DRBC was taking its first step in the early 1960s towards implementing the comprehensive development plan, another crisis developed—this time a drought—that provided further impetus for proceeding with the Tocks project. In 1961 the spring runoff needed to fill the Basin reservoirs and sustain water supplies through the dry summer months dropped drastically. In the next four years the entire Northeast received 25 percent less rainfall than normal, and by April 1965, as a result of the 44-month dry spell, New York City's reservoirs were at 40 percent capacity. Worried about the serious shortage, City officials instituted a series of emergency ad hoc conservation measures—street cleaning was halted, the use of garden hoses was restricted, and the filling of backyard pools was prohibited—while the more fundamental problems of waste and leakage remained untouched.

In May, City restaurants were instructed to stop serving water to customers unless specifically requested. The City banned lawn sprinkling in June, and one month later, at the height of the drought, two blimps began flying around the city every night with flashing signs imploring New Yorkers to "Take Brief Showers Instead of Baths" and "Stop Running Hot Water on Dishes." Although some of these measures, such as the ban on serving water in restaurants, were more effective psychologically than in reducing consumption by a significant degree, New York City did manage to force water use down from 1,100 to 900 million gallons a day by the end of June.

But pleading with water users to reduce consumption was not enough to alleviate New York City's worst water shortage ever. More direct action was needed to increase the Delaware reservoirs' water supplies. City officials accomplished this by continuing to divert the full 490 million gallons a day from the Delaware watershed—as permitted by the 1954 Supreme Court decree—while ceasing, on June 14, 1965, the compensatory releases to augment the river's flow required by the same Court decision. By July 1, the flow at Montague had dropped to less than half the 1,525 cfs guaranteed by the 1954 decision, causing the "salt front" in the Delaware Bay to inch its way up towards the Camden well fields and the water supply intake for Philadelphia at Torresdale.[c] Although the salt front, at its closest, was still ten miles from Torresdale, local newspapers in New Jersey and Pennsylvania printed sensationalistic reports of the salt front daily advance and of its threat to municipal and industrial water supplies, fanning the passions of the general public.

New York's flagrant violation of the 1954 Supreme Court decree, which required that certain minimum flows be maintained at Montague and Trenton under all conditions, sparked immediate reactions:

New Jersey's Governor Hughes, who was the current chairman of the DRBC and seeking re-election in the fall, accused New York City of "illegal" action and threatened to reopen the court litigation. Pennsylvania's Secretary of Forests and Waters, Maurice Goddard, leveled charges of "water piracy" and his counterpart in Philadelphia, Samuel Baxter, indi-

[c]A discussion of the salt front—what it is and what to do about it—is found in essay 5 in this volume.

cated that the emergency was forcing the issue of New York City drawing upon Hudson water.[20]

On July 7, 1965, a cautious DRBC finally entered the renewed fracas between New York and its downstream neighbors over allocation of the Delaware's water. The commissioners met in an "extraordinary" session and declared a four-state water emergency; this provided the DRBC with absolute authority to ration and allocate water use in the Basin. Asserting that it was "hydrologically impossible" for New York to satisfy both its diversion and release requirements, the DRBC enacted three critical temporary modifications of the 1954 decree: (1) the Montague flow requirement was lowered from 1,525 to 1,200 cfs (i.e., from 1,000 mgd to 800 mgd); (2) New York City's diversions from the Delaware were cut from 490 to 335 mgd, and (3) New York City was directed to resume its 200 mgd releases. To boost flow levels, the Commission directed private electric power companies in Pennsylvania and New York to release up to 266 mgd from their hydro-power reservoirs. The combination of these stop-gap measures produced some beneficial effects, but New York City's water consumption plus the imposed releases continued to exceed its buildup of supplies.

In early August New York City officials announced that, if maintained, the DRBC's water use policies would force the Delaware reservoirs dry by the end of November. Mayor Wagner, reacting to this inauspicious prediction, initiated steps to buy and borrow water from private companies in order to sustain the City's supplies until the spring. In another emergency meeting, on August 18, the DRBC recognized New York's desperate plight and proceeded once again to juggle the Basin's water resources. The DRBC's intervention this second time, followed by late August rains, alleviated the immediate drought crisis. By late October the danger of salt contaminating Philadelphia's water supplies no longer existed; by Mid November New York's reservoirs had reached a level equal to the previous year; and in March 1966 the crisis was officially declared over.

For a young, untested agency, the Delaware River Basin Commission performed well in its handling of the drought and the various interstate complications. Joseph Sax, a noted legal scholar, reviewed the DRBC's activities during this period, writing:

> In the broadest sense the lesson deals with the function of law. We are used to considering the law as an institution which resolves disputes by defining relative rights and obligations upon a set of facts which are both known and static. And this, indeed, is what the Supreme Court decision did.

We are not accustomed to viewing law as a device for promoting creativity; yet this, in essence, is what the Delaware River Basin Commission, as a law-making and law-enforcing body, did. Instead of simply dividing the water "available". . .on the basis of an analysis of some previously existing legal rule, such as the Court's decision or the compact terms, it changed the facts by seeking out, and inducing the parties involved to seek out, additional water supplies. Instead of merely allocating a scarce resource, it resolved the conflict to a significant degree by making the resource at issue less scarce.[21]

Sax thus praises the DRBC as an institution for its success in promoting a "creative search for alternatives" and considers it to be a better conflict resolving mechanism than the Supreme Court. But he adds that:

[On] the other hand, one must be more than a little troubled by the fact that the Commission was in existence all during the time that the drought was developing, beginning in 1961, and that it did nothing to keep the crisis from coming to a head; that it was not mobilized to action until the crisis was at the disaster stage; and that when it did act, its solutions were ad hoc and temporary.[22]

From its first days, the DRBC also gave much of its attention to another area—controlling water quality in the Delaware Bay. The federal government in 1962 had funded a four-year, $1.2 million, comprehensive analysis of pollution problems known as the Delaware Estuary Comprehensive Survey (DECS). This investigation, which had grown out of the Public Health Service study of Delaware pollution for the Corps' HD 522, was staffed by young, mathematically oriented engineers. Using the latest analytic techniques, DECS developed four alternative plans and presented them in 1966 to the political decision makers on the DRBC. As has been pointed out by one careful observer of DECS, its development and implementation appeared to represent the "frontier of applied scientific fact-finding in 1966."[23] However, in fact, the DECS had a critical structural flaw: the division of bureaucratic responsibilities into a "thinking" agency (DECS) and an "action" agency (DRBC). This split discouraged serious refinement of the technical analysis once the technical plan produced by the DECS group was turned over to the DRBC for implementation.[24]

The function of the DRBC has thus been varied. It has acted sometimes as a compromiser seeking to resolve conflicts among the Basin states, and sometimes (as in the instance of DECS) as the chief framer of a Basinwide policy. In the instance of Tocks, the DRBC role may best be characterized as that of an expediter, seeking to implement the comprehensive development plan developed by the Corps of Engineers. For the DRBC to be an effective expediter, however, it must operate by consensus—something, as will be seen, that was never achieved for the Tocks Island Dam.[25]

V. THE STRUGGLE RESUMES

No one likes to have his home condemned and to have his community reduced to ruins—particularly when he lives in an area as beautiful as the Delaware River Valley. Thus, it was completely predictable that the first signs of opposition to the Tocks Island Dam project would come from the local residents. They were the ones most directly affected and they were the ones who had the most to lose.

But for a long time, even the local people seemed passively to accept the plan to flood the Minisink Valley. Hardly a handful of people in 1960 opposed the dam; and in 1962, when Congress held hearings on HD 522, no one was active enough to make a real fuss. Many people living around the taking area believed that the project would contribute to the region's and their own economic betterment. Others felt that it was hopeless even to try to influence the government's plans, that they "couldn't fight city hall." Local residents reluctantly accepted the Tocks Island Dam and waited to see what would happen.

The first postauthorization public hearings on the Tocks project, held by the DRBC and by Congress in 1964, marked the beginning of more vocal dissent. Soon after these hearings, several local residents opposing the dam founded the Delaware Valley Conservation Association. In four days, they had gathered 1,000 signatures on a petition asking the House Appropriations Committee to hold hearings in Stroudsburg. The Committee granted the request, and the Congressmen appeared in Stroudsburg in April 1965 though with no noticeable effect on the character of the project planning then underway.

In the fall of 1966, local landowners were confronted by the first tangible evidence of the dam. Although Congress had yet to appropriate any funds for land acquisition for the project, the Corps notified 208 landholders by letter that their properties were being considered for the initial year of purchases for the Recreation Area only. In November, 604 landowners became plaintiffs in a class action suit to stop the Tocks Island Dam project and the Delaware Water Gap Recreation Area. The landowners' suit began in the federal court in Philadelphia, went to the Court of Appeals in the spring of 1967, and reached the Supreme Court in August 1968. The suit was finally dismissed in October 1968 on the technical grounds that the government had not consented to being sued.[26]

While landowners organized their legal and political opposition to Tocks, environmentalists began protesting plans to transform a 44-acre glacial pond located atop the Kittatinny Ridge and inside the DWGNRA into the upper reservoir of a pumped-storage facility. A pumped-storage facility (as explained more fully below in essay 7) is a system for storing electric power. At night, when demand is low, electricity is used to pump water from a lower to an upper reservoir, and the stored water is then allowed to fall to the lower reservoir during the daytime, generating peak demand electricity. Although the comprehensive plan in HD 522 included provisions for development of pumped storage by private utilities as well as for public conventional on-stream hydropower, the plan authorized by Congress and by the DRBC provided only for the latter. Private development of pumped-storage by private utilities as well as for public

In March 1961 the first steps towards private pumped-storage were taken when the State of New Jersey and the New Jersey Power and Light Company agreed to an exchange of land, the utility receiving in the swap over 700 acres of state park land on Kittatinny Ridge in Worthington State Park, including the 44-acre Sunfish Pond. By 1966 the Corps was proposing that the Basin comprehensive plan be amended to allow the power companies to proceed. Although local newspapers in the early 1960s published occasional stories on the plans for constructing a pumped-storage facility, until 1965 few people even realized that Sunfish Pond had been sold. One reason for this ignorance is that engineering reports and public announcements commonly referred to the Pond, not by its known name, but as the "Upper Labar Reservoir," since it was directly above a small island of that name.

In 1965, Glenn Fischer, a local resident concerned about the fate of the Pond, sat on the edge of the Appalachian Trail collecting signatures and began writing protest letters to newspapers and politicians demanding that the Pond be returned to the state. Fischer then formed the Lenni Lenape League and, through press publicity, the group gained members and supporters; and in April 1966, a Warren County chapter was formed. One month later, on Mother's Day, the League organized its first protest pilgrimage up the two-and-one-half-mile mountain path to Sunfish Pond. The Lenni Lenape League conducted a vigorous campaign with the support of the New Jersey Audubon Society, Sierra Club, and other groups. "Save Sunfish Pond" bumper stickers and lapel pins began appearing all over the state. The preservation campaign reached a climax in the spring of

1967 when opponents to the project marched to the Pond with Supreme Court Justice William O. Douglas, making the Pond's future a major public issue.

A public hearing held in August 1967 by the DRBC to consider the utilities' proposed amendment to the comprehensive plan marked a turning point in the pumped-storage debate. For the power companies the main issues were to determine which customers would receive preference in the delivery of the additional power, to decide on charges for water use, and to allocate construction fees for the dam and reservoir. For the citizen groups the main issue was whether Sunfish Pond should be used as the upper reservoir. They argued that Sunfish Pond should be preserved for two basic reasons. First, if it were used as the upper reservoir, river water would have to be pumped into and drawn from the lake. This would of necessity destroy the Pond's pristine purity, change its water quality and ecology, and reduce its attractiveness due to extreme fluctuations in the water level. Second, as the largest New Jersey lake inaccessible by car, Sunfish was an important wilderness retreat that would be downgraded by facilities associated with the power station. The area's natural qualities, argued the conservationists, deserved preservation in the increasingly urban northeast megalopolis.[27]

By December 1967, Secretary of Interior Stewart L. Udall, responding to a barrage of letters from conservationists, had declared that the federal government would do everything possible to save Sunfish Pond and would press for modifications of the storage plant's design to avoid damaging the glacial lake. The press exerted a powerful force to save the Pond. In a late May 1968 editorial, *The New York Times* declared its support for two bills in the New Jersey legislature to repurchase Sunfish Pond, "a small but irreplaceable natural asset, which for that reason alone, deserves preserving."[28] Finally, in July, in a hearing at Trenton on the "Save Sunfish Pond" bill, the power companies announced a compromise plan for pumped-storage that did not use Sunfish Pond but instead expanded the existing Upper Yards Creek reservoir. Conservationists still opposed this scheme, however, claiming that the enlarged reservoir would leak and contaminate Sunfish Pond, and that the twenty-stories-high retaining dikes within 1,000 feet of Sunfish Pond and "smack in the middle of Appalachian Trail" would irreversibly mar the environment. Nonetheless, the companies' retreat from plans to use the glacial lake seemed to most of the public a victory for the conservationists.

But the Sunfish Pond issue was not completely resolved. As part of the compromise, the comprehensive plan had to be amended to allow pumped-storage facilities. On October 22, 1968, the DRBC issued its amendment, known as Resolution 68-12, which contained a fairly strict list of conditions for approval:

> Sunfish Pond could not be used as a reservoir, and its recreation and conservation values could not be impaired. Construction of an upper reservoir was to occur with a minimum disruption of the natural environment. The Department of the Interior was to designate the exact location of the reservoir, and was to supervise restorative landscaping. Penstocks between the upper and lower reservoirs, and transmissions lines, would be buried underground; excavation scars would be restored and landscaped. The Corps and the DRBC would determine the pumping schedule, to correspond with the requirements of river management. Services and facilities to mitigate fishery problems would be paid for by the utilities.[29]

In March 1969, the New Jersey State Assembly voted to buy back the lake and property sold eight years earlier. Although the Senate never approved this bill, the power companies offered to return the Pond to the state without charge. On July 1, 1969, Governor Hughes accepted the deed to Sunfish Pond and 68 acres of surrounding woodland. The power companies retained over 600 acres on the Kittatinny Ridge.

Both the DRBC and the power companies came out of the Sunfish Pond controversy looking like "good guys." DRBC's Resolution 68-12 proclaimed, in effect, that the Commission was siding with environmentalists and giving primacy to saving natural resources from abuse and destruction. The utilities' gift of the Pond back to the state was equally good public relations. The environmentalists lost much of their support. The issue of regaining the remaining park land, for all practical purposes, disappeared from public view.

It is difficult to determine exactly how the compromise over Sunfish Pond was actually reached. Casey Kays, one of the Pond's most devoted protectors, maintains that it was pressures on the DRBC from Secretary Udall in Washington. Henry Smith, a later director of the Lenni Lenape League, hypothesizes that the legislative activities in the New Jersey State Assembly compelled the power companies to relinquish the Pond. Thomas Kean, the legislator who sponsored the bill to buy back the state property, believes that the major factor, in addition to pressure from Washington and the State Assembly, was public opinion. According to Kean's interpretation, the DRBC withdrew support for the power companies' position when citizen protest reached the offices of Congressmen and began to threaten the whole Tocks project. "The DRBC cares about one thing," says Kean, "And that is the Tocks Island Dam. They see their future as the 'Czar of the Delaware' dependent upon the continuous source of revenue provided by Tocks. Resolution 68-12 was an attempt to short-circuit environmental opposition and prevent the transition of protest from Sunfish Pond to the Tocks project."[30]

But just as Sunfish Pond–related environmental concern was beginning to fade, a new controversy erupted. On January 1, 1970, President Nixon signed the National Environmental Policy Act (NEPA) into law, revolutionizing environmental control procedures in the United States. Section 102(2) (c) required all federal agencies to assess and make public the environmental impact of each major action. NEPA also established a Council on Environmental Quality (CEQ) in the Executive Office of the President to investigate environmental conditions in the nation, develop and coordinate new federal programs and policies, and generally advise the President on solutions. CEQ was also charged with overseeing the environmental assessment process and reviewing the final impact statements after the drafts were commented on by federal, state, and local government agencies as well as the public.

In 1970, pursuant to the National Environmental Policy Act, the Corps prepared an Impact Statement on the Tocks Island Dam project and in November presented its preliminary draft to the CEQ and the public. This preliminary Environmental Impact Statement, a cursory eight-page discussion of the dam's influence on the environment, seemed to invite public outrage. After the landowners' class action suit, and the Sunfish Pond dispute, the Impact Statement initiated the third round of the Tocks Island Dam Controversy. Proponents for the dam included no one who was particularly new to the Tocks dispute. The nucleus of those urging an early construction start included the Corps of Engineers, the Delaware River Basin Commission staff, and various industrial and business interests. Local citizens and local county officials organized two pro-dam lobbying groups: the Tocks Island Citizen Association and the Tocks Island Regional Advisory Council.

While the aftermath of the November 1970 Impact Statement came as a shock to the dam's proponents, it was a boon to the opponents. It gave them something concrete to react to, to criticize and to organize around. In December, three groups already opposing the dam—the Lenni Lenape League, the Delaware Valley Conservation Association, and the eastern Pennsylvania chapter of the Sierra Club—formed the Save-the-Delaware-Coalition. This organization of organizations set out to coordinate the various groups which opposed all main stem dams on the Delaware and supported the preservation of a free-flowing river.

From that time on, the two camps have battled. And they have turned out to be evenly matched.

NOTES

1. *The New York Times*, August 18, 1955, p. 1.
2. *Ibid.*, August 20, 1955, p. 1.
3. House Document No. 522, Delaware River Basin Report, U.S. Army Corps of Engineers, Vol. 1, 1962, pp. xxi–xxii.
4. Luke W. Brodhead, *Delaware Water Gap, Its Legends and Early History* (Philadelphia: Sherman and Co., 1870).
5. *Ibid.*
6. House Document No. 179, *Delaware River*, 73rd Congress, 2nd Session, 1934, pp. 70–73.
7. *The Fourth Annual Report of the Water Supply Commission of New York*, for the year ending February 1, 1909, State Water Supply Commission of New York, 1909, p. 424, in *Delaware Diversion Case*, vol. 7, p. 589.
8. House Document No. 179, *op. cit.*, p. 103.
9. A detailed history of water management before 1955 may be found in Roscoe C. Martin and others, *River Basin Administration and the Delaware* (Syracuse, N.Y.: Syracuse University Press, 1960), pp. 277–306.
10. New Jersey's Counsel, Duane Minard, equated New York's initial attempt to negotiate a diversion of the waters—which New Jersey claimed it owned by riparian rights—with the following story:

> "It's just like going to a man who owns a farm and saying, 'I will give you $10,000 for your farm.'
>
> The Owner says: 'Why, I couldn't take $10,000 for my farm.'
>
> The proposed purchaser puts his money back in his pocket and says: 'All right, I'll take it anyway.'"

In *Delaware Diversion Case*, vol. 48, p. 36.
11. *Delaware Diversion Case*, vol. 44, p. 4785.
12. *Ibid.*, p. 4786.
13. *Ibid.*, p. 4961.
14. *Ibid.*, p. 4902.
15. *New Jersey v. New York*, 283 U.S., 342-43 (1931).
16. House Document No. 179, *op. cit.*, pp. 3–4.
17. Incodel, *Report on the Utilization of the Waters of the Delaware River Basin*, prepared by Malcolm Pirnie Engineers and Albright and Friel, Inc., September 1950, p. 8.
18. Vernon D. Northrop, "The Delaware River Basin Commission. A Prototype in River Basin Development," *Journal of Soil and Water Conservation* 22 (2) (1967): 3.
19. Bruce Ackerman, Susan R. Ackerman, James W. Sawyer, Jr., and Dale W. Henderson, *The Uncertain Search for Environmental Quality*, New York: Free Press, 1974, p. 4.

20. Richard Hogarty, *The Delaware River Emergency*, cited in Joseph Sax, *Water Law, Planning and Policy* (New York: Bobbs-Merrill, 1972), p. 174.

21. Joseph L. Sax, *Water Law, Planning and Policy* (New York: Bobbs-Merrill, 1972), pp. 178–179.

22. *Ibid.*, p. 180.

23. Ackerman and others, *op. cit.*, Chapter 4.

24. *Ibid.*, Chapter 5.

25. Richard Hogarty, *The Delaware River Drought Emergency*, Inter-University Case Program #107 (New York: Bobbs-Merrill, 1970).

26. *Delaware Valley Conservation Association and the 604 Additional Plaintiffs v. Stanley R. Resor, Stewart C. Udall, and W. F. Cassidy*, 378 U.S. (October 1968).

27. Interview with Mr. Henry Smith, present director of the Lenni Lenape League.

28. *The New York Times*, May 24, 1968, p. 46.

29. William Hillhouse and John DeWeerdt, *Legal Devices for Accommodating Water Resource Development and Environmental Values* (Springfield, Va.: Technical Information Service, 1971), p. 187.

30. Interview with Mr. Thomas Kean, New Jersey State Assemblyman.

✳ *Chapter 3*

Conflict and Irresolution

Harold A. Feiveson

The Tocks project followed a more or less routine course until the Corps' initial Environmental Impact Statement, issued in the fall of 1970, set off a shock of opposition. The rush of events that followed gathered into the controversy a variety of actors: public agencies supporting the dam, various competing private interests, the White House and Executive Office of the President, the governors of the Basin states and their staffs, and congressional chieftains. It was during this period also, when the protagonists were striving hardest to reach decisions, that a large fraction of the technical, economic, and political analyses relevant to the Tocks project were produced and examined.[a]

I. FLOODS, DROUGHT, POWER, AND PLAY: THE PROFESSIONALS

A. The Corps and the Water Professionals

It was not surprising that the precipitating event was a study done by the Army Corps of Engineers. Throughout the Tocks controversy, the Corps has been the major planning agency, the major source of analytic studies, the most visible government agency in the region, and, consequently, the major target of people and groups opposed to the dam.

The Corps is a highly structured agency with a rigorous chain of command. The Washington headquarters, at the top of the com-

[a]The full citations for studies referred to in this essay and in the volume generally are given in a list at the end of this volume, pp. 407–411.

mand, maintains a close liaison with Congress and provides the final review and approval of plans developed at the Division and District levels. Although the Washington office is directed by a three star general and a thin layer of other Army officers, the office is mainly staffed by civilians. This is true as well at the regional levels, albeit with corresponding rank reductions for the military command; the Division offices are directed by one star generals, the District offices by colonels. The Washington headquarters report formally to the Secretary of the Army, although in practice most of their dealings are directly with Congress, from whom they derive the greater part of their political support.

Serious planning for and direction of Corps projects occur at the regional level, at the Division and District headquarters. The Tocks project falls within the jurisdiction of the North Atlantic Division headquarters, which includes the District offices from Norfolk, Baltimore, Philadelphia, and New York, and which has responsibility for all Corps projects in the Northeast. In early 1971 the Division came under the direction of General Richard H. Groves, a powerful advocate of Corps projects (and incidentally the son of the Army general who directed the WWII Manhattan Project to develop the atomic bomb). In this position, Groves presented the Corps testimony before the congressional appropriations committees in support of the Tocks project, and he was also the chief Corps contact with the Basin governors regarding the project.

Groves's message in these briefings was clear: Tocks was needed to protect people on the Delaware flood plain and to provide water for the growing population in New Jersey. Whatever the benefits of power and recreation supplied by the project, it was the flood control and water supply purpose that *really* counted. To Groves, although recreation accounted for about 50 percent of benefits in the Corps' formal benefit-cost calculation, recreation was "not something we will fight and die over." This idea was also echoed by the chief of planning of the Division, Herbert Howard, who believed that the inclusion of recreation in the multipurpose project, although economically justified, had actually made more enemies for the project than friends, and had deflected attention from the critical issues of flood control and increased water supply.

These views of Groves, Howard, and others were not lightly based. They had grown out of two long range planning studies for the Northeast, the North Atlantic Regional Water Resources Study (NAR) and the Northeastern Water Supply Study (NEWS), which vividly portrayed the growing demands for water in New Jersey and the difficulties of meeting this demand without Tocks. These studies were not done in great detail, however; the responsibility for the detailed investigation of water supply alternatives had been delegated to the District Office.

From the beginning of the Tocks project as a component of the Delaware Basin Comprehensive Survey, the detailed planning and engineering design had been the responsibility of the Philadelphia District Office. Here, Tocks had assumed an important role in the District's planning. The Tocks Island Dam is a large project by any standard: it would be the eighth largest public works project of any kind undertaken by the Corps in the United States. It was by far the largest Corps civil project contemplated for the Northeast, and it represented 15 percent of the total value of authorized civil projects in the North Atlantic Division and 40 percent of those in the Philadelphia District.

By 1971 the Philadelphia District Office had lavished years of attention and effort on the planning of the Tocks project; the chief responsible officers were deeply committed to its fulfillment and were resentful of what appeared to them to be shallow and irresponsible criticism of the project. The civilian officer who perhaps best exemplified this attitude was Gordon Dilley, then Acting Assistant Chief of the Engineering Division. Previously, Dilley had been the Tocks project officer and in one way or the other intimately involved in the detailed planning of the project since the early 1960s. Dilley is a quiet, earnest person, trained as a civil engineer, with a reputation for thoroughness, integrity, and persistence (his Tocks adversaries would say stubbornness). He maintained a strong feeling for the outdoors and wild unspoiled areas; he liked to mention how his father, who often took him fishing as a youth, always thought the Corps "a catastrophe for trout fishing." But Dilley also grew up in Wilkes Barre, a community ever threatened by floods, which in the summer of 1972 was struck by one of the worst in American history. The desolation and anguish it brought in its wake were observed by Dilley in a sad visit soon afterwards.

Whatever the reasons, Dilley certainly felt deeply about the project's benefits, especially flood control and water supply. He saw the Corps' mission as stated in the preamble to the congressional charge to the Corps to develop land to its highest and best use for the benefit of its citizens. This meant to Dilley managing the river, not only for flood protection but also to make more water available, if that was what the citizens of the Basin states were demanding. Beyond the explicit economic benefits to be provided by the project, Dilley saw in it also a stirring accomplishment. He would comment how he hoped to find a way to have cable cars run up the sides of the embankments and across the top of the dam so visitors could look down the dramatic spillways and onto the distant vistas. In this romantic and attractive vision, Dilley conceived of the dam as a magnet for tourists both young and old, a landmark that would draw visitors from all parts of the Northeast.

Dilley also recognized that there would be certain unavoidable adverse consequences, notably the disappearance of 37 miles of the flowing river and the mostly unpleasant impacts on the local people near the dam; but he rejected the notion that the project would do all sorts of other environmental harm, and he sharply resented the charge that he and the Corps were indifferent to environmental concerns. Indeed, Dilley took pride in the Corps' efforts to protect the shad and the oyster, and to survey historical and archaeological sites. Under his direction, the Corps incorporated into the Tocks project fish ladders to get the shad over the dam and a water release schedule that would leave the spring flows to the estuary unimpeded, a condition generally recognized as helpful to the oysters. The Corps also had sponsored detailed archaeological studies of the region, the first such studies done in the area, but whose findings were (perversely, in Dilley's view) then used by the dam opposition as another argument against the project.

The most important studies of the Tocks project by the Corps were done out of the Philadelphia office. These included the initial Basin Survey, contained in House Document 522, a series of benefit-cost calculations, and the Environmental Impact Statements. The final Environmental Impact Statement was much more thorough than the eight-page preliminary version; it involved substantial coordination with other agencies, most notably the Department of the Interior, who assessed the impact of the dam on fish and wildlife. Released in October 1971, the final statement contained in appendices a wide variety of public comment on the initial draft statement. The body of the statement was a reasonably thorough assessment of environmental problems that might be expected to accompany the project, but presented in a way that suggested that most of these were subject to control, compromise, and solution. In this sense the statement was rather upbeat and supportive of the Tocks project.

Environmental Impact Statements are also supposed to analyze alternatives to the project under study that conceivably could be less environmentally troublesome. This was not done systematically in the Corps statement, as was soon pointed out by several critics. In this respect it was not different from similar reports then being prepared in other parts of the country. Accompanying the Impact Statement was a study commissioned by the Corps under prodding by the

President's Council on Environmental Quality. This study, "An Appraisal of the Potential for Cultural Eutrophication of Tocks Island Lake" by Jack McCormick and Associates, played a critical role in the next act, which is described in section III below.

The Army Corps of Engineers provides a meeting ground for three kinds of sensibilities of a vivid stamp: that of the professional, the military, and the bureaucrat. The water professionals in the Corps, in fraternity with their colleagues elsewhere, take a marked pride in their hard-headed realism, above all in their willingness to think unblinkingly about the violence unleashed by a flooding river, and to gainsay any easy wishful thinking about human nature. They looked knowingly and without surprise at how the citizens' memory of the 1955 flood faded with time, until only they, the professionals, were able to keep clearly in mind the full flood dangers to the region. They noted, with perhaps a tinge of mock sadness, the general irresponsibility of the populace, not only forgetful of the potential power of an unshackled river, but quite willing against all common sense to dwell and build in the flood plain.

Could people really be relied upon to cooperate in the various nonstructural alternatives to flood control that the environmentalists so tirelessly harped upon? People cannot be controlled, but nature can. The professional's task, and what marked him as a professional, was fully to understand this—to look out for the citizen too careless to look after himself. Consider this engaging observation by Maurice Goddard, Secretary for the Environment of the Commonwealth of Pennsylvania, a strong supporter of the Tocks project and an exemplar of the old water professional:

> Make no mistake, the forgotten man in the so-called Tocks Island controversy is the average citizen of the Basin who knows little, and cares less, about Tocks Island. He won't be heard from until he is flooded, until his tap runs dry, until he travels all day for recreation and gets turned away, or until his power fails.
>
> He takes no part in the "controversy," but expects these things to be provided.[1]

To the Corps professional, the proper defense against a flood is a dam. It represents and makes forever visible the direct counterattack. A dam is an elegant structure, a vivid and enduring symbol of the accomplishment, service, and engineering ingenuity of its builders. (Essays 5 and 6 in this volume capture well the truly stirring aspects of dams.) A dam is also what the Corps knows best how to build, what its experience has taught is the response to a flood; it is the flood control measure over which the Corps has the clearest and least encumbered authority, in contrast to nonstructural approaches, which require multijurisdictional strategies mixing technical and social measures. Large dams also permit the design of multipurpose projects. Notwithstanding the Corps professionals' emotional focus on flood control and water supply, they are, as well, caught in the mainstream of the water resource field, which since the 1920s had placed emphasis on multipurpose dams, such as Tocks. Alternative packages of several single-purpose projects appear scarcely to have been considered.

The Corps' preoccupation was really more with floods, violent, one-shot events, than with drought, a gradual, more complex phenomenon. As noted in the preceding essay, until the great flood of 1955, the Corps was hardly interested in a dam on the Delaware; and since then, it was always the flood that was in the forefront in the Corps' sense of the rationale for the dam and its own sense of duty. As water supply came gradually to occupy a more important role in Corps planning, this sense of professional identity had to be translated to a new area. Thus droughts, in the imagination of the Corps professionals, came gradually to be thought of in the same sudden, cataclysmic terms as floods. The fact that a drought in the northeast United States meant essentially summer shortage and inconvenience was lost sight of in the drought's translation into a "disaster" and "catastrophe." This image of disaster was not restricted only to the Corps; it was shared fully, as noted below, by the water resource planners of the Delaware River Basin Commission.

The military ambience in which the Corps finds itself reinforces all these attitudes—a preoccupation with a violent antagonist, a pride in thinking about the unthinkable, a search for technical counters, and a disdain for a lazy thinking and uncontrollable populace. There is as well in the Corps a militarylike tendency to assume the worst of the adversary (in this case, nature) and to prepare to combat extreme though unlikely contingencies. The Corps, like the military, plans with prudence—there is little penalty to being overprepared or overcautious. Also like the military, the Corps is impatient with the adversary's counterattack. If predicted growth of odorous algae (eutrophication) in the Tocks reservoir seemed to call into question the value of the Tocks project, the Corps response was not to rethink the dam, but rather first to downgrade the importance of, and then to devise a plan to attack, the eutrophication.

The Corps is also a bureaucracy, with its own standard operating procedures and its own political ties. Like the other bureaucracies involved in the Tocks controversy, and indeed no more than the others, the Corps has wished to protect its own expertise from the disorder of public and critical scrutiny. None of its procedures has been more protected than the benefit-cost analysis, which is discussed and, one hopes, demystified in the following essay. The Corps is also a political animal and it does try to respond to congressional wishes and, to a lesser extent, to local and regional interests. As long as Congress and the Basin state politicians appeared to want the Tocks Island Dam, the Corps felt a strong obligation to pursue its development.[2]

B. The Delaware River Basin Commission

By 1971, the staff of the Delaware River Basin Commission was hardly less enthusiastic in its support of the dam than the Corps of Engineers, although their ardor was perhaps somewhat less expected. The Tocks project certainly appealed to the staff on its merits. The staff saw the project as the keystone of their effort to resolve three problems that had marked the DRBC's prehistory and first decade: floods, drought, and pollution in the estuary. The potential impact of the project on the first two were direct and obvious. Less evidently, the project promised to bolster the DRBC efforts to abate estuarine pollution, by permitting the maintenance of a high flow of 3,000 cfs at Trenton at the top of the estuary. The DRBC believed that such flow enhancement would help to validate their abatement program, which was based on a specific mathematical model of the estuary keyed to the 3,000 cfs minimum flow at Trenton.

From the perspective of an agency trying to control pollution in the face of severe industrial and municipal opposition, the DRBC view was understandable. Environmental standards are notoriously difficult to justify and contain an inevitable degree of arbitrariness. They are thus especially subject to challenge. The DRBC control program for pollution in the estuary requires industry to reduce biological oxygen demand (BOD) discharges by significant amounts, the precise amount derived largely from the mathematical model. To the extent that the operation of this model could be shown to contain arbitrary or unsound features (such as the 3,000 cfs assumption), the easier it would be for industry to challenge the abatement program. Beyond this, to the extent that the model and abatement program were taken seriously, any substantial relaxation of the 3,000 cfs requirement might require increased abatement from industry, a change difficult to achieve for political reasons.

This concern of the DRBC, for example, is strongly, though somewhat obliquely, stated in a staff study completed in November 1971:

Nonetheless, unless the Trenton flow can be sustained at a minimum of 3000 cfs, the indications are that the pollution-abatement program established on the basis of that flow would have to be redesigned to increase the degree of treatment or to allow a lower level of water quality with the current program. To avoid this *environmental disaster*, it will be necessary to replace from storage reservoirs any water that is diverted from the Basin or consumed within the Basin before it reaches the tidal river[3]. (emphasis added)

As against these real advantages, the alleged drawbacks of the project did not appear very compelling. The charter of the DRBC has been interpreted by the staff as charging the Commission to manage the waters of the Delaware to ensure adequate water supply and quality; it did not, in the view of the staff, charge the Commission to investigate changing patterns of land use in the Basin brought about by the development of water resources. Thus, not surprisingly, the DRBC adopted the comprehensive plan of the Corps, and later, specifically, the Tocks project, without any serious examination of the impact of the dam on roads, real estate transactions, land conversions, or economic development—all problems that were later to be of great concern to the governors of the Basin states. As a consequence, the DRBC commissioners (the governors) have in recent years relied for staff advice on Tocks principally on their own state oriented staffs.

The dam also promised the DRBC an interesting potential source of revenue independent of grants from the states—the ability to devise water rates and to sell water. This could be done without the dam, but the Tocks project would vastly increase the potential amounts that could be collected under such a scheme. This kind of enterprise would also reinforce the staff's ability to lead the Commission toward development of a regional perspective. The more the regional functions undertaken by the DRBC, the less important would seem the occasionally parochial points of view of the member states.

These claims of history, of the Charter, of a regional perspective, were all heightened by the character of the DRBC staff, above all by its remarkable stability, especially in comparison to the frequent changes in the Commission itself. Without exception, all the key members of the staff in 1971 were there at the DRBC's inception or very shortly thereafter. No other group or agency involved in the Tocks controversy had anything approaching such a record. The legal counsel to the DRBC, William Miller, was one of the Commission's architects in 1961; and the Executive Director, James Wright; the secretary, Brinton Whitall; the Chief Engineer, Herbert Howlett; the Director of Public Information, Dawes Thompson; and the Chief of Water Resources, Seymour Seltzer, all had held these positions since

1963. The vivid recollection of the 1963–65 drought was not just a product of an institutional memory.

The personalities and pre-DRBC background of the key staff members also helped to shape the DRBC position. James Wright came to the DRBC after graduate training in public administration at Syracuse and a career in public works administration in New Jersey and California where he was involved in water projects that dwarfed the Tocks enterprise. Wright, a rather droll and impressive person in his fifties, had been raised in a water resource tradition that scarcely questioned the subtle problems of environment and growth that now bothered so many. Although he would agree that in principle a new facility (a new source of water, for example, or a new power plant) could hasten future growth and create new demands, he felt there was no way to determine this in practice; a responsible bureaucrat has to act to ensure that any expected future demand will be met. Before coming to the DRBC Buzz Whitall had been on the executive staff of the Tennessee Valley Authority and also participated in the creation of the Delaware River Basin Commission. A reflective, precise thinker with a philosophic bent, Whitall was especially imbued with the innovative character of the DRBC as a regional institution; and he was sharply impatient with conservationists and others who argued for preservation of the "natural" river, while conveniently overlooking the tremendous changes already wrought by man along the Delaware. Both Howlett (who, like Wright, had worked on water projects in California) and Seltzer had long backgrounds in water resource engineering before joining the DRBC. Not until 1972 did the staff add a full-time ecologist.

The principal DRBC staff analyses supporting the Tocks project dealt with water supply needs; the other purposes of the dam received relatively little attention. The most complete and clear example of the water analysis was the staff report issued in November 1971, "Water Demands in the Delaware River Basin as Related to the Tocks Island Reservoir Project," which set forth systematically the projected growth of demand for Delaware water and the reservoir capacity this growth appeared to require. The DRBC staff attitude expressed in this report and elsewhere was clear: confronted with a rising demand, it was the DRBC's responsibility to ensure that it be met even under improbable conditions of severe drought; any shortfall would be unacceptable. How deeply this attitude was imbedded in the DRBC's perspective may be gauged from its response to a suggestion (forwarded in 1973 in a paper by a university-based observer of the Tocks controversy) that since the Tocks reservoir, above all, provides assurance against drought conditions, one should ask how costly it would be to pay the penalty of falling substantially short in water suppy for (say) five or six months every decade—and compare this cost to the cost of the Tocks reservoir. Falling short if there were no Tocks, so one might argue, would not be catastrophic, since one is talking at worst about shortages of perhaps 20 percent; shortages of this magnitude may require some temporary change in summer life style and some rationing but would not endanger the health of the community or its economic well-being.

The DRBC staff response to this speculation was sharp:

It is stated that the Tocks Island reservoir storage capacity will not be needed under normal conditions of rainfall. This is correct and true of all water supply projects. They are designed, like flood control projects, to meet adverse conditions that occur infrequently but which can be devasta-ting. To suggest that we should live with those risks, and change our summer life style and accept rationing, instead of providing storage capacity which is physically and economically feasible, may be good theory but that's all. How does one effect change in summer life styles, under whose authority, and with what degree of assurance that they will actually change? How does a public official rationalize rationing as an alternative to a storage reservoir that could have been constructed? How does one know that the costs of falling short (if we do not have Tocks Island) would not be catastrophic? Does the paper really intend to say we should have *another disaster* before we see if we should have done some-thing to prevent it? We suggest that while such assumptions are easy to make, they are totally speculative and unsubstantiated as real alternatives.[4]

The DRBC staff, like the Corps, has the professional's image of disas-ter. The constricted view of legitimate alternatives suggested by the response does reflect, however, the reality of politics and institutions in the Delaware Basin. The DRBC does not have an explicit charge to devise emergency preparedness plans, and the public does not, in fact, take kindly to enforced changes in life style. Nevertheless, emer-gency plans were instituted by the Basin governors in 1965, and it would not have been unreasonable, although it would have been out of character, for the DRBC staff to have investigated and refined such plans even while promoting the Tocks Island Dam. But they did not do this.

C. National Park Service

Since 1965, upon authorization by Congress of the Delaware Water Gap National Recreation Area, the National Park Service (NPS) of the Department of the Interior had, along with the Corps, been one of the two planning agencies for the Tocks project. The NPS had been purchasing land for the recreation area under a separate appropriation, although the Corps had acted as agent for the NPS in the actual land acquisition process. Also, the NPS, in coordination with the Corps and state planning agencies, had devised a master design for the recreation area. It was essentially complete by 1971, when the headquarters for the fledgling recreation area were established and a Superintendant, Peter DeGellecke, designated. DeGellecke and his small staff had participated in the park design and were enthusiastically looking forward to its fulfillment. They were imbued with the idea of using the reservoir and swimming beaches as a sort of lure to attract people to the area where they could then be exposed to the less popular and familiar joys of hiking, camping, and nature study.

The Department of the Interior was not an altogether happy family, however. There were some people in the bureaucracy, even in the Park Service itself, who didn't like dams, didn't like mass recreation, and above all, didn't like Tocks. Such a person was Nathaniel Reed, the Assistant Secretary for the Bureaus of Outdoor Recreation, Sports Fisheries and Wildlife, and National Parks. Reed, who never thought much of the Tocks Island Dam, was attracted to the idea of a Delaware Water Gap National Recreation Area based on the *river* rather than on a reservoir. In this attitude, he was joined by several others in the bureaucracies under his direction. Many staff members of these bureaus were outdoorsmen of one sort or other, hunters, fishermen, and hikers. They were naturally sympathetic to the arguments of the conservationists, although they also felt a responsibility to their bureau charter, so that, for example, members of the Bureau of Outdoor Recreation found it difficult to argue against a high density recreation plan unless it could be found ecologically harmful. Members of the NPS also felt something of this split sensitivity; although the designers of the recreation area took pride, of course, in their designs, others in the Service were attracted to a natural systems design for the area.

In early 1971, Reed encouraged a small group in the Park Service, including DeGellecke, to examine the possibility of such a "natural systems plan." Since Interior had no special authority from Congress to implement this kind of plan, which also would appear to undercut the project as then conceived, the study was kept low key and confidential. It was completed in a week during the spring of 1971, undated and anonymous; only 200 copies were made, which were then distributed selectively to several government agencies. The study, "A Natural Systems Plan for the DWGNRA," sketched in broad outline the concept of a recreation area organized around the free-flowing river with emphasis on hiking, biking, canoeing, and swimming in small offstream impoundments.

No numbers for the capacity of such a plan were given in the study, but the authors had privately calculated that it would be sufficient to accommodate about four million visitations annually, the number projected for the first stage of the reservoir-based design. This number evidently passed by word of mouth, for several people who subsequently read the study were sure that the design assumed a four-million capacity, although they could not recollect how they learned this. The study could not long be kept locked in the government, and it eventually leaked to the public. This greatly pleased the dam opponents, who believed the natural systems plan would provide an alternative for those who did not want the dam but who did want a park. By the spring of 1972, Reed was stating publicly that the law that created the Recreation Area in no way depended on the construction of the dam, an interpretation of the legislative history not accepted by the Corps.

Notwithstanding these events, the main line of the NPS effort was the design of the recreation area with a dam and reservoir. To park planners like DeGellecke the reservoir was attractive from many points of view. Above all, based on previous experience, DeGellecke believed that a park with a lake would attract several times more visitors than one without a lake. Furthermore, since most of the visitors to the area would concentrate at the lake, the rest of the recreation area, which would be far more fragile, could be better protected. Exactly how fragile it would be and thus how many visitors could be permitted in the recreation area were professional judgments made by the park designers. There is no published analysis to show how the estimate of a ten-million visitation carrying capacity for the area was derived. The design finally settled upon envisioned a three-stage development to accommodate four million annual visitations initially and ultimately the ten-million upper limit upon completion of the recreation area ten years later. Thus, by 1971, the Delaware Water Gap National Recreation Area was ready to be developed, along with the dam and reservoir.

By late autumn 1971, after the completion of the environmental impact statement, the Tocks project at last appeared ready to go. The proponents of the dam believed they had a strong case. The benefits appeared clear: water, power, recreation, and flood control. And the costs appeared minimal. All the critical supporting analysis—the benefit-cost calculations, the detailed planning, the demand

projections, the search for alternatives, the environmental assessment—had been completed; and there was scarcely any political
opposition to the project. The Corps planned to start construction in
early 1972.

II. RESERVOIRS OF DISTRUST:
THE PUBLIC RESPONSE

With the issuance of the final Impact Statement and refinement of
the engineering design for the project, the private interests both supporting and opposing the dam grew increasingly active.

A. Proponents
The water and power professionals in the Basin generally rallied
behind the project, and for much the same reasons as their counterparts in the public agencies. Such support also reflected their own
special interests. Thus the several local water supply authorities in
the region, separately, and collectively through their umbrella organization (the Water Resources Association of the Delaware River
Basin), were constantly engaged in a variety of lobbying activities in
favor of the dam. Their fundamental argument was simply that the
Basin needed more water; they believed that the safe yields of the
present system were under strain and that without new sources
growth in the Basin would be stifled.

Similarly, the electric power utilities supported the Tocks project
as a way to ensure cooling water for the substantial number of power
plants planned for construction on the Delaware downstream from
the Tocks dam site. Without such assurance, the utilities would either
not be able to expand as vigorously as they hoped or would themselves be responsible for providing the requisite water storage. The
utilities were also attracted by the prospect that the Tocks project
would permit the construction of a utility owned pumped-storage
facility near the dam site to help meet peak demand requirements.

In addition to these professionals, business and labor organizations
strongly supported the project. They wished for strong economic
expansion in the region—more people, more factories, more jobs—
and this seemed to call for more water and more power. Thus, virtually every Chamber of Commerce and organized business association in the region favored the Tocks project, and it was water and
power, not flood control and recreation, that lent urgency to their
concerns.

For much the same reasons as business, organized labor throughout the Basin region supported the project. Although this support

was often nominal, labor did lobby consistently for Tocks both in the state capitols and before congressional committees in Washington; and as the recession in the construction industry deepened, some members of the construction unions engaged in still more forceful actions: on one occasion they organized a "March on Trenton," in which thousands of construction workers surged through the streets of New Jersey's capitol to the steps of the governor's office, where they issued a series of demands for the thawing of frozen construction projects (Tocks included). On another occasion several dozen workers provoked a nearly violent confrontation with a citizen group reviewing the Tocks project: they surrounded the group's bus, punctured its radiator, and demanded the chance to present their case directly to the citizens group and to the local politicians and planners whom the group was visiting. (Frank Sinden, co-editor of this volume, was present at this latter incident.)

Part of the workers' concern was, of course, jobs, and especially construction jobs. But this concern was not directed merely to the dam itself; nor could it reasonably have been so. The dam, expected to take seven years to construct, would at a maximum employ a few hundred workers, as compared to a construction labor force of over 100,000 in New Jersey alone. As noted by one political observer, "there were more jobs in a half-dozen highway improvement projects than in Tocks." The concern of organized labor was more symbolic and indirect. Although Tocks would not produce substantial numbers of jobs, it was one of several projects in the Basin region—and one of the most visible—that appeared to be stymied by environmental measures and opposition. Tocks thus became symbolic of a long list of grievances and of the imagined unconcern of environmentalists for the plight of the working man. This apparent indifference seemed further galling to many members of the labor organizations who thought also about the recreation area. In supporting the reservoir-based and auto-accessed recreation promised by the project, they believed also that they were supporting the wishes of the average working man. They had little patience with the concerns and interests of the environmentalists and backpackers.

The construction opportunities afforded by the project were less important to labor than the water and power it promised. Tocks as a symbolic and real impulse to economic growth in the region formed the main part of labor's position on the project. Along with the water user associations, utilities, and businessmen's groups, labor believed that a rejection of Tocks would diminish the material basis for growth in the Basin—and worse, would signal a success for the naysayers, for all those who opposed growth either in the name of some elusive environmental purity or for selfish and elitist reasons.

B. The Environmentalists

The field of public action was of course not left only to project supporters. The opposition was substantial, and as time went on became increasingly colorful and inventive. The concerns raised by the opponents were many: the impact of the dam on shad and oysters in the estuary; the potential for eutrophication of the reservoir; the loss of a 37-mile stretch of the river; the destruction of a wild and lovely valley; the destruction of historical homes, many dating back over 200 years.

These specific objections, however, grew out of a more amorphous sensibility. To many opponents of the project, what really counted was the precedent and symbol. They saw the Corps as a sort of malevolent agent of "progress" all over the countryside, running away with the few wild, unspoiled areas left in the Northeast. They wanted to halt this momentum, to have the community face more thoroughly than it had ever done the costs of growth. The opponents of the dam, convinced of the real and symbolic costs of the project, looked hard and skeptically at the alleged benefits; indeed, these benefits to the extent that they were a measure of still more economic growth were not considered real benefits at all. Nor were the opponents appeased by reassurances of the professionals. They believed that the dam supporters were so persuaded of the project's benefits that they largely rationalized away its attendant costs.

Opposition to the project also continued to grow out of local grievances, especially in reaction to the Corps' land acquisition techniques. Many local citizens were coming slowly to believe that the project was not likely to bring the economic prosperity to individuals and to the community initially expected. Much of the concern of the local populace was directed at the recreation area as well as the dam. A good part of the land acquisition was, after all, due to the recreation plan. It was the planned expansion of recreation that would provoke the expected deluge of visitors to the region, and with it all sorts of requirements for new roads and new service facilities. The descent of outsiders to the region was especially upsetting to some. People simply did not fancy an influx of intruders into their quiet valley; and to a small minority there were perhaps ethnic and class overtones to this feeling, for they especially looked askance at urban visitors from New York and Philadelphia.

Reflecting these varied sentiments, a variety of citizens' groups employing a variety of tactics marshalled their forces in 1971 and 1972 to combat the Tocks project. Most of them have remained active from that time to the present, although their composition, their motivation, their relationship to technical analysis, and their tactics have sometimes shifted.

The locally-based opposition groups which march so visibly across the history of the controversy—the Save-the-Delaware-Coalition, The Delaware Valley Conservation Association, the Lenni Lenape League, and others—were really less groups than loose clusters of volunteers lending some financial, some moral, and some technical support to a few persons of great energy and dedication who did much of the work. The activity of any given group would thus wax or wane with the energy and engagement of a very few individuals. Very few individuals and even less money! An impressive aspect of the opposition movement was the vast imbalance in resources available to them as compared to those at the disposal of the public agencies promoting the project. With few exceptions, the project's opponents fought the dam on their own personal time, mainly with their own money, and with a passion that grew out of strong personal convictions or grievances.

Consider, for example, the Delaware Valley Conservation Association (DVCA). The DVCA thrice was at the frontier of the struggle against the dam: first in the early days of the controversy in the late 1960s under the leadership of a resident of Stroudsburg, Nancy Shukaitis, who later became an elected Commissioner in Monroe County, Pennsylvania, bordering the dam site; then in 1970 and 1971 when another local resident, Joan Mathieson, took up the cudgel; and last, when the controversy reached its peak, under the leadership of Mina Haefele. An intelligent and intense woman, Haefele was living as a tenant in her family's ramshackle old farmhouse overlooking the River several years after the house had been purchased by the Corps when she turned full time to the Tocks controversy. Full time in this case meant a flurry of varied activities—attending hearings in Washington, organizing mailing and telex campaigns directed at the Basin governors and Congress, writing articles, distributing press releases, and soliciting funds. She tried successfully to engage the attention of Washington-based environmental organizations, and with them helped coordinate Congressional lobbying efforts. Although (in the view of Haefele and her colleagues) analysis counted a lot less to the relevant policymakers, governors, and congressmen than did simple citizen pressure, she was herself most successful in marshalling evidence—to wit, in producing an analysis—suggesting that the Corps was trampling on the rights of individuals in the taking area, and through its destruction of historical homes, trampling also on the rich historical legacy of the valley.

Quite generally, the environmentalists did not shun the idea of technical and political studies. On the contrary, when the occasion arose, they jumped at the chance to encourage analytic work on the project, and especially work on possible alternatives to the project. The two groups which most vigorously pursued this path were the regionally based Save-the-Delaware-Coalition and the more nationally oriented Environmental Defense Fund (EDF).

Save-the-Delaware Coalition:
Recreation Without a Dam

The Save-the-Delaware-Coalition, with representatives from dozens of conservation groups, was formed in response to the initial Corps Impact Statement, and soon came to play the most important coordinating role in focusing the environmental opposition. Under the direction of its chairman, Harold Lockwood, a lawyer from Philadelphia, the Coalition from its inception played a critical part in mobilizing political opposition to the dam. Members of the Coalition, especially Lockwood, tirelessly sought out policy makers in the state capitols and in Washington and otherwise lobbied strenuously against the dam. Lockwood—affable, energetic, imaginative—also persistently sought to encourage analytic work on the dam, and on possible alternatives to it, that he trusted would call the entire project into question. One of the Coalition's early efforts was to assign two of its members to put together and edit a series of papers prepared by several different authors over the previous years, which, taken together, sketched out a plausible picture of ways to achieve flood control, water supply increases, and recreation without a dam and reservoir. The volume that emerged, "Papers in Support of a Free-Flowing Delaware River" (October 1973) sought to question and counterbalance in some measure the massive studies done by the exuberant supporters of the dam.

In a second venture, the Save-the-Delaware-Coalition sought to sketch a vivid and attractive vision of the valley without a dam. Opponents of the Tocks project on Congressional staffs in Washington suggested that it would be helpful to them to have in hand a substantial report on the positive aspect of the opponents' position—that is, on the future of the land to be acquired by the government if no dam were built. It was taken for granted that this future meant a federal park of some sort. The Save-the-Delaware-Coalition eagerly took up this suggestion and immediately set about raising a special fund and seeking a professional consultant to prepare a plan. The prospect of a constructive, even creative, project contrasted refreshingly with the necessarily negative character of much of the Coalition's previous work. Each member, moreover, saw the opportunity of finally expressing his or her own vision of the Delaware's future in more concrete form.

Their visions, as has been noted earlier, were by no means uniform. Conservationists long concerned about creeping commercial encroachment on rural land at first welcomed the Tocks Island Dam and recreation area because it promised to take a large piece of especially attractive land off the market. As they became aware of the physical magnitude of the reservoir and of the numbers of people it was supposed to attract, however, the conservationists changed their position and opposed the dam while continuing to support federal acquisition of the land.

The landowners who joined the opposition were largely resigned to losing their own land, but hoped in some sad, altruistic way to preserve the land they were sentimentally attached to, at least for others. They did argue for remnants of private ownership or leasing on principle, avoiding positions that would benefit them personally in order not to weaken the opposition as a whole with the appearance of special pleading. Most landowners, it must be said, did not join the organized opposition, because they rightly saw little support in it for their interests. Of course all members of the opposition believed that the area should be preserved, but there was no consensus on what form the preservation should take. Indeed there was no occasion to establish a consensus, since all hands were occupied with opposing the dam. As it later appeared, each individual had formed in his own mind a vision of the Upper Delaware's future, embodying his own tastes and values. In addition, each person had made his own internal compromises with what he imagined to be reality.

Although the visions of the opponents differed in many ways, they were all similar in one fundamental and surprising way: virtually all reflected compromise on the issue of numbers of visitors to be provided for. They were willing to support a plan that called for just as many people as the first phase of the official plan they aimed to challenge, namely four million visitor-days per year. This is surprising not merely because conservationists are notorious crowd haters, but because it was precisely the large numbers of visitors envisioned in the official plan that was responsible directly and indirectly for the most severe and widespread impacts of the Tocks project—the impacts that most concerned the conservationists. People meant cars, and cars mean highways, and highways mean almost certainly the destructive, chaotic, and explosive development of Sussex and Warren Counties.

Every step in this sequence was in itself anathema to the conservationists, yet most of them shared the simple conviction that no plan without large crowds could compete in the political arena. Nevertheless, the "Concept Plan for a Delaware River Park," which emerged from the Coalition's efforts, provided an intriguing park design based upon the river, and one that could not so easily be expanded to accommodate the ten million annual visitor-days then envisioned as the final target of the Corps and National Park Service plan. The concept plan also served as the starting point for the Park Service's later intensive planning for a damless park. After some study, the Park Service concluded that the number of visitors should be no more than about two million per year.

Environmental Defense Fund: Flood Control and
Water Supply Without a Dam

During 1971 and 1972 another environmental group, destined to play an important role in the controversy, entered the fray. The Environmental Defense Fund (EDF) had been formed in 1967 as a national organization supported by private contributions and dedicated to mounting legal challenges to projects that appeared environmentally damaging. The usual modus operandi of EDF was to combat a project in the courts; but this time, the technical director of the Long Island Office, Leo Eisel, a young, serious, hard-driving water engineer, saw an opportunity to influence the decision before it reached the courts.

Eisel's first line of attack was to try to show that even apart from the adverse environmental consequences, the Tocks project did not add up in simple economic terms. To this end, EDF commissioned Gardner Brown, an economist at the University of Wisconsin, to undertake a critical study of the Corps benefit-cost analysis. The Corps had wielded its benefit-cost analysis as an argument for the dam, and the environmentalists believed they needed a public response that would at the least show the tremendous flexibility possible in such calculations. The resulting analysis did tend to neutralize somewhat the political potency of the benefit-cost analysis, although few persons probably took the structured benefit-cost analysis very seriously anyway.

The EDF emphasis then shifted, as had the Save-the-Delaware-Coalition's, to a search for alternatives. Eisel decided that flood control and water supply were the real driving purposes behind the project, and that unless one could show that these goals were unnecessary or could be achieved in other ways, the project would surely go forward; he chose flood control as the first object of investigation. Thus, in the summer of 1972, in cooperation with the New Jersey Department of Environmental Protection, Eisel and an assistant, Laurie Burt, launched a study of flood control in the Delaware

Basin below the dam site, poring over aerial photographs of the flood plain and counting structures, doing field surveys to document the substantial effect of flood plain zoning on the most vulnerable towns, like Burlington, which had reduced the potential damage from flooding on the main stem, relative to the Corps' projections of ten years before.

These investigations resulted in two studies, a preliminary report, "Flood Control—A Field Investigation," September 1972, and "Flood Control and the Delaware River," April 1973, both of which cast doubt on the importance of the flood control purposes of the Tocks Island Dam, and, above all, documented the potential of non-structural approaches. Eisel was encouraged in these studies by some of the policy makers, both in Congress and at the state level, who would soon be making the critical decisions respecting the dam, and to whom Eisel had easy access during the research phase of the enterprise.

Later in the controversy, EDF determined to pursue a concept known as high-flow skimming as a nondam alternative to water supply. The concept was sparked by the imagination and persistence of a physicist at the R.C.A. research laboratory in New Jersey, Smith Freeman; and it was carried out by Freeman and two Princeton University professors: Edwin Mills, an economist, and David Kinsman, a geologist. The three produced a study which suggested that sufficient water to provide an alternative to the water supply functions of the dam could be assured by offstream storage in existing reservoirs, with the water pumped out of the Delaware during high flow periods. This unconventional notion, introduced by three "amateurs," received little notice from the water professionals; and EDF decided that the idea, to get a fair hearing, would have to be examined by a recognized consulting firm who would play by all the traditional rules.

The contractor given the task was Disko Associates of New Jersey, and their report was released in October 1972. The study did conclude that high-flow skimming had substantial potential to increase the water yield of the Delaware, but the study proposed damming one of the most beautiful tributaries of the Delaware, Flatbrook Creek. Although the area flooded by this proposal would be significantly less than the Corps' plan for the main stem, the remedy appeared to many environmentalists almost as bad as the illness. The report presented a straightforward technical solution to a problem, but one that may have missed the central point of undertaking the study in the first place.

PIRG

Later in the controversy, still another environmental group entered the arena, this one with an even more pugnacious attitude than most of the older environmental activists. The New Jersey Public Interest Research Group (PIRG) was founded in the fall of 1972 as a student funded "watchdog" research organization of the kind Ralph Nader had been encouraging. The board of directors, made up mostly of students from Rutgers and Seton Hall Universities, soon had identified the Tocks project as a priority study area, and Chris Burke, the Executive Director and only full-time operative of PIRG, turned full time to the project. Burke, a recent graduate of Oberlin College, brought a clear and definite bias to the Tocks project: "We are suspect of the Corps and certainly suspect of power companies."

PIRG was concerned not simply with preserving the environment in the Delaware River Valley, but also with the broader social and economic impacts of the development on people living in the area. In land acquisition, for example, Burke maintained that the Corps had unjustly treated local landowners and had, to boot, adopted practices that flouted federal law. This deep-rooted distrust of government and big business provided the impulse to PIRG activities and the theme of the numerous press releases put out by PIRG. To Burke, the Tocks project had to be stopped not only because of its specific consequences, but also because it would simply add to what he perceived as a growth mania in the country (more water, more energy, more nuclear power plants) and deflect attention away from energy conservation and controlled growth strategies.

The Squatters

Although not an environmental group or even a group in league with the environmentalists, one other fragment of the public deserves brief mention — the "squatters," a band of some 40 to 100 illegal occupants of abandoned or condemned properties on the Pennsylvania side of the Delaware near the dam site. Feared by some, cheered by many, this small group of counterculture enthusiasts were a continual dramatic focus of journalistic interest. The origin of the squatters is subject of some local debate. Many residents on the New Jersey side claim that hordes of pop music fans, bound for a New Jersey rock concert that was cancelled at the last minute, stopped at the Delaware River and occupied some vacant farmhouses there.

Some original squatters, however, were once legal tenants of their properties. When the Corps of Engineers found itself faced with an indefinite delay of contruction plans, it decided to rent several of the properties it had acquired. Attracted by ads in the *New York Times*, a handful of Greenwich Village residents moved to Shawnee-on-Delaware for the summer. Finding the peaceful and pastoral setting ideal for a pioneer or commune type of life style, the squatters refused to vacate when their leases ran out. Passively resisting eviction attempts, and contesting government action in the courts, they had stayed on for years.

The local residents had somewhat mixed but mostly hostile reactions to the squatters. They believed them to be the source of countless illegal acts, widespread vandalism, and occasionally more violent crimes in the area. Their attitudes became more sympathetic and complex when (in an episode described in Essay 10) the Corps moved on the squatter homes with bulldozers in the dead of night.

With very little money and few active participants, the band of environmental activists opposing the dam were able to keep up a constant hubbub of criticism; and along with the criticism, they sometimes raised new ideas, new alternative possibilities to the dam and reservoir. Some of their anger, criticism, and ideas reached the policy making level and there provided valuable ammunition for their natural allies in the state capitals and in Washington.

However, whatever their abilities, the opposition activists could scarcely have had the success they did in confronting such a solidly supported establishment project if they hadn't also tapped some hidden springs of sentiment. There was, in fact, a constituency of ideas that the activists were able in some inchoate way to speak for and speak to—concerns about growth, pollution, overbearing technology, that were shared by many citizens and many policymakers.[5]

III. CLOUDS OVER WASHINGTON: THE POLITICIANS

Although the activities of the environmentalists were important, the main arena of opposition to the dam shifted unexpectedly in 1971 and 1972 to Washington: unexpectedly, because hitherto there had been no serious dissent to the project emanating from Congress or the Administration. Virtually every congressman with a district in the Basin supported the project, and perhaps more importantly, the project was strongly backed by the key public works subcommittees.

As with all legislation, public works appropriations must run a gauntlet in both Houses of Congress, from subcommittee to committee to the full House or Senate, to Senate-House conference, back to the full Congress for approval, and thence to the President. And, as with all but the most extraordinary legislation, the fate of the bill is largely determined in the subcommittee and committee deliberations. Congress had authorized the Tocks project in 1962 and the DWGNRA in 1965. Thenceforward, the annual appropriations had each year to go through the two appropriations committees.

Appropriations bills must originate in the House: for Tocks, in the Subcommittee on Public Works of the House Appropriations Committee for funds appropriated to the Corps; and in the Interior Subcommittee for funds appropriated to the National Park Service for further land acquisition. These subcommittees then report to the full Appropriations Committee for "mark up" sessions in which the subcommittee reports are frequently amended. After approval by the full House, usually a formality, the journey begins again in the Senate, first in the Subcommittees on Public Works and on Interior and Insular Affairs of the Committee on Appropriations, then to the full Committee, and finally to the Senate. Differences between the House and Senate versions are then worked out in the House-Senate Conference.

The dominant factors in this process were the crusty and canny chairmen of the two Public Works Subcommittees, Joe Evins in the House and John Stennis in the Senate. These veteran congressional chieftains strongly supported public works in general, and their support for the Tocks project seemed to ensure an uneventful and successful passage of the project from the drawing board to the first bulldozer. But this easy state of affairs was suddenly disrupted, in large measure by a single study on eutrophication, the McCormick Report, which the Corps had commissioned in March 1971. The study achieved prominence due to the importance attached to it by the President's newly formed Council on Environmental Quality (CEQ), a small group in the Executive Office of the President responsible for reviewing the Environmental Impact Statements required under the new National Environmental Protection Act.

The McCormick Report resulted from a series of informal discussions between members of the Corps, CEQ, and others during the late fall and winter of 1970, at the time of the initial Environmental Impact Statement concerning the possibility of eutrophication (unwanted algal blooms) in the Tocks reservoir. (Essays 8 and 9 describe and discuss eutrophication in considerable detail; in fact, as is noted there, eutrophication is a complex phenomenon and can mean different things to different people). Eutrophication was a phenomenon often observed in other reservoirs and certain lakes, and despite the Corps' assurances that it should not be a serious problem for Tocks, it was a natural concern to the CEQ. The Army agreed that construction would not begin until there was an independent study of eutrophication, and turned to Jack McCormick and Associates, a newly formed consulting group in Philadelphia directed by a terrestrial ecologist, Jack McCormick. The firm hired as chief consultant to the study Tom Cahill, a water ecologist, who actually wrote much of the report. The study was initiated in the spring of 1971, and released along with the Corps' Final Impact Statement in October 1971. Its main conclusion, that "accelerated cultural eutrophication is likely to occur after creation of the proposed Tocks Island Lake," had immediate impact.

The McCormick Report was received at CEQ in October, where it was reviewed by a young, thoughtful staff analyst, Steve Sloan, who at the time was responsible for reviewing *all* water resource projects in the eastern United States. In Sloan's view, the report suggested clearly the dangers of eutrophication of the Tocks lake and the foolhardiness of proceeding with the project before that danger was fully addressed; and he persuaded CEQ chairman Russell Train to so notify the Army. This Train did, adding in his comments CEQ's additional concern also that reservoir drawdown during the summer would expose mud flats and create a variety of detrimental impacts on recreation, water supply, fisheries, and downstream water quality.

After some further exchange of correspondence between CEQ and the Army, CEQ hardened its position, noting that its approval of the project depended upon assurance from the Basin governors that the environmental problems raised by CEQ, especially the eutrophication problem, would be adequately handled. Such a request by CEQ had no force in law and its influence on the Army depended on the degree of support CEQ could obtain from the White House and from Congress. The Army, on the other hand, would have liked the White House especially to direct the Corps to go ahead. But 1972 was an election year and the White House, as we now well know, was preoccupied with the coming election campaign.

The President's contact men (John Whitaker and John Ehrlichman) did not want to rock any boats unnecessarily; they neither wished to endorse the project over the objections of the President's chief environmental advisor and project opponents in the Basin states, nor to antagonize the congressional and local supporters of the project. They thus did not try overly hard to impose a decision one way or the other, but suggested rather that the Corps and CEQ work things out themselves. At the same time, the Office of Management and Budget, presumably acting under similar White House guidelines, also took a hands-off attitude. This benign neglect forced, but also permitted, CEQ to look to Congress for support.

And in Congress CEQ discovered important allies: Howard Robison, a Republican representing the 27th District in New York, and a member of the Public Works Subcommittee of the House Appropriations Committee; Clifford Case, Republican senator from New Jersey, whose administrative assistant, Gar Kaganovich, had independently become wary of the eutrophication danger; Congressman Pierre duPont, Republican from Delaware, who had in the previous year been virtually alone among congressmen in speaking against the Tocks project; and James Buckley and Jacob Javits, senators from New York. But the key role in translating the CEQ misgivings into an effective constraint on the Corps was played by Robison, who managed both to place the CEQ stipulations into the Appropriations Bill for the Tocks project, and to persuade Governor Rockefeller not to issue an assurance that New York State would move quickly to meet those stipulations.

During all these maneuverings, the only analytic works that seemed to have had any real consequence were the McCormick study, and to a lesser extent the Impact Statement; even these studies appear to have been read by a mere handful of people: by Sloan at CEQ, and, in parts at least, by legislative assistants to Robison, Case, and duPont. Most of the concerned congressmen also had available as background a miscellany of studies produced by the Corps and DRBC, namely the 1961 Corps HD522 Survey, the most recent Corps benefit-cost analysis, and various DRBC staff studies and public information releases. However, it is doubtful that any of the congressmen had read these studies in any detail. Whatever the readership of these other studies, the eutrophication issue certainly became the most dominant politically, far surpassing in importance other environmental concerns touching, for example, the effect of the dam on oysters or shad.

There were probably several reasons for this. Perhaps most important, eutrophication (if it occurred), unlike the other problems, would significantly diminish one of the main benefits of the Tocks project—recreation. It thus seemed to undermine one positive argument for the dam. This perverse character of eutrophication was probably more important in its political impact than simply the calculable reduction in the monetary benefits of recreation it implied. Moreover, the impact on recreation affected a fairly clear constituency: those who would use the recreation area and those who would live nearby. It was also important politically that the eutrophication issue could not simply be absorbed by the project. To combat (or at least ameliorate) the shad problem, the Corps incorporated a fish ladder; to ensure that the oyster beds would not be adversely affected, the Corps agreed to change the planned operation of the Tocks reservoir so that the spring flows into the estuary would not be diminished (a decision with a real, but largely hidden, cost). With eutrophication, however, the Corps could not on its own meet the environmentalists' objections; actions by the involved states in establishing effective sewage systems appeared necessary.

Moreover, eutrophication presented a vivid symbol of ecological hazard for those who were searching for such symbols. By comparison, the shad and oyster were deficient symbols: both resources had already suffered enormous injury from water pollution, and it was difficult for an urban populace to take the preservation of natural systems in their backyards as seriously as, for example, they might take the preservation of virgin areas of Alaska. Shad runs up the Delaware do not provoke the imagination of the Basin populace the way salmon runs have elsewhere. But eutrophication, as nature's backlash, was well matched to the East Coast's urbanity and skepticism.

The intellectual journeys that brought key figures in Washington to support or oppose the Tocks project were varied. Most congressmen on the public works subcommittees tended to trust the Corps' analysis and, in general, to favor public works projects, especially in a case such as Tocks where the project also appeared to have the support of a crucial regional body like the DRBC. The environmental mood of the 1970s had not yet descended on most of Congress. In a mini-debate on the Tocks dam on the floor of the House in 1971, James Wright of Texas doubtless spoke for many when he described with a religious fervor the case for intervention:

> We cannot keep people from intruding upon the earth. and the interests of people must come first. Nature sometimes, as in this case, needs the corrective surgery of intelligent men, under the injunction given to us in the Book of Genesis, to subdue the earth and husband its resources.

And Wright also spoke for many congressmen in his contempt for those who argued for further study of projects such as Tocks. They reminded him, he said, of Kipling's description of old men:

> They peck out, dissect, and extrude to the mind
> The flaccid tissues of long-dead issues

Offensive to God and mankind
Like vultures over an ox
That the army has left behind.

Such attitudes were further reinforced by the personal experience
of the congressmen with districts in the Delaware Basin. Some, like
Frank Thompson of New Jersey, remembered vividly the floods of
1955, and others, like Fred Rooney of Pennsylvania, saw the project
as an economic and recreation boon to their districts. Thompson also
was attracted to the idea of establishing the precedent of public
power in the Northeast; the 70 megawatts of electric power to be
produced by the dam, trivial in economic terms, in this sense took on
symbolic importance.

The chief congressional foe of the Tocks project in 1971—and
virtually the only one at that time—was Pierre duPont. Through
discussions with scientists at the University of Delaware, duPont and
his administrative aid, Austin Olney, became convinced that the dam
might cause a serious ecological imbalance in the estuary, robbing it
of nutrients and fresh water flows and eventually affecting adversely
oysters and other fish life. This concern in turn led duPont to question the apparently casual way in which the Corps had performed the
environmental assessment required by NEPA; and this formed his
main argument in support of an amendment he offered on the floor
of the House to strike the $3.7 million construction funds the
Appropriations Committee had designated in the Public Works Bill.

It was this amendment that inspired the hyberbole of Congressmen Wright quoted above, in a debate that ended with a crushing
rejection of the duPont amendment in a voice vote. (In duPont's
recollection, the " 'Noes' rolled across the Chamber like thunder.")
By this time, however, the CEQ had entered the controversy, and
duPont was soon to have several allies both in Washington and in the
Basin states that now had to act on the Tocks decision.[6]

IV. THE GOVERNOR AND THE ADVISOR

A. Introduction
The events in Washington put off for a time the start of construction by throwing the responsibility for decision back to the DRBC.
There appeared little question that Congress would appropriate the
necessary funds to initiate the construction once the DRBC Commissioners approved the project and satisfactorily resolved the
environmental issues raised by CEQ. The focus of decision thus

moved to the Commission—that is, to the four Basin governors, especially the governors of New Jersey and Pennsylvania, whose states would be most affected by the project.

Not until this time (early 1972) did New Jersey Governor Cahill begin to think seriously about the Tocks Island project. Until then, there was little reason for the Governor to focus on the dam. No decisions were necessary; the Corps had been implementing the various procedures required by the National Environmental Protection Act, and was otherwise gradually purchasing land and refining the project design. Whatever Cahill now decided would likely be decisive; his approval would almost certainly set the project in motion. Although the governor of New York and his chief environmental advisor saw some potential problems, virtually all other involved politicians appeared to support the project. The governors of Delaware and Pennsylvania were in favor of the dam, as were all the New Jersey and Pennsylvania congressmen with districts along the Delaware. The previous New Jersey governor, Richard Hughes, had also, while in office, formally endorsed the Tocks project.

There was, however, little political pressure on Governor Cahill to make the decision one way or the other. Outside the impact area itself, most of the public scarcely knew about the project, and its benefits were sufficiently diffuse and nonimmediate to discourage the formation of any strong pressure group (although, as already noted, there did exist some ardent bureaucratic sentiment in favor of the project). There was nominal support for the dam from labor, industry, the utilities, and some newspapers, but these groups never could make the project widely visible to the public. Although the Governor had supported the dam while he was a congressman from southern New Jersey, a change of sentiment now would cause him no more than a momentary embarassment. For why shouldn't he have earlier been in favor of the project? It had appeared then as an excellent idea, an unmixed blessing of water supply, flood control, power, and recreation—for which, moreover, the federal government would pay almost entirely.[b] Thus, in the spring of 1972, Governor Cahill believed himself open-minded on the project and politically unencumbered. With this frame of reference, he turned for advice to his Commissioner of Environmental Protection, Richard Sullivan.

Sullivan had become Commissioner in 1970 at the outset of the Cahill administration. Before this time he had been in the state government for over two decades, starting out as a $2,900 per year air pollution control officer in 1951, and rising to the chief environ-

[b]This last was a delusion, as noted in section VI below.

mental position in 1969. Previous to his government career, Sullivan had studied engineering and also held graduate degrees in Public Health and English. By 1972 he had become an extremely effective advocate for an increased government role in environmental protection—an advocacy marked by a particularly affable and witty style of public speaking. His views on the environment were thoughtful, searching, and always reasonably pragmatic. Although a strong proponent of increased environmental protection, Sullivan remained aware of the economic, social, and political costs frequently associated with such protection, and he sought compromises.

Sullivan's views were moderate in another sense. While he had developed a lively respect for nature (illustrated, for instance, by his conviction that there were ecological benefits to be gained from a flooding river: "A river is not just a transportation corridor, but a biological system"), he was by no means a conservation purist. He personally enjoyed tent trailer camping, for example, and hoped that the planned Tocks recreation area would have provision for trailer camps—a prospect that appalled the Sierra Club and most other conservationists. From the beginning of his interest in the Tocks project, Sullivan was much more alert to the ecological arguments advanced by the project opponents than to the anguished notes struck by the backpackers and wilderness buffs, to whom he felt the state owed no special obligation.

The Department of Environmental Protection (DEP), which Sullivan headed, was formed in 1970 (on "Earth Day") at the time Sullivan became its Commissioner, by combining the agencies from the Division of Clean Air and Water (which Sullivan had directed previous to 1970) with several agencies from the Department of Conservation and Economic Development, including the agencies responsible for the development of water resources in the state. Thus DEP contained within it the two bureaucratic interests that would tend to feel most strongly about Tocks, pro and con. Much of the argument with respect to Tocks would therefore be worked out at Sullivan's level rather than the governor's. By 1972, Sullivan and DEP had established a strong reputation as environmental advocates. In several areas they had pioneered widely popular policies that had placed New Jersey at the forefront of the national attack on environmental despoliation (for example, the establishment of a motor vehicle emissions testing program). Although there was some grumbling from within the state, the environmental program of the Cahill administration was, in general, considered a definite political plus.

It was against such a background that Sullivan and his personal staff undertook their investigation of the Tocks issue. This review was actually carried out in two distinct phases. In the first phase, during the spring of 1972, Sullivan, working more or less alone and without any substantial review of the relevant documents, concluded (for reasons to be indicated) that the project raised several serious issues that required more study prior to any decision to proceed. Governor Cahill accepted this view and announced it at the annual meeting of the DRBC in May to his startled colleagues, who had had no inkling of Cahill's doubts up to that point. The second and more intensive phase of the review then began in DEP. The staff person most responsible for working with Sullivan in this endeavor was Thomas O'Neill. O'Neill, like most of Sullivan's staff, was far more interested in the environmental aspects of DEP's responsibility than in the Department's residual responsibility for economic development. He had once been a U.S. Army intelligence analyst in Berlin, and before joining Sullivan's staff in 1971 had spent two years at Princeton University studying various techniques of social analysis. This background prepared O'Neill to be somewhat skeptical of professional analysts working in the bureaucracy, which when coupled with a view of the environment similar to Sullivan's, shaped the way he tackled the Tocks issue.

B. The Analyses

The analytic work on hand, as O'Neill and Sullivan initiated their review of the project, was sparse; it included, most importantly, the massive eleven-volume Delaware River Basin Report (HD 522) prepared by the Corps in 1961 (described above in essay 2); the Corps' Environmental Impact Statements; the ubiquitous McCormick Report on eutrophication; water demand estimates by the Delaware River Basin Commission; and two consultant studies of the expected social and economic impact of the project, one by Robert Nathan Associates investigating economic growth implications, and one by Edwards & Kelcey, analyzing the impact of the recreation area on new road requirements for New Jersey. Actually, at the time Sullivan initiated his review of the Tocks project, this last report was buried in the depths of the Department of Transportation; it was not known to Sullivan or the Governor, nor apparently even to the planners designing the recreation area.[c]

In addition to these documents relating specifically to Tocks, Sullivan and staff were aware most significantly of the 1969 Report to the President on Flood Control by the special ad hoc committee asked to examine federal flood control programs. This report noted

[c]The annotated list of technical studies at the end of this volume contains the full citations of the studies referred to here.

that despite vast sums being spent on flood control structures, annual flood damage was rising dramatically in the United States for the reason that development on flood plains continued to grow. They were also aware of the work underway at the Environmental Defense Fund which indicated that in the fifteen years since the floods of 1955, development along the Delaware tributaries had risen markedly while the number of persons and structures in the mainstem flood plain (the part of the Basin that would be protected by the Tocks Island Dam) had stabilized or perhaps even declined. Coupled with this work, EDF had also helped to persuade Sullivan's group that flooding along a river provides ecological benefits, by fertilizing the lands adjacent to the river. This ecological argument was made most dramatically to Sullivan in a film, "The Flooding River," prepared by Lincoln Brower, an ecologist at Amherst. It is interesting to note in passing that EDF approached Sullivan on these matters, not the reverse; and only after Governor Cahill's announcement in May that he had doubts about the project.

These then were the expert documents and ruminations on the Tocks project available to Sullivan and staff. What story did they tell? In sum, the story seems to have been very spare. The entire array of analysis had almost no influence on the *personal* position of Sullivan or even (eventually) Cahill toward the dam, though it did, as will be noted, play an important political role nonetheless. In the first place, some of the studies were clearly contrived to support a particular goal, for or against the dam, and were consequently discounted by the DEP staff. The DRBC staff papers, for example, appeared to be building a case for the dam, and did not seem thorough or balanced in their arguments. Similarly, the Corps environmental impact assessments were organized to support the Tocks project. They displayed the impacts in as narrow a framework as possible while always counterpointing them with possible ameliorative measures (fish ladders and such).

Of course, not all the studies had this adversary character (for example, the Edwards and Kelcey Report, the Nathan Associates Study, the McCormick Report) and some that did contained interesting analyses that could not cavalierly be discounted simply because they were partisan. But much of the analysis also had insignificant impact because it did not seem to address the issues that really mattered to Sullivan and the DEP staff. For example, with the exception of the Nathan report, the studies never confronted the impact of the project on the future pattern of development in the rural areas of northwest New Jersey. Nor did the studies really say much about the manifold ecological implications that must follow from the dam. Above all, the studies said very little about who wins and who loses if the dam is built.

Certain of the analyses did have an impact; at least they supported what O'Neill and Sullivan already believed, and were frequently referred to by the DEP group in ensuing discussions. Thus, the Edwards and Kelcey Report gave estimates of the massive costs of new roads required by the project, costs which had nowhere entered the Corps' benefit-cost analyses. The McCormick study seemed especially important, as already suggested, for if it became necessary to control the nutrient flows into the reservoir, New Jersey's plans for the construction of sewage facilities for effluents draining into the lake behind the dam would probably be significantly affected. (Also, New York State would have to become involved in the project in a much more direct and perhaps less neutral way than hitherto.) However, in sum, even the best analytic work available to O'Neill and Sullivan did little more than suggest that many secondary impacts of the project had not yet been fully considered.

C. The Bureaucracy

The skepticism toward the alleged project benefits engendered by these analyses was also reinforced in the eyes of Sullivan by the apparently far from disinterested positions taken by the water resources group within DEP and by the DRBC staff. The Corps of Engineers position had already been almost automatically discounted as deriving from a bureaucracy that would willy-nilly promote dams. But DEP's own water resource group might have been expected to hold a less committed view on the project. This expectation, however, gradually eroded as the DEP water professionals appeared to Sullivan consistently and uncritically to reject possible alternatives to the dam such as the high-flow skimming concept described earlier. Sullivan (and Cahill) also did not believe they could rely upon the DRBC staff—in principle available to the Governor qua Commissioner—for a critical assessment of the project. In particular, they did not think that the staff could comfortably adopt the more parochial statewide view Cahill needed, or capture the concern with land use that was appearing increasingly important to the Governor.

D. The Uses of Analysis

Persuaded by neither the available analyses nor the experts as to the proper fate of the Tocks project, O'Neill and Sullivan had to construct their own position. In doing so, they took a rather cool view of the project, perceiving in it little romance or drama. If it was to be built, it should be simply as a means to an end. And what was this end? Was it worth the environmental complications the dam promised? The DEP group came increasingly to the view, as O'Neill later recalled, that "the project simply did not add up."

The benefits were derived from both implicit and explicit assumptions of continued growth in the demand for energy, for water, for recreation, and for flood plain development, while at the same time the costs of this growth were hardly addressed. The project appeared to be encouraging a haphazard development in rural northwest New Jersey in return for some highly dubious benefits. The local politicians and planners in the primary impact area felt completely at a loss to cope with the expected rampant development in the region and ensuing pressures on local services of all types—fire, police, hospital, solid waste collection, road repair, and so forth.

As the DEP staff looked in such detail at the problems the Tocks impact region would experience, they began to question both the inevitability and the value of growth in that part of New Jersey, a process perhaps not clearly defined in their own minds, but certainly including the continuous conversion of rural and farm lands to more intensive uses. It is doubtful that any of the analytic work on hand at that time had any significant role in this growing skepticism, with perhaps the exceptions of the Nathan Study and the EDF work on flood control, especially the latter, which did suggest the paradox of flood control programs that encouraged the further development of the flood plains.

Notwithstanding these deficiencies, the available analytic work did have an influence. The analyses posed projections and Basin needs for water that had to be answered. Although these analyses were flawed and often unconvincing, there they were! And, politically, it is difficult to fight something with nothing. If Sullivan and staff were to oppose the Tocks project, they would have to do more than merely criticize the existing analytic work. In particular, the Commissioner, and ultimately the Governor, were faced with two apparently very strong arguments *for* the dam: (1) the dam would provide additional assured water supply from the Delaware; and (2) the dam would provide flood control protection for people and structures already on the main-stem flood plain.

The water supply argument was a blend of two separate points: first, that there was a requirement for more water; second, that Tocks was the best way to meet the requirement. Perhaps no argot of analysis is as misleading as the notion of "requirement" or "need." Above all, the concept hints ominously of disaster should the requirement not be met. The concept supports powerfully the bureaucratic and political syndrome of prudence, of not being caught short;

and it also supports the professional's concentration on disaster. The political system finds it difficult to accept the costs of shortages, even when these are neither too severe nor too frequent (a point made more fully in essay 1). To use them deliberately as a planning tool to discourage growth is even more difficult for politicians to accept. For these powerful political reasons, the DEP staff's response to the water supply argument for the Tocks project was to stress the possibility of some alternative to the dam: perhaps high-flow skimming, perhaps something else. But in the absence of any systematic investigation of alternatives, Sullivan and staff felt hard pressed to oppose the dam outright.

The flood control argument in favor of the dam was still simpler, and perhaps more powerful. Two pieces of analytic work appeared to be crucial in shaping the Governor's and Commissioner's views in this case: the detailed study of past and potential flood damage in the Basin by the Environmental Defense Fund, and the Corps' own benefit-cost analyses. The key points made by the EDF studies (reviewed earlier in this essay) were politically useful to Sullivan and the Governor. The studies had noted that there were continuing and rapid developments in the flood plains of the Delaware tributaries, where all the loss of life in the 1955 floods occurred, and that would not be directly protected by the Tocks Island Dam; by contrast, over the past decade there had been a substantial decline in the number of structures on the main-stem flood plain below the dam site. The Governor could safely argue, if he wished, that were flood control the goal, Tocks did not appear the most effective way to achieve it.

The importance of the Corps' benefit-cost analysis derived from its relatively low assessment of the project's flood control benefits—about $2 million per year. This reflected the Corps' judgment that very severe flooding on the Delaware capable of causing hundreds of millions of dollars of damage was highly improbable. The low estimate, of course, markedly deflated the political potency of flood prevention as a major purpose of the dam. It stood, for example, in engaging contrast to the Corps' attempt to emphasize the costs of a single flood, probabilities aside, when it released a calculation estimating the effects of Hurricane Agnes had it struck the Delaware (above the dam site) rather than the Susquehanna Valley in 1971.

E. The Alternatives

O'Neill and Sullivan had now to translate these various perspectives into a defensible position for the Governor to adopt at the special DRBC meeting to be convened in September. They chose a threefold strategy. First, they did not confront the DRBC and the

Corps' analyses directly; although they were themselves skeptical of the benefit-cost and other studies, they chose not to emphasize this publicly. Second, they selected from the analyses already available certain problems which, they argued, required safeguards before the project should be undertaken; in particular, the analyses suggested that something would have to be done about control of flood plain development, new road construction, regional sewage facilities, and prevention of eutrophication. Finally, they stressed the importance of dealing also with problems only glancingly studied previously, especially the danger of uncontrolled growth in the impact area, which the local communities seemed ill equipped to handle. This threefold strategy did not include any call for new studies.

The arguments were woven first by O'Neill and then by Sullivan into a paper for the Governor setting forth six possible alternatives, ranging from an unconditional go-ahead for the project to outright opposition. By this time, O'Neill and Sullivan had personally reached the conclusion that the dam should not be built. They recommended, however a middle-of-the-road position, where the Governor would approve the project only if seven specified conditions were met. These conditions, which articulated the wanted safeguards (many of which they knew well would be difficult to achieve) were as follows.

1. That New Jersey and Pennsylvania enact legislation to give authority to the state governments (rather than to local zoning boards) to control land use in the Delaware Basin flood plains.
2. That the DRBC authorize the construction of a dispersed sewage plant system.
3. That a plan be devised to control nutrient flows into the Tocks reservoir for the purpose of preventing eutrophication.
4. That state and local units of government in New Jersey be given authority to control land use in the primary impact area.
5. That the federal government provide substantial funding for the construction of highways required to access the recreation area.
6. That the recreation plan be scaled down to accommodate a maximum annual user load of four million day visits (from ten million).
7. That the federal government consider payments in lieu of taxes to local units of government for loss of ratables as a result of federal acquisition of lands.

The question may be asked why this rather than the more drastic alternative was chosen. One reason certainly was the hope by both Sullivan and the Governor that the occasion could be used to wrest from the New Jersey Legislature some legislation that would be desirable even were there no Tocks Island Dam: for example, the flood plain and primary impact area zoning authority. However, Governor Cahill has since also made it quite clear that he did not want all the conditions to be met too readily; they were deliberatedly framed to ensure a long breathing spell for people to think through the Tocks project anew. Probably the main reason why Cahill chose the more moderate alternative was that he was not yet ready to question sharply the value of more growth in the state.

F. The Decision

By the end of the summer of 1972, Governor Cahill had come to share Richard Sullivan's concern with the social impact of the project on northwest New Jersey and had fully accepted his suggested alternative. He now essentially shared Sullivan's perspective on the environmental hazards and was even more skeptical than his Commissioner of the alleged benefits of the project. For example, unlike Sullivan, who strongly supported the establishment of a recreation area, albeit without the dam, Cahill remained skeptical even of this. Moreover, the political dangers of opposing the dam still remained low. Not only was the project something most of the states' citizens hardly knew existed, there were now other politicians opposing the dam, notably Joseph Mariziti (R), who was running for Congress in the thirteenth Congressional District, bordering Tocks.

Before Governor Cahill announced his decision, he wanted to obtain a firsthand feel for the problem as it was perceived by local politicians. Consequently, on the weekend before the special DRBC meeting, at a breakfast meeting in an inn near the dam site, Cahill met informally with over 100 county freeholders, planning board members, and other local politicians from the Tocks region. Cahill later described this meeting as "electrifying." Cahill now heard the anguished laments of communities not prepared for the influx of ten million visitors per year to the recreation area. The politicians and planners had real and specific concerns: loss of tax revenue due to federal condemnations, not enough fire protection, insufficient police, no capability for solid waste disposal, not enough ambulances or hospital beds. Above all, without any effective zoning authority, the local communities seemed to stand completely helpless before a haphazard sprawl of motels, restaurants, and trailer camps, which the recreation area and new road construction would threaten to bring.

The vividness with which Cahill recalls this meeting is interesting. In a talk at Princeton after he left the governorship, Cahill commented that one of his greatest mistakes as governor was not undertaking more such personal visits—whether to hospitals, schools, prisons, or reservoirs. Indeed, even the *trip* (by helicopter) to the breakfast meeting had an impact. The Governor recalled his shock at the extent of the land to be flooded by the project as, for the first time, he flew low over the 37-mile stretch of valley above the dam site.

The Governor duly announced his decision on September 13, 1972, listing the seven conditions that would have to be met before he could approve the project. It was a decision that neither supported nor opposed the dam outright.[7]

V. FROM IMPASSE TO STUDY

The period after the Cahill decision was a time of lazy maneuver and of general frustration. While the professionals sought somewhat desultorily to respond to the Cahill conditions, the Basin state governors each undertook still another review of the project: Malcolm Wilson of New York, now more than ever concerned about the impact of the project on the poultry and dairy farms of New York; Milton Shapp of Pennsylvania along with his old pro Secretary for the Environment, Maurice Goddard, steadfastly in favor of the dam; Sherman Tribbitt of Delaware, steadfastly uncommitted; and in New Jersey, a new Governor and new Environmental Commissioner, Brendan Byrne and David Bardin, hewing for the time to the Cahill holding pattern.[d] For the environmentalists this was the season for looking for alternatives: the Save-the-Delaware-Coalition's alternative recreation plan and the Environmental Defense Fund's study of high-flow skimming, both previously mentioned, were done during this interlude.

But no one was happy with the impasse. The project hung over the environmentalists like a sword, and to the local populace surrounding the dam site, the indecision and frozen expectations were perhaps worse even than a determination to construct the dam. The Corps, the Delaware River Basin Commission, the water companies, and the utilities could not set their own plans in order until the project was finally approved or rejected once and for all. In the states, as long as the Tocks project remained in suspension, there could realistically be no sustained investigations or implementation of alternative water

---

[d]Cahill had lost in the Republican primary in the summer of 1973 on issues unrelated to Tocks. Byrne, a Democrat, entered office in January 1974, and Bardin replaced Sullivan soon thereafter. Tom O'Neill remained as staff assistant to the Environmental Commissioner and continued throughout this period to play a principal role in defining the state's position toward Tocks.

supply and recreation schemes. And in Congress, Joe Evins and John Stennis wanted the Tocks project resolved and off their subcommittees' agendas—one way or the other. In their view, each year's delay merely increased the cost of the project. They believed that the environmentalists wanted the project environmentally perfect before it even began, and that they would probably never be satisfied.

How to get the project off dead center had therefore become everyone's question by the spring of 1974. To Evins the answer was to precipitate a court test—vote out construction funds, set the first steam shovel into operation, and then let the environmentalists dare to seek an injunction; their arguments were, he believed, frivolous and overstated and would soon be seen as such. Partly to forestall such a maneuver by Evins in the House and by Stennis in the Senate, some of the dam opponents (or at least skeptics) in Congress launched a competing idea of how to break the impasse: an intensive, comprehensive, year-long study, after which the decision would be made.

Another study! Did anyone really expect that any study, no matter how thorough and imaginative, would change people's attitudes toward the project or goad reluctant politicians toward decision? And yet a study did promise some benefits. It might in fact make it easier for the skeptics in Congress and the states to find a basis for finally opposing the project outright, and it would anyhow forestall the start of construction still another year. To project supporters in Congress, the significance of the study promised to be its insignificance—with its completion, the policy makers would lose their last excuse for delay. There was also a fond (and small) hope held by some on both sides of the controversy that perhaps the study would in fact finally resolve the outstanding issues and persuade the *other* side that *it* was in error.

It could certainly not be denied that there were such outstanding issues. Indeed, despite the vast number and variety of studies that had been undertaken during the previous decade, a substantial fraction of the issues which policy makers and citizens really cared about still remained unclear, uncertain, and in many instances, altogether unexamined. The clearest such issue was whether the project was in fact needed—whether without the dam there were ways to achieve the project benefits of water supply, flood prevention, power, and recreation.

This question had both a narrow and a broad interpretation. In the narrow view, the issue was whether the benefits defined by the Tocks project could be met otherwise if the dam were not built. Could other ways be found to reduce flood damage on the main stem, provide mass recreation at the Water Gap site, implement large scale storage of energy, provide water for power plant cooling, and, above all, make water available for export out-of-Basin to northern New Jersey? These questions had to some extent been addressed, but for the most part not very thoroughly. The agencies responsible for studying the alternatives and with the resources to do so were also the agencies most committed to the project; they displayed a coolness in pursuing alternative possibilities that could undercut the dam.

The search for alternatives could also be given a broader interpretation, and one in fact more nearly touching the kinds of arguments the protagonists in the controversy were actually forwarding. The analyst need not restrict himself to the specific purposes defined by the Tocks project, but could instead inquire more generally into ways to achieve a balance of water supply and demand in the Basin service region, flood reduction not only on the main stem, and so forth. Thus, for example, instead of investigating a natural systems alternative for the recreation area, one could instead consider ways to maximize recreation opportunities throughout the entire region, not merely at the Water Gap. Such an investigation would have been especially appropriate as a response to the often stated concerns of some of the dam supporters that a recreation area at the Water Gap should cater to the urban poor and working classes in Trenton, Philadelphia, Newark, and New York; it seemed rather to those who opposed the project that such concerns could better be resolved by a series of recreation opportunities close to the people, not by a relatively distant park to be reached only by automobile. But neither side of this dispute undertook a systematic regional analysis of recreation.

The water supply alternatives above all seemed to require the broader perspective. Even a casual examination called into doubt the uses to which the Tocks-created water supply were to be put. None of the major projected demands—water for cooling power plants, exports of water out-of-Basin to northern New Jersey, and enhanced stream flow to prevent a salt intrusion up the estuary—had been critically examined. Nor had the region's water supply potential been thoroughly explored.

Many of the environmental and social consequences of the Tocks project also remained in dispute, their analysis having inspired little field research, little theory, and little attention by scientists, economists, and other professionals. For example, the eutrophication issue, under study since 1970, remained unresolved. The best available water models were completely inadequate, and the data relevant to the Delaware Basin were markedly deficient. Also, at least one new environmental issue had been raised that needed some further study. The Medical Society of New Jersey, under the prodding of one of its members, Dr. Gerald Rozan, had suddenly passed in May 1974 a resolution opposing the Tocks project. The basis of the opposition was the Society's concern that upstream runoff of chicken effluent into the reservoir might lead to salmonella contamination, the spread of a communicable disease caused by the salmonella bacilli.

With respect to the expected social consequences of the dam, no one had a clear picture of the probable secondary impacts: the expansion of roads, commerce, industry, and residential sprawl in northern New Jersey. Although the Nathan Associates study of 1966 had made an excellent initial attempt at such an analysis, there had been no systematic study since that time. There never had been a study of the project winners and losers, especially of the residents in the taking area, who would be the most deeply affected by the project. In sum, for reasons both simple and subtle (anticipated in essay 1 and discussed in detail in the final seven essays of this volume), a substantial variety of salient issues remained unresolved.

So the idea of a study finally did come to appear attractive to many, especially if its sponsorship and terms of reference could be widely agreed upon. These were no small tasks, however. Those who had doubts about the project wanted an independent agency to sponsor and define the scope of the study. But which agency? The Council on Environmental Quality, an initial candidate, did not have the staff or the experience to conduct a study of the character envisioned; nor was it a disinterested party who would be acceptable to the project supporters. The Environmental Protection Agency had the staff, but it also was suspect by some; John Stennis especially objected—EPA's budget is reviewed by the Interior Subcommittee of the Senate Appropriations Committee, on which Stennis does not serve. Another candidate, the National Academy of Sciences, objected to doing a study of such scope in the time allotted.

Beyond the difficulty of finding an appropriately independent and capable agency, several Congressmen felt that any review not piloted by the Corps would be a slap in the face to the Corps, and would provide a bad precedent of having outside agencies review Corps projects. Of course, the project opponents were not eager to have the Corps direct the project. However, since it was mainly the project skeptics who wanted the study, they finally had to give in somewhat. Congress resolved the question of sponsorship at last by appropriating the study funds of $1.5 million to the Corps, but specifying that the Corps was to conduct the investigation in cooperation with the Delaware River Basin Commission—that is, in practice, with the concerned Basin states. This last was an important stipulation, for it permitted the states to fight successfully for broad terms of reference, and to insist that the contractors examine a wide range of alternatives to the dam rather than merely review past procedures and studies. It also led to state representatives joining the Corps on the study management team; and it gave the states some input into the selection of the study contractor.

By January 1975 the contractors had been chosen (URS/Madigan-Praeger, and Conklin and Rossant, Manhattan-based engineering consultant and architectural consultant firms, respectively) after a competitive bidding process. They had $1.5 million and eight months to complete the study. Almost twenty years after the floods that inspired the comprehensive survey by the Corps, and after over a decade of research and planning and four years of intensive controversy, there was to be still one more study, again under the direction of the Corps. Was anybody listening?[8]

VI. FROM STUDY TO DECISION

The idea of a million and a half dollar study was viewed skeptically on all sides. To the Corps of Engineers and the DRBC staff, the very existence of a new study would imply that their own long years of effort—including, for example, those eleven data-packed volumes of H D 522—were not sufficiently thorough or were otherwise deficient. They regarded the study as entirely unnecessary—a waste of time and money perpetrated by the environmentalists.

The environmentalists, on the other hand, were equally skeptical, but for a different reason. They regarded the conflict of interest created by putting the Corps of Engineers in charge of the study as so blatant, as such a clear case of the fox being set to guard the chicken coop, that they could expect no honest or objective information to be produced by it. In caucus they debated whether they should disassociate themselves from the whole undertaking and simply seek to discredit it, or whether they should cooperate in the hope of counterbalancing the bias (as they saw it) of the other side. They finally chose the latter course, and were surprised and somewhat disarmed when the consultants approached them in an earnest and respectful way rather than in the perfunctory way that they expected. Herbert Howard, the civilian officer of the Corps of Engineers who was given the delicate job of overseeing the study, was acutely conscious of the conflict of interest and took great pains to see that everything was done openly. Nevertheless the conflict of interest was real, and the dam's opponents retained a substantial degree of skepticism.

A less well defined third group was also skeptical for yet another reason. This was the group of people who, potentially, could do the work. Many of these people felt that the six or seven months of real working time that would be available was too short to find convincing answers to the important questions. Thus, the consultants who finally agreed to undertake the study found themselves in an ambience of universal skepticism. Among other ways, they met it by announcing that their work would rely mainly on existing studies rather than on de novo research. This tended to excuse them with their colleagues who thought the time was too short to do new research, and it simultaneously tended to relieve the apprehensions of the dam's proponents who thought the past work adequate. It disappointed, however, those who had hoped the study might really attempt to resolve some of the nagging uncertainties that genuinely bothered the more conscientious decision makers. As it turned out, there were some exceptions to the policy of relying upon past work. Perhaps the most notable of these concerned the salinity of estuarine water, a problem crucial to the project rationale, which the study did tackle in a novel manner. (The story of this analysis is told in Essay 5.)

The study was taken seriously by the analysts and planners in each of the Basin states responsible for review of the Tocks project—but especially so by the New Jersey analysts. The project had always been more important to New Jersey than to her sister states in the Basin, and it remained so. New Jersey's review was far more intensive than those in the other states, particularly in its investigation of water supply. The review in New Jersey was under the direction of Bardin and O'Neill; and the themes and institutional setting shaping their outlook were similar to those that had guided the analyses of Sullivan and O'Neill two years previously. Above all, water supply again loomed as the issue crucial to the state's position on the entire project.

In a roundabout way, the consultants' study did finally provide an outline of what many in New Jersey had been seeking—an acceptable water supply alternative to Tocks. The study, first of all, projected future demand for water at levels much lower than those used previously by New Jersey planners, or by the Corps. The water demand projections were lower for two reasons: The population projections on which they were based reflected the latest U.S. government estimates, which were lower than the population data hitherto used by the state. Second, the consultants, again on the basis of the latest evidence, projected a much diminished demand for water for industrial use. They stressed in particular the relatively high fraction (about two-thirds) of industrial demand that would be self-supplied by industry, thus reducing the demand for publicly supplied water. The consultants also calculated the sensitivity of water demand to projections of future economic growth in the region. In addition, the consultants' report contained a long list of relatively small water supply projects that could be undertaken in each of the Basin states, as supplements or, possibly, as alternatives to Tocks.

Although the consultants themselves had not done so explicitly, the New Jersey analysts reviewing the Tocks project under the direction of Commissioner Bardin and Tom O'Neill were able to extract from the consultants' study an interesting finding—that a plausible combination of intrastate projects *without Tocks* would probably serve to meet all the state's water needs for at least the next 25 to 50 years. Furthermore, the state analysts suddenly realized that the cost of these projects to the state would not exceed that of Tocks, even though the federal government would build Tocks at no initial cost to the state budget! The reason was simply that it would cost a vast sum of state money to bring the Tocks-supplied water from the Delaware to the northeast part of the state where the water would be needed. Through a good part of the Tocks debate, this cost had been forgotten—it never, for example, appeared prominently in the criticisms of the project's benefit-cost analyses. The belief that the federal government would be, in effect, financing state water needs was indeed one reason the states had found it so difficult to give up the Tocks projects.

Commissioner Bardin reported the results of the New Jersey analysis to Governor Byrne:

> *In summary*, New Jersey seems unlikely to need the Tocks increment for from 25 to 50 years, as current projections indicate. From the standpoint of water supply, it would be desirable to preserve the option to build the dam and lake, but to defer the actual construction for as many years as practicable while perfecting the contingent right to divert (water from the Delaware). . . . From the environmental standpoint, building the intrastate projects ahead of Tocks would delay the impact on the existing valley and could preserve the free-flowing river for a substantial period at least. From the water supply standpoint the dam and lake project seems a "bird in the hand" which is painful to relinquish. . . .
>
> If you believe that a large new lake would be an attractive amenity in place of the existing valley, and if you believe it is worth $311 million of federal tax money to build it over the next few years . . . you will favor the dam and lake project.
>
> If you prefer a free-flowing river for at least a generation, you will

nonetheless weigh the likelihood that New Jersey would need this water supply within 25–50 years, and its chances of securing it nearer to the time of need via this dam versus the risks you feel New Jersey should take. . . .[9]

One detects here still a reluctance to let the Tocks project—"a bird in the hand"—slip away altogether even if it isn't needed for a while. To the environmentalist, the building of a dam is an irreversible action; it cannot be undone. And to a policy maker responsible for water supply, the final deauthorization of a project as significant as Tocks must also appear irreversible; it could be undone but at what a political cost![e]

The consultants' study was completed in June 1975, and the governors of the Basin states had now to decide. On balance, the study appeared to have had little direct effect. In New Jersey, for example, the governor and his staff apparently assumed from the beginning that a study sponsored by the Corps would naturally favor the dam. Evidently no one in the governor's office took the study seriously, an attitude that clashed oddly with the detailed attention paid to the study by the Department of Environmental Protection and its Commissioner. There had evidently been little contact between DEP and the governor's office on this issue.

The study did, however, confirm the views of the policy makers and help steel them to decision. The study had also, as had previous studies, altered the terms of the decision in several significant ways. Approval of the project would not mean the same thing in 1975 as it would have in 1971, for the project had been much altered in the interim, as had the perspectives of those responsible for guiding and coping with its consequences. Similarly, a rejection of the project would lead to a different train of alternatives from that which would have ensued four years previously. Each study had its own small impact on these redefinitions of the project. Thus, for example, whether or not the dam were built, the design of the recreation park, the ways of bringing people to the park, and the sorts of things people would do once there had all changed in concept during the preceding years (gradually and grudgingly) under a steady flow of studies and criticisms, lengthy and short, technical and political. The water supply picture for New Jersey had also shifted markedly in focus during the years of controversy, no more so than in the preceding few months. This is a recurrent theme captured in several of the subsequent essays of this volume.

[e]New Jersey's options were set forth with considerable dexterity in a companion report from Bardin to Byrne. An abridged text forms the Afterword of this book, pp. 403–405.

Some altogether new concerns had also been generated during the period of the consultants' study, notably through the intervention of the Medical Society of New Jersey noted previously. The Society, through an ad-hoc committee formed to review the consultants' study, suggested several potential public health problems that might follow in the wake of the Tocks project, including various dysentery-type infections caused by lake-bathing as well as by the possibility of salmonella contamination mentioned in its initial resolution. These health issues were particularly noted by Governor Byrne at the decisive DRBC meeting.[10]

On July 31, 1975, at a special meeting of the Delaware River Basin Commission, the Commissioners voted three to one *not* to request Congress to provide construction funds for the Tocks project. The governors of Delaware, New Jersey, and New York[f] voted against construction; the governor of Pennsylvania voted in favor; and the Federal Commissioner to the DRBC abstained. By a vote of three to zero, with New Jersey, New York, and the United States in favor and with two abstentions, the Commissioners then approved a motion that the DRBC request Congress to provide continued funding for land acquisition.

This then was the decision. Few believe it was the final decision. The chief protagonists in the controversy were as divided at the end as they were at the beginning on its wisdom, and many of the issues which have bedevilled the controversy remain yet unresolved. It is still too early to tell whether another flood, another drought, or a new personality in one of the Basin statehouses or in Washington couldn't again revive the idea of a dam at Tocks Island.

NOTES

This chapter in part derives from several personal interviews, including importantly, with the following persons: Chris Burke, New Jersey Public Interest Research Group; Governor William Cahill, former Governor of New Jersey; Richard Curry, Special Assistant to Assistant Secretary for Outdoor Recreation, Sports Fisheries and Wildlife, and National Parks, Department of Interior; Robert Cyphers, Water Resources, Department of Environmental Protection, State of New Jersey; Gordon Dilley, U.S. Army Corps of Engineers, Philadelphia District; George Gardner, Special Assistant to Assistant Secretary for Outdoor Recreation, Sports Fisheries and Wildlife, and National Parks, Department of Interior; Mina Haefele, Delaware Valley Conservation Association; Herbert Howard, U.S. Army Corps of Engineers, North Atlantic Division; Jack Isenogle, National Park Service, Department of Interior; Gar Kaganovich, Staff, Senate Committee on Appropriations; Harold Lockwood, Save-the-Delaware-Coalition;

[f]Hugh Carey replaced Malcolm Wilson as New York Governor in January 1975.

Austin Olney, Administrative Assistant to Congressman Pierre duPont (R-Del.) (telephone); Thomas O'Neill, Special Assistant to the Commissioner, Department of Environmental Protection, State of New Jersey; Dr. Gerald Rozan, Medical Society of New Jersey (telephone); Chip Seeger, Administrative Assistant to Congressman Joseph McDade (R-Penn.); Nancy Shukaitis, Commissioner, Monroe County (interview with Lynn Anderson); Lawrence Siegal, Staff Assistant to Congressman Howard Robison (R-N.Y.); Steve Sloan, former staff analyst of the President's Council on Environmental Quality; Hunter Spelling, Staff, House Public Works Subcommittee of Appropriations Committee (interview with Michael Reich); Robert Steenhagen, National Park Service, Department of Interior (telephone); Richard Sullivan, former Commissioner, Department of Environmental Protection, State of New Jersey; Robert Teeters, U.S. Army Corps of Engineers, Washington Headquarters; Jack Vandenberg, Assistant to Senator Clifford Case (R-N.J.); Brinton Whitall, Delaware River Basin Commission; Gary Widman, Staff analyst, President's Council on Environmental Quality; Edward Wisniewski, U.S. Army Corps of Engineers, Philadelphia District.

In addition, several of the participants in and observers of the Tocks controversy convened at Princeton in January 1973 for a highly illuminating discussion which I have drawn upon in preparing this chapter. The non-Princeton participants in this conclave were as follows: Joseph Browder, Environmental Policy Center; Hope Cobb, Sierra Club; Terance Curran, New York State Department of Environmental Conservation; Peter De Gelleke, National Park Service; Gordon Dilley, Army Corps of Engineers; Steve Ebbin, George Washington University; Smith Freeman, Environmental Protection Agency; Alan Gitelson, Loyola University; Jerry Gollub, Haverford College; John Harte, Yale University; Herbert Howlett, Delaware River Basin Commission; Richard James, Schuykill Nature Center; Gar Kaganowich, Office of Senator Clifford Case; Richard KixMiller, New York, N.Y.; Lee Merrill, Rutgers University Institute for Environmental Studies; Thomas O'Neill, New Jersey Department of Environmental Protection; Leonard Rodberg, Institute for Policy Studies; Ann Satterthwaite, Washington, D.C.; Corinne Schelling, American Academy of Arts and Sciences; Donald Scott, New Jersey Chamber of Commerce; Robert Strassler, Alford, Massachusetts; Richard Sullivan, New Jersey Department of Environmental Protection; Robert Teeters, Army Corps of Engineers; Laurence Tombaugh, National Science Foundation; Francesco Trama, Rutgers University; Laurence Tribe, Harvard Law School; John Voss, American Academy of Arts and Sciences; William Whipple, Rutgers University Water Resources Research Institute; Brinton Whitall, Delaware River Basin Commission; Christopher Wright, Rockefeller Foundation; James Wright, Delaware River Basin Commission.

I also wish to acknowledge a special debt of gratitude in the preparation of this chapter to Lynn Anderson, who sensitively investigated impacts of the Tocks project on the local communities bordering the dam site, and to Tom O'Neill, whose contributions were many and were especially marked in section VI.

1. Letter from Maurice Goddard, Secretary of the Department of Environmental Resources, Pennsylvania, to Harold A. Feiveson, December 19, 1974.

2. This section derives from several personal interviews, among them Gordon Dilley, Herbert Howard, and Robert Teeters. The statement by General Richard Groves quoted in the text was made at the Princeton University Conference on Water Resources, April 1973.

3. Delaware River Basin Commission, Staff Study, "Water Demands in the Delaware River Basin as Related to the Tocks Island Reservoir Project" (1971).

4. Delaware River Basin Commission, "Staff Comments on Paper Entitled: 'The Tocks Island Dam Project,' Report No. 1, by H.A. Feiveson," Center for Environmental Studies, Princeton University, Princeton, New Jersey, October 1, 1973, p. 9.

5. This section derives from several personal interviews, among them Harold Lockwood, Mina Haefele, Chris Burke, Leo Eisel, and Smith Freeman.

6. This section derives from several interviews, among them Steve Sloan, Jack Vandenberg, Gar Kaganovich, Lawrence Siegal, and Austin Olney (telephone). See also, letter from Russell Train to Secretary of the Army, Robert Froehlke, October 20, 1971. Letter from Russell Train to General Counsel of Army, Robert Jordan, April 7, 1971. Pete duPont, "The Tocks Island Dam Fight," Sierra Club Bulletin, July–August 1972, pp. 13–18. The statements by James Wright were taken from this article.

7. Interviews with Governor William Cahill, Richard Sullivan, and Thomas O'Neill. See also William Cahill, "Statement Concerning the Tocks Island Dam," September 13, 1972, Delaware River Basin Commission. The film *The Flooding River*, by Lincoln Brower (1972) is available from John Wiley and Sons, New York.

8. Interviews with Gar Kaganovich, Lawrence Siegal, Jack Vandenberg, and Hunter Spelling. See also letter, from Malcolm Wilson, Governor of New York, to Congressman Joe L. Evins, May 10, 1974; letter, from Sherman Tribbitt, Governor of Delaware, to Harold Lockwood, Chairman, Save-the-Delaware-Coalition, July 9, 1974. The resolution of the New Jersey Medical Society was #39, "Opposition to Tocks Island Dam Project," May 15, 1974.

9. Discussion paper, David Bardin, July 1975.

10. Letter, Gerald H. Rozan, Chairman, Ad Hoc Committee, Medical Society of New Jersey on Tocks Island Dam Project to Governor Brendan T. Byrne, July 29, 1975 .

Part Three

Technical Analysis and Human Values

In this central section the reader is asked to look in on the professionals who are planning the future of the Delaware River Valley. Like their counterparts around the country, they are applying techniques that are rigidly circumscribed by rules not entirely of their own devising; and they are making judgments about what to consider and what not to consider that are strongly influenced by the extent to which the experts can measure (or think they can measure) the subjects under investigation.

Each of these four essays is partly a primer, written for people who want to check the "experts" in their backyards, and partly an exploration of alternatives, usually from a fairly fundamental level. The first essay, by David Bradford and Harold Feiveson, introduces the reader to benefit-cost analysis as it is currently done by the U.S. Army Corps of Engineers. But a considerable portion of the essay examines benefit-cost analysis more generally, explaining the assumptions that underlie the calculations and that, in principle, define a procedure for carrying out an "ideal" benefit-cost analysis.

The next three essays explore three of the Corps' four "benefits": water supply, flood control, and electric power. Their points of departure are the past studies that have been directed at understanding and measuring the respective benefits. But the essays attempt to move beyond the traditional approaches to show the effectiveness of looking at much-studied problems in fresh and innovative ways. The fourth benefit, recreation, appeared to us to require such a complete reformulation that it deserved a section of its own; it is treated, in conjunction with the issue of transportation access, in the final essay of this volume.

Water supply, flood control, and electric power share a grounding in physical laws; a return to such fundamentals as "water has to go somewhere" has proved to be extremely useful as we have strived to isolate the fundamental issues at stake in each area. As human problems, the three subjects also are dominated by somewhat rare events: droughts, floods, and power shortfalls. Frank Sinden develops a number of relatively untried concepts for dealing with the unequal flow of water, and these return in less explicit form in Allan Krass's essay on floods and Thomas Schrader's and Robert Socolow's essay on electric power. Policies that directly address "peak and valley" problems are bound to receive renewed emphasis in the near future as our society starts to do strict accounting of how its water and energy are being used. We may well discover that the marginal watts and cubic feet per second are almost absurdly costly.

✳ *Chapter 4*

Benefits and Costs, Winners and Losers

David F. Bradford
and
Harold A. Feiveson

I. INTRODUCTION

Should a project that will generate the equivalent of $9.5 million per year in net benefits necessarily be undertaken? Must a person who opposes such a project be regarded as in muddle-headed opposition to a rigorous chain of argument from universally accepted first principles and obvious facts? Must we regard the opening up of rural regions to commercial development as a good thing in spite of the apparent loss of amenity? The answer to all these questions is no.

Is economic analysis fundamentally incompatible with a regard for such intangible values as the complexity and variety of a free-running river? Must refined sensitivity be suppressed to permit the crass calculus of dollar gains and losses to proceed? Is the Tocks Island Dam decision a choice between "economic values" and other, higher values? The answer to these questions is also no.

The term "benefit-cost analysis" refers to an ideal procedure for resource allocation and to its embodiment in practice as a management tool. Theory and practice go back at least to 1844, when Jules Dupuit made his contribution to improving bridge investment decisions in France. However, relatively little development of them took place until the 1930s, when the United States government officially adopted benefit-cost analysis in water resource investment choices. Although this policy has remained in effect since then, and the area of application has been extended as the techniques of analysis have been refined and improved, there remains widespread misunderstanding about what one validly can and cannot expect of it. This is our subject in this essay.

Below, in Part II, we introduce benefit-cost analysis by discussing the procedures the Corps of Engineers has actually used to evaluate the costs and benefits of the Tocks Island Dam project in the formal reports it has submitted annually to Congress. Much of what goes on, the reader will learn, is narrowly circumscribed by federal guidelines, and still other inflexibility is a product of the bureaucratic context within which these analyses are developed. If we are successful, the reader will have grown anxious about the outer limits of benefit-cost analysis that persist even after all such institutional constraints are removed and an analyst can do whatever he or she likes. The remainder of this essay addresses several of these limits.[a]

II. CALCULATING BENEFITS AND COSTS IN THE TOCKS PROJECT

1. The WRC Guidelines

The *Federal Register*[1] presents a set of principles and standards to be applied by federal agencies in the planning of federal water resource projects. These principles provide the guidelines for the benefit-cost calculations that must accompany any plan for water resource projects submitted by federal agencies to Congress for authorization and appropriations. The most recent principles and standards were developed by the federal Water Resources Council (WRC) and ultimately were amended and approved by Congress. The WRC is an independent executive agency formed in 1965 and responsible for coordinating water resource planning and development in the United States. It is composed of Secretaries of Interior; Agriculture; Army; Health, Education, and Welfare; Transportation; and the chairman of the Federal Power Commission; and it includes also participation of several other executive agencies, including the Environmental Protection Agency and the Council on Environmental Quality.

The principles and standards define the guidelines by which federal agencies are to develop a stylized balance sheet of project benefits and costs. Although the agencies are directed to list intangible factors not readily monetizable, the heart of the analysis is the display of benefits and costs measured in dollar units. The ensuing ratio of benefits and costs (the B/C ratio) is intended to play a twofold role. It should first form a loose guide both to the federal agencies and to

---

[a]The reader who is not especially interested in the Tocks case may wish to skim Part II of this essay.

Congress as to the priorities of projects, and second, play the role of a filter.[b] Projects with a B/C ratio less than one will not be considered for authorization. The guidelines imposed by Congress, therefore, may be seen as a way of limiting the number of projects with which Congress must contend, but not so much that Congress loses discretion over which projects to fund. In this sense the guidelines represent a compromise: there should be a filter but one not too fine. In this screening process, seldom if ever does Congress inquire into the basis of a benefit-cost evaluation, faulty though it might be. Rather, it has used benefit-cost analysis as a tool for controlling the bureaucracy, for imposing at least some modest amount of discipline on a set of agencies it otherwise has great difficulty controlling. The filter role for the B/C ratio is far more significant than its use in setting priorities. By all accounts, so long as the B/C ratio is above one, and "comfortably" so, Congress pays relatively little attention to it.

The Tocks project was planned and authorized under guidelines formulated by Congress in the late 1950s. These guidelines specified planning parameters, such as the discount rate to be applied to water projects (3 1/8 percent) and the average recreation value to be attributed to swimming, hunting, hiking, etc., which now seem out of date. And indeed, after a very substantial review, the WRC formulated a new set of guidelines in September 1973 that adduced several significant changes, among them the establishment of a discount rate consistent with the average cost of federal borrowing (6 7/8 percent),[c] an escalation of recreation benefits, and the establishment of a dual bookkeeping system in which planners must display *two* alternative plans—one maximizing "national economic development" (the old method) and one maximizing "environmental quality." This last change in practice permits consideration of a project with B/C ratio less than one if the reason is that a penalty has been paid for enhancement of environmental quality. Although it has been under

[b]Note that the *difference* between benefits and costs is more important and more meaningful than the B/C *ratio* itself since the ratio is affected by the somewhat arbitrary decision of whether to count factors as benefits or negative costs. Consider, for example, a project undertaken in a depressed area with an abundance of unemployed labor and resources. Here the utilization of these unemployed resources can with logic either be considered a net benefit or a negative cost, that is, a factor that will reduce the net costs of the project. To limit the discretion of the federal agencies undertaking the analysis, the principles and standards require in this case that the factor be considered a benefit—a conservative stipulation that minimizes the benefit-cost ratio.

[c]Congress afterwards established the discount rate at 5 5/8 percent to be applied to projects evaluated after March 1974. However, with this one exception the WRC principles and standards as published remain in effect.

almost continual review, the Tocks project has so far remained subject to a sort of grandfather clause: the earlier guidelines operable at the time of the project authorization are taken to apply.

In assessing the benefit-cost analysis of the Tocks project it is important to note the degree to which the guidelines—of whatever vintage—limit the discretion of the Corps of Engineers and other federal agencies in the calculation of benefits and costs. In several crucial respects, such as the choice of discount rate where the benefit-cost calculation may be subjected to criticism, the choice of assumption has been outside the Corps' control.

2. The Tocks Project: Summary Data

Summary of the Formal Calculation. As described in the preceding essays, the Tocks project is multipurpose, designed to provide recreation, water, power, and flood control. The recreation is provided by a national recreation area, centered about the reservoir and to be constructed in stages over several years. The recreation benefits will thus grow gradually as the recreation area is completed. The other three benefits will remain roughly constant over the entire life of the project. On the cost side, most of the project expenses will be incurred before and during the period in which the dam and reservoir are constructed. The most recent formal calculations of the project benefits and costs by the Corps are summarized in Table 4-1.

The assumptions that underlie these numbers have recently been clearly set forth by the Corps. Until 1974 these assumptions had, remarkably, never been made publicly available. For the first time in

Table 4–1. Summary Benefit-Cost Calculation for Tocks Project

Average Annual Benefits (millions of dollars)	
Recreation	11.7
Power	3.2
Water supply	10.2
Flood reduction	3.8
Total	29.0
Average Annual Costs (millions of dollars)	
Associated with the initial construction and recreation	15.9
Associated with future recreation	2.4
Total	18.3

Note: These calculations are based on a discount rate of 3-1/8 percent and a project life of 100 years.

the history of the Tocks project, it is possible for outsiders to replicate with confidence the benefit-cost calculations. This is done below, with the more technical aspects of the calculation put into boxes offset in the text. The reader can safely skip these technical excursions, though we hope some will want to work through the calculations—a fine way to dispel any lingering mystery they may hold. The two elements of Table 4–1 that may be unfamiliar to some readers are the discount rate and the concept of average annuities.

Discount Rate. The discount rate, which is discussed more fully in section IV, measures the rate of exchange between dollars in one period (today) and dollars at a later period. To say that a group uses a 3 1/8 percent discount rate is to say that it is indifferent between an additional dollar today and an additional 1.03125 dollars one year hence. Looked at the other way around, a dollar one expects to receive in the future is less valuable than a dollar one receives today—with the discount rate measuring how much less valuable.

The discount rate used in these calculations has been established by Congress; it is 3 1/8 percent, the rate applicable to projects authorized in 1962. The rate designated by Congress for projects authorized in fiscal year 1975 is 5 5/8 percent. Whether projects such as Tocks, authorized in the early 1960s but not yet under construction, should be reevaluated using current discount rates has been a matter of controversy. What is clear is how important the discount rate is to the benefit-cost calculation.

For example, Table 4–2 shows how the annual average construction costs would be affected by changes in the discount rate. The remaining annual costs and all of the annual benefits are nearly constant over future years and hence are hardly altered by a change in the discount rate. Assuming for ease of illustration that they are strictly constant, the sensitivity of the Tocks benefit/cost ratio to

Table 4–2. Discount Rate Sensitivity, Tocks Construction Costs

Discount Rate (%)	Average Annual Construction Costs (millions of dollars)
3-1/8	13.1
5-5/8	22.3
6-7/8	27.5
10	40.0

Note: These calculations are based on a project life of 100 years and a total construction cost at the start of the project of $400 million.

Table 4–3. Discount Rate Sensitivity, Tocks Benefits and Costs

Discount rate (%)	Average Annual Benefits (millions of dollars)	Average Annual Costs (millions of dollars)	Benefits/ Costs
3-1/8	29.0	18.3	1.6
5-5/8	29.0	27.5	1.1
6-7/8	29.0	32.7	0.9
10	29.0	45.2	0.6

Note: These calculations are based on a project life of 100 years, a total construction cost of $400 million, and the approximation that average annual benefits and operating costs are not significantly altered by changes in the discount rate.

the discount rate may be readily calculated. The results are displayed in Table 4–3 (which may be compared to Table 4–1).

Because of the power of a change in discount rate to affect the benefit-cost ratio, great significance is attached to the discount rate by both advocates and opponents of federal projects, and it becomes an instrument in the political debate. Often the underlying allocative role of the "price" is overlooked as, for example, when conservationists opposing dams will argue for a high discount rate, although this contradicts their normal sensibility, which attaches great weight to the future. Similarly, persons who advocate federal projects at the time of slack economic conditions are often tempted to support low discount rates as a shortcut means of enhancing the calculated economic benefits of the projects.

The Concept of Average Annual Benefits and Costs.   The benefit and cost figures in Table 4–1 are average annual equivalences to the variable stream of benefits and costs one will encounter in practice. Roughly speaking, an average annual benefit may be thought of as that constant amount of dollars one would be willing to accept each year instead of the real, variable stream of benefits. An average annual cost similarly represents the constant annual payments one would be willing to expend instead of the real, variable payment schedule. The mathematical details are in Boxes 1 to 6.

3. Calculation of Costs

The Average Annual Costs.   The initial construction of the dam, reservoir, and first stage of the recreation area is estimated to take seven years and to cost approximately $400 million including inter-

Box 1. The Calculation of Average Annual Benefits and Costs

If B_1, B_2, and B_3, ..., B_N represent the stream of real benefits for years 1, 2, 3 ..., N where year 1 is the first year after the dam/reservoir construction is completed and year N represents the project life, then the average annual benefit Ba is derived by the expression:

$$\sum_{i=1}^{N} \frac{B_i}{(1+r)^i} = Ba \sum_{i=1}^{N} \frac{1}{(1+r)^i}$$

where r equals the discount rate. In words, Ba is the constant annual dollar flow, over the project life, which has the same discounted value as the actually anticipated flow of dollar benefits. Usually, the stream of benefits varies from year to year; if it should be constant, $B_1 = B_2 = B_3 = \ldots = B'_N$, and then the average annual benefit Ba would be, as we would expect, simply this constant.

Average annual costs are calculated in an analogous way, although, for apparently traditional reasons, the flow of construction expenditures and operating expenditures are usually calculated separately.

Thus, if initial construction costs are C_O, the average annual construction cost, $\overline{CCa}$, is calculated by:

$$C_O = \overline{CCa} \sum_{i=1}^{N} \frac{1}{(1+r)^i}$$

And, the average annual operating cost, $\overline{OCa}$, is calculated by:

$$\sum_{i=1}^{N} \frac{C_i}{(1+r)^i} = \overline{OCa} \sum_{i=1}^{N} \frac{1}{(1+r)^i}$$

est charges paid during the construction period. The composition of this $400 million figure is summarized in Table 4–4.

The average annual cost associated with these capital costs is $13.1 million. If one adds to this, the annual costs for operations and maintenance and for planned expansions of the recreation area, one ob-

Table 4–4. Summary of Capital Costs of Tocks Project (1973 prices)

First Cost	(millions of dollars)
Lands and damages	93.5
Relocations (roads)	44.2
Reservoir	10.5
Dam	98.2
Fish and wildlife	7.1
Power plant	28.4
Roads	0.3
Levees and floodwalls	20.0
Pumps	6.5
Recreation	24.4
Engineering and design	14.2
Supervision and administration	11.8
Miscellaneous	1.4
Total	360.5
Interest During Construction	39.5
Total	400.0

tains the total average annual costs of the Tocks project, $18.3 million.

The Losers. The cost figure that most needs explanation is the first one in Table 4–4—the $93.5 million associated with lands and damages. This refers primarily to the purchase of private lands by the federal government. However, a moment's reflection will persuade the reader that it is a figure that very imperfectly measures the human costs of the purchases. As with most benefit-cost analyses, the Tocks calculations tend to conceal how the benefits and costs of the project will actually be distributed over individuals—who will win and who will lose.

It is especially striking in the Tocks case how little analytic attention was devoted to the impact of the project on the people who live in the immediate vicinity of the dam, the group who would be most deeply affected for good or for ill. Some of them would gain from the project and welcomed the dam, but many of the local residents saw themselves as victims. They viewed the costs of the dam not in terms of expended public monies but in terms of lost homes, dissolved communities, and a vanished life style. The very act of government purchase of land in the vicinity of the dam site carried with it untold bitterness toward the government. In almost every phase of the purchasing process, local residents claim that the government has acted unwisely or unfairly.

Several of the property owners were simply unwilling to move at

---

Box 2.   Calculation of Costs

The total initial construction cost in year 1 = \$400 million. This is turned into an average annual construction cost $\overline{CCa}$ by:

$$\$400\,M = \overline{CCa} \sum_{i=1}^{100} \frac{1}{(1+r)^i}$$

For r = 3 1/8 percent, $\overline{CCa}$ = \$13.1 million.

To this number must be added the average annual costs, $\overline{OCa}$, due to operations and maintenance (O & M), major replacements, etc. These total to \$2.8 million annually making a total of \$15.9 M average annual cost associated with the dam, reservoir, and first-stage recreation plan.

The expansion of the recreation area from its initial capacity (four million annual visitations) to its final planned capacity (ten million annual visitations) is assumed to occur in ten equal annual increments costing \$3.2 million each starting in year 1. Given an annual charge of \$1.8 million for O & M, replacements, etc. associated with the additional recreation facilities this gives an average annual cost $\overline{CRa}$ associated with future recreation construction of \$2.4 million:

$$\sum_{i=1}^{10} \frac{3.2 + 1.8}{(1+r)^i} M + \sum_{i=11}^{100} \frac{1.8M}{(1+r)^i} = \overline{CRa} \sum_{i=1}^{100} \frac{1}{(1+r)^i}$$

For r = 3 1/8 percent, $\overline{CRa}$ = \$2.4 million.

The total costs of the project are, thus, $\overline{CCa} + \overline{OCa} + \overline{CRa}$ = \$13.1 M + \$2.8 M + \$2.4 M = \$18.3 million.

---

any "reasonable" price. They felt that the taking of intangible or uniquely personal attributes of their property could not be compensated by the market assessment. In addition, some of them felt unfairly overwhelmed by a bargaining situation which pitted them as individuals against the apparently infinite, impersonal, implacable, and experienced resources of the federal government. This was especially true of the many elderly persons in the population not accustomed to pressure tactics and adversary procedures; the personal costs of fighting the government's assessment in time, legal fees, and mental anguish seemed higher than any monetary gain they could expect from protracted bargaining.

Missing from the calculation of costs is any accounting of the unusual delays and uncertainties which have plagued the Tocks project. The slow and sporadic removal of scattered properties has had a particularly debilitating effect on the provision of services in the valley communities. When a property is purchased, it is removed from the tax rolls, although the residents often remain. These circumstances hamstring the local authorities, and the maintenance of adequate police and fire protection and of road services for the tourists and remaining residents becomes nearly impossible. The police situation was alleviated in part by the appearance of federal marshalls and rangers, but they were usually on duty during daylight hours only, and fear of violence from vandals and squatters became widespread among the citizenry.

The impact of the project, however, is more than unfair assessments, reduced police services, and vanishing jobs. Listen to the words of two local residents discussing the land acquisition:

> They've made a ghost town of Bushkill. They've bought our land and torn down all our buildings in favor of a national park. Most of the people here don't like to see it come. We seen the store go, we seen the village go . . . and the people we've known all our lives, we seen 'em moving out. We don't like it. It makes all of us sad to see these beautiful things torn down (Ray Steel, age 66).

> . . . we had to move my parents. They tore it down, the government. It's been leveled—the wood house, the smoke house, the hog pen, the outhouse, the spring house. That spring house was worth a million dollars. It had never gone dry. And that was good water. . . . (Charlie Garriss, age 38).

Such rootedness and sense of stable community are common throughout the valley. Much of the charm and uniqueness of the valley is in these people and their structures, a charm the residents did not believe could be preserved by a "wilderness" preserve or nature enclave. The valley had been settled, farmed, and subtly altered by man since the 1600s, and the bottom land farms and stone houses seem as much a part of the valley as the maple trees and river.

This simple description of some of the human costs that lay behind the first item of Table 4–4 tries to touch a note usually and deliberately kept out of benefit-cost calculations. The information and feelings conveyed by such descriptions are surely less objective then the $93.5 million. But are they therefore any less valid? We return to this question in section IV.

4. Calculation of Benefits

Recreation. The WRC guidelines (with the grandfather clause) stipulate an average recreation benefit of $1.35 per visitor day; the annual benefit for a given year would thus be $1.35 multiplied by the expected number of (net) visitations for that year. In the calculation, the Corps assumed that in year 1 (the year the dam is completed) the annual visitation would be approximately four million and that it would grow in ten equal stages to approximately ten million by year 10. This is consistent with relatively long-standing Corps and Park Service plans to expand from four large beaches at the outset of the project to an eventual ten such beaches.[d] With these assumptions, the calculation of recreation benefits is straightforward: the average annual net recreation benefits are $11.7 million.

Box 3. Calculation of Recreation Benefits
(in millions of dollars)

$$\sum_{i=1}^{10} \frac{(4 + \frac{6}{10} i) \times \$1.35}{(1+r)^i} M + \sum_{i=11}^{100} \frac{10 \times \$1.35}{(1+r)^i} M = B_R \sum_{i=1}^{100} \frac{1}{(1+r)^i}$$

For $r = 3\,1/8$ percent, $B_R = \$11.7$ million.

There are several critical assumptions behind this apparently simple procedure. Perhaps the most problematic is the average value adduced for a visitor-day. This average follows directly from the schedule set forth by Congress in Senate Document 97, the guideline to benefit-cost calculations preceding the recent WRC publication. However, the numbers so set forth are highly arbitrary; the first director of the national recreation area believed they could as well have been ten times as high ("it's all make believe to put these things in dollars and cents anyway"); and indeed there has been hitherto little persuasive work on recreation benefits one way or the other. The recent WRC guidelines suggest a somewhat higher scale: $0.75 to $2.25 per day for "general" recreation (swimming, picnicking, most fishing), and $3.00 to $9.00 per day for "special" recreation (certain types of fishing, hunting, etc.).

[d]The recreation plan is described more fully (and more critically) in Essay 10.

Table 4–5. Values of a Recreation Day

Activity	Percent of Visitors	Value	Benefit
Sightseeing	20	$0.65	$0.130
Fishing	6	1.20	0.072
Camping	7	1.40	0.098
Hunting	4	2.50	0.100
Swimming and picnicking	50	1.50	0.750
Power boating	9	1.50	0.135
Sailing and canoeing	3	1.50	0.045
Hiking and nature study	1	2.00	0.020
Total	100		$1.35

Source: General Accounting Office, "Review of Tocks Island Reservoir Project," October 1969.

The schedule of dollar values arrived at appears to be a political compromise among the several federal agencies concerned with recreation, and Congress, the guidelines for the determination being quite arbitrary. That is, the value of a recreation day should not be so high as to overwhelm the other benefits of dam building (and thereby make the whole calculation look ridiculous), nor so low as to fail to represent at least some of the real worth of recreation. The result is an interesting phenomenon, a "political number." It is, of course, questionable whether *any constant value* for a visitor-day makes sense, since such a value implies a linear relationship between visitations and recreation benefits: the more the merrier.

The assumption regarding the expected number of annual visitations is also problematic. The estimates presumably reflect a judgment of the environmental carrying capacity of the recreation area, a judgment that has nowhere been explicitly defended. Nor do the plans provide any guide to how the recreation load will actually be limited if the demand for recreation (as expected) outstrips the design load of the park.

Yet another critical issue associated with the recreation calculations is the determination of the recreation alternatives to be compared. The Corps compares the benefits of a recreation area centered about the reservoir with the present relatively low intensity recreational use of the Water Gap region. This is sensible if one is trying to determine whether to attach a recreation area to the project *after construction of the dam and reservoir have been assumed.* But the procedure is not acceptable if one believes that a recreation area of some sort will be developed regardless of the fate of the dam. In that case, the benefits of the reservoir-based recreation area should be compared to the benefits of a natural systems recreation plan based upon the river. Were this done, the recreation benefits attributed to the project would almost certainly be significantly reduced.

The calculation, like nearly all benefit-cost analyses, says nothing directly about the distribution of benefits: for example, whether the visitors to the recreation area will be predominantly urban poor, suburban affluent, working class, or white collar. Although some of the dam proponents have argued that the recreation park will serve mainly the less affluent urban dwellers in the New York, Philadelphia, and Trenton areas, the little relevant analytic work that has been done does not support such a contention. On the contrary, the urban poor especially could not be expected to travel the distances necessary unless very good public transportation were provided, contingencies not in the project plans.

Water Supply. Water supply benefits are based on the costs of a most likely alternative equivalent water supply facility. This has been judged to be a single-purpose dam/reservoir at Wallpack Bend and a subimpoundment at Flat Brook, the total storage capacity of which would be identical to that of the Tocks reservoir, 425,600 acre feet. It is assumed for purposes of calculation that this alternate water supply would be privately financed at a discount rate of 4 1/2 percent, or 1 3/8 percent above the 3 1/8 percent used for the Tocks project.

The focus on private finance (if not necessarily the discrepancy in discount rate) is partly justified by the absence of any express congressional authority for the Corps to build single-purpose water supply systems. It is also noteworthy that the least cost alternative is, like the discount rate, fixed at the time of authorization; thus, even if new technology in the past decade permitted an even better single purpose alternative, this would presumably not be reflected in the calculation. However, it is not these grandfather clause issues that govern the calculation. The requirement of identifying and pricing the least cost alternative makes sense only if one is certain that an equivalent amount of water will be supplied regardless of the fate of Tocks.

This method of calculation makes the calculated water supply benefits independent of the actual demand schedule for water in the Delaware Basin service area. The method also disguises the uses to which the extra water is to be put. The actual calculation of water benefits derives from an assumed construction cost of an alternative facility of $211 million. The total average annual cost for the alternative, and therefore the total average annual benefit for water supply is then $10.2 million.

Box 4.   Calculation of Water Supply Benefits

$$\$211\,M = \overline{CCw} \sum_{i=1}^{100} \frac{1}{(1+r)^i},$$

where $\overline{CCw}$ = average annual cost of constructing the lowest cost alternative dam and reservoir.
For r = 4 1/2 percent, $\overline{CCw}$ = \$9.6 million.
Annual operating costs = \$0.6 million.
Total cost of alternative water supply = \$10.2 million.

Power.   The power benefits are also derived by calculating the cost of the most likely alternative power plant. The Federal Power Commission supplies the Corps with the necessary data—the cost per installed kilowatt for dependable (i.e., continuous) and for interruptable capacity, as well as a cost per kilowatt hour for fuel. The benefits are based on the average annual net benefits of the least expensive alternate steam plant, financed by the federal government at a discount rate of 3 1/8 percent. Table 4–6 summarizes the data.

Table 4–6.   Power Benefits

Dependable capacity	38 MW at \$24/KW = \$0.9 million
Interruptable capacity	32 MW at \$12/KW = \$0.4 million
Energy value	300,000 MWH at \$.006/KWH = \$1.9 million
Total average annual benefits	\$3.2 million

Box 5.   Calculation of Power Benefits

The expected annual benefits are a constant \$3.2 million. The average annual benefits are thus the same, \$3.2 million.

$$B_P = \sum_{i=1}^{100} \frac{1}{(1+r)^i} = \sum_{i=1}^{100} \frac{3.2M}{(1+r)^i}$$

B_P = 3.2 million.

These benefits derive from the 70 MW directly obtainable from the dam and waterhead; they do not include consideration of the pumped-storage potential provided by the Tocks project (as described in Essay 7).

Flood Control. Flood control benefits are defined as the expected flood damage to those structures in the Delaware flood plain that are protected by the Tocks project but are not without it. The total value of the structures in jeopardy has four components: (1) the current value of the structures in the flood plain, (2) new developments to be expected, (3) increases in damageable assets (consumer goods) attributable to increased affluence of flood plain inhabitants, and (4) increases in land value due to increased or higher utilization of property in the flood plain made possible by the provision of flood protection. The benefits attributed to the dam weight these components by the probability of various levels of flooding in the absence of a dam. The average annual flood benefits thus calculated is $3.8 million, or less than 14 percent of the total project benefits. Given the historic importance of flood prevention as a driving force to the Tocks project, this is a surprisingly low figure.[e]

Box 6. Calculation of Flood Control Benefits

Flood Plain Benefits (Benefits at year shown, in millions of dollars)

	0	*50*	*100*
Downstream (Penn.)	1.3	1.7	1.7
Downstream (N.J.)	1.0	1.0	1.0
Upstream	0.5	0.7	0.7
Affluence (18.83% of above)	0.5	0.6	0.6
Land Enhancement	0.1	0.2	0.2
B_i = Total Annual Benefits	3.5	4.1	4.1

Then:

$$\sum_{i=1}^{100} \frac{B_i}{(1+r)^i} = B_F \sum_{i=1}^{100} \frac{1}{(1+r)^i}$$

For r = 3 1/8 percent, and using a linear extrapolation between years 0 to 50, B_F = $3.8 million.

---

[e]The politics, economics, and physics of floods are discussed further in Essays 2, 3, and 6.

Two additional features of this calculation deserve mention. First, it is implicit in the calculation that if the dam encourages people to move into the flood plain, this increase in flood plain usage would increase the estimated flood reduction benefits. Conversely, flood plain zoning diminishes the calculated flood control benefits. Thus, if Pennsylvania were to follow New Jersey in enacting such zoning legislation, the benefits of the Tocks project would thereby be reduced.

It is interesting to note that the potential saving of lives and the feeling of security that flood protection could bring do not enter the computation, even though they are undoubtedly the primary reasons for spending money on flood control and the generators of much of the political pressure for it. Instead, the protection of property, which can be calculated with some objectivity and consistency, becomes the target of analysis.

5. Why Just These Benefits and Costs?

A large number of benefits and costs are not considered in the national income balance sheet of the benefit-cost calculation. These are most evidently those factors for which it would be impractical and unpersuasive to assign a monetary value.

Most kinds of environmental damage or improvements caused by the project, such as the expected attrition of shad, are examples of such kinds of intangibles. Scientists cannot predict the ultimate scope or effects of these impacts, much less attribute an economic cost to them, a predicament recognized in the new water planning guidelines that establish a separate balance sheet for the environment. Even when one can trace the changes in the environment to be expected, it remains unclear how to attribute costs—whether even to try to measure harm to animals, plants, and the natural landscape in homocentric terms.

Large scale, systemic social impacts also cannot readily be measured. Everyone recognizes, for example, that the dam would alter the rural character of the communities near the dam site, affecting the life styles of the inhabitants, but whether for good or for ill, substantially or slightly, appear questions beyond the reach of the economists. Still another class of factors that seems to defy benefit-cost measurements are the elusive changes in the values and attitudes of the affected parties that may be expected consequent to the dam. For example, the dam will remove a burden of insecurity from the flood plain inhabitants, alter the recreational values of many in the wider impact area, expand and constrict the horizons of varied groups of citizens in the Basin states, all consequences not readily countable in monetary terms. In addition to these intangibles, certain benefits and costs are circumscribed by the congressional guidelines: for example, a monetary benefit for improved water quality (say, in the Delaware Estuary) due to increased fresh water flow provided by a dam project can be claimed only under extraordinary conditions.

6. Development of the Tocks
Benefit-Cost Calculation

The Corps included an elaborate benefit-cost study in its massive HD 522 review of Delaware Basin water resources published in 1961. This was prelude to congressional authorization of the Tocks project in 1962, and since that time the Corps has each year presented to Congress an updated benefit-cost calculation of the Tocks project. After the initial study, this updating has been mostly routine except for 1970 and 1973–74 in which significant changes were either effected or considered.

Reflecting the new water resource planning guidelines then being formulated, the Corps, at the time it undertook its review of the Delaware Basin, placed considerable emphasis on multipurpose planning, and especially on the recreation potential of federal water projects. Thus, although the Delaware Water Gap recreation area was not authorized until 1965, three years after Congress authorized the Comprehensive Plan, such an area was contemplated by the Corps from the beginning, and indeed, even in 1962, recreation represented a high fraction of the expected benefits of the Tocks project. The initial benefit-cost analysis, therefore, already displayed the essential shape of all subsequent analysis, the listing of the four specific benefits—recreation, power, water supply, and flood control. The initial study also employed benefit-cost analysis as a planning device, to optimize within rigid constraints the distribution of projects within the Basin. The formal benefit-cost framework was thus used not so much to justify a particular project, but rather as a means of comparing a large number of alternatives.

Between 1963 and 1969, the summary Corps benefit-cost calculation for Tocks looked as shown in Table 4–7. The sudden jump in benefits between 1969 and 1970 was due to a reestimate of the recreation benefits. When it appeared in 1969, it led the chairman of the Senate Public Works Sub-Committee of the Committee on Appropriations, Senator Ellender, to request an audit by the General Accounting Office of the Corps' plan for Tocks. The audit was duly published in 1969. The chief findings of the GAO study were that the Corps: (1) had inappropriately invoked benefits and costs relating to the ultimate development of recreation facilities

Table 4–7. Schedule of Estimated Annual Benefits and Costs

Fiscal Year	Total Annual Benefits (millions of dollars)	Total Annual Costs	B/C Ratio
1964	11.6	4.9	2.4
1965	11.6	5.0	2.3
1966	12.0	5.1	2.4
1967	12.5	6.9	1.8
1968	13.9	9.1	1.5
1969	14.4	9.1	1.6
1970	22.9	11.3	2.0

Source: GAO Study, "Review of Tocks Island Reservoir Project," October 1969, Appendix IV.

in the recreation area, not just those facilities immediately bordering the reservoir; and (2) had substantially understated present recreation visitation to the area. The major GAO claim was that the Corps did not have authority to include the entire recreation area in its calculation: the benefits flowing from the facilities not directly related to the reservoir that would have to be built and operated by the Park Service should not be claimed by the Corps. In effect, the GAO would have reduced the claimed recreation benefits by deleting benefits for the upland part of the park that could be used for recreation with or without a reservoir.

The corps responded that its procedures were in fact reasonable: that the increase in recreation benefits did reflect a past error in the calculation of recreation benefits, but that the new procedures correctly followed congressional guidelines in planning for the best use of water resources "to meet all foreseeable short and long term needs within the projects' zone of influence over its economic life"; and that the Corps' figure of current visitation (183,000) still seemed more reasonable than the GAO estimate (1,200,000).[2] The Corps' first argument rested on the presumption—not shared by the dam's opponents—that the recreational value of the uplands was largely dependent on the presence of the reservoir. Upland recreation benefits were therefore seen by the Corps as attributable to the reservoir. In any event, the Senate took no action as a result of the GAO study and the Corps essentially ignored the findings of the study.

As described in Essay 3, the New Jersey governor, William Cahill, insisted in 1972 that the recreation plan design load be reduced from ten million annual visits to four million. Pursuant to this Cahill condition, there had been persistent speculation that the Corps and NPS were redoing the benefit-cost analysis. It was thus somewhat of a surprise that the calculation released for fiscal year 1975 did not reflect this scaledown at all. This has been defended by the Corps on grounds that the park plan *at the outset of the project* did meet the Cahill concerns; the expansion would presumably take place as planned only if the initial influx of visitors was not unduly disruptive. The Corps thus argued that Cahill and his supporters simply did not fully appreciate the several step development anyhow contemplated for the recreation area. The Corps' belief is that the demand for recreation will be so intense once the first stage of the recreation area is constructed that its expansion will be inevitable whatever the wishes or presumptions of an ex-governor who would be at least a decade out of office at the time the dam construction was completed.

Thus neither the plans for the recreation area nor the accompanying benefit-cost calculation was changed significantly. However, since the Corps analysis was accompanied by detailed assumptions, it did permit an easy calculation of the benefits and costs should the recreation area, despite all, be frozen at four million visitations annually. Such a situation with other assumptions intact would reduce average annual benefits by $6.3 million and costs by $2.4 million. The benefit-cost ratio would be reduced from 1.6 to 1.4.

7. Open Questions

Even this briefest summary raises several questions regarding the character and power of benefit-cost calculations. These may be grouped into two classes of issues, each of which will be addressed in the following sections.

1. What in principle can benefit-cost analysis tell us about the project under investigation; what is its prescriptive power? In particular, how can benefit-cost analysis deal with the problem of equity and distribution; how can the analysis treat unrepresented actors, such as future generations, potentially affected by the project; and how can an analysis which purports to measure the benefits and costs of a future project and its uncertain train of developments deal with a situation in which peoples' conceptions of that future and their values are in a continual state of flux?
2. What are the principal limitations of benefit-cost analysis in practice? In particular, can the complex web of benefits from a project such as Tocks be rationally partitioned without serious distortion of the results; can there be a satisfactory means of defining all the relevant alternatives to the project; are the methods of measuring benefits, such as for recreation and water

supply, persuasive when there is no direct market test; and in what instances can intangibles be incorporated into the central benefit-cost calculation?

III.   THE BOUNDARIES OF ANALYSIS: CONCEPTUAL PROBLEMS

1.   The Ideal Benefit-Cost Analysis

In principle, a benefit-cost analysis may be constructed in the following way: for each member of the relevant group there is calculated the maximum amount of money he would be willing to give up to see the action in question (say, a dam) undertaken. For some people, this amount will be positive (they favor the project), while for others it will be negative. In the latter case, a negative amount may be thought of as the minimum compensation that person would accept to see the action undertaken. If the *sum* of these amounts over the entire society is positive, the action is said to pass a benefit-cost test. In the case of mutually exclusive alternative actions, the one for which the sum is highest is said to maximize net benefits.[f]

This brief characterization of benefit-cost analysis ignores some fine points, but the basic logic of the statement is correct. One thing that might be noted right away is that the consequences of the public decision to be taken account of here include absolutely everything that anybody in the relevant group cares about. There is no distinction to be made between tangible and intangible values or effects, nor is there any reference to the type of consideration that may legitimately be considered. One person's deep sensitivity to nature is as valid as another's wish for economic development.

2.   The Prescriptive Power of Benefit-Cost Analysis

Why "should" the decision that maximizes net benefits thus defined be undertaken? The argument runs as follows: If the project P has larger net benefits than another action A, it will, by the use of compensating payments, always be possible to make everyone better off under P than under A. For example, suppose that a benefit-cost

---

[f]The technique of analysis is to reduce everything to a common denominator which we have called dollars but which could be some other numeraire, provided it is a "commodity-like" substance in the sense of being redistributable from person to person. Strictly, it may matter whether this numeraire is dollars or apples or ice water. But the analytical problems introduced by this choice are not crucial to the logic of the claim that those decisions should be made which pass a benefit-cost test or, in the case of mutually exclusive alternatives, that the decision should be made which maximizes net benefits.

analysis of the various alternative possibilities of the Tocks Island site were to reveal that a particular configuration of dam, park, and water supply system generated a net benefit of nine million dollars per year relative to some no-dam plan.[g] And let us suppose that the people who would be the main gainers from the no-dam plan would be the hikers and campers and the people who would gain most from the dam plan would be boaters and developers. Our study would then have told us that it would be possible, if we wished, to build the dam, take money away from the boaters and developers, and distribute that money to the hikers and campers, with the net result that after the transaction *everybody* would consider the outcome preferable to the recreation area plan without the dam.

The idea that in every situation one should choose the alternative generating the largest net benefits is sometimes called the criterion of hypothetical compensation. It is a criterion that makes a certain amount of sense when the distribution of gains and losses is so organized that it satisfies some principle of fairness or justice. In this case the overall social well-being might fairly convincingly be said to be maximized when the social pie is as large as possible. But real world projects such as the Tocks Island Dam do not come equipped with schemes for distributing the benefits and costs in any way significantly separable from the particular pattern that comes naturally with the project.

Returning to our hypothetical choice between the dam and no-dam plans, in the one case the people to benefit would be boaters and developers, and in the second case hikers and campers. Even though compensation is a logical possibility, in choosing between two such plans we are frequently choosing between benefits to one group of people and benefits to another. Where the assurance of the equitable distribution of benefits is not plausible, the criterion of maximizing the benefits is not very compelling ethically.

Indeed, benefit-cost studies scarcely ever include substantial information about the identity of gainers and losers from the project; when these individuals are known, any given policy maker might properly reject one proposal in favor of another with smaller net benefits if he favored the distributional effects of the latter. This is of course also true of the individuals who see that they will be among the losers. Their objection to the analysis is entirely legitimate, and it is to be expected, as is well illustrated in the Tocks controversy.

---

[g]It is a well known proposition of welfare economics that we cannot, strictly speaking, measure the "size of the pie" independently of its distribution. We would like to pretend that this analytical problem does not arise here, in the interest of isolating our more fundamental (and simpler) point.

Nevertheless, there may well be reason to be concerned with the size of the total benefits apart from any explicit redistribution scheme. This is especially so if the political system *as a whole* operates to effect the redistribution. It may be argued, for example, that while it is true that in any one case there may be no particular virtue attached to the gainers, nor any particular reason to subject the losers to the losses from a given decision, over the long run a sequence of decisions will occur such that any one individual is randomly situated with respect to decisions. That is, following a rule over time of choosing actions to maximize the net benefits will also eventually maximize everyone's real wealth. About this claim it can only be said that it might be correct. One could argue that those economists who favor a free enterprise system on the grounds of its efficiency do so with some such argument in mind. It is a position that deserves to be stated in an operationally testable form.

In general, people probably are partially aware of the sharing arrangements and of the way in which the political process functions to reallocate gains and losses. It seems clear that politicians are going to pay attention to the identities of the gainers and the losers and not simply to the aggregate sum of the gains. They are not likely to be persuaded of the virtue of a project whose gainers all live in another district. But the fact that a project has positive net benefits does tell politicians something, namely that there is the potential for a profitable agreement with other decision makers that would produce mutual benefits. The losers from the project will agitate for compensation and sometimes get it.

In the Tocks case, the recent proposal of the Delaware River Basin Commission to include the 75-mile stretch of the Delaware just above the Tocks reservoir in the Scenic River Preservation Act might be viewed as a compensating adjustment favoring many of the conservationists especially outraged by the Tocks project. In familiar economic language, such a finding of positive net benefits implies the possibility for gains from trade. In the political context, trade may occur in the form of log-rolling.

The prescriptive power of the benefit-cost calculation is further undermined by the realization that the ability of a project to pass a benefit-cost test could depend sensitively on the present income distribution of the affected citizens and more particularly on the preferences of very tiny minorities. That is, the values people will place on a projected change will in general depend on their income, and for some persons (with sufficient current comfort), no practical compensation may be sufficient to persuade them to support a given public project. In such a case, given our idealized definition, the project could not pass a benefit-cost test, which may or may not suggest whether the project should be undertaken anyway. One's feelings here are again dependent on how one assesses the merit (and political power) of the project's beneficiaries and victims.

3.   Who Counts?

The benefit-cost analysis ideally reflects the preferences of all the individuals and agents in "the relevant group." But who are they? Who should, in effect, vote on the Tocks Island Dam? Should the analyst take into account the preferences of persons far from the dam site—and what of the claims of animals, trees, stones? Welfare economics is mute on this issue, a silence connected with the ethical weakness of the criterion of hypothetical compensation. If one takes the view that the object of the analysis is to determine whether the status quo is capable of modification in a way that is beneficial to all agents, this question is in principle answerable for any given group of agents, and that is all there is to the matter.

On the other hand, if one has decided to use the principle of hypothetical compensation as the basis for decisions, then it becomes very important to establish which individuals and agents are included. Most economists would have some difficulty in imagining an analysis that included the preferences of stones, for the simple reason that it is rather difficult to attribute any meaning to the idea, and western economics, at least, regards the evaluations of individual human beings as paramount. However, it must be conceded that for purposes of welfare economics the concept of "agent with preferences" is rather like the concept of a point in Euclidian geometry: the mapping of theoretical constructs onto real, existing entities is a matter of art, not of logic.

A special problem, which applies to the ethical force of benefit-cost analysis, is the representation of future generations. This problem is principally a practical one: from a logical point of view there is little question that future generations can count. The monetary measures of benefits and costs attributable to alternative courses of action in the present, but incident upon individuals not yet part of the consulted individuals and agents, can count as much as any others and be added into the reckoning-up of aggregate benefits and costs in an ideal analysis.

But future generations' interests are necessarily looked after by those alive today, and there is the practical problem of predicting how future generations would evaluate alternatives. Most environmentalists at least will guess that future generations would value the environment highly. Future generations, the argument goes, are likely to be wealthier than the current generation, more able to afford environmental protection, more inclined to sustain a lesser rate of economic growth—and likely to have less natural environment to protect. The practical problem of weighting the future is distilled in the discount rate, the choice of which has long been a subject of controversy. This aspect of the problem is discussed later in this essay.

IV. THE BOUNDARIES OF ANALYSIS: PERSISTENT LIMITATIONS IN PRACTICE

It is all well and good to construct an ideal benefit-cost analysis through a series of interviews with everyone in the relevant group, but in practice the necessary data must be inferred by indirect means. The practical difficulties, we shall see, are only a minor extent those of economic theory. It is useful to distinguish four steps that must be undertaken, explicitly or implicitly, in implementing benefit-cost analysis.

1. Define the zero point: that is, attempt to specify the developments that will take place in the absence of any positive alternative decision by the political agency involved.
2. Define and describe the set of mutually exclusive alternatives open to choice by the agency.
3. Decide which of these alternatives are to be analyzed and determine a classification of the benefits and costs which makes the analysis manageable.
4. Develop methods of producing answers to the question: How much net numeraire good is equivalent in the aggregate for each of the alternative choices available relative to the baseline status quo.

For the most part, economic theory is called into play only in the last step.

1. Defining the Baseline
Although it is unusual for a benefit-cost study to include any detailed description of the baseline from which the alternatives are measured, greater precision in this respect could reduce ambiguity and confusion in subsequent steps. In one respect, fortunately, the precise choice of baseline is unimportant. Benefits and costs are like electric potential—it is only differences or changes that count. As long as *some* consistent baseline is adopted, the results should not be sensitive to which one it is.

Normally the baseline adopted by an agency doing benefit-cost analysis, at least implicitly, is a future in which the agency takes no action. This future, then, by definition has net benefit zero. Naturally, estimates of what will happen if the agency does nothing are subject to great uncertainty. If, in the absence of the Tocks Island Dam project, the state governments might construct a recreation area at the same site, should this be considered part of the description of the baseline? If the null action has uncertain consequences that can be expressed as some distribution of probabilities, then ideally all alternative actions should have their benefits expressed as distributions corresponding to the distribution of baselines.

2. Defining the Alternatives

The invention of alternatives is probably the most crucial step in benefit-cost analysis. Analysts, for example, will almost always have considerable discretion to choose the boundaries of the project under consideration. In the Tocks case, the Corps of Engineers, following accepted practice, did not include in the benefit-cost analysis either the network of highways required to service the recreation area or the sewage treatment plants required to make any Tocks Island reservoir useful for recreational purposes. It is perhaps an interesting commentary on the use of analysis in actual decision processes that the inclusion of some of these "external" effects of the construction of the project have been forced into the analysis by its users. It needs little thought to convince oneself that these secondary influences of a project are just as integral a part of it as the primary ones from the point of view of an ideal benefit-cost analysis.

The problem of developing and defining a set of alternatives is one of the most difficult steps in doing analysis, relative to which the other aspects are in principle mechanical. But here science has little to say and art and imagination are the critical factors. The discovery of institutional methods for generating useful and imaginative alternatives in any decision situation is an area that, while it has commanded considerable imaginative thought already, no doubt will reward further efforts at innovation. For example, devices such as the design competitions conducted traditionally in architecture might be usefully extended to stimulate the generation of alternative designs in other contexts.

3. Choosing Which Alternatives to Analyze

When one considers the extraordinary complexity and difficulty of performing the analysis of even one specified alternative relative to the status quo, one comprehends the tendency of agencies to reduce an analysis to the close scrutiny of a single plan. Given this difficulty, perhaps the most important point to recognize is that analysis must continue beyond a first effort and should not simply stop after one particular study has been completed. One should view a given study as merely one part of the process of economic analysis and not imagine that one study is *the* economic analysis.

We have already mentioned the utility of subsequent criticism in revealing undiscussed or unanalyzed alternatives, and we must add that subsequent controversy is likely also to encourage analyses of the alternatives discovered. These are commonsense notions, which are nonetheless not fully accepted by public agencies such as the Corps, who have tended to see each of their benefit-cost analyses as the last word, beyond improvement, refinement, and criticism by others—not as the first step in a series of ever more fertile inventions and analyses.

4. Doing the Calculation

In the absence of a direct interrogation such as suggested by the ideal benefit-cost analysis, the analyst must seek indirect clues of peoples' preferences. The most useful by far of these clues are provided by market prices. The basic approach is simple: if individuals are observed in the market place to exchange one apple for two pears, we conclude that giving anyone an apple is as good as giving him two pears. We can therefore use the observed market price of two pears per apple to place a pear value on changes in apple quantities. Suitably elaborated, this is the logic of using prices to place dollar values on various physical changes.

This is actually the single most important principle used in developing estimates of the answers people would give to the question of how much they would value specified changes in the world. These values are revealed in an indirect way, from individual behavior in the market place. In many instances, it is clear that this manner of discovering preferences cannot so easily be applied. This will be so where there is no established price or market mechanism—that is, when no exchange or trade is feasible. In the Tocks controversy three difficulties of this sort stand out: the choice of discount rate, the calculations of water supply and recreation benefits, and the treatment of intangibles.

5. Discount Rate

It may seem odd to speak of the discount rate as a price, but it is one, exactly like the price of water or electricity, and it has the same function in the analysis: to indicate the rate at which people are willing to exchange one thing for another. As noted in section II, the rate of exchange being referred to is between dollars of consumption in one period (today) and dollars of consumption at a later period. The difficulty is that the market on which this price is set, usually called the capital market, appears to permit a great variety of exchange rates, from the 15 or 20 percent per annum rates paid on installment loans to the 6 percent earned on savings accounts. Furthermore, there are individuals who are unable to participate in the exchange in question. Generations in the future are not able to participate in the exchange of dollars today for dollars tomorrow.

For this reason, economists have not been able to settle on a definitive discount rate. Even though it is possible under certain precise constraints to decide on a specific discount rate appropriate to those conditions, analysis leads to the conclusion that no single discount rate can be appropriate for evaluating all projects. For practical purposes, some sort of compromise discount rate is necessary, however. Most economists would favor using a discount rate that falls somewhere between the rates received on secure assets by savers and the rates of return earned by profitable corporations. But there is no general agreement on where in-between it should be; and unfortunately—as strikingly shown in Table 4–2 in section II—the choice can make a great deal of difference.[5]

6. Least Cost Alternative: Water Supply

As noted in section II, the water supply benefits of the Tocks Island Dam were derived by calculating the cost of the most probable least cost alternative. It was assumed that certain physical services would somehow be rendered by the economy—delivery of certain quantities and qualities of water—and the question was asked, What costs are *avoided* if these services are obtained from the Tocks Island project? In this case the required services are estimated by relating water use to certain indices of population and industrialization, and projections of the latter are used to project future consumption of water, with no reference to the price of water. The difficulty is that the amount of water used is subject to the economist's familiar first law of demand. When the price is high, less is used. An analysis that takes the quantity of water required as rigidly fixed is therefore not likely to lead to an efficient outcome. Even if one accepts this approach as a reasonable approximation to the ideal, one can ask whether the actual methods used to identify alternative costs are appropriate.

Ideally, one would like to know which are the least expensive methods of producing water that would, in fact, be used if the water were not provided by the Tocks Island Dam. These would then represent the cost savings produced by the dam. It is rather difficult to know whether the average cost estimates from currently operating water systems are likely to be appropriate measures of these costs. One would suspect that currently used sources are of lower cost than those which would have to be used in the future were the Tocks Island Dam not available as a source of water. The problem of identifying the least expensive alternative ways of obtaining water that would otherwise be used requires identifying how much water would be used, how we would provide it, and in particular how this provision would be provided in sequence over time. None of these steps is easy.

7.   Shadow Prices: Recreation

The case of recreation presents an interesting contrast to that of water supply. Whereas there the object of the analysis was to estimate potential cost savings made possible by the presence of the Tocks Island Dam, the recreation services are treated as a net addition to the available totals of recreation services in the economy.[5] The incremental "visitor-days" provided by the full capacity utilization of the Tocks Island recreation facilities were treated as net additions to recreation in the region. Since some of the recreation benefits from the dam would seem likely to take the form of cost savings (just as was the case with respect to water supply), the treatment of recreation services as purely a net addition to the total introduces a possibly significant factor of uncertainty into the calculation.

Available studies rely on a variety of indirect methods for placing a dollar value on a visit to a facility such as the Tocks Island Dam. Necessarily such studies are prepared infrequently and for a very diverse set of recreation opportunities. And while considerable ingenuity has been applied to measuring the value placed on visits in the various cases studied, transferring the results to the particular time and place of the Tocks project is clearly subject to a wide range of error. All the calculation methods attempt, in effect, to establish a "shadow price," which corresponds to answers people would give to our ideal benefit-cost calculation, in which each person who came to the recreation area would be asked the value of the recreation experience to him. This value would be a net figure, with the respondent comparing the value of recreation at the Water Gap with his other recreation alternatives.

It is clear from this perspective that the admission price, and, in general, the method by which visitors to the park are rationed could affect the calculation of benefits. If the number of daily visitors is rationed (limited) by the admission charge, then the last person who will want to enter the park will be indifferent whether he enters or not: the net value of the Water Gap recreation experience compared to his other alternatives will be roughly equal to the admissions charge, and his "consumer surplus" will be zero.[h] The total social benefits in this case will be the consumer surplus aggregated over all the visitors, plus the public net revenue collected through the admission charges.

If the rationing is effected in some other way than price, the social benefits are likely to be different, depending on the rationing scheme actually adopted. For example, a first come, first served procedure may under some circumstances fill up the park with marginal visitors with no strong preference for the visit, but who live in convenient range of the park. A calculation of benefits that does not explicitly consider the means of rationing the visitors will thus be unreliable. The analysis employed in the Tocks case is flawed in this manner.

8. Intangibles

In practice, most benefit-cost analyses will not deal systematically with factors that are difficult to measure in monetary terms. In the Tocks case there are many such examples: the value placed by a substantial number of citizens on their ability to hike in unspoiled rural countryside, or on the security they would derive from living on an unthreatened flood plain, to name only two. A review of the available instruments for practical benefit-cost analysis does not make one sanguine about the possibility of including these values in a systematic way, even though the theory is unambiguous that such preferences count as much as any others.

While one should perhaps not give up hope of improving upon our indirect measures of the value that people place on such aspects of public choices, there is likely to remain a large element of judgment that must be exercised by those legislators or public officials responsible for making such choices. This gives to the benefit-cost analysis a "residual" character. Since the analyst will be unable to provide an estimate of the equivalent monetary value to (say) losses of amenity, the recipient of the benefit-cost study (say, a public official) must provide his own estimate of the appropriate monetary equivalent of

---

[h]For present purposes, "consumer surplus" may be defined as the difference between the consumer's net benefits and the price (or admissions charge) he must pay to receive the benefits.

these amenity changes. In effect, the benefit-cost study measures the value not of the actual change, but of that change minus the intangible benefits and costs.

All fields of inquiry relevant to public policy are plagued by this issue of intangibles, in which factors apparently relevant to an assessment of costs and benefits simply cannot be given a measure in dollars or any other common numeraire. National security debates are often dominated by reference to nationalism, national pride, flexibility, etc.—certainly not concepts that can be measured in any sensible way. Similarly, analysts of social welfare programs have never been able to make the benefits of these programs (health care, cancer research, Headstart programs, special remedial reading, etc.) commensurable in dollar or any other terms.[7] Such intangibles will most often stand outside the formal benefit-cost analysis.

Sometimes, as with recreation benefits, there will be an attempt to provide a measure that will permit the benefit or cost at stake to be put into the monetary benefit-cost framework. But in most instances, this will not even be attempted. The value a person places on various experiences crucial to an assessment of environmental issues, such as canoeing, security against floods, solitude, well-watered lawns, backpacking, swimming, visits to historical sites, etc., often does not have an echo in the market place. They are thus intangible, and much of the work on intangibles involves attempts to find surrogate ways for such preferences to be revealed. This effort is sensible (to a point), for it is in principle possible for persons to indicate the value—a money value if necessary—that they place on these experiences. Recreation at Tocks Island is clearly not a priceless experience; and it is well to estimate even imperfectly the cumulative benefits the public attaches to such recreation. Individuals can and do place values on personal experiences, and these values ought to be of prime interest to an analyst.

Certain kinds of personal experiences do not lend themselves at all easily to such analysis, however. Consider experiences that drastically alter the values and preferences of the affected party. (Remedial reading programs for adults could be placed in this category, for example.) It seems much less interesting and less reliable in these cases to learn the monetary value the individual places at a given instant on the experience. It appears equally unrewarding to discover the value a person places on (say) being cured of cancer, as part of an analytic effort to determine how much funding should be put into cancer research.

The impracticality of finding reliable monetary measures becomes even more evident when the alternative futures confronting the affected parties are complex and not well specified. What are the ecological hazards of the dam? What will be the social impact of the project on the way of life in Warren and Sussex counties? In instances such as these, the preferences of individuals, while important to probe, will depend significantly on the degree to which the alternatives can be understood and made vivid. Preferences will depend sensitively on the individual's degree of knowledge and experience, and may change drastically as the individual thinks more about and learns more about the alternatives actually open to his community. For these decisions involving an entire community, peoples' preferences are likely not only to be unstable and unformed but not easily additive as well. An individual's preference for a particular community life style will, in general, depend on the values his neighbors place on that life style. The collective value a community places on some alternative future will not simply be the sum of the individual preferences of its citizens.

The inability of analysts to construct monetary surrogates for important intangible values has had little perceptible effect on the degree to which they will be regarded or disregarded by policy makers. In the Tocks controversy, for example, policy makers generally seemed appropriately skeptical of the formal benefit-cost studies and perfectly willing to judge the relative importance of intangible benefits and costs without the analysts placing dollar values on them. Whether or not intangible factors get woven into the decision making process depends upon considerations other than the degree to which analysts can concoct some illusory monetary measure for them.

In the Tocks case (as well as others with which we are familiar), four such considerations appeared of particular importance: (1) the analytic richness and vividness with which the intangible benefits and costs could be described in physical terms, (2) the relative importance of the political and bureaucratic constituencies holding strong feelings respecting these benefits and costs, (3) the legitimacy of discourse about the intangible factor, and (4) the preferences and values of the policy makers themselves.

In the first instance, the policy maker seeks as clear and as vivid an understanding of issues as possible; he will want a clear statement of the benefits and costs in whatever terms are possible quite apart from any attempt to assign monetary values. For example, rather than trying to find a monetary measure to describe the unpleasantness of a eutrophic lake, the policy maker will want to have that unpleasantness and the probability it will occur described as clearly as possible. In short, the policy maker seeks more science, not esoteric and subtle social indices and ways to monetize elusive values.

Second, intangible factors tend to be weighed by policy makers to the degree that the factors have strong political and bureaucratic constituencies. Flood control, for example, is much studied and much heeded by policy makers partly because it is a politically salient issue. Floods, and politicians' responses to floods, are highly visible. The beneficiaries of a flood control program are well identified and often well organized. These include not only the flood plain inhabitants, but real estate groups, building trade unions, and other interests who would profit by the construction of flood control structures. Moreover, flood control has vigorous spokesmen in the Corps of Engineers, a strong and aggressive bureaucracy with ties to Congress and to many local interest groups. Factors, however intangible they may be, will be considered by analysts and weighed by policy makers if they are supported by a politically important constituency.

Third, a sense of "legitimate discourse" prevails in the relevant political community. For a variety of reasons, certain kinds of arguments or values cannot easily be conveyed or invoked. Thus politicians will be more likely to stress hard data (such as construction costs and tax benefits) than they will concepts such as beauty or solitude. In this sense, intangibles are at a disadvantage. To say that the Tocks project will flood a quiet and beautiful valley might open a politician to argument and derision—"who says the valley is beautiful?" To be sure, there is some circularity here. If enough people care about certain values, then it will be possible for politicians to discuss them. But the circularity is not complete; certain kinds of discourse invoking elusive and esthetic and elitist values do not seem to have equal standing in the political arena, a situation which often reinforces the prevailing political alignments. The values that appear most tainted are those that are nonquantifiable (beauty), are not associated with American self-confidence (skepticism toward economic growth), or are associated with esthetic minorities (quiet brooks).

Still other types of considerations appear to be off limits—possibly because they are too complex. For example, the Tocks project would attract considerable automobile traffic, a circumstance that would with statistical certainty increase markedly the number of traffic accidents on north New Jersey roads. It may or may not also cause a comparable reduction in traffic accidents elsewhere, but unless there is a perfect match in this increase and reduction, the effects are likely to be significant in any rational balancing of benefits and costs. Yet they are never considered.

Finally, the values of the decision makers, while not unalterable, form a crucial determinant of the weight they will give an intangible factor. In the field of social welfare, the allocation of funds (say) between preschool education and cancer research will depend strongly on the deepest values of the decision makers; no contrived measure to compare benefits is likely to affect significantly this choice. How national security managers will weigh the various imponderables of risk, commitment, and honor will also ultimately depend on their values and their world view. Similarly, in the Tocks case, the policy makers typically have had strong intuitive ideas about the trade-off among various intangible benefits and costs— wilderness, flood control, social stability, and so forth.

V. CONCLUDING REMARKS

Even in principle, benefit-cost analysis cannot automatically make public choices for us. Because alternative policies will typically have important distributional effects in which some people will gain and others will lose, the decisions are intrinsically political, and they must be decided through the political process. The choices cannot be taken out of the political arena and made subject to the control and judgment of experts and bureaucrats. Political problems cannot be turned as if by magic into economic problems by waving a wand of benefit-cost analysis.

This is all the more true for analyses far from the ideal, such as those currently attained or attainable for projects of the complexity of Tocks. Combined with information about the distributional effects of alternative actions, however, benefit-cost analysis can usefully contribute to democratic decision making, by enhancing the ability of policy makers and citizens to predict the consequences of alternative policy actions. Unfortunately, the analysis too often conceals distributional effects and wraps the problem in a web of technical formulae and quantitative techniques that neither policy makers nor the public can penetrate. This permits the bureaucratic analysts to proceed undisturbed by the clamor of interest groups.

To become a component of genuine democratic decision making, and to improve significantly the reliability and completeness of predictions of consequences of alternative public choices, benefit-cost analysis must be executed in ways that encourage wider public participation in decision making; and to this end it must appropriate new styles of analysis and presentation that would make information more accessible and understandable to affected citizens and better clarify the consequences of the choices set before them. Rather than disguise the host of arbitrary assumptions and biases that necessarily inform any practical benefit-cost analysis, a proper study would clearly present differing approaches and divergent conclusions.

One cannot help but be distressed by the illusion of precision the summary numbers in typical benefit-cost analyses present. At worst, these summary data are the resultant of a large number of possibly large errors; at best they will be merely clues about the consequences of a particular action. Instead of the crisp column of figures displayed in most benefit-cost analyses, perhaps what is needed is a sort of Rube Goldberg machine, with numbers popping out at odd times and places, to remind us of all the loose connections. A somewhat more modest suggestion (from editor Frank Sinden) is set forth below, as an appendix to this essay. It would be especially helpful to have various alternative plans and analyses drawn up for any project by competing agencies and interests who believe in them. The notion that a single agency such as the Corps can honestly set forward detailed analyses of alternative plans (most of which are not favored by the agency) seems unreasonable. The generation of many benefit-cost analyses by diverse groups might be disorderly, but it would almost certainly yield more comprehensive, more inventive and wiser results.

NOTES

1. The most recent listing is found in *The Federal Register*, vol. 38, no. 174, September 10, 1973.

2. Letter from Robert Jordan, III, Special Assistant to the Secretary of the Army, to Elmer B. Staats, Comptroller General of the United States, November 20, 1969. Reprinted in *Public Works, Hearings* before the Sub-Committee of the Committee of Appropriations, House of Representatives, Part I, 1971, p. 288. ·

3. This issue is discussed in greater length in D.F. Bradford, "Constraints on Public Action and Rules for Social Decision," *American Economic Review* LX (September 1970): 642–654.

4. On the problem mentioned, see, e.g., E.J. Mishan, "A Survey of Welfare Economics 1938–59," *Economic Journal* (1960), reprinted in E.J. Mishan, *Welfare Economics: Ten Introductory Essays*, 2nd ed. (N.Y.: Random House, 1969).

5. These issues are examined at greater length in D.F. Bradford, "Constraints on Public Action and Rules for Social Decision" *op. cit.*

6. The evaluation of recreation benefits is the subject of considerable literature. For some discussion of the literature, see the DRBC study #24-49-69, *Economic Studies of Outdoor Recreation*, "Economic Evaluation of Outdoor Recreation Benefits"; T.L. Burton and Margaret N. Fulcher, "Measurement of Recreation Benefits — A Survey," *Journal of Economic Studies* (July 1968): 35–48; Jack L. Knetsch and Robert K. Davis, "Comparisons of Methods for Recreation Evaluation," in *Water Research*, A. V. Kneese and S. Smith, eds. (Baltimore: Johns Hopkins Press, 1966).

7. See, for example, Alice Rivlin, *Systematic Thinking for Social Action* (Washington, D.C.: Brookings, 1971).

APPENDIX: ABOLISHING THE B/C RATIO

Benefit-cost analysis is widely regarded as a black box that produces a single number—the B/C ratio. It is as if a trial lawyer made his entire case with a single sentence: "From incontrovertible evidence I have deduced by impeccable logic that the defendant is guilty." No jury, of course, would accept that. It is the evidence and logic themselves that the jury wants to see. So it should be with benefit-cost analysis. The best way to deflect attention away from the B/C ratio would be to abolish it. This appendix outlines briefly a way of organizing a benefit-cost analysis and displaying its results without the aid of the ratio.

A benefit-cost analysis can be regarded as a list of additive components, each generating a stream of positive and negative benefits over time. The components can be displayed as follows:

			time $\longrightarrow$		
components	construction	- - -	−\$	−\$	- - -
$\downarrow$	power benefit	- - -	+\$	+\$	- - -
	flood benefit	- - -	+\$	+\$	- - -
	.		.	.	
	.		.	.	
	.		.	.	
	overall net benefit	- - -	Σ	Σ	- - -

No time horizon needs to be imposed; even distant events such as probable machinery replacements decades hence or siltation of a reservoir centuries hence can be indicated. Individual components can be further disaggregated in other renderings of the same format. The ultimate starting data or formulas should be measured relative to a precisely and explicitly defined base case.

The output of the analysis is the bottom line of the final table, the overall net benefit function $B(t)$. This function can be summarized by the single number

$$\overline{B}_\alpha = \alpha \int_o^\infty B(t)e^{-\alpha t}dt = \text{``average annual net benefit''}$$

where α is the "discount rate."[i] This has the two drawbacks of creating a golden number and suppressing useful information.

I suggest instead that $B(t)$ not be summarized at all, but that it be plotted against a certain series of distorted time scales as shown in Figure 4-1. These scales (one for each discount rate α) are such that

---

[i]See Box 1, where a discrete form is given (p. 131).

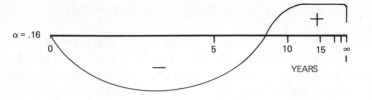

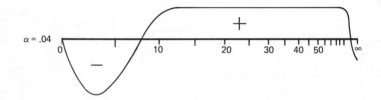

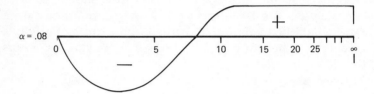

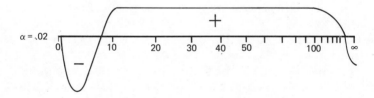

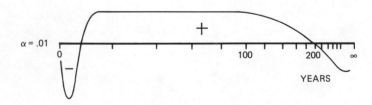

the net area under the curve (the area above the horizontal axis minus the area below it) is always just equal to $\overline{B}_\alpha$.[j] It is not difficult to judge this area roughly by eye. In most cases not much more precision than this would be justified anyway. In the example shown $\overline{B}_\alpha$ is positive for $\alpha \leqslant .04$, but not at the other values. The B/C ratio is simply the ratio of the positive area to the negative area. The graphs show intuitively what it means to take the short or long view. Note that the artificial idea of a "project life" is avoided: Events in the distant future simply do not show up in the short view graphs, yet they can always be made to appear by taking a sufficiently long view.

[j]For discount rate α, the semi-infinite t-axis is mapped onto the unit τ-interval by $\tau = 1 - e^{-\alpha t}$. Hence $d\tau = \alpha e^{-\alpha t} dt$.

Figure 4-1. The Same Hypothetical Net Benefit Stream Plotted on Different Time Scales. Construction lasts almost a decade, during which time money flow is negative (investment). Thereafter steady positive benefits are realized for a time. At about 100 years siltation begins to reduce the dam's effectiveness, and 150 years after that, the dam is completely useless, and since the river and valley are left in a less valuable state than if no dam had been built, a negative benefit is registered each year thereafter. Such distant future effects begin to show up on the right at very low discount rates. In the five cases shown, comparison of positive and negative areas shows the project to be uneconomic at $\alpha = .16$, marginal at $\alpha = .08$ and economic at $\alpha = .04, .02, .01$. At even lower discount rates, far below those conventionally considered, the project would again be uneconomic as the distant future effects take hold. Even though they profess to take a longer view of the future than most other people, Sierra Club members urge high discount rates and the Corps of Engineers urges low discount rates. It is easy to see why.

✳︎ *Chapter 5*

The Water Cycle, Supply and Demand

Frank W. Sinden

I. THE USES OF WATER

During the energy crisis of 1973, prudent householders caulked their windows, closed their chimney dampers, and turned down their thermostats in order to impede the flow of energy through their houses and thus to get more out of each BTU as it passed through. Some analysts predicted that the energy shortage that induced this behavior would soon be followed by a water shortage, which, in an analogous fashion, would induce householders to impede the flow of water through their houses by such measures as fixing leaky faucets, shortening shower baths, and putting bricks in toilet tanks. But in contrast to the energy saving measures, the seemingly analogous water saving measures would, under some circumstances, be ineffective.

On the surface, the analogy between energy and water is almost perfect, since both may be thought of as fluids. Indeed, early physical theories asserted that at least one form of energy—heat—was literally a fluid. Both energy and water flow more or less continuously through the household, performing useful functions on the way. One would suppose, therefore, that the cause of conservation would be served in both cases by reducing the flow. This is true in the case of energy, but, as we shall see, not necessarily in the case of water. When we view the world as a whole and not just the household imbedded in it, we find that the analogy between energy and water is no longer so exact.

Consider, for example, two identical toilets, one in New York and one in Philadelphia, each with a brick in its tank placed there by the owner with the aim of reducing the tank's volume, hence the amount of water used for each flush. What, in fact, does each brick accomplish? New York takes its water by pipeline from the upper reaches of the Delaware Valley and discharges its waste water into the lower Hudson River. The New York toilet brick, by reducing the drain on the upper Delaware reservoirs, allows more water to flow down the Delaware River. On its way to the sea, this water performs many useful functions whose value can be credited to the New York toilet brick.

The Philadelphia toilet brick is different. Philadelphia takes its water out of the lower Delaware and puts its waste water back into the same lower Delaware a little further downstream. The effect of the Philadelphia toilet brick is simply to reduce the rate of circulation of water through the system. In no way does the brick increase the quantity of water in the river. Nor does it improve the quality of the river's water either, since the amount of pollution added to the river is the same with or without the brick. Thus the toilet brick in Philadelphia, unlike that in New York, accomplishes no effective water conservation (although it may save some pumping energy).

The difference here is that in one case the water use is cyclic and in the other case it is not. Water conservation cannot be understood without taking account of the cycles in which the various uses are imbedded. In this respect water is more complex than many other resources, such as energy, which can reasonably be treated by one-way, source-sink models. Since practically every use of energy irreversibly increases entropy, recycling is impossible. The best we can do is to place certain uses in tandem—for example, we can keep houses warm with the low temperature heat discharged by power plants—so as to get as much good as possible out of the one-way energy flow. This one-way character of energy makes for a relatively straightforward conception of conservation that is not applicable to water.

By the same token, the economics of water is less straightforward than that of other commodities. This is true both in theory and in the market place. Economics is permeated with the one-way model implied by word pairs such as resources-consumption and supply-demand. Although we often break out linear pieces of the water cycle and talk about "water resources" and "water consumption" or "water supply" and "water demand," our actual use of water is much too cyclic and interactive to be adequately described in an aggregate way by such terms. The example of the toilet bricks should suffice to illustrate the point.

Another related problem with the economics of water is ownership. Conventionally, ownership attaches to physical objects or to batches of a commodity. In the one-way flow of iron from mine to junkyard, for example, ownership passes from hand to hand, with price reflecting at each stage the value added (or subtracted) by whatever physical or chemical modifications may have occurred since the last sale. Even such an intangible commodity as energy lends itself readily to clear-cut ownership: as coal, the energy is locked in a physical commodity; as electricity it can be metered to a consumer, who is free to dissipate it to the environment in whatever manner suits him. Ownership of specific masses of water, on the other hand, is in many cases infeasible. The riparian law, for example, has long recognized the impossibility of attaching absolute ownership to the water flowing in a stream.

How, then, are we to deal with water as a commodity? A thing cannot be bought and sold unless it can be owned. To deal with water it is necessary to go to a more abstract concept of ownership, namely the ownership of *rights*. The riparian law recognizes the right of a streamside landowner to divert and use the stream's water in various ways, provided the net deleterious effect on downstream owners is held within specified bounds. The water is not owned, only rights with respect to its use are owned.

Of course, all ownership is ultimately a matter of rights; nothing is owned absolutely. Though a man may have a deed to his home and even regard his home as his castle, he is still constrained in most places from using it for certain kinds of otherwise legitimate business. His rights of ownership are not absolute. Nevertheless, for most things and most purposes, the inexact but concrete and convenient conception of physical ownership is adequate. Water is one of the exceptional commodities (land is another) for which the more abstract conception of rights ownership must be taken explicitly into account.

What then is the economic value of a water use? How much should be paid for it and to whom? In principle, competition between uses should establish prices for water rights so that these can be bought and sold like physical commodities. And to some extent markets for water rights do exist and, for better or worse, do determine for society which uses shall take precedence. But the device of attaching ownership to rights, even though it has often been applied with considerable ingenuity, has not been able to draw all water decisions into the market place. In many cases, including those involving the most urgent environmental issues, water rights are too ill-defined or broadly held to be marketable. In these cases, choices about what uses are to take precedence inevitably devolve upon planners and political leaders. It seems to be in the nature of things that the economics of water must give way to the politics of water.

To appreciate in a vivid way the bewildering variety and subtlety of the interferences and interactions between water uses that must be taken into account if planning is to be rational, it is good to consider some examples. Although the following examples are couched in hypothetical terms, several of them illustrate real problems on the Delaware River.

1. Evaporation

A power plant with an evaporative cooling tower and an irrigated farm withdraw water from the same stream. Both operations intervene in the water cycle in the same way: they short-circuit to the atmosphere water that would otherwise flow to the ocean. The two operations are also in direct competition: if one depletes the stream, then the other is precluded from operating. The conflict is simple and direct. One can imagine a market mechanism, perhaps an auction, for allocating the water between the two uses on the basis of economic value. On each side the additional productivity made possible by the availability of the water would determine the bid.

2. Pollution

Two cities are located some miles apart on the same river. Both take water out of the river for municipal use and both release their waste water back into the river. In the stretch between the cities the river purifies itself to some extent, but tap water in the downstream city smells more of chlorine and costs more than in the upstream city because of the more elaborate treatment made necessary by the residual pollution. In this case there is an economic and esthetic conflict between the two uses but neither one precludes the other. The conflict here is more oblique and subtle than in the first case. Where should the treatment be done? At the outlet of the first city or the inlet of the second? Which city should pay? Before heaping the entire burden on the upstream city, note that if *either* city were absent (ignoring any other considerations) the other city would be free of any cleanup burden.[1]

3. Quality versus Quantity

As in the previous example, two cities take their water from the same river. One city, as before, releases its waste water into the river, but the other city is located some distance away and releases its waste water into the estuary of another river. The first city diminishes the *quality* of the river's water, the second its *quantity*. Although both interventions are for "municipal use" and thus are often lumped together in statistical compendiums, they impose very different burdens on the river, and conflict therefore in very different ways with alternative uses. For many purposes, "municipal use" is not a very helpful category; neither is "industrial use," for similar reasons. In fact the prevalence of such categories makes meaningful estimates of water "supply" and "demand" very difficult to construct.

4. The Weather and Uncertainty

A town is supplied by a reservoir. The system is of the once-through type with no recycling. The probability of a drought severe enough to cause a shortfall is small but not zero. Various insurance measures can be taken: a supplementary reservoir can be built, standby wells can be drilled, a pipeline to a neighboring system can be laid. Or, the risk can be ignored. How much should the town be willing to pay (including environmental costs) to reduce the risk of shortfall? In principle it should be willing to pay no more than the discounted expected loss from shortfalls. In practice this quantity is virtually impossible to calculate because both the probabilities and the losses are so imperfectly known, especially the latter. Difficult trade-offs involving risk are inherent in the economics of water.

5. Aquatic Life and Ignorance

A reservoir catches the high spring runoff for later use by a municipality. In the estuary, the boundary between fresh and salt water, which used to move downstream in the spring, is now stabilized by the reservoir's action. Certain organisms which had adapted to the seasonal salinity changes are affected. In particular, oysters, which can stand the salinity change, are now attacked by oyster drills, which cannot. Previously, the oyster drills were held in check by the springtime rush of fresh water.

The estuarine life is highly complex, and we do not know all of the consequences of changing the fluctuations of flow. We do know that the estuaries are a vital link in the whole oceanic web of life, and we know that in at least one instance a dam (Aswan) has caused a massive ecological disaster in an estuary. Should we worry? The difficulty here is that the conflicts between uses (where "uses" is taken in a broad sense) fade out into the dark fringes of our ignorance, so that we are not even sure what the conflicts are.

6. Ground Water and the Unknowable

A town in an arid region "mines" water from a large aquifer. It releases its waste water to a stream, which runs into the ocean. In fifty years the aquifer will be dry. This water use precludes whatever opportunities the full aquifer might have offered to unborn generations. The conflict is difficult to adjudicate fairly because the unborn generations have no representative in court.

This example illustrates a subtle point. Not only must existing uses be taken account of, but also potential uses. But potential uses exist only in the imagination, and the imagination (or potential imagination) is virtually infinite. The unborn generations could conceivably invent a use for the ground water that we would admit is better than our present use. For example, they might find a way to use the water conservatively (i.e., with recycling) so that the aquifer would not run out. Or, conceivably, living arrangements might so change that the ground water would be of no interest to the unborn generations.

Though subtle, the question of potential use is by no means academic. The water planners in New Jersey are saving the potential sustained yield of the Pine Barrens (whatever that may be) for imagined future development in the southern part of the state, and they therefore resist suggestions that the water be shipped north where it could be used now. But the future of southern New Jersey can be imagined in many ways, not all of which involve development. What image of the future should guide us?

7. Esthetics

A city has a choice between a dirty lowland source and a clean upland source. Although the lowland water can be treated for less than it costs to develop the upland source, the city chooses the latter for "esthetic" reasons.

C. H. J. Hull, an engineer with the Delaware River Basin Commission, believes that this was a major factor in New York's decision to take Delaware rather than Hudson water.[2] He believes, moreover, that the esthetics of drinking water relate not to its chemical composition, but to its history. He was brought to this view, he says, by the fastidiousness of his family:

> They simply could not—and have not to this day—overcome their repugnancy toward second-hand water, no matter how well renovated. Don't bother to point out that second-hand water may be used in making some soft drinks. I've tried this argument too; it doesn't work. There is just no rationalizing an intangible thing like esthetic sensitivity.
>
> Although I haven't yet admitted it to my family, living with such fastidi-

ous creatures has had its effect on me. I seldom drink a glass of water without experiencing an involuntary thought about its history. The result is that my intake of water, at least in its undisguised state, has diminished.[3]

The attitude of Hull and his family seems at first sight to be similar to that of the organic gardeners: only nature's product, untouched by technology, will do. This view seems rather out of keeping with the usual image of the engineer as a no-nonsense type devoted to technological miracles. But perhaps Hull is merely expressing a preference for one technology over another, since the purveyance of nature's untouched product usually requires engineering works of at least as great magnitude as the processing of man's mess. The organic gardeners, on the other hand, tend to eschew technological miracles of any kind. They are the sort who take pleasure in drinking rainwater collected from their own rooftops according to instructions found in the *Mother Earth News*. The thought that the water might have trickled over bird droppings on its way down the roof probably only increases their sense of contact with nature. Esthetics has many facets.

The Tocks Island controversy has generated a great deal of talk about esthetics, though mostly of a more visual kind—the beauty of clear water running over stones, of the teardrop shape of an island, of a drooping tree along the riverbank, of other such images associated with a free-flowing river. Some have even tried to focus the issue by presenting it as a simple choice between abundant drinking water and the beauty of the natural river. While this has hardly any real validity, it does rightly recognize the central role esthetic considerations have played in the controversy. But it wrongly implies that these considerations are all on one side.

Engineering is an extremely esthetic pursuit. In fact, the element of esthetics in engineering is just about as great as in architecture, though its nature is a little different. In engineering, beauty is not only visual, but also abstract. It is a matter of clarity, simplicity and subtlety—what in mathematics is called elegance. The mechanism of the combination lock (the kind you turn alternately right and left) is beautiful, not because its metallic embodiment is especially pleasant to gaze at, but because the *idea* it is based on is so incredibly simple. (If you don't know how it works, try to figure it out. It is an amusing puzzle.) The clavichord mechanism, the crystal radio, the automobile differential are further examples of devices with abstract elegance. Early steam locomotives and modern racing catamarans are appealing in both an abstract way and in a sensory way. So are dams.

Elegant devices embody clear and simple solutions to clearly perceived problems. But clearly perceived problems are necessarily based on an idealization of some segment of reality. And although it is the ability of science to idealize that gives it its power, it is nevertheless often true that when an elegant solution to an idealized problem is embedded in the real world, the effect is less than elegant. Thus, although steam locomotives are very beautiful to look at, to listen to, to ride on, and to contemplate, they are an environmental abomination. The first ones ran on wood and denuded entire mountainsides. During their later, coal burning heyday, they spread a thick blanket of grime over practically every city of the industrialized world. The best of them wasted most of the energy stuffed into their fire boxes.

As a solution to the clearly perceived problem of bringing a steady supply of pristine water to the people, the dam is elegant for its conceptual simplicity. Indeed, for sheer simplicity it rivals the wheel. When the realization of the simple concept is placed in the unidealized real world, however, it, like the steam locomotive, fails to fit in a number of ways. It is, for example, incompatible with the habits of anadromous fish, disruptive of the estuarine shellfish balance, and excessively hospitable to bluegreen algae. And its useful life is limited by siltation. Such awkward aspects of reality are not included in the idealization which lends the dam its elegance. Moreover, any special measures taken to cope with the difficulties detract from the simple elegance of the original concept.

In their failure to fit perfectly into the real world, dams are no different from any other device ever invented by man. None has ever fitted perfectly. On the other hand, dams are very large scale devices, so that the inelegances stemming from their lack of fit are also large scale.

In the Tocks controversy, as in other environmental controversies, esthetics is much more than a matter of natural beauty. It pervades our processes of thought.

8. Growth

A region can dam its river at some economic and environmental cost in order to provide water for continued conventional growth, or it can leave its river alone, conserve water, and limit conventional growth.

In the minds of the participants this is surely Issue One in the Tocks controversy. It nevertheless hardly ever surfaces in any sustained, coherent way, but only in passing remarks. Probably it seems too fraught with values, prejudices, and political pitfalls to be much good for legalistic case making. But since it is really Issue One, it deserves some discussion here.

In the 1930s, the Tennessee Valley Authority (TVA) was seen by its creators as a shining humanitarian enterprise that would bring order and prosperity to an impoverished people and set an example for the whole country. The image was neat new farms on a fertile, protected flood plain, lighted by electricity from humming water turbines. All this to replace moonshiners' shacks.

The spirit of TVA progressivism is well captured in a film made by Pare Lorenz in 1937 entitled "The River." The film shows how the earlier clearing of midwestern forests had led to soil erosion and disastrous flooding and how people suffered as a result. The need was clear: the natural flood control previously provided by the forests had to be replaced by the works of man. Elegant concrete structures with water gushing over their faces in controlled torrents appear on the screen. Then the power lines, then the newly prosperous farmer plowing his field against a scenic backdrop. The film is low key but stirring. There is not the slightest trace of cynicism and not the slightest trace of doubt about what is the right course of action. Our ancestors may have been imprudent when they cut the trees, but the dams will atone for their error and will repay their debt to nature. The progressive spirit of TVA has continued to motivate the government dam builders to this day.

Odd, then, that it is just those who imagine themselves to be most progressive who are now berating the Corps of Engineers for building too many dams. The images have changed. The term "progress" has gone somewhat out of style and has been more or less replaced by the more technical-sounding term "economic growth." And this concept in recent years has lost so much of its luster that it no longer raises eyebrows to say that economic growth is a mixed blessing. The governor of Oregon has even made the braking of growth an official state policy.

The images which have brought about this change have been negative. "Progress" was to bring gradually more wealth to each individual, but "economic growth" is now perceived by some as gradually diminishing each person's wealth, or at least certain components of it such as his share of open space, clean water, clean air, natural beauty, quiet, and health. Hardly anyone who has lived more than two decades can have escaped seeing a beloved hilltop invaded by houses, a familiar country road transformed by commerce, a swimming place ruined by scum, a peaceful town split by a highway and suffocated by its traffic, or a favorite valley flooded. Such perceived retrogression conflicts with the deep feeling, especially characteristic of Americans, that life should get gradually better. This sense of inexorably creeping loss is surely the real engine driving the opposition to the Tocks Island Dam.

Opponents of conventional development believe that under present circumstances real wealth can be increased only by improving the *efficiency* with which environmental resources are used—for example, by using less water for each ton of steel, less steel for each passenger-mile of transportation, and less transportation to conduct our business. Or less land for each ton of coal, less coal for each kilowatt-hour of energy, and less energy for each square foot of office space. And so forth.

Achieving such gains is not necessarily a matter of frugality: redirected technology can do a great deal. Nevertheless, a renewed sense of frugality does seem to be accompanying the current environmental awareness. Will the old Puritan slogans be revived? ("Use it up, wear it out, make do, or do without.") Will people be perverse enough to see frugality as improving the quality of life in some moral sense, as the Shakers and others once did?

Frugality brings us full circle—back to the problems of water conservation with which we began. As we saw, the conservation of water is not quite so obvious a matter as it may seem. The trouble is that water is already conserved by nature. With negligible exceptions, water is neither created nor destroyed; it just moves endlessly around a grand hydrological cycle. Although we say we do, we never really consume water; we merely intervene in the natural cycle by short-circuiting, delaying, or polluting parts of it. Unfortunately our various interventions conflict with one another in a bewildering variety of ways. Conserving water merely means modifying one intervention so that another, conflicting one may be larger.

II. WATER'S PATHWAYS

Figure 5–1 shows the main water cycle in a stylized way. Rain water striking the earth is driven by gravity to the sea. A typical path passes first through the ground, then out into a stream, and finally into the saline ocean.

1. Diversions for Human Use

For a variety of reasons, man diverts water from its natural pathways into others of his own making. These diversions can be classified as forward, local, or backward according to the relative locations within the cycle of the points of withdrawal and discharge. A

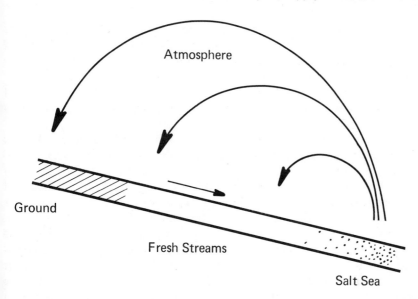

Figure 5–1. The Main Water Cycle

forward diversion is one whose discharge point is further along in the cycle than its withdrawal point (assuming the path tracing starts and ends with the atmosphere). A local diversion is one whose withdrawal and discharge points are close enough together to be regarded as identical, and a backward diversion is the opposite of a forward diversion.

Forward diversions are the most conventional kind. A typical example is a municipal supply system, such as Newark's, that takes water by aqueduct from an upstream point on a river and discharges it after use at a downstream point. From the point of withdrawal to the point of discharge, the river's flow is diminished by the amount of the diversion. A cooling tower that short-circuits river water directly to the atmosphere is another example. From the site of the tower to the sea, the river is diminished by the amount of the tower's diversion. In general, a forward diversion has the effect of diminishing flow along some segment of a natural path. It is usually this effect that limits the volume of water that can be allowed to flow through a forward diversion.

Local diversions are not limited in this way. Since the points of withdrawal and discharge are the same (by definition), such a diversion is in effect an independent circulation whose rate of flow does not affect any other flow rates. In principle, then, the rate of flow through a local diversion can be arbitrarily high. A typical example of a local diversion is a municipal system, such as Philadelphia's, that withdraws and discharges at nearby points on the same body of water. Another example is a farm that takes ground water from a well and puts its waste water back into the ground through a septic system. A third example is a seacoast town that desalts seawater and puts its waste water back into the ocean. All these systems could be run arbitrarily fast without diminishing natural flows.

Local diversions are, however, limited by contamination. Almost every water use except evaporation introduces some foreign substance into the water, and in a cycle such substances tend to accumulate. The accumulation is mitigated somewhat if one link in the cycle is dispersive (the river, in Philadelphia's case) or if one link is a filter (the ground, in the case of the farm). But the capacity of such helpful links is usually limited, so that the allowable magnitude of the contaminating water use is also limited. This magnitude has been exceeded, for example, on Long Island, where the well–septic tank system, multiplied by hundreds of thousands, has resulted in a slow accumulation of soluble nitrates in the ground water, until now hazardous levels have been reached.

Expanding the capacity of a local diversion, then, is usually a matter of pollution control. Thus pollution control has a direct bearing on the magnitude of potential water supplies. It also has an indirect bearing in that forward diversions are often undertaken, despite their great cost, in order to avoid pollution (see the comments of C.H.J. Hull in Section I-7). Thus it is not possible to estimate the water supply potential of a region by means of volumetric calculations alone; cleanup possibilities must also be taken into account.

Backward diversions are the least common kind. A hypothetical example would be the pumping of water from a lake to the top of a mountain, with waste water discharged at the top into a natural stream. Another example would be the shipment inland of desalted water from a seaside plant, with the waste water discharged into a river. In all cases, the flow along some segment of a natural path is *increased* by the diversion. Despite this dividend, backward diversions are uncommon because they necessarily require energy: they must do the work the sun would otherwise do. In driving the water cycle the sun does two kinds of work: it lifts the water against gravity and it separates the water from salt. Backward diversions must also do one or both.

A transfer of water from one stream to another is neither a forward nor a backward diversion, since it diminishes the flow in one stream and augments it in the other. Such a transfer can, however,

be regarded as the sum or simultaneous occurrence of a purely
forward and a purely backward diversion.

2. Conservation—Limiting the Diversions

Traditionally, water engineers have devoted their efforts to
diverting ever more water for human use. But as the diversions have
grown and their environmental effects have become more evident,
people have begun to ask if so much diversion is really necessary, and
have suggested various measures for reducing the demand for it. Such
measures can reasonably be called conservation measures.

Conservation measures, in contrast to projects for increasing diversions, tend to avoid the destructive chain reaction effect, so common
in our technological society, wherein the solution of one problem
creates another. Increased diversions, for example, tend to increase
the burden on the sewer system, whose expansion creates further
problems, and so forth. Conservation measures, on the other hand,
tend to relieve such problems.

Within our framework, conservation measures fall into three main
types: (1) those that reduce the *volume* of a forward diversion,
(2) those that reduce the *length* of a forward diversion, and (3) those
that reduce contamination. There appear to be significant opportunities for measures of all three types. This section discusses some
examples.

Cooling of many kinds constitutes one of the largest components
of water use. Any serious effort to conserve water must consider
cooling. Water is especially useful for cooling because of its high heat
of vaporization. In evaporating, a single gram of water absorbs about
580 calories of heat, or enough to cool 58 grams of water or 542
grams of steel by $10°C$. Thus, from an engineer's point of view, the
evaporation of water provides a very attractive way to transfer heat
to the atmosphere.

In a study of three Massachusetts towns during the drought of the
1960s (the most severe of record) Russell, Arey, and Kates[4] estimate
the annual per capita loss due to a 15 percent water shortage to be
only about $10. One important reason for this startlingly low value
was that in many cases measures undertaken by industries to save
cooling water were found to be profitable, so that over the long run
they generated net gains, which offset some of the drought losses.
The savings were achieved, according to the authors, by "recycling"
cooling water. Though no explanation of this is given, it may mean
that water flowing in a forward diversion (e.g., municipal water from
an upland source) was being used for cooling in such a way that only
a small fraction was actually being evaporated, with the rest simply

passing through. This would be characteristic, for example, of the simple and common "once-through" method. By rearranging their systems to evaporate a larger fraction of the input water, so that less total input water was needed, the industrialists reduced their demands on the forward diversion. This would be an example of a Type 1 conservation measure, since it reduced the *volume* of the diversion.

The diversion it relieved, however, was that associated with the municipal water supply; it did nothing to relieve the diversion of water to the atmosphere by evaporation. Indeed, the rate of evaporation is determined by the cooling load, so that as long as evaporative cooling is to be used, the volume of this diversion cannot be reduced. Nevertheless, a Type 2 conservation measure might be applicable in a case such as this: if the cooling tower could be moved closer to the sea, then the *length* of the evaporative diversion could be reduced.

This possibility has become important in the Tocks Island Dam controversy. A Delaware River power plant originally planned for an upstream site has been moved to the estuary, where its forward diversion, being shorter, has less impact on the river's flow. Though the move was made primarily for reasons other than water conservation, the conservation effect has pleased some environmentalists, who are urging that other plants be moved as well.

Going one step further, evaporation can be abandoned altogether and heat can be transferred to the atmosphere through conductive metal surfaces, usually of copper or aluminum. While this is feasible, the dry surfaces, operating without the benefit of those 580 calories per gram, must be very large. Lots of metal and lots of space are needed.

Ideally, of course, "waste" heat should not be dissipated by cooling, but should be put to good use. Schemes to do this go by the name of "total energy systems." These usually use the waste heat for direct space heating, for indirect cooling by means of an absorptive cycle, or for chemical processes. Their more widespread adoption is inhibited by the fragmentation of planning: power plants that make the heat, and houses or factories that could use it, are planned by different people.

A spectacular piece of evidence that conservation has large potential in industry is provided by the Kaiser steel plant in Fontana, California, which uses only 4 percent of the water used by conventional plants.[5] In spite of the cost of special equipment required to achieve this, Kaiser is able to compete in the market for steel.

Sunday supplement articles on water conservation tend to concentrate on the universally familiar household segment of use. (Such articles generally assume tacitly that the household is imbedded in a forward diversion so that reductions in volume are effective.) It may seem startling that the average American uses 75 gallons per day. Thus a family of four uses 300 gallons per day, or two brimming bathtubs full.[6] Households in other industrial countries use less. According to one text:[7] ". . . some water authorities in Britain maintain that 25 [30 U.S.] gallons per head per day is an adequate supply for domestic needs, while many American engineers do not blink at supplying up to 70 [84 U.S.] gallons per head per day for exactly the same purpose." Part of the explanation, no doubt, is that machines for washing clothes and dishes, especially abundant in the United States, use more water than hand methods, though other aspects of life style are probably also important.

How much water does a comfortable standard of living really demand? No one knows for sure, but there are some inventive people who think we could get along with much less water than we now use. One proposal is to use the waste water from washing for flushing toilets. Since each of these uses accounts for about half the indoor total, this measure in principle could cut indoor consumption by 50 percent. A similar saving would be achieved by the Swedish composting toilets, which use no water at all. Another proposal, for which a variety of small savings totalling 25 percent is claimed, is centralized, electrically operated valves.[8] Further proposals concern various means for improving the efficiency of washing.

A more immediately effective Type 1 conservation measure, however, would be the repair of leaks in municipal distribution systems supplied by forward diversions. A 1960 analysis of New York City's decision to build the Cannonsville reservoir in the upper Delaware Basin concluded that more than Cannonsville's yield could have been obtained by fixing the leaks in New York's pipes.[9] About one-third of the saving would have come from fixing street mains and two-thirds from fixing pipes on customers' premises. The per gallon cost of the former would have been less than one-hundredth, and of the latter less than one-third, the cost of Cannonsville water. The Cannonsville reservoir was nevertheless built, and the leaks were never fixed.

This odd decision was consistent with a venerable tradition in New York City politics. At least since 1900 the City has been more or less continuously criticized for failing to fix the leaks in its mains and for failing to install meters so that customers, who now pay a flat rate, would have an incentive to fix their own leaks and maybe even moderate their notoriously profligate water using habits. Other cities, after installing meters, have experienced reductions in consumption of as much as 40 percent.[10] To date, New York City officials have successfully resisted all such criticism, even though at times of crisis it has sometimes been intense. Their reasons for doing so are apparently rooted in the Catch-22 logic of bureaucratic politics. They are certainly not economic.

Whatever its cause, New York City's negligence has a direct bearing on the Tocks Island project, even though it is seldom mentioned in debate. New York takes much of its water from the upper Delaware. Water not taken by New York could be released down the Delaware River and could serve precisely the same functions as water released from the proposed Tocks reservoir. For the sole purpose of feeding its leaks, New York City is taking at least enough water to cover the 300 million gallons per day (mgd) New Jersey would like to export out of the Delaware Basin into its northeast region.[11] The provision of this 300 mgd (which we will discuss in more detail later) is seen by the Tocks proponents as a major justification for the dam.

Although the physical sense in which the Tocks Island Dam is to service New York's leaks is clear, the connection is hardly ever pointed out by the dam's opponents, for a decidedly nonphysical reason. The reason is that a U.S. Supreme Court decision of 1954 allocating 800 mgd of Delaware water to New York City is seen as an insuperable barrier. It is as if the Himalayas had sprung out of the earth under the river, cutting off a piece of the upper Basin from the rest and permanently diverting its water to the Hudson. No one has yet observed that no such mountain range exists. If New Jersey had to pay for the Tocks Island Dam, and if all parties pursued their own economic interests, then New Jersey and New York might well find it advantageous to strike a bargain under which New Jersey would pay for fixing New York's leaks and installing meters there, in return for additional water releases down the Delaware from New York's reservoirs. But since New Jersey does not have to pay for the Tocks Island Dam, it has no incentive to consider such a bargain and it may as well believe in the Himalayas.

III. FLUCTUATIONS

The previous section on the routing of water—its natural pathways and manmade detours—allowed, for simplicity, the tacit assumption that flows are uniform in time. This, of course, is not the case. Natural flows fluctuate widely in response to fluctuations in the weather.

It was observed that forward diversions borrow water from natural pathways, and that such diversions are usually limited by the need to avoid excessive reduction of the natural flow. A variety of physical, biological, and economic circumstances impose constraints on natural flows that cannot be violated without environmental or dollar cost. In planning diversions, therefore, water engineers must find means for raising the minima—that is, for filling in the troughs of the graph of flow versus time. With the troughs filled in, greater diversion is considered allowable up to the point where the borrowing it entails brings the minima back down to a specified limit. The traditional source of water for filling in a trough is a preceding peak, or set of peaks, and the traditional device for accomplishing the transfer of water from peaks to troughs is the dam. Dams, then, are devices for raising minimum flows and thus permitting expansions of forward diversions. The "safe yield" of a dam is the magnitude of the forward diversion the dam permits under some constraint on minimum flow and some criterion of safety.

This, in brief, is the traditional way of dealing with one kind of fluctuation in one context. It is not the only way or kind or context. From noise to business cycles, man is beset by unwanted fluctuations on every hand, and he has invented dozens of ways of dealing with them. But one often finds in widely different contexts methods that are similar or analogous in some way. Certain time series taken from the stock market are indistinguishable from certain others taken from nature; insurance and electric grids use similar kinds of averaging; a mathematical "theory of storage" applies with minor modifications to dams, inventories, and queues. And so forth. But even taking account of such analogies, there remain a number of fundamentally different ways of dealing with fluctuation. This section briefly examines some of these in the context of water.

1. Getting at the Source

It is fashionable these days to list weather modification (cloud seeding) among the means for increasing water supplies. This gets right to the ultimate source of irksome hydrological fluctuation. To level out the weather into one monotonous drizzle is a delightful science fiction possibility that the rain makers have not failed to achieve through lack of enthusiasm. Edith Weiss, who has looked seriously at the possible consequences of a really effective weather modification technology, has discerned a hair-raising tangle of legal, political, and international problems.[12] Although bringing rain in times and places of genuine drought would have undoubted humanitarian benefit, it is difficult to imagine mankind stopping with that.

In our present state of civilization it is perhaps just as well that weather modification is still a nonresource.

2. Filling in the Troughs

Dams are the traditional trough filling devices, but there are others too, for which a convenient generic term is "standby sources." Standby sources are common in utilities such as electric power that face a fluctuating difference between demand and supply.

Electric power engineers distinguish between base load generators, which run continuously, and peak load generators, which run intermittently. Typically, different types of plants with different economic characteristics are used for the two functions. Base load is provided by plants (e.g., nuclear reactors) that have relatively low operating (e.g., fuel) costs and relatively high capital costs; peak load is provided by plants (e.g., gas turbines) with the opposite characteristics. The reason for the trade-off is clear: since standby sources such as peak load generators produce relatively little yearly output for their capacity, the burden of their capital cost falls relatively heavily on each unit of output. Hence, the relative premium on low capital cost.

Some water supply systems are seemingly analogous. New York City's water is supplied by reservoirs, supplemented by a standby pumping station on the Hudson River at Chelsea, which is used only if the reservoir supply runs low. Like the peak load generator, the standby station at Chelsea has relatively low capital cost and relatively high operating cost (energy).

But the analogy is far less accurate than it might seem, for the reservoirs are, in fact, not continuously operating base load plants, but rather are standby devices, like the Chelsea pumps. If the river flows were uniform and unfluctuating, the aqueduct alone could purvey the water to New York City and no reservoirs would be needed. In the same sense that a pump is idle unless its blades are turning, a reservoir is idle unless its level is declining, for only then is it providing any water that is not otherwise available. Since its level declines only at times of low flow, a reservoir operates as a standby device. Its economic characteristics, however, are those of a base load plant. This can make a reservoir relatively uneconomic compared to other standby devices.

The output of a reservoir is conventionally stated as an addition to "safe yield." The cost of the reservoir is often divided by this quantity to give a normalized cost—so many dollars per mgd of additional safe yield. The cost is thus spread out over a constant, uninterrupted flow, most of which, typically, could have been obtained without the reservoir. Although this procedure is conceptually more appropriate for a base load rather than a standby plant, it is not really wrong, provided the same procedure is applied to all alternatives.

Consider, for example, a comparison between a reservoir and aqueduct on the one hand, and a standby well and aqueduct on the other hand. We will assume that the aqueduct is the same in both cases so that its cost cancels out of the comparison. In the second case the aqueduct brings water from the (undammed) river whenever it is available; the well is brought into action only on the relatively rare occasions when the river flow is inadequate. Even though the well actually produces little water on the average, it *makes possible* an uninterrupted supply, just as the reservoir does. To make a consistent comparison, then, we must spread the cost of the well over the whole flow, including the flow when the well is idle. The result, as before, is so many dollars per mgd of additional safe yield.

It is equally correct, and perhaps conceptually better, to allocate the cost in both cases to just that portion of the water actually supplied by the standby source. This merely sets a new baseline: the natural flow in the undammed river is taken as given, so that only the water needed to fill the gaps is counted. This water can reasonably be called "insurance water." When the cost of a reservoir is allocated only to the insurance water it actually supplies, the per gallon cost can be startlingly high. In a report prepared by the Institute of Public Administration for the Corps of Engineers as part of the NEWS study,[13] the cost of providing insurance water by means of reservoirs in the New York metropolitan region is estimated at $22 per thousand gallons (1970 dollars)—or about 100 times the normal price! While this number can hardly be taken literally (it is based on a very simple aggregate model of runoff variation), its magnitude does not appear implausible. The implication, of course, is that even expensive means for supplying insurance water could compete with reservoirs. At $22 a thousand gallons, water could almost be brought in by truck.

Such a high number should spur every inventor to seek better ways of obtaining insurance water. Two general sources are the sea and the ground. Though much inventive effort has gone into the desalting of sea water, costs remain high and environmental problems persist. Ground water, whose technology (so far) is simpler, appears more promising.

A. Desalting.   During the 1960s the federal government, through its Office of Saline Water, mounted a major effort to make desalting economically competitive. The reports of this agency fill a bookcase six feet high and six feet wide. In recent years, however, the effort has greatly diminished and in 1972 the Office of Saline Water was dissolved.

A fundamental difficulty with desalting is that it requires a great deal of energy. On the basis of fundamental physical principles it can be shown that at least 2.6 kwh must be expended to extract 1000 gallons of fresh water from sea water by any method whatever. Ingenuity cannot reduce this limit any more than it can create perpetual motion. Moreover, no practical method has even approached the limit; an efficient existing plant requires 145 kwh per 1,000 gallons.[14] The reason for this is also fundamental: to approach the theoretical limit it would be necessary to perform the extraction very slowly, and the slower the extraction, the greater the capital cost of the plant per gallon per day of output.

Apparently, an important stimulus to the efforts of the Office of Saline Water in the 1960s was the seeming imminence of abundant nuclear power. It was hoped that by using the waste heat from the nuclear plants to desalt water, both electricity and water could be produced at competitive costs. Unfortunately, a variety of technical, environmental, and political problems that have gradually come to light in recent years have diminished the promise of both technologies, although the combination may still find uses in special situations (islands) where fresh water is especially scarce and costly.

Aside from the land use problems associated with any large industrial installation, desalting plants have their own special environmental problem, namely the disposal of prodigious quantities of concentrated brine. This is especially acute inland (where the source of salt water might be the ground), but even along the seacoast the effects on aquatic life might be troublesome.

In 1966 a group of investigators called the "Northeast Desalting Team,"[15] who looked into the potentialities of desalting for New York City and northern New Jersey, estimated that desalted sea water could be produced at about twice the cost of standby pumping from the Hudson. Their estimate assumed a 300 mgd standby plant using heat from a power plant. This leaves a factor of two to go on the economic side and a substantial problem to overcome on the environmental side—not a hopeless gap to close, but still a discouraging one.

A more immediate prospect is the use of dilute salt water; if the salt concentration is low, then the energy required for desalting is correspondingly low. Thus, mildly brackish water from estuaries, or waste water containing small amounts of dissolved solids, are both promising candidates for desalting. In fact, desalting of dilute solu-

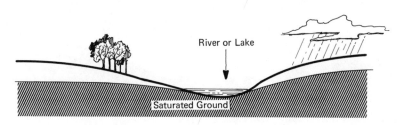

Figure 5-2. Ground Water Under Virgin Conditions

tions is a necessary step in many recycling procedures. The membrane method, which is applicable especially to dilute solutions, shows considerable promise. The development of a really good, inexpensive membrane could have a major impact on water technology.

Although every method of desalting requires a substantial plant, capital costs are low enough (and operating costs high enough) to make desalting usually look better as a standby source.[16] Relative to reservoirs it has the capital cost advantage that its plants can be built in stages as needed, while reservoirs must be built all at once.

B. Ground Water. The second commonly mentioned standby source is ground water. More fresh water is stored in the ground than anywhere else except the polar ice caps—more than in all the lakes and rivers and more than in the atmosphere. But it has many peculiar properties that make its role in water supply complex.

Physically, surface and ground water form a single system. The water table is continuous with the surfaces of rivers and lakes, as shown in Figure 5-2. Water is readily transferred between surface bodies and the ground. Under virgin conditions, the system fluctuates about an equilibrium state with fluctuating rainfall. Rain raises the water table, thereby creating a pressure head that drives the water out of the ground into the lakes and streams. After the rain, the water table slowly subsides as the streams drain away the excess water. It is the ground water, not direct surface runoff, that keeps the rivers going between rains.

The soil above the water table may be periodically moist, but it is not saturated. Only the water in the saturated zone is normally counted as ground water. Most plants take their water from the upper zone, intercepting it on its way down. But a few, called phreatophytes, reach right down to the water table and drink ground water. That portion of precipitation that reaches the water table is called recharge. In virgin equilibrium, the recharge equals the sum of

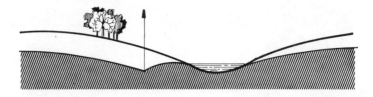

Figure 5-3. Equilibrium Water Table with Well

streamflow and the evapotranspiration of phreatophytes. Removal of ground water through a well causes the volume of stored ground water to decline until a new equilibrium is established. The lowering of the water table eventually reduces the flow in nearby streams, and, if there are phreatophytes, it may reduce their evapotranspiration. After a new equilibrium is established, the well discharge is just equal to the reduction in stream flow and evapotranspiration.

It is important to realize the significance of this simple fact. In equilibrium all water taken from wells is, in effect, stolen from streams and plants. Thus the capacity of an aquifer to yield water depends less on the rate of recharge than on one's willingness to reduce stream flows and the welfare of phreatophytes, if there are any. Of course there are other constraints on groundwater use also. Among them are salt water intrusion (esp. along seacoasts), land subsidence over mined-out aquifers, manmade pollutants, and interference between neighboring wells.

If water is sucked at a moderate rate from the center of a pond, the surface, so far as the eye can see, remains flat as it recedes. But there must in fact be a slight depression toward the middle— otherwise there would be no pressure gradient to drive the water in from the edges. Since the resistance to the inward flow is slight, only a slight distortion of the surface develops. In the ground, where the resistance to the flow of water is high, a very deep depression of the water surface (or of the potential head in the case of a confined aquifer) called the "cone of depression" develops around a withdrawing well. As time passes the cone slowly expands until it reaches a lake or stream. The surface ultimately comes to rest in a new equilibrium in which the flow through the lake or stream is reduced by the amount of the well withdrawal. Figure 5-3 shows the equilibrium shape of the water table after a well has been introduced into Figure 5-2.

The time from a disturbance to a new equilibrium may be very long. A well in permeable ground right next to a river may stabilize in days or weeks, but in other places only after decades or even centuries. Thus almost everywhere where the water table has been disturbed by man, it is in a state of disequilibrium. In some places, particularly in the West, aquifers are being "mined." These aquifers will go dry before a new equilibrium is established.

In the East the prospect is for ultimate equilibrium with surface flows. In this state, as we have seen, water taken from wells is merely subtracted from rivers (assuming phreatophytes are not a factor), and thus does not add to available supplies. But this does not mean that aquifers are useless. They can serve any or all of three functions: they can act as filters, as conduits, or as reservoirs. In the last role they are smoothers of fluctuation.

In nature, aquifers provide a great deal of smoothing of surface flows. Indeed, without them streams would be torrential during rains and dry in between. But the storage capacity of the ground is very large and it could provide even more smoothing than it does under natural conditions. In order to realize this extra smoothing, however, it is necessary to operate wells intermittently, just as it is necessary to operate the gates of an off-stream surface reservoir intermittently if it is to equalize the flows in a stream. Constant withdrawal from a well accomplishes only a diversion of water, but no smoothing of surface flows.

To set up an effective schedule of well withdrawals, one needs to know the effect of each well on surface flows. Figure 5-4 shows in a hypothetical case the surface flow deficit resulting from the short term pumping of a well. The effect can be spread out over weeks, months, or even years, depending on the permeability of the ground and the distance of the well from the nearest streams and lakes. If these parameters are right, then the well water can be taken during a period of low surface flow and the flow deficit can occur largely during the following high flow season. A nice application of this principle is proposed by Young and Bredehoeft for a stretch of the Platte River:

One can design a pumping system to take advantage of the delay between groundwater pumping and its effect on the stream and thus use the aquifer as a storage reservoir. The aquifer underlying the South Platte Valley represents the largest available reservoir remaining on the river. A properly designed conjunctive use system will store water during the nongrowing season for pumping during the growing seasons. By using the delay time of the aquifer, the groundwater reservoir can be operated so that it will have only a small effect on the stream during the growing season.[17]

Even without precise location of wells and timing of withdrawals, however, some smoothing of surface flows can be achieved. If a well is far away from the streams it affects, the intermittent use of the

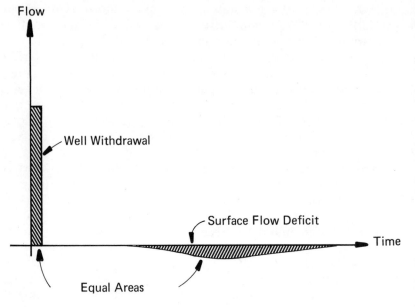

Figure 5–4.   Effect of Well on Surface Flow

well may produce a nearly uniform reduction in surface flows. Using such a well during low flow periods in conjunction with a pipe that takes surface water during high flow periods can produce a steady supply of water that depletes high flows more than low flows. The net smoothing effect is similar to that of a surface reservoir.

The region that would be served by the Tocks reservoir contains a great deal of ground water, much of it now withdrawn in a continuous way that uses the aquifers only as pipelines but not as reservoirs. To assess the real potential of the region to produce a continuous flow of water, it would be necessary to postulate an extensive system of conjunctive use of ground and surface water. This apparently has not been done. The NAR Study[18] does give estimates of total potential ground water yield by region, but these are based on annual recharge rates. As we have seen, recharge rates do not contain the information we would really like to have. Bredehoeft and Young comment on the recharge approach as follows:

> Commonly, hydrologists make a water budget in which estimates of the virgin rate of recharge and discharge are made. Some think that the magnitude of the virgin rate of recharge and/or discharge indicates the size development that can be made in the system. Theis (1940) pointed out the difficulties of such an approach. A water budget is usually of little or no

value in assessing the capability of wells in the system to yield water, the water levels at any point in the system, and changes in the rates of discharge and/or recharge.[19]

3. Putting the Eggs in Many Baskets

Insurance companies and portfolio managers count on averaging fluctuations from many sources. If the sources are sufficiently independent, then, on the average, the peaks and troughs from different sources will tend to cancel out so that the aggregate is smoother than any typical component. In a similar way, electric power companies attempt to average fluctuating demands in different places by means of large interconnection grids.

Unfortunately, dry spells tend to be widespread, so that the analogous interconnection of neighboring water systems, unless done on a very large scale, would accomplish relatively little smoothing. However, there is some local variation in the difference between demand and capacity that could be leveled by better interconnection. In particular, northern New Jersey, which is served by dozens of small independent companies, could increase its effective margin of safety by better interconnection arrangements.

4. Shifting the Burden

Unwanted fluctuations tend to propagate through whatever system they infect. This is true whether the system is an electronic circuit subjected to noise, or a production process subjected to fluctuating demand or supply. Fluctuating rainfall leads to fluctuating grain yields, which leads to fluctuating income to the farmer. In such systems the unwanted fluctuations are often attacked at various points by various means. Reservoirs level out the water supply, grain storage levels out the grain supply, and insurance, or its equivalent, levels out the farmer's income. Ultimately, these disparate undertakings are all aimed at the same fluctuation, and they therefore tend to trade off against one another: Do you store the water or do you store the grain? Or some of both?

One way of dealing with fluctuation, then, is to transfer it from one part of a system to another where it will do less harm. In some manufacturing industries it is common practice to match output to a randomly fluctuating demand by means of frequent layoffs and rehiring. To counteract the untoward effects of this on their members, some labor unions have demanded a guaranteed annual wage, whose effect is to transfer the burden of the fluctuation from the employees to the stockholders, who, they argue, are better equipped to absorb it.

A case involving water occurs in the Northwest, where electricity generated by water is used, among other things, to make aluminum. When water is short, aluminum production is interrupted, and demand is met from aluminum stockpiles. This effectively substitutes aluminum storage for water storage. At the economic optimum the marginal cost of enlarging the power reservoirs would be equal to the marginal cost of equivalently increasing the aluminum stockpile. Fluctuations within systems, then, can be suppressed at various points or can be transferred to other points. To recognize all the options this implies, it is necessary to look at whole systems at once and not just pieces.

In water supply planning, institutional, political, and conceptual constraints have often restricted the view to something less than the whole system. Attention has been focussed primarily on physical hydrology and the engineering of dams and conduits, and much less on the economics of demand and the technology of water use. Demand is usually estimated by simple extrapolation of aggregate quantities, while supply systems are designed and optimized with elaborate sophistication to insure that they will meet the estimated demand "safely." The reliability of the supply—which, in spite of the language, is not perfect—tends to be measured primarily by the probability of its failure and not by the sizes of the deficits, or their costs to water users. Demand for water tends to be seen as rigid and inviolable so that any deficit is a disaster. Water, it is said, is essential to life.

A consequence of this view is that fluctuation is suppressed as close to the source as possible by means of storage. As little fluctuation as possible is allowed to propagate out into the rest of the system. But it may be that the rest of the system is less intolerant of fluctuation than we might have thought. Some water is indeed essential to life and its supply cannot be interrupted, but this is only a small fraction of what we use. For most purposes water is no more than a valuable commodity, among many others. In a well ordered economy the cost of handling fluctuation at various points in the system would be traded off against the cost of eliminating the fluctuation at the source.

5. Living with It

The idea of tolerating fluctuation is directly contrary to the concept behind the phrase "safe yield." Under the safe yield concept a sharp distinction is drawn between continuous and intermittent supplies, and in principle only the former are regarded as having any economic value. Since absolute continuity cannot be achieved in

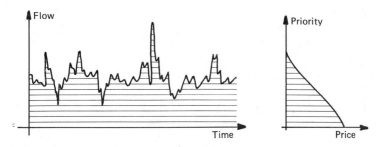

Figure 5-5. Subdivision of Flow

practice, an arbitrary risk level is set to distinguish the valuable from the worthless supply streams.

It may well be, however, that the distinction is not sharp, and that the real economic value of supply streams falls off gradually with increasing intermittency, i.e., with increasing frequency and length of gaps. Consider, for example, a fluctuating source as depicted in Figure 5-5. If the flow is divided into layers as in the figure, the lowest layers are least intermittent and the highest layers are most intermittent. If the layers were sold separately (in the form of priority rights) the price would diminish monotonically from the lower to the higher layers. A reservoir, or other smoothing device, would create more of the high value layers at the expense of the low value ones, thereby increasing the value of the whole supply. This formulation presents us with a classic economic optimization problem. At the optimum, the cost of a further increment of smoothing exactly equals the increase in value the smoothing generates. In general the optimal smoothing will be less than total.

The economic value of the smoothing achieved by a reservoir depends not only on the size of the reservoir but also on the way in which it is operated. This can be illustrated by contrasting two operating rules: (1) Water is released at a constant rate r, so long as the reservoir is not empty; (2) water is released at a rate $r(Q)$ that varies with the quantity Q of water stored in the reservoir. The output under the two rules is shown qualitatively in Figure 5-6. Thus, Rule 1 produces infrequent severe shortfalls; Rule 2 produces more frequent but milder shortfalls. Which one is economically preferable depends on the character of the market for intermittent supply. If a surface reservoir is operated conjunctively with a well field, Rule 2 might be advantageous for the following reason: the capital cost of the well and pump depends on its yield. A small well operated for long periods is cheaper than a big well operated for

Figure 5-6. Effects of Different Reservoir Operation Rules

short periods. Thus the conversion of short severe shortages to long mild ones reduces the cost of the well.

Instead of slicing the flow graph horizontally, as in Figure 5-5, one can slice it vertically and attach prices to the vertical slices according to their height. In times of shortage (short slices) the price would be high and in times of plenty (tall slices) the price would be low. This is similar in principle to the "peak load pricing" telephone and power companies use to encourage their customers to level their demand over time. If the economist's device of exponential discounting for comparing values at different times is accepted, then horizontal and vertical slicing of the flow graph are nearly equivalent.

With an appropriate pricing scheme in effect, what might the market for water of graduated intermittency look like? If the cost of reservoir supplied insurance water is really $22 per thousand gallons as the Institute of Public Administration report maintains, then the incentive to buy relatively low priority water for some uses would seem to be substantial. Would a car washing establishment improve its profit by buying low priority water along with insurance against business lost during rare dry spells? Could a water using manufacturer of a storable product (soft drinks) profitably use low priority water and sell from inventory during gaps? A great deal of summer demand is for lawn watering in some places. How much is it worth not to tolerate a brown lawn every few years? How uniform must our habitat be?

Making our habitat uniform is a primary human occupation. As Socolow observes in Essay 1 (p. 19), "The thrust of most of industrial society has been ... to reduce man's vulnerability to nature's excesses, and, by extension, to reduce man's subordination to nature's variability." The devices we have invented to reduce our subordination to nature's (and man's) variability are legion. Air conditioning levels out the varying temperature, electric lights level out the vary-ing illumination, and Muzak levels out the mood. Mutual funds smooth out the financial bumps of the market place and accident insurance, however lamely, attempts to smooth over some of life's pain. The drive for uniformity and regularity is very general: it ex-tends to spatial as well as temporal fluctuations. The irregular cave is replaced with planar floors, walls, and ceilings; the superhighway cuts straight and level through the undulating landscape. Corners are square, lines are straight, circles are round; the works of Euclid are visible on every hand.

Science fiction writers, extrapolating the human striving for regularity to its limit, have created visions of totally uniform environ-ments, usually underground. In E.M. Forster's story, "The Machine Stops," each person lives alone in an underground cell, which he seldom leaves:

> Imagine, if you can, a small room hexagonal in shape, like the cell of a bee. It is lighted neither by window nor by lamp, yet it is filled with a soft radiance. There are no apertures for ventilation, yet the air is fresh. There are no musical instruments, and yet, at the moment my meditation opens, this room is throbbing with melodious sounds. An arm-chair is in the centre, by its side a reading-desk—that is all the furniture. And in the arm-chair there sits a swaddled lump of flesh—a woman about five feet high, with a face as white as a fungus. It is to her that the little room belongs. . .
>
> Night and day, wind and storm, tide and earthquake, impeded man no longer. He had harnessed Leviathan. All the old literature, with its praise of Nature, and its fear of Nature, rang false as the prattle of a child.
>
> Few travelled in these days, for thanks to the advance of science, the earth was exactly alike all over. Rapid intercourse, from which the previous civilization had hoped so much, had ended by defeating itself. What was the good of going to Pekin when it was just like Shrewsbury? Why return to Shrewsbury when it would be just like Pekin? Men seldom moved their bodies; all unrest was concentrated in the soul.[a]

IV. WATER SUPPLY IN THE DELAWARE BASIN

1. Original Tocks Planning

Although it was the sense of urgency created by the 1955 flood that stimulated the planning for Tocks Island Dam and its sister projects, three other purposes—water supply, recreation, and power —were pursued simultaneously. This was in accord with the pre-

[a]E.M. Forster, *The Eternal Moment and other Stories* (London: Sidgewick and Jackson, 1928).

vailing view that water projects should be as "multipurpose" as possible. Moreover, the accelerating and seemingly endless growth visible on every hand could easily be seen as demanding water development of all kinds. Before long, each of the purposes acquired its own sense of urgency in the minds of the planners quite apart from the urgency of flood control.

The drought of the 1960s, which came just a few years after the eleven-volume House Document 522 was published, lent further urgency to the water supply purpose, which soon overshadowed flood control as the main concern of the politicians and planners. Even today, with the memories of both the flood and the drought considerably faded, water supply remains the dominant theme of the dam's supporters.

Two quite different analyses of water demand in support of the dam were undertaken. The first, done before the drought by the Corps of Engineers, is contained in House Document (H D) 522, Appendix P, published in 1960.[20] The second analysis was done eleven years later (1971) by the DRBC. In the intervening decade, changes in technology, changes in public attitudes, new political pressures, and changes in the DRBC's own perceptions produced a new water use picture. Thus the sources of demand included in the DRBC analysis were almost entirely different from those included in the earlier one done by the Corps. In spite of this difference the demands projected by the DRBC neatly absorbed just the amount of water that was to be provided by the Corps' reservoir system over the 50-year planning period.

Although finding demand to fit supply, rather than the other way around, may seem backwards in this context, it is not, in a larger sense, necessarily the wrong way to look at things. As the finite size of the earth makes itself felt, our perception of progress is beginning to change. We are beginning to see progress in the adaptation of demands (hence of life style) to the finite supplies offered by the earth rather than in endless growth of supplies to meet arbitrarily given demands. In a curious and certainly inadvertent way, the DRBC adopted the viewpoint of the conservationists.

Among the motives of the DRBC in reanalyzing demand may have been a desire to correct the errors in the Corps' original analysis. As we shall see, certain conceptual faults in this analysis rendered its results virtually meaningless. The DRBC largely corrected these faults. Very briefly, the procedure in HD 522 is the following: The basin is subdivided into "problem areas," in which water "requirements" are estimated separately. Then the yields of the various reservoirs are assigned to the different areas so that the requirements of the latter will be covered. All the yield of the Tocks Island reservoir is assigned to the problem area labeled "Trenton-Philadelphia."[21]

Within each problem area, requirements are broken down into four categories: (1) domestic and municipal, (2) self-supplied industrial, (3) agricultural, and (4) upstream surface losses. Requirements in the four categories are added together and the sum is compared to the minimum flow in the stream. The excess of the requirements over the minimum flow is called "required augmentation." Reservoir yields are assigned until their sum at least equals the "required augmentation."[22] It is not clear what conception of river flows inspired this calculation. The calculation can conceivably make sense only if "requirements" are somehow reduced to the flow *in the river* necessary to accommodate all the various contemplated uses. Because of the great variety of these uses and the complexity of their interactions, such a reduction to river flow is not simple and, in fact, was not done by the Corps.

The point is sufficiently illustrated by the Corps' treatment of the first category, "domestic and municipal" requirements. Except for a numerically minor adjustment, domestic and municipal requirements are set equal to the sum of all domestic and municipal withdrawals from the river. But the riverside communities put almost all the water they withdraw back into the river as waste water. Moreover, the points of withdrawal and discharge are distributed along a considerable stretch. The city of Trenton, for example, withdraws and discharges several miles above Philadelphia. The quantitative effects of the various withdrawals and discharges on the river's flow are at once complex and slight. They have no relationship whatever to the "required augmentation" calculated by the Corps.

In any case, the details of the Corps' calculation, which concerned only water quantity, are largely beside the point, because the real problem for Trenton and Philadelphia is not water quantity, but pollution. To be sure, augmentation of flow may have an effect on pollution control, but the effect is not simple. It depends, among other things, on the local patterns of mixing and diffusion, which in the Trenton-Philadelphia area are complicated by tidal oscillations. By pushing pollutants downstream, it is even possible for low-flow augmentation to worsen pollution at some places and times.

In Appendix C, prepared by the Public Health Service, House Document 522 does discuss water quality in some detail. With respect to low-flow augmentation the Health Service concludes the following:

> It was indicated above that an increase in fresh water flow to the estuary from the present minimum monthly of 2,610 cfs to a regulated minimum

of 4,060 cfs in 1980 will result in a relatively small increase in dissolved oxygen above the [Delaware] State line and an even smaller decrease in dissolved oxygen below the State line. Although it is anticipated that the quality of the estuary in 2010 will be somewhat less than at present, it is believed that the further increase in regulated flow from 4060 to 4720 will not result in a further significant increase in dissolved oxygen. Nor is it believed that the additional increase in fresh water inflow will significantly decrease further the dissolved oxygen levels below the State line. Further, it is not anticipated, then, that the increase in fresh water flow augmentation will change the dissolved oxygen levels in the estuary to such an extent that additional sewage treatment facilities can be deferred. As was pointed out in Part B, the quality of the estuary can be maintained at least at present levels only by substantial increases in waste treatment measures. Undoubtedly, the addition of low flow regulation will supplement the waste treatment programs, but it is estimated that the quality of the estuary will not be altered materially by the augmentation of low flows. A tangible monetary benefit can not therefore be ascribed to the increase in flow, although an intangible supplemental benefit should be recognized.[23]

It appears, then, that H D 522 did not provide any really clear and convincing uses for the prodigious quantities of water to be stored behind the Tocks Island Dam. In addition to the Trenton-Philadelphia water supply, H D 522 does mention briefly three other possible uses of Tocks water, but for various reasons it dismisses them as unimportant. It is precisely these three uses that dominate the DRBC's 1971 report.

A. Electric power plants. Power plants use enormous amounts of water for cooling. In the late 1950s, at the time H D 522 was being prepared, the standard cooling technique (called "once-through") was to withdraw water from a river, run it through the power plant's condensers, then discharge it back into the river. The Corps dismissed this water use "as imposing no specific demands on developments for augmenting stream flows since the return to the stream is equivalent in quantity and quality to the withdrawals in each instance of such use."[24] On close scrutiny, this seemingly obvious proposition turned out to be false. In passing through a typical condenser, the river's water is heated by about 20°. After discharge to the river, the water dissipates this heat in part by evaporating some of itself. Until the late 1960s, it was apparently not widely recognized that the water thus lost is appreciable.

In the meantime, another more serious side effect of once-through cooling came to light. Very large power plants created such large masses of heated water in the downstream stretch that fish could not escape, and some susceptible species were killed in large numbers. This effect, among others, forced the power companies to look for alternate methods of cooling. One commonly considered method evaporates water in huge hyperbolic towers. No hot effluent is discharged into the river, but evaporative losses are about twice as high as with the once-through method. Another technological change—the coming of nuclear power—threatened to drive the evaporative losses even higher. Because of their lower thermal efficiency, nuclear power plants generate in the condensers almost twice as much waste heat per useful kilowatt-hour as fossil plants; hence they must evaporate almost twice as much water (see Essay 7).

These two technical developments, each contributing almost a factor of two to water losses associated with power plants, occurred, or became prominent, during the decade following the publication of H D 522. Together with the apparently burgeoning demand for electricity, they created the raw material for truly horrendous projections of evaporative water consumption. Thus it came about that an element of water demand that was dismissed in one sentence by the Corps in 1960 played a major role in the analysis of the DRBC in 1971.

B. **Salinity Control.** Downstream from Philadelphia, the estuary becomes gradually saline. Water is considered unsuitable for drinking (i.e., salt can be tasted by some people) when the concentration of chloride ions exceeds 250 parts per million (ppm).[b] Therefore, one is especially interested in knowing the location of the boundary between water that is more and less saline than the 250 ppm standard. This boundary is often called the "critical isochlor" or "salt front," though the latter term is misleading since the salinity change is gradual. Tidal motion causes the critical isochlor (along with all its noncritical companions) to make daily excursions up and down the estuary. In addition, the volume of fresh water coming down the river influences the position of the isochlors. Spring floods drive them down the estuary; droughts allow them to creep upstream.

During the drought of the middle 1960s the critical isochlor reached the most upstream point of record and caused the authorities some concern that it might reach the Torresdale intake of the Philadelphia water system, or that saline water might seep into certain riverside wells used by the city of Camden. Emergency

---

[b]It is common practice to measure salinity by the chloride ion concentration. In seawater, the chloride ion concentration is 15,000 ppm. Most sea salt is sodium chloride.

releases of fresh water from upstream reservoirs were made in an effort to hold the salt back, and contingency plans for running Philadelphia's intake pipes upstream were drawn up. Although the 250 ppm isochlor was still ten miles downstream from Torresdale at its highest point, and the maximum salinity observed at Torresdale was about 50 ppm of chloride, the experience was felt by the DRBC and other water authorities as traumatic, and it strongly influenced their subsequent thinking.

Back in the days of H D 522, the dramatic image of salty water coursing through the Philadelphia mains seems to have been absent. H D 522 treats salinity control almost casually as a mere convenience for estuarine industry:

> Of particular interest to the water users in the tidal section of the Delaware River is the contribution that may be secured through the control of salinity. The salinity front, while not affecting sources of water currently being utilized for domestic supplies, continually poses treatment problems for water-using industries downstream from Eddystone in the Chester-Marcus Hook area.[25]

As we saw, salinity control was not an element in the Corps' 1960 calculation of "required augmentation." In the DRBC's 1971 analysis it constituted the largest single element.

C. Out-of-Basin Exports Within New Jersey. Of all the "golden numbers" associated with Tocks Island, perhaps the most golden of all is 300 mgd. The meaning attached to this number varies somewhat, but usually it is taken to be the amount of water northeastern New Jersey will some day have to import from the Delaware Basin. Most people profess ignorance of its origins, but some water resources officials claim that it goes back to the mid 1920s, which means that the famous number will soon be celebrating its fiftieth (or golden) anniversary.

Its true origins are somewhat obscure. The 300 mgd per se seems to go back only to about 1955, though its ancestry may well extend all the way back to the 1920s. One researcher, examining the question for the DRBC, found that reports from 1922 to 1955 consistently projected a diversion from the Delaware to northeastern New Jersey of about 400 mgd.[26] Apparently it became customary in water supply planning to supplement various reservoir schemes in northern New Jersey with a diversion from the Delaware of this amount, despite the varying projections of demand and advancing time horizons. How the 400 mgd got translated into 300 mgd is not clear, but it may have resulted from subtracting off the diversion through the Delaware and Raritan Canal, whose capacity is generally taken to be about 100 mgd.

In the 1955 TAMS report,[27] the Delaware and Raritan Canal diversion was indeed separated from a 300 mgd, which figured prominently in the conclusions. This latter figure, however, was not the amount of water northeastern New Jersey would have to import from the Delaware Basin, but was rather the amount northeastern New Jersey would need by the year 2000 from *all* new sources beyond what it could obtain by expansion of its existing sources. The report believed that the entire 300 mgd could be obtained from the interior of the state if necessary, though the plan preferred by TAMS provided for 100 mgd to be obtained from the Delaware and 200 mgd from the interior of New Jersey. According to the summary of the report given in H D 522:

> The final report on the [TAMS] survey stated that specific studies of surface and ground water resources show that there are sufficient potential water resources available to the State of New Jersey to provide for predictable needs. All of the State's water requirements to the year 2000 can be met entirely from resources within the boundaries of the State. These can be developed without interstate agreements, or approval of the Supreme Court of the United States. There are, however, economic advantages in using water from the interstate Delaware River to provide the additional supplies which will be needed in the State's Northeastern Region after 1966.[28]

In spite of the "economic advantages," the Corps did not include any exports to New Jersey in its demand projections, as we have seen. In fact, it regarded exports to New Jersey as outside the limits of its responsibility:

> Since diversions from the basin are authorized by the U.S. Supreme Court, it would be presumptive to project, for purposes of this investigation, diversions to satisfy, wholly or in part, the water needs in adjacent areas at designated dates in the future. Therefore, except for current diversions, the water uses of primary interest are those within the basin's boundaries. Furthermore, this approach was supported by the fact that local water resources and their capabilities to satisfy the water needs in the areas adjacent to the basin were beyond the scope of this investigation.[29]

Putting New Jersey beyond the scope of the investigation is particularly striking in light of the dominant role New York's diversions had played in the history of the Delaware Basin starting as far back as the court battle of 1930. The possibility of a New Jersey diversion was not entirely forgotten, however. After the comprehensive plan was set, the Corps simulated its operation on paper, applying water input data from the 1930–31 drought, and found the safe yield for the year 2010 to be 367 mgd higher than they had expected. This excess, they remark, could be drawn upon for diversions to Wilmington and northern New Jersey.[30] Though not entirely forgotten, northern New Jersey clearly had low priority in H D 522.

At the time of the preparation of H D 522, there was no controversy and the 300 mgd had not yet become a golden weapon. This role came later as the number was passed about among the adversaries in the ensuing controversy. In hearings it was repeatedly quoted by proponents of the project with authority and urgency, and was often associated with this or that deadline. So formidable did it become that opponents of the dam chose not to challenge it but instead expended great effort in devising schemes for diverting the golden 300 mgd from the Delaware without the Tocks Island Dam.[31] The State of New Jersey lent it official status by formally requesting permission of the DRBC to make the 300 mgd diversion some time in the future. To date, permission has been neither granted nor refused. By 1971, when the DRBC staff undertook its reanalysis of demand, the 300 mgd diversion had become so well established that the DRBC could confidently include it as a major element in demand without detailed justification, although privately emphasizing that its willingness to grant New Jersey's request could not be considered a foregone conclusion.

During 1975, as New Jersey officials prepared for the DRBC decision on Tocks that was to be made in August, water supply in the northeastern part of the state was uppermost in their minds. The main question was whether imported Delaware River water would really be needed.[c] Comparing the cost of transporting Delaware water to northeastern New Jersey with the cost of developing a series of local sources, the officials found, somewhat to their own surprise, that the former was higher. This discovery played a role in New Jersey's negative decision on Tocks in 1975 and, for the time being at least, it put the golden number on the shelf.

2. The DRBC Projections of 1971

It is not clear to what extent the DRBC's reanalysis was motivated by a desire to correct the faults in H D 522. Certainly these faults had been criticized many times, but there is little evidence that the

[c]For the political context of this story, see Essay 3.

criticism was of much concern to the dam's proponents. As late as 1971, in testimony submitted to a committee of the Pennsylvania legislature, the Corps included a verbatim copy of the key Table P-10 from H D 522, which summarizes the faulty calculation outlined above.[32]

Whatever the DRBC's motivation, its reanalysis did in fact correct the conceptual errors in HD 522. Instead of vaguely equating water withdrawals with water "use," it clearly specified depletive uses so that inputs and outputs could be treated in a consistent fashion.

The DRBC analysis is implicitly based on what might be called the "bathtub model:" The river from Montague to Trenton is seen simply as a tub with the sum of the inputs balanced against the sum of the outputs. Only water not returned is counted in the outputs. This of course, drastically reduces the amounts attributed to municipal use by Trenton and Philadelphia. The DRBC somewhat arbitrarily takes municipal losses (i.e., net consumptive use) to be 10 percent of withdrawals.

Although the bathtub model is adequate for many purposes, complications arise when the water is taken from the fresh-salt transition region. For some time the DRBC staff treated water evaporated from any location as a simple withdrawal from the bathtub:

> It is worth noting that the consumptive use of brackish water from the Tidal Delaware River and Bay, *no less than* consumptive use of fresh water, unless compensated by regulation of fresh water inflow during critical low flow periods, will result in greater concentration of sea salts in the estuary and upstream advance of any isochlor. [Emphasis added.][33]

This statement is not correct. Water evaporated from the saline part of the estuary has less effect on the upstream salt distribution than the evaporation of an equal amount of water from the fresh part of the river. The effect diminishes gradually with position downstream. There is, in fact, substantial conservation gained by moving power plants to the estuary. In 1974 the DRBC staff modified their excessively conservative position as a result of a consultant's study.[34]

The DRBC demand and supply projections are summarized in Figure 5–7. The figure brings out clearly the importance of the three depletive uses discussed above: electric power, exports, and salinity control. Without these, present capacity (no Tocks) is more than adequate well beyond the year 2000. Even including electric power and exports, present capacity serves until 2010. The really critical item, dwarfing all the rest, is salinity control. The salinity control

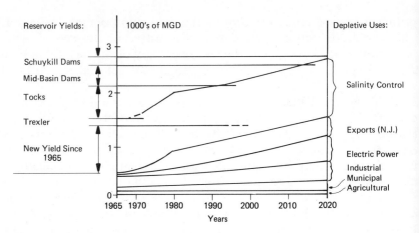

Figure 5-7. Water Demand and Supply as Given by the DRBC Staff Report of 1971.

This figure does not appear in the DRBC report but is derived from the data in the report. By "reservoir yield" the DRBC apparently means the amount by which the minimum flow at Trenton could have been increased during the worst drought year if the reservoir had existed. Unfortunately, this amount depends on how much other storage capacity is already there: the first increment of storage increases the minimum flow more than the second and so forth. Thus the first interval on the chart, "new yield since 1965," seems disproportionately large. Most of this interval represents the difference between the minimum flow at Montague now required by the Supreme Court decision and the actual minimum flow at Montague that occurred during the drought. The DRBC study assumes that the present minimum flow requirement would be met in a future drought.

layer in Figure 5-7, of more than 1,000 mgd, represents the *additional* margin of low flow, above that which occurred at the depth of the 1960s drought, that the DRBC wanted to have. The DRBC's water supply justification for the Tocks Island Dam rested heavily on the validity of this margin.

The DRBC's projection of water use for salinity control shown in Figure 5-7 was based on their minimum flow standard of 3,000 cfs at Trenton. This number had become firmly imbedded in the Tocks controversy and had assumed the typical golden hue. Skeptics of the dam tended to dismiss it out of hand with comments such as: "It was pulled out of a hat; they might as well have chosen 2,000 or 4,000," or: "They used 3,000 because they thought they were going to get the dam, and that's how much the dam could provide," or: "During the drought the flow was way below that and the salt never got anywhere near Philadelphia," or simply: "It's just a golden number." The DRBC defended the number as essential to both pollution and salinity control in the estuary, giving three specific reasons: (1) to protect Philadelphia's water supply from excessive salinity; (2) to protect the aquifers, particularly in Camden, that are recharged by the river, from excessive salinity; and (3) to maintain the waste assimilative capacity of the upper estuary.

The last reason is somewhat different from the other two. The DRBC's pollution control plan was based on mathematical modelling of the estuary done by the Delaware Estuary Comprehensive Study (DECS). The particular calculations supporting the DRBC's dissolved oxygen objectives assumed the 3,000 cfs minimum inflow at Trenton. The figure therefore became embedded in the pollution abatement program.

In principle, the purpose of maintaining a minimum flow is to provide a minimum degree of dilution of the river's pollution load. But dilution tends to be unsatisfactory for two reasons: first, because large amounts of clean water are usually needed to have much effect, and second, because the extent of the polluted water is increased in the same ratio that the concentration of pollutants is decreased. Congress, in its Water Resources Act of 1972, specifically forbade government agencies to substitute dilution for control of sources:

> In the survey or planning of any reservoir by the Corps of Engineers, Bureau of Reclamation, or other Federal agency, consideration shall be given to inclusion of storage for regulation of stream-flow, except that any such storage and water releases shall not be provided as a substitute for adequate treatment or other methods of controlling waste at the source.[35]

On the Delaware, the beneficial effects of dilution appeared to be small in any case. According to a 1966 report based on DECS work there is no improvement in the minimum level of dissolved oxygen when a steady inflow of 6,000 cfs is compared to the DRBC's 3,000 cfs. The effect of the increased flow is merely to move the oxygen sag downstream. At points downstream of the Philadelphia Navy Yard, the dissolved oxygen is actually reduced by the higher inflow (see Fig. 5—8).[d] Dilution was not, in fact, a large part of the DRBC's abatement program. This program depended primarily on reduction of effluents. In the minds of most people, and indeed in most DRBC documents, the dominant reason for the 3,000 cfs minimum was control of salinity.

In the context of salinity control, the 3,000 cfs had tended to assume an absoluteness that belied its true probabilistic nature. Since salinity is strongly related to fresh inflow, it can be stated more or less absolutely that maintenance of flow at Trenton above 3,000 cfs will keep the chloride concentration at the mouth of the Schuylkill

[d]This agrees essentially with the earlier HD 522 (see above, p. 193).

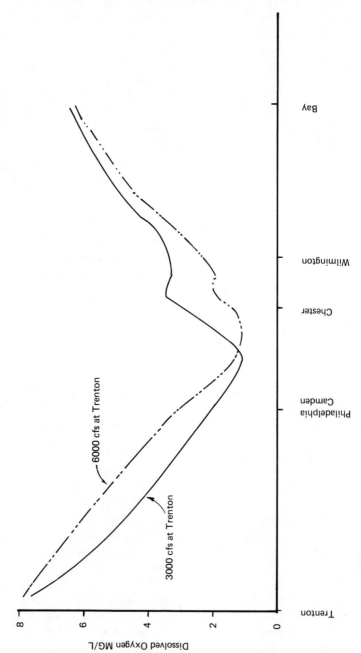

Figure 5-8.   Dissolved Oxygen for Different River Flows[36]

Oxygen is depleted by pollution. The oxygen "sag" below Philadelphia inhibits the migration of fish and thus affects aquatic life in the whole river. Adjustment of river flow affects mainly the position of the sag rather than its severity. To raise the minimum oxygen level significantly requires not more flow, but abatement of pollution sources.

River below the 250 ppm drinking water standard.[e] The absoluteness was reinforced by statements such as that made by a member of the DRBC staff: "We set the 3,000 cfs minimum because we want to be sure that salt *never, ever* gets into the Philadelphia system." As Robert Socolow observes in Essay 1: "Public discourse is dominated by solutions offered as risk free."

Despite the stout words of the DRBC staff, the 3,000 cfs standard is not absolute but probabilistic, and like all probabilistic standards it has an inevitable degree of arbitrariness. Moreover, it is not, despite appearances, a flow standard at all, but a *storage* standard. Its precise meaning is the following: it is the amount of reservoir storage required to maintain a minimum flow of 3,000 cfs at Trenton in an otherwise exact replay of the 1960s drought. Its guarantee, then, is not absolute: in the improbable event of a drought more severe than that of the 1960s the minimum flow at Trenton would be less than 3,000 cfs, and the chloride concentration at the mouth of the Schuylkill would presumably rise above 250 ppm. Thus the control of salinity by means of reservoir releases, like any other water use depending on finite storage, inevitably involves risk. And the level of risk that one deems to be acceptable or unacceptable is inevitably somewhat arbitrary.

Risk is always composed of two elements: (1) the nature and cost of the dreaded event, and (2) the probability of its occurrence. There are, therefore, two ways of dealing with risk: (1) by preparing to cope with the event if it should occur, and (2) by reducing the probability of its occurrence. If the event is taken to be the appearance of saline water high upstream, then the DRBC's proposal of providing reservoir water to hold it back is an example of the second way.

There is some arbitrariness in defining the dreaded event. One could, for example, define it to be the occurrence of a drought of given severity, or the actual contamination of water supplies, or some other event. The choice of definition affects the assignment of countermeasures to the categories (1) and (2) given above, but aside from this inessential semantic effect the choice is largely one of convenience. I will arbitrarily define a dreaded event to be the occurrence of salinity S at point P for duration T. Associated with each such event, i.e. with each triple (S,P,T) is a probability p. The risk is determined by the set of event-probability pairs, or, equivalently, by the function $p(S,P,T)$. Before turning to the probability side, let us consider the nature of the events and their consequences.

[e]This is only more or less absolute because factors other than inflow, such as wind, also have an effect.

A. **Philadelphia Water Supply.** One event of obvious interest is the occurrence of water containing 250 ppm of chloride at Philadelphia's Torresdale intake for a period of days or weeks. Water of this salinity can be approximated roughly by dropping a pinch of salt into a quart of pure water. What happens if the tap water gets that salty? According to a compendium of water quality criteria published by the State of California, "restrictions on chloride concentrations in drinking water are generally based on palatability rather than health."[37] Thresholds of taste, however, are apparently highly variable, as are other physiological effects. The California compendium lists the following reports for sodium chloride:

> ... taste threshold values from 200 to 900 mg/1[f] have been reported. Water containing more than 500 mg/1 of sodium chloride may be unpalatable and cause appetite disturbances. Although an excess of sodium chloride induces thirst or can act as a diuretic, water containing up to 1,410 mg/1 has been used by some communities for many years without appreciable harm; however, 1,000 to 1,500 mg/1 of sodium chloride generally renders water unpalatable. It has also been reported that 7,500 mg/1 of salt is harmless and that 10,000 mg/1 causes vomiting.

These figures presumably apply to healthy people. Heart and kidney patients on low salt diets have other requirements not based on taste. For water uses other than drinking, problems would arise at a wide variety of salinities, some at levels below 250 ppm, others only at much higher levels. Many of these would depend strongly on the duration of high salinity. Salinization of tap water, then, is far from a sharply defined disaster; on the contrary, it shades off gradually through a series of diverse problems from mere inconvenience to real disaster over a wide range of salinities and and durations. It is unlikely that this range is adequately represented by a single standard based on taste.

What are the real threats? To understand the nature of the event we are trying to deal with, we should examine each of the diverse problems in the series in its own right. And this should be done not only for sea salt, but also for soluble industrial substances, which, unlike sea salt, might *suddenly* appear in the river through some accident. How much does it cost to get pure water (or a substitute beverage) to people with special sensitivities or to feed fussy boilers in a pinch? We should know. The amounts of water needed for some

---

[f]One mg/l (milligram per liter of water) is the same as one ppm (part per million by weight). Because of the extra weight of the sodium, the drinking water standard, 250 ppm of chloride ion, is equivalent to about 400 mg/l of sodium chloride.

purposes, such as drinking, are miniscule compared to the whole supply.

Although Philadelphia has elaborate and effective plants for purifying the river water it uses, it lacks facilities for removing salts. As we saw above, desalting requires an expensive plant, and, for fundamental reasons, considerable energy. The energy required for dilute solutions such as 250 ppm of chloride or even 1,000 ppm, however, is much less than that required for sea water. One way Philadelphia could protect itself against salt would be to build a standby desalting plant. The probability of its being needed, even without Tocks, is so small, however, that this solution is unattractive. Much simpler alternatives are available in any case.

The salinity of tap water in Philadelphia would not necessarily be as high as that in the Delaware River. Philadelphia takes about half its water from the Schuylkill River, which is isolated from the Delaware estuary by a dam, and the water department is able to mix the water from the two sources. This mixing could provide a reduction in salinity by as much as a factor of two. It should be noted, however, that the Schuylkill has limited capacity. At one point during the 1960s drought the entire fresh flow was being taken so that no water at all went over the dam.

In 1950 an engineering firm, as part of one of the many Delaware development plans, proposed among other things an aqueduct running straight north from Philadelphia's Torresdale intake to a point just upstream of Trenton.[38] The purpose was not to avoid salt water, which was not considered a serious problem in those predrought days, but to avoid some of the manmade pollution in the lower part of the river. An alternative plan in the same report proposed a much longer aqueduct all the way to Wallpack Bend, some 70 miles away. An aqueduct to avoid salt water would not need to be as long as either of these.

A permanent aqueduct might not be necessary, however. During the drought, the Army Corps of Engineers made plans for constructing a temporary pipe of rubberized material stiffened by steel hoops to be submerged in the river itself. Fortunately, saline intrusion is not a sudden event, but one that develops gradually during the spring and summer, generally reaching its peak in the fall. In drought years the normal movement is merely exaggerated; thus there is time to undertake temporary construction, particularly if well prepared in advance. The temporary pipe has the economic advantage that much of its cost can be discounted by a factor depending on the probability of its being needed. Since this probability is very small, the discounting is heavy. To make a rational economic choice, one needs to compare the discounted cost of the temporary pipe with the cost of providing reservoir storage to achieve equivalent risks.

B. Ground Water in the Nearby Aquifers. From the vicinity of the Delaware estuary, where it is near the surface, the bedrock slopes gently downward to the southeast under southern New Jersey. It is overlain by a wedge-shaped series of unconsolidated strata that are saturated with water. The billions of gallons contained in these strata constitute by far the largest reservoir of ground water in the region. Virtually all the towns and industries along the New Jersey side of the river below Trenton take their water from wells.

Originally, the ground water, derived from precipitation, flowed out of the aquifers into the rivers and streams. In many places along the lower Delaware, however, pumping from nearby wells has reversed the gradient, causing water to flow from the river into the ground. Most of the water from wells very close to the river is in fact river water. Such wells are using the aquifer simply as a filter to remove some of the river's pollution. While the ground is very effective in removing bacterial and other suspended particles, it does not remove dissolved substances such as salt. The DRBC staff feared that if the river became saline, nearby wells would also.

Unfortunately, sea salt is not the only substance that passes through aquifers. Nitrates from septic systems and agriculture, as well as acids, metallic salts, some organic compounds, and other substances produced by industry all seep into the ground, forming blobs of contaminated ground water that slowly expand and drift down-gradient over periods of years or even decades. Nassau County on Long Island has recently issued bonds to construct a plant to remove the nitrates that have slowly accumulated in the ground water from the thousands of septic systems that dot the surface.[g]

Under southwest Philadelphia there is a blob of ground water several square miles in extent that is contaminated with sulphates. It is thought to have originated many decades ago with the dumping of sulphuric acid by a company that has long since gone out of business. But more recent accretions are thought to have occurred also. It is slowly expanding toward the south under the river and may ultimately pollute many wells in Camden. Chromium salts from within Camden itself forced the closing of a municipal well in January 1973. Other local spots of pollution have been discovered all up and down the heavily industrialized strip along the river. Camden is currently

[g]Removal of nitrates is essentially desalination, which, as we have seen, consumes a good deal of both capital and energy. Both of these are in short supply. Thus a technical fix of one problem aggravates another.

looking outside its city limits for new places to drill wells. As far back as 1955 the engineering firm TAMS,[39] in a comprehensive report on the Delaware Basin, suggested the possibility of running an aqueduct from Camden some 25 miles back into the pine barrens where water could be taken from the very large and still pure Cohansey aquifer.

Virtually all the wells within a few miles of the river draw from the Raritan-Magothy formation, which is near the surface there. It is this formation also which is suffering pollution under the industrial areas. Thus the possibility of saline intrusion into it from the river during a severe drought is only one of the threats to its purity—and by no means the most urgent. Protection of ground water from all sources of pollution should be given at least as much attention as the protection of surface water. But as one geologist remarked, ground water is not visible; you can't swim in it and you can't paddle a canoe in it. It is easy to ignore.

Drought induced saline intrusion from the river differs from most other ground water pollution in that it is temporary. During the 1960s drought, brackish water lay in the river for many days opposite nearby wells that were believed to draw much of their water from the river. Yet the well water did not become seriously brackish. In some cases the salinity rose temporarily, but only to a much lower level than that observed in the river. This was probably due to time averaging, which is explained in a USGS report with regard to a particular well as follows:[40]

> [T]he water reaching the well at any time is probably a composite of water that left the river at various earlier times over a period of as much as several months, depending on the length of flow paths over which individual particles of water traveled.

Such averaged water would be much less saline than that momentarily in the river.

In order to devise a rational plan for protecting the aquifers against the effects of drought, it would be necessary to determine how severe conditions would have to get—i.e., how saline the river would have to be for how long—before any wells would be seriously contaminated. More generally, one would need to know how many wells would be affected to what degree and for what period over a range of river conditions. Since actual conditions have never been severe enough to provide this information directly, it would have to be obtained by indirect means. The problem does not appear to be beyond the power of modern mathematical techniques.

The movement of ground water (along with any contaminants) is governed by the gradient of the head,[h] and this in turn is strongly influenced by the pattern of pumping from wells. By coordinating pumping rates at many wells over an extended area, it is possible to some degree to guide or stop the movement of contaminants. This technique is now used and will be needed increasingly to control industrial pollution.

In the case of temporary salt intrusion from the river, one has the additional parameter of time. To minimize the intrusion of saline water into the aquifer, one would want to minimize the gradient of head at the junction of river and aquifer during the period of high salinity. One might be able to do this, for example, by leaving nearby wells idle for some period ahead of time, replacing their yield with direct withdrawals from the river. During the idle period the aquifer would tend to fill and its gradients to diminish. Alternatively, inland wells could be substituted temporarily or permanently for those strongly connected to the river. As in the case of Philadelphia, the alternatives need to be examined quantitatively and their costs and risks compared to the costs and risks of salinity control by reservoir storage.

Let us turn now to the second element of risk—the probability that a dreaded event will occur. The probability of observing a drought of given severity in a randomly selected year is difficult to estimate. By definition, a "severe" drought is one whose like has rarely occurred, and about which, therefore, little is known. As with floods, one is faced with estimating the tail of a probability distribution with very little to go on. Moreover, human intervention (e.g., deforestation) may cause the probability distribution itself to change over time.

The severest drought of record in the Delaware Valley is that of the 1960s. According to an estimate made by TAMS, apparently conservative enough to justify positive language: "It is quite certain that the runoff in the driest year has a return period of at least 100 years and may increase to several hundred years in the lower reaches of the main river."[41] During this rare event, salty water reached higher up the river than had ever been recorded before, but it did not reach high enough or remain long enough to contaminate water supplies.

It is difficult to estimate how much rarer a drought it would have taken to actually cause contamination. In any case, the DRBC wished to provide a very large amount of reservoir storage—more

---

[h]"Head" at a point is the elevation to which water would rise in a well drilled at that point; "gradient of head" is the rate of change of head with position. Water moves in the direction of steepest downward gradient of head.

than all of Tocks, according to the DRBC's study (Fig. 5—7)—to reduce even further the probability of high salinity. In view of the already low probability and in view of the alternative means for dealing with salinity, the DRBC's proposal seems, on the face of it, excessively conservative and costly.

There is, however, in addition to the uncertianty of nature expressed in estimates of drought probabilities, a human uncertainty that needs to be taken account of. That is the uncertainty of New York City's behavior under the pressure of a water shortage. The Supreme Court decree requires New York City to maintain a certain minimum flow in the Delaware under all circumstances, but that is, despite its august auspices, only a human rule, which can be and has been broken by humans (see Essay 2). If one looks only at the map and the unbreakable rules of nature, then the direct conflict between New York and Philadelphia is clear. Any drop that New York takes is unavailable to rush down the river and help drive the salt from Philadelphia's door. During the 1960s drought the Supreme Court rule was temporarily suspended and the DRBC refereed the conflict by imposed compromises.

In the event of a severe drought, maintenance of a high minimum flow at Trenton, such as 3,000 cfs, might seem wasteful to competing water users, since it might mean sending several gallons of water down the river for each gallon protected. There is merit in policies that would tend to defuse such a conflict, and more particularly to decouple New York in a physical rather than a merely legal sense from Philadelphia, Camden, and other lower Delaware users. Displacement of Philadelphia's intake upstream, on either a permanent or a standby basis, management of the aquifers along the lower Delaware with conjunctive use of the river and nearby wells, provision by New York City for standby use of the Hudson all would have a decoupling effect.

3. The Consultants' Study of 1975[i]

Among the few pieces of new research done by the consultants who carried out the million-dollar study mandated by Congress in late 1974, was an attempt to estimate salt intrusion probabilities. This was undertaken largely through the efforts of an unusually ambitious and energetic young engineer name Charles Kohlhaas. The analysis made use of a sophisticated statistical technique on which Kohlhaas enlisted the aid of a respected expert, Michael Fiering of Harvard, with whom he had worked before.

[i]URS/Madigan-Praeger and Conklin-Rossant.

The results of the analysis were startlingly unfavorable to the dam, and appeared to constitute a major break for the opponents. Indeed, for a short while it appeared that a technical analysis, done at the eleventh hour, might decide the issue in a dramatic fashion, almost as if it had happened in the imagination of Walter Mitty. But in the end, the breakthrough did not occur after all, for reasons that shed light on the limitations of analysis in the pressure of controversy.

As noted above, the DRBC had set the absolute-sounding salinity standard of 250 ppm of chloride at the mouth of the Schuylkill, but had neglected to estimate the probability of its being violated. Moreover, there remained a substantial margin between this standard and actual salinization of important sources. The really pertinent information was the probability of actual damage of a given extent. And to determine this it was first necessary to find the probability of the occurence of salinity of given concentration, duration, and location along the river. It was to this question that Kohlhaas addressed himself.

The problem fell into two parts: first, finding the relation between river flows and the distribution of estuarine salinity, and second, estimating the probabilities of different river flow patterns. Putting the two parts together, one could estimate the probability that any specified salinity event would occur—for example, finding more than 250 ppm of chloride, the accepted maximum for drinking water, at Philadelphia's Torresdale intake.

A number of circumstances render the problem less straightforward than it might seem, most notably these: (1) the salinity distribution at any time depends not just on the momentary river flow at that time, but on the past pattern of flows extending back at least two or three months; (2) the historical record is not long enough to give a statistically adequate sample of the more unfavorable flow sequences that occur during droughts; (3) river flows are not determined entirely by nature, but in part by the human operation of tributary dams, both present and future. Although circumstances such as these complicated the analysis, they were by no means insurmountable.

The first part of the problem—the relation between flow and salinity—had been much studied, and although the available results were not in a form Kohlhaas could use, the tools were there. In fact, two different sets of tools were there, offering a fundamental choice of method. On the one hand there was a mathematical model of the estuary that expressed the governing physical mechanisms as differential equations; on the other hand there was a group of standard statistical techniques for establishing a purely empirical relationship between flow and salinity.

A similar choice confronts almost every analyst of a complex system. The first approach has the great conceptual advantage that it embodies the best theoretical understanding of the phenomenon being modeled and the great practical advantage that it is adaptable to hypothetical variants of the real situation or to parameter values outside the observed range. The second approach has the advantage that it reflects all the real world effects, including those that are necessarily neglected for the sake of simplicity in the mathematical-physical model. It often has the added advantage of being quick and simple to apply.

It is not difficult to cite cases in which either one of the approaches is better than the other. In the present case, in which the physics is well understood, there can be little doubt that the mathematical-physical model was the best for Kohlhaas's purpose,[j] and he did, in fact, prepare to use a computer version of a respected model of the Delaware estuary. But before these preparations were complete, he ran across some statistical work that convinced him that he could do the job more simply by means of a regression empirically relating past average flows at Trenton with measured salinities at the Torresdale intake.

This empirical relationship turned out to be a weak link in the argument. The difficulty was that significant amounts of sea salt had never really reached as high upstream as the Torresdale intake. It was therefore difficult to separate definitively the changes in salinity due to sea salt movement from changes in the background salinity due to varying pollution. Kohlhaas also used salinity observations at points downstream of Torresdale, where the sea salt effects were much larger, but it was difficult to extrapolate these results back upstream with sufficient confidence. This was a case where the practical advantage of the mathematical-physical model—its adaptability to hypothetical variants of the real situation (more extreme salinity events than had ever really occurred)—would have been especially helpful.

The second part of the job—estimating the probabilities of different river flow patterns—could not be done directly from the historical record because the record was too short and because future flow patterns would be influenced by future tributary or main stem dams. To solve this problem, Kohlhaas, in cooperation with Fiering

[j]For an opposite example, see Daniel Goodman's discussion of eutrophication models in Essay 9.

and with the aid of a computer, constructed a "synthetic streamflow sequence"that is, a sequence of numbers that had the same statistical characteristics as the sequence of historical natural flows and that conformed to the known behavior of river basins. Such a sequence, made sufficiently long, will in theory display all possible flow patterns of given length (say three months) with the right statistical frequency.

This sequence represented the natural flows as they would occur in the basin without dams. To get the effect of existing and possible dams, Kohlhaas ran the synthetic sequence through an existing computer model that can simulate any flow regulation scheme. When Kohlhaas put this together with his flow-salinity regressions, he found that the probability of even the most minimal salt intrusion in the Philadelphia-Camden area in any given year was only one in several hundred (the exact number depending upon the assumptions about upstream regulation), and further that the Tocks Island Dam would only reduce the probability moderately.

The opponents, needless to say, were jubilant. But the New Jersey state officials, who bore the burden of making a decision, were more cautious. Recognizing the potential importance of the result, they arranged for the DRBC to call a meeting of eminent hydrologists and others with a knowledge of the Delaware. For the reasons mentioned above, these experts were unwilling to accept Kohlhaas's relationship between Trenton stream flows and Torresdale salinity. Thus his startling results were largely nullified for political decision making.

This did not mean, however, that the experts thought that Kohlhaas's probability estimates were necessarily too low, only that they were not convincingly established. As one of them pointed out, the flows at Trenton in 1965 were not only below the DRBC standard of 3,000 cfs but in fact were below 2,000 cfs for several weeks without causing contamination of the Philadelphia and Camden water supplies. Moreover, the Kohlhaas-Fiering synthetic streamflow analysis assigned a very low probability to this flow event. That much could be said without the regressions.

The experts were unanimous in the view that a probabilistic streamflow model could and should be joined to the mathematical-physical model in order to obtain estimates of the probabilities of salinity events.[k] They agreed that Kohlhaas had identified and formulated an important question amenable to technical analysis. Thus Kohlhaas's energetic effort did achieve what rushed studies

[k]The DRBC has asked its staff to look into this. Another case of the fox guarding the chicken coop, though eminently logical according to the organization chart.

sometimes do: it forced a new question into the arena. This is not to say, of course, that the golden numbers (250 ppm at the mouth of the Schuylkill, or, more or less equivalently, 3,000 cfs at Trenton) will tarnish easily. Old hands among the dam's proponents were at pains to restore the gilt that Kohlhaas had temporarily knocked off. Said one: "The 250 ppm standard must be regarded as a fact of life."

Kohlhaas's effort did not achieve what rushed studies practically never achieve, namely the resolution of an outstanding question. Under the press of controversy, there never seems to be enough time to undertake the kind of sustained research that the resolution of issues usually requires. A most ironic instance was Tom Cahill's plea (in the McCormick Report on eutrophication) for the collection of nutrient data over several seasons. Since the Tocks decision seemed continuously imminent, it never seemed worthwhile to launch such a long term effort. Yet the decision remained hanging in part because of the missing data. Had the data collection been begun back in 1971, when Cahill recommended it, we would now be a long step ahead on the eutrophication issue.

The incident brought together in one room a group of scientists with intimate knowledge of the Delaware, and inevitably the discussion went beyond the narrow question at hand and raised the more basic one: How much do we *want* to deplete the river? The conservationists want to take as little additional water as possible (just as they want to pollute as little additional air as possible and pave over as little additional land as possible, etc.). Their opponents, the promoters of growth, want to take as *much* additional water as possible, with compensating releases from a dam.

The trouble is that the compensation is not complete, since it applies only to low flow: both the average flow and the variance of the fluctuations are necessarily reduced. The estuarine biologists among the experts were convinced that these effects could only be detrimental to the aquatic life. Inevitably, the issue came down to the costs and benefits of growth, or at least of conventional growth. The answer to the salinity question, if it were known, would set one of the terms of this trade-off.

NOTES

1. For a discussion of the economics of this sort of situation, see Coase, "The Problem of Social Cost," *Economics of the Environment,* ed. Robert Dorfman and Nancy Dorfman, (New York City: Norton, 1972), p. 100.

2. "The decision not to use the Hudson River was based on the poor quality of water in that source. As treatment processes could have been provided to

correct the quality deficiencies at far less cost than that of importing mountain water, it is reasonable to assume that a high value was placed on the esthetic quality of the more remote source." C.H.J. Hull, "Control of Raw Water Characteristics," Proceedings, 11th Sanitary Engineering Conference on Influence of Raw Water Characteristics on Treatment, University of Illinois, February 5, 6, 1969, p. 82.

3. *Ibid.*

4. Russell et al. *Drought and Water Supply, Implications of the Massachusetts Experience for Municipal Planning* (Baltimore: Johns Hopkins Press, 1970).

5. 1,400 gal/ton of steel vs. 35,000 gal/ton of steel. Ray K. Linsley and Jos. B. Franzini, *Water Resources Engineering*, 2nd ed. (New York: McGraw-Hill, 1972) p. 426. Presumably these figures represent net forward diversion.

6. Linsley and Franzini, *op. cit.*, p. 425.

7. A. C. Twort, *A Textbook of Water Supply*, (New York: American Elsevier, 1963).

8. Ultraflo Corp., Sandusky, Ohio.

9. Jack Hirshleifer, James C. De Haven, Jerome W. Milliman, *Water Supply, Economics, Technology and Policy*, (Chicago: University of Chicago Press, 1960), pp. 261–263.

10. Linsley and Franzini, *op. cit.*, p. 427.

11. Hirshleifer, et al., *op. cit.*, p. 264.

12. E.B. Weiss, "International Responses to Weather Modification," *International Organization* 29 (3) (Summer 1975): p. 805.

13. Appendix on Economic Analysis, prepared as part of Northeastern U.S. Water Supply Study (NEWS), Contract No. DACW-52-69-C0002, by the Institute of Public Administration, 55 W. 44th St., New York, pp. 30–31. This report, which is highly critical of conventional water resources planning, was not included in the published version of the NEWS study.

14. Clair Engle Plant, Calif.; see California Department of Water Resources, Bulletin #134–69, "Desalting State of the Art," June 1969. See also John Harte, Robert H. Socolow, *Patient Earth*, (New York: Holt, Rinehart & Winston, 1971), p. 174.

15. Northeast Desalting Team (B. Johnson, et al.), "Potentialities and Possibilities of Desalting for No. N.J. and N.Y.C.," February 1966, Clearinghouse for Federal Scientific and Technical Information, Dept. of Commerce, Springfield, Va. PB170568.

16. V.A. Koelzer, "Desalting," National Water Commission, National Technical Information Service, Dept. of Commerce, Springfield, Va. PB 209942.

17. John D. Bredehoeft and Robert A. Young, "Digital Computer Simulation for Solving Management Problems of Conjunctive Groundwater and Surface Water Systems," *Water Resources Research* 8 (3) (June 1972): p. 536.

18. *North Atlantic Regional Water Resources Study*, Appendix D, North Atlantic Division, U.S. Army Corps of Engineers, May 1972.

19. John D. Bredehoeft and Robert A. Young, "The Temporal Allocation of Groundwater—A Simulation Approach," *Water Resources Research* 6 (1) (February 1970): p. 5.

20. Appendix P, "Gross and Net Water Needs," *Delaware River Basin Report*, House Document 522, Vol. IX, 1960.

21. H D 522, vol. IX, Appendix P, Plate 17.

22. H D 522, vol. IX, Appendix P, Table P-10.

23. H D 522, vol. III, Appendix C, p. 230.

24. H D 522, vol. I, Main Report, p. 59.

25. H D 522, vol. I, Main Report, p. 51.

26. Memorandum from L.J. Warns to H.A. Howlett of the DRBC, dated April 2, 1974.

27. Survey of New Jersey Water Resources Development, for State of New Jersey, Legislative Commission on Water Supply, by Tippetts-Abbett-McCarthy-Stratton (TAMS), December 1955.

28. H D 522, vol. II, Appendix A, Exhibit C, p. 11.

29. H D 522, vol. I, Main Report, p. 49.

30. H D 522, vol. VI, Appendix M, p. M-96.

31. "New Jersey Water Supply, Alternatives to Tocks Island Reservoir," M. Disko Assoc. (West Orange, N.J., October 1973). See also, Smith Freeman, Edwin Mills, David Kinsman, "High Flow Skimming," Chapter 2 of *Papers in Support of a Free-flowing Delaware River*, Save-the-Delaware-Coalition, 1973.

32. Joint Legislative Air and Water Pollution Control and Conservation Committee, Hearing on Tocks Island Project, East Stroudsburg, Pa., October 28, 1971, pp. 4–6.

33. Draft Environmental Impact Statement for Newbold Island Generating Station, Atomic Energy Commission. Discussion prepared by DRBC staff for AEC.

34. Englesson, G. A., and Anderson, R. H., "The Impact of Consumptive Use of Water on the Salinity Distribution in the Delaware Estuary," United Engineers (Subsidiary of Raytheon Co.), June 1974.

35. Federal Water Pollution Control Act, Amendments of 1972, Public Law 92-500, Section 102 (b) (1).

36. Water Quality Control Study, Tocks Island Reservoir, Delaware River Basin, Federal Water Pollution Control Administration, Department of Interior (New York, June 1966), Figure VII-1.

37. J. E. McKee and H. W. Wolf, "Water Quality Criteria," California State Water Quality Control Board, Publication No. 3-A, 1963, 2d ed. p. 160.

38. Report on the Utilization of the Waters of the Delaware River Basin, for INCODEL, Malcolm Purnie Engineers–Albright and Friel, September 1950.

39. Survey of New Jersey Water Resources Development, *op. cit.*

40. Barksdale, et al., Groundwater Resources in the Tri-State Region adjacent to the Lower Delaware River, N.J. Div. of Water Policy and Supply, Special Report 13, 1958, p. 123.

41. *Water Resources Study for Power Systems*, Tippetts-Abbett-McCarthy-Stratton New York, March 1972.

Chapter 6

Floods and People

Allan S. Krass

On Friday night, June 10, 1972, a flash flood descended upon the city of Rapid City, South Dakota. At least 10% of the city's homes were destroyed with 235 people killed and over 5000 made homeless. The following quotes were obtained from residents of Rapid City by B. Drummond Ayers and published in the *New York Times* of June 13, 1972.

Frustrated by the lack of success [at pulling buried automobiles out of sand and gravel], Mr. [Dennis] Waltz fell to his knees in the muddy water and started clawing at the sand and rocks with his bare hands. "They say a woman and her baby are in one of these cars," he yelled over his shoulder.

* * *

"You know this is a terrible thing to be involved in, but since I've been in the [National] Guard, this is the first time I've ever felt I was doing anything worthwhile."—National Guard private

* * *

"We're down on our hands and knees like animals. I've had enough of the smell of death in this awful, awful mire."—Rapid City housewife

* * *

"It's unbelievable. Everybody is pitching in, giving us more equipment and help than we know what to do with. I've done construction work all over the world but I've never seen people like the folks in Rapid City."
—State Highway Department employee

I. THE URGE TO CONTROL

Most people have a reasonably clear image of what is meant by the phrase "natural disaster." Under this rubric we usually include earthquakes, forest fires, hurricanes, tornadoes, and floods. The pejorative connotation of the word "disaster" used in this context is very potent, and society's image of these natural events has been formed over a period of some five thousand years, since human beings first organized themselves into large, complex, urban societies.

It does not take a great deal of thought to recognize that these events are "disasters" only to the extent that they interfere with the aspirations and tranquility of human societies. An earthquake is a disaster in San Francisco or Anchorage but is little more than a curiosity along the sparsely populated coast of Baja California. A brush fire is a disaster in the hills above Los Angeles but provides an ecological service to a redwood forest by periodically burning away accumulated underbrush and saving the large trees from really serious fires.

A flood is somewhat like a forest fire in this respect. Periodic flooding of a river serves to bring beneficial deposits of sediment to the flood plain and to clear away accumulated debris in the channel. There is now good evidence that the river and its flood plain form an interdependent ecosystem and that the prevention of floods and augmentation of low flows may distort and oversimplify the river's ecosystem and possibly do it irreversible damage. However, it is difficult for normal people to keep this subtle, ecological principle in mind when entire cities are inundated by floods causing hundreds of millions of dollars in damage or when, for example, vacationers, most of them children, are swept away and killed, as they were by the raging flood waters of Brodhead Creek near Stroudsburg, Pennsylvania, in 1955. (The story of the 1955 flood is told in Essay 2.)

The loss of homes, jobs, or possibly even of loved ones and friends in a flood can cause severe psychological and emotional damage to people. Noticeable increases in divorce and suicide occurred in the aftermath of the great spring floods on the Mississippi River in 1973,[1] and some of these same effects were noted after the Rapid City, South Dakota disaster in 1972. At the same time other observers have noted the tendency for people to draw together in mutual aid and sympathy when such disasters strike, and there are many inspiring stories of courage and strength that renew one's faith in human resourcefulness. In no way do I wish to make light of these effects. Nevertheless, it is clear that floods are disasters only because people choose to live, work, or play on flood plains. They do so for very old reasons: the river is a source of food, drinking water, and water for irrigation; it is a transportation route, a recreation area, and, of course, a sewer.

There was a time, before the great technological civilizations of the Bronze Age, when the human response to the periodic flooding of rivers was primarily adaptive. The flood plain was kept extremely fertile by the floods, and the neolithic societies which farmed the flood plains learned to predict the floods and move to high ground to avoid them, returning to their farms as the waters receded. There are many areas in the world, including the United States, in which this kind of behavior still goes on to some degree.

But as human technological capabilities grew and as civilizations became increasingly urbanized and specialized, this kind of adaptive behavior became less and less convenient, and the motivations toward controlling and managing the flood cycle for human benefit grew apace. The Egyptians and Sumerians devised and constructed elaborate flood control and irrigation projects, whose purpose was to maximize the benefits and minimize the costs of the yearly flood cycle.[2] As a result of these projects, great cities were built on the flood plains of the Nile or the Tigris-Euphrates, and, as has occurred with every flood plain development since that time, these cities must have occasionally suffered severe damage in those years when the flood discharge exceeded the design capabilities of the control works. One can even speculate that the biblical story of Noah may have originated in what might now be called the "1,000-year" flood of the Tigris and Euphrates Rivers.[3]

One might reasonably expect modern societies, with this 5,000-year backlog of bitter experience, to approach flood plain development with considerable caution and to demonstrate a healthy respect for the river and the awesome and unpredictable devastation of which is capable. In "primitive" cultures such respect is often expressed in worship, in which the river is a god, to be placated and appeased rather than challenged and manipulated. But "civilization" has repudiated belief in such natural deities and has substituted instead a belief in its own technological omnipotence. The enormous economic benefits to be derived from exploitation of the river and its flood plain have led to a chronic shortness of memory and what dramatists might call a willing suspension of disbelief in the efficacy of flood control technologies.

In the United States the flood control problem has evolved with the parallel growth of agriculture and urbanization. The conversion of vast areas of highly water retentive forest to easily eroded farm-land has caused large increases in the ratio of runoff to infiltration in most major drainage basins. At the same time cities on downstream flood plains have grown rapidly, placing an ever increasing number of people in the direct path of flood discharges. And through it all the few voices warning that flood plain development should be controlled have been overwhelmed by the far greater number of voices demanding that the floods be controlled instead.

Engineers who build dams take great pride in their accomplishments. Their dams are usually designed with great care and with large margins for safety, and, as a result, the failure rate in the United States has been very small.[3] The desire to build spectacular, enduring, and socially beneficial projects is a very human one and one that gives the agency responsible for construction a powerful motivation to advocate the building of large dams. One ought not to be too critical of these motivations, especially in the light of our entire society's preoccupation with spectacular technological feats.

The excitement and awe inspired by a great dam is captured well in this selection from *Rivers in Harness* by Allan H. Cullen:

> [Hoover] Dam's hydroelectric facilities are open for inspection. First you can look out at Lake Mead and see the four intake towers, 390 feet high, jutting into the lake. Then you can descend, in an elevator that goes right down through the heart of the dam, and visit the powerhouses. The elevator ride is somehow a disturbing one, for you know that leaping, straining masses of water are only a matter of yards from you. You feel a sense of apprehension at the fragility of man and his works. But it gives way, as you continue to descend, to a new feeling of exhilaration and confidence, as you realize that the dam will protect you after all. You feel sudden wonder at the knowledge that small weak creatures very much like yourself somehow succeeded in damming this potent river. By the time you reach the bottom of the shaft, you feel like a giant, holding back the rush of water yourself with one contemptuously outstretched hand![4]

It would be difficult to find very many engineers who would express these feelings, as Mr. Cullen has, in such openly emotional terms. Most engineers are not given to this kind of hyperbole. One senses, however, that these feelings must exist in even the most outwardly reserved of dam builders. But it would be unfair to attach too much importance to these subjective motivations. The building of big dams has for many years been seen as a socially useful and laudable activity by all but a small minority of our society. The majority emphasizes the role of a dam in protecting life and property and its

[a]The Washington office of the Corps of Engineers claims that there has never been a failure of a Corps constructed dam and that there have been no major levee failures.

contribution to the economic growth and well-being of the river basin in which it is built.

As discussed much more fully in Essay 4, only a dam's role in protecting property is quantified in the conventional benefit-cost analyses performed by the water resources professionals. The benefits from lives saved and from disruption and anguish avoided are treated as "intangibles," incapable of being quantified in dollar terms in any satisfactory way. The benefits from promoting regional development are not included in benefit-cost analyses because these benefits typically occur beyond the project's boundaries and also because the economist worries that development in one region may occur at the expense of development in another, with no net benefit in "national income" accounts.

Yet it is clear that both a dam's role in reducing the toll on human beings and its role in promoting regional development loom large in the decision to build it, far larger than does its role in protecting property.[b] In the case of the Delaware Valley, everyone who has ever read the heartbreaking story of the 37 people who were killed at Camp Davis in 1955 finds it unforgettable and wants to have something done to prevent a recurrence of such a tragedy.[c] And anyone who has watched the debate over the decision to build the Tocks Island Dam knows that among the strongest supporters of the dam are the labor unions, who see in the control of the Delaware River a major spur to new jobs. Their position was well captured in the Corps of Engineers' basic report on the valley back in 1958:

> Whether or not this region can achieve the high level of economy projected for it over the next half century will depend on the favorable operation of a highly complex set of factors. The historical and projected levels of economic development show that a potential for major expansion already exists within the region as well as for the country as a whole. One factor upon which the service area will rely to sustain and nourish its growth will be the reasonable exploitation of its water resources.[5]

Over the twenty years since the great floods took place, memories of these floods have been slowly fading. In order to help reinforce these memories the Corps conducted a study of Hurricane Agnes,

[b]The most recent cost-benefit study done by the Corps of Engineers for the Tocks Island Dam project states that flood control will provide only about 13 per cent of the annual benefits to be gained from construction of the dam (see Essay 4, Table 4-1, p. 128)

[c]As explained in more detail in Essay 2, Camp Davis is located on a tributary that enters the Delaware just below Tocks Island. The proposed dam would have had no effect on that tributary.

which struck eastern Pennsylvania in 1972 and caused severe flood damages. The Corps made an estimate of the flood damages that would have resulted had Agnes centered over the upper Delaware Valley instead of over the Susquehanna Basin and estimated that Agnes would have caused about $190 million in damage in New Jersey and Pennsylvania. Then the Corps went one step further and calculated that about 80 percent of this hypothetical damage would have been prevented by the hypothetical Tocks Island Dam. That the Corps saw fit to publicize this report and give it wide circulation among responsible officials in the Delaware Valley lends further support to the assertion that flood control has played a role in the dam's promotion far in excess of its purely quantitative importance.

In the next two sections I concentrate on the quantitative tools used by the water professionals to describe floods and the damage they do to property. Any participant in a controversy about flood control is at a disadvantage if he or she has no familiarity with the concepts in use, and the important concepts are considerably less difficult than I had first thought. (There are no introductory science textbooks on floods that I am aware of.) Section II explains how one can estimate the amount of flooding associated with a storm, given its location and intensity. Probabilistic aspects of calculations of flood damage, derived of necessity from statistical treatment of the historical records, are discussed in section III. The two sections contain the essential ideas that lie behind the dollar figure for flood damage that gets reported in a benefit-cost analysis. Section IV describes some nonstructural alternatives to dams that offer protection, in varying degrees, against the monetary and human toll of floods. And in section V, I take a try at sorting out what seems to be at stake in choosing between structural and nonstructural approaches to flood control.

II. HOW DO FLOODS HAPPEN?

A flood is a dramatic manifestation of a very simple physical principle—the conservation of water. In order to illustrate this in a quantitative way let us consider a highly simplified model of a river drainage basin and ask what happens to the rainwater during and after a heavy rainstorm.

Let us choose a moderately sized basin of area 1,000 square miles. If it is roughly circular in shape it would have a diameter of about 36 miles. Examples of basins of this size in the Delaware Valley are the Lehigh River basin above Bethlehem, Pennsylvania (1,279 square miles) and the Schuylkill River basin above Pottstown, Pennsylvania

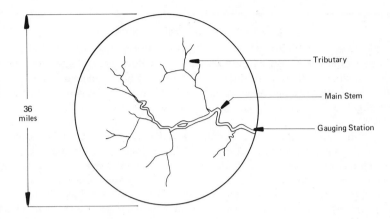

36
miles

Tributary

Main Stem

Gauging Station

Figure 6-1. A Model Basin — Perfectly Circular

(1,147 square miles). Next let us suppose that a rainstorm complete-ly covers this area and drops four inches of rain uniformly onto the basin during a period of five hours. We can easily compute the total amount of rain that falls on the basin by multiplying the rain's depth by the basin's area, and we obtain a total of 9.3 billion cubic feet of water. The average rate at which it fell is obtained by dividing by the duration of the storm (five hours) and this rate is called the *intensity* of the storm. In our example the intensity is 0.8 inches per hour, which yields for the whole basin 516,000 cubic feet per second (cfs).[d]

We have obviously chosen a very simple storm pattern, and it should not surprise the reader to learn that real storms are a great deal more complicated than this. One real storm, which figures prominently in the planning for flood control in the Delaware Valley, is discussed in Box 1 below.

Hydrology textbooks characterize storms by three quantities: intensity, duration, and area. The complex structure of a real storm is usually smoothed out by averaging all of these quantities over the area under consideration, usually a particular drainage basin. If the basin is small this averaging is a reasonable technique, but for very large basins taking an overall basin average can obscure important local effects. To avoid substantial errors, the big basin must be broken into smaller basins.

Four things can happen to the rain: (1) it can infiltrate into the soil, (2) it can be stored on the surface in puddles and ponds, (3) it

[d] A useful conversion factor in this type of calculation is one inch per hour = 645 cfs per square mile.

Box 1   The Basin Project Storm

Figure 6–2 is a picture of the "basin project storm" used by the Corps of Engineers in the design of the Delaware Basin flood control system.[1] The general shape and rainfall values of this storm are based on an actual storm that occurred over the Basin in May of 1942. It is a reasonable prototype of the kind of large, severe storm which can occur over the Delaware Basin.

The lines of constant total rainfall are called *isohyetal* lines (iso = same, hyetos = rain) and these are obtained by connecting all rainfall gauges which record the same total rainfall. In 1958, when the report was written, there were 153 official rain gauges in the basin. This averages out to about 80 square miles per gauge, which means that local variations in rainfall patterns of a smaller scale than this cannot be detected. So the isohyetal pattern which is plotted for any given storm is only an approximation of the gross features of the storm.

The rainfall depths, which are shown on the map, are total depths and therefore, unless we know something about the duration of the storm, we cannot obtain the intensities along the isohyets. Intensity is as important as total depth, because the faster the rain falls, the less the ability of the ground to soak it up. A given depth of rainfall produces more total runoff if it falls in a short period than if it falls over a long period.

A second variable absent from the map is the direction of motion of the storm over the basin. A storm that moves *down* a river basin piles the runoff water upon itself, and increases the severity of the flooding, relative to the flooding that would result from the same storm hovering over the basin. Although we assume there is no such nonuniformity of rainfall pattern over time in our model storm, the avid reader may want to enlarge the treatment in Appendix 1 to this Essay, to incorporate this potentiality.

The central role of the "basin project storm" in water resource planning should give us pause. If one concentrates on designing structures to meet one single threat, in what sense can one claim to be optimizing the basin's ability to withstand the variety of storms that will in fact occur? The basin project storm, although clearly a convenient mechanism to force some reality on planning, can be a dangerous concept if given too much emphasis. With high speed computers it becomes at least conceivable to try to optimize a basin's flood control strategy relative to a variety of threats, each with some associated probability of occurrence, and thereby to avoid the pitfalls of designing defenses against a single form of attack.

1. Taken from House Document 522, U.S. Army Corps of Engineers, Delaware River Basin Report, vol. 6, Appendix M, Plate #70.

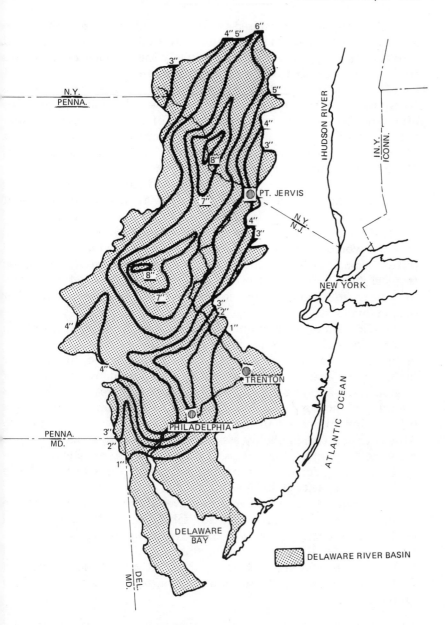

Figure 6-2. Basin Project Storm. (Contours show inches of rainfall.)

can evaporate or be transpired back into the atmosphere through the leaves of plants, and (4) it can run off over the surface of the ground into the stream system of the basin. Only the last factor contributes to flooding; the first three contribute to reducing the amount of runoff. Of these three the least important in a large storm is evapotranspiration, which takes place too slowly to have any appreciable effect on the runoff during the hours of a single storm. Evapotranspiration is important, however, in considerations of long term water balances, since losses due to this mechanism can, and often do, exceed total runoff over the period of a year.

The ability of the ground to absorb and store water is called its infiltration capacity, and it is usually given in units of inches of rainfall per hour that can be absorbed.[e] Infiltration capacity is a very strong function of the nature of the soil and ground cover. At one extreme would be a shopping center parking lot, which has an infiltration capacity of zero, and at the other extreme would be a dense tropical rain forest with several distinct layers of vegetation overhanging a soft, spongy soil covered with fallen leaves and other organic material.

We will assume that our model basin has an average infiltration capacity of 0.15 inches per hour during the storm we have postulated. This is a number typical of the Lehigh and Schuykill river basins in the regions mention earlier, as reported by the Corps of Engineers in H D 522. In our sample storm, where rain falls at 0.8 inches per hour, the infiltration and storage are holding back 0.15/0.8 or 19 percent of the rain from participating in the runoff. Note that we have implicitly assumed that the infiltration capacity is constant during the storm. This assumption is often made in hydrologic modeling, for the sake of simplicity, but it is a weak one: the infiltration capacity is lowered drastically if the ground has already been saturated by a previous storm; even during a single storm the infiltration capacity drops as the soil saturates, and therefore rainfall of a given intensity is far more effective at producing runoff at the end of a storm than at the beginning. Any flood prediction model that aspires to reasonable accuracy must incorporate sufficient data on the properties of soil and ground cover to take these factors into account.[f]

[e]It is customary to lump surface storage and infiltration capacity together for the purpose of runoff calculations. Water stored on the surface eventually either infiltrates or evaporates, but this is clearly irrelevant in flood calculations.

[f]Responsibility for the acquisition of such data in the United States rests with the weather service.

Now let us follow the runoff, starting when the storm begins and continuing until long after it stops. If we keep track of the discharge at the mouth of the basin, we will see it first grow and then diminish. We are able to work out a complete description of the runoff for our model basin if we assume that the runoff travels down the basin at a constant average velocity. A typical average velocity for sluggish basins is about 0.5 miles per hour and for flashy basins is about 1.5 miles per hour. We choose an intermediate velocity, such that a drop of water will travel a distance equal to the radius of our basin (eighteen miles) in twenty hours; its velocity is 0.9 mph.

A graph of water flow versus time for any single point on a river is called a hydrograph, and it is one of the standard tools of the professionals who assess the relationship between storms and flood damage. The hydrograph of the flow at the mouth of our model basin for our model storm is shown in Figure 6-3. It has the general features of hydrographs measured at real gauging stations following real storms. The essential features of the hydrograph can be deduced from a relatively simple geometric model, and this is presented in Appendix A.

The principle of conservation of water tells us that the area under the discharge curve must equal the total runoff. Since the area under the curve is fixed, it is obvious that a flashy basin that discharges all the water very rapidly must have a hydrograph with a very high peak discharge. In Figure 6-4 a hydrograph for a flashy basin with a sixteen-hour lag time is superimposed on the more typical hydrograph from Figure 6-3. One sees that a given rainstorm will produce a far more serious flood in a flashy basin. Some of the small tributaries of the Delaware, like Brodhead Creek, lie in flashy basins. It was on Brodhead Creek, during Hurricane Diane in 1955, that the water level at Camp Davis rose some 25 feet in about one-half hour and swept 37 people to their deaths.

If we choose our stream to be 250 yards wide at the gauging station, assume that the water is flowing by at a rate of about 5 mph (7.5 feet/second), and assume that the banks rise vertically at the edge of the stream (so that the width of the stream is fixed), we can compute how much the river will rise when the peak discharge of 75,000 cfs comes past. (We simply divide the total discharge by the width and by the average velocity.) The result is a rise of 13.3 feet in the river at the mouth of the basin.

Notice what happens if we assume no infiltration capacity for the basin. (This situation could arise if the storm we are considering followed closely upon the heels of a previous storm which had

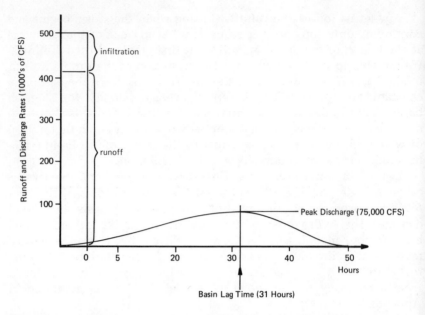

Figure 6-3. Hydrograph for a Five-Hour Storm at the Edge of a Circular Basin

saturated the ground, as happened in the Delaware Basin in 1955.) A total absence of infiltration would mean 19 percent more water appearing as runoff, so that all points on the hydrograph would have to be raised by 19 percent. This would give a peak discharge of 89,250 cfs and a maximum depth of 15.8 feet, an increase of 2.5 feet in gauge height. It is usually unrealistic to assume that the river will stay within vertical banks while it rises thirteen to sixteen feet above its normal gauge height. However, this is the situation if levees or dikes are in place, and thus we see how engineers go about determining how high dikes should be built. They use the information we have so far analyzed plus one other important datum, the frequency with which floods of this magnitude are expected to occur. This important step is probably the weakest link in the entire chain, and we will return to analyze it in more detail in the next section.[g]

If there are no local flood protection works and the river is not in a

---

[g]The flood we have just calculated would be classified by the Corps of Engineers (using 1956 data) as a 35-year flood on the Lehigh River at Bethlehem, Pa. and about a 200-year flood at Pottstown on the Schuylkill. If we assume zero infiltration capacity in the Lehigh basin then the 89,000 cfs discharge is equivalent to a 70-year instead of a 35-year flood. (An N-year flood is a flood whose severity is expected to be exceeded once in N years.)

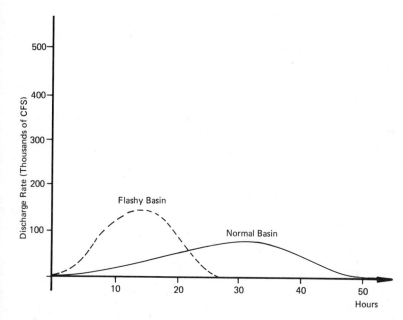

Figure 6-4. Hydrograph for a flashy basin superimposed on the hydrograph from Figure 6-3. Because the runoff has to flow out of the basin eventually, the areas under both hydrographs are equal to the area of the runoff rectangle (Figure 6-3). The flashy basin produces higher floods, sooner after the storm, but of shorter duration.

deep channel, the river will spill over its banks and spread the excess discharge over a larger area. This larger area, whose boundary varies with the discharge, is called the flood plain, and it is here that flood damage occurs if humans have built structures or planted crops close to the river. When the water spreads out over the flood plain, its velocity generally decreases. Relative to vertical banks, moreover, its depth does not increase nearly so rapidly with increasing discharge because the width of the effective stream bed keeps growing.

For any given point on a stream it is possible to plot a curve, called a *stage-discharge* relation, which displays the stage (depth) of the river corresponding to any value of its flow; in particular, this curve allows the peak stage to be predicted if the peak discharge is known. The stage-discharge curve is more or less constant over time, being determined essentially by the topography of the river bed and flood plain; it evidently can be altered rapidly by the passage of very high discharges or slowly with sediment accumulation. The stage-discharge relation is very difficult to derive from first principles, and it is determined empirically, for any fixed location along a river, using topographic maps and devices that can monitor the instantaneous flow velocity of the water. In order to predict flood stages at all significant points on a river, one generally needs a great many stage-discharge relations, and this implies a very substantial data acquisition program.

When the river overflows its banks there is not only a substantial decrease in the average flow velocity but also a substantial increase in the effective surface storage. Both consequences are highly beneficial for points downstream, because the warning times in the basin are increased and the effective storage-infiltration rate is also increased. Conversely, local flood control works (such as channel straightening, levees, and dikes) often have just the opposite effects and make downstream locations more susceptible to flooding than they were before. Furthermore, if a levee ever is overtopped, it becomes downright harmful, since it prevents the flood waters from draining back into the stream bed when the stage falls.

Let us now use the model drainage basin we have been analyzing to show how a dam will reduce flooding downstream. We build our dam at the point where we have calculated the hydrograph in Figure 6–3, and we embed our model basin within a larger basin. Downstream of the dam, at the mouth of the larger basin, we place a city (see Fig. 6–5). At the location of our city the river has been swollen by the addition of water from other tributaries downstream of the dam, so that the 75,000 cfs peak discharge that passes the dam site is only a fraction of the expected peak discharge at the city. Just how large this fraction is will be determined by the dimensions in space and time of the storm and its location over the larger basin. This is why it is impossible to make any general statements about the downstream effects of the dam. For any particular storm, the analyses performed for each subbasin may be combined, in what is called a routing study.

We will assume that the storm we have used so far forms a portion of some larger storm over the basin above the city, and that a routing study of this storm has shown that flooding at the city can be held to acceptable levels if the peak discharge at the dam can be held below 20,000 cfs. (Not only is the magnitude of the peak important ordinarily, but so is its timing; the inclusion of time dependent effects requires a full routing study.) This requirement is enough to tell us the short term storage capacity that must be allowed for. Referring to Figure 6–6 we can see that the required short term storage capacity, represented by the shaded area, reflects the difference between the discharge expected from the project storm in

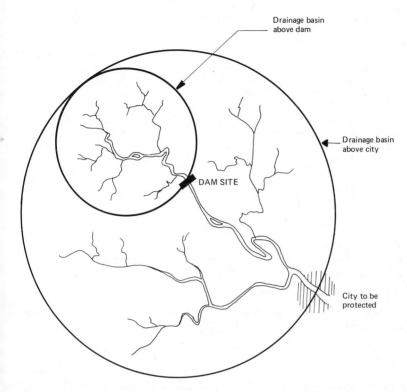

Figure 6-5. The drainage basin of Figure 6-1 embedded in a larger basin, and a dam placed where the gauging station was.

the absence of a dam and the discharge permissible with the dam in place. The stored water continues to flow out of the reservoir considerably beyond the time when the river, in the absence of a dam, would have fallen back to its base flow. In this way the natural discharge in excess of 20,000 cfs is spread out over a longer time and made harmless.

Either from the formulas in Appendix A, or by graphical methods applied directly to Figure 6–6, one may verify that the short term storage capacity of our dam must be about three billion cubic feet, or 69,000 acre feet. This much water would create a lake with an average depth of twenty feet and a surface area of 3,450 acres or 5.4 square miles. If this water is now discharged at 20,000 cfs the flow must be maintained for about another 40 hours, as seen in Figure 6-6.

In Appendix A, the Tocks Island Dam is subjected to a similar analysis, and, indeed, the required storage capacity calculated by the

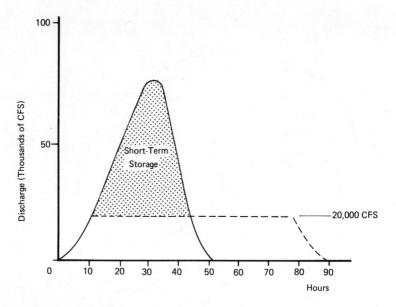

Figure 6-6. A dam delays the flow. The solid curve is the same as the hydrograph in Figure 6-3 (rescaled). The dashed curve shows the flow past the dam when the maximum flow is constrained to be 20,000 cfs.

Corps of Engineers is found from a few simple properties of the drainage basin. Thus, simple models have a certain usefulness in gaining intuition about how floods arise and about how big they get. But the reader should not be unduly impressed with such drastically oversimplified models—predicting floods from real rainstorms is far from a simple process. There are a great many complications that can arise in a real flood, such as sudden local fluctuations in rainfall or in infiltration rates, that make prediction far more difficult in practice than in theory. These difficulties increase rapidly as the size of the basin increases.

III. PREDICTING ANNUAL FLOOD DAMAGES

The techniques used in the previous section are necessary in the development of an accurate flood prediction program, but they do not nearly suffice to decide whether it is worthwhile to build a flood control dam on a particular river. One clearly must know something about how often and with what severity floods occur on the river and what damages can be expected from these floods. Such information is used to quantify the annual dollar benefits from flood control associated with the building of the dam in the benefit-cost analyses that are the subject of Essay 4. In this section I outline how these benefits are conventionally calculated; some further details are found in Appendix B to this Essay.

If next year a flood causing one million dollars worth of damage had one chance in ten of occurring, and a flood causing five million dollars worth of damage had one chance in one hundred of occurring, the expected value of the damage for the year would be $150,000.[h] More generally, if we know the numerical probability associated with every possible level of damage to a basin from flooding, we can calculate the expected value of the damage in an analogous fashion. The art of producing damage-frequency curves, which contain just these probabilities, proceeds in three steps.

1. Discharge-Frequency Relations. The historical record of large floods is restated mathematically so that every value of peak discharge from a future storm has an associated probability. Actually, one conventionally plots not the probability that a flow of given magnitude will occur, but the probability that a flow of a given magnitude will be exceeded (the exceedence frequency), during any year-long interval.

2. Stage-Discharge Relations. As discussed in the previous section, the topography and soil characteristics of a basin, as well as the historical records of floods, are used to associate a given peak discharge with a given "stage" or height of the river.

3. Damage-Stage Relations. The physical structures in the flood plain are surveyed, and the dollar damage each can be expected to sustain when the river is at various heights is estimated. The possible appreciation or depreciation in the value of these structures over time, and the possibility that new structures will be built, are handled separately.

The first step is the most difficult and unreliable. There is almost by definition no reliable way to determine the frequency of rare events, and it is just the rarest (and most damaging) events that are most important.

Typical graphs for each of the three steps are presented in Figures

[h]$0.1 \times \$1,000,000 + 0.01 \times \$5,000,000 = \$150,000.$ We assume these two floods are the only ones conceivable, in this highly oversimplified example.

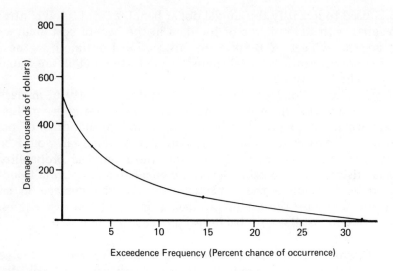

Figure 6-7. Damage Frequency Curve

6B-1, 6B-2, and 6B-3 in Appendix B. When the three are combined Figure 6-7 results. This figure gives the percent chance that a storm will occur in the basin in the next year that will produce an amount of damage to property (in dollars) in excess of the damage shown on the vertical scale.

It may be seen from Figure 6-7 that completely negligible damage has about two chances in three of occurring. It may also be seen that, as almost always, severe damage is associated only with rare events.[i] The largest source of unreliability of estimates of "flood benefits" quite generally can be traced to the fact that rare events are intrinsically difficult to treat statistically. (For further evidence, see Box 2, below.)

Damage-frequency relations must be calculated both in the presence and in the absence of control structures if the benefit associated with a structure is to be estimated. The construction of a levee at a damage center, or of a dam upstream of this center, will generally cause the damage-frequency curve to be displaced downwards, thereby reducing the expected annual damages from floods. The problem is to attempt to estimate just how much the damage-frequency curve will be displaced.

---

[i]By a rough measurement of the relevant areas under the sample damage frequency curve shown on Plate 7 of Appendix D of H D 522, I find that 70 percent of the expected yearly damages from flooding on the Delaware is caused by floods with greater than ten-year recurrence intervals.

Box 2   Rare Events

To get a feeling for the uncertainties involved, I compared six different methods that have been designed for attaching recurrence intervals to rare floods. I applied all of them to the historical data for the Lehigh River at Bethlehem, Pennsylvania.[1] The six methods were (1) a simple fit to the normal distribution, (2) the Beard Method,[2] (3) the Gumble Method,[3] (4) the log-Pearson type III method,[4] (5) the method used by the Corps in H D 522 employing a joint distribution of normal and hurricane discharges, and (6) the simplest method of all, simply assuming that the previous period of record will be repeated, on the average, in the future, the period of record being 1902–1970 (data for 1906–09 not available). The results are shown in Table 6–1 below.

Table 6-1.   **Recurrence Interval for Worst Flood or Record (approx. value)**

Method of Computation	No. of Years
Fit to normal curve	180
Hurricane + normal	75
Beard	95
Gumble	160
Log-Pearson type III	70
Repetition of previous period of record	66

This wide range of recurrence intervals obtained by differing but basically reasonable methods cannot provide a quantitative measure of the range of uncertainty, but it does serve to give the reader some feeling for the difficulties involved in making even approximate statements about the probabilities of rare events.

1. USGS Water Supply Papers, #1672 and #1902.

2. See H D 522, Appendix M.

3. See, e.g., R.D. Linsley and J.B. Franzini, *Water-Resources Engineering*, 3rd ed. (N.Y.: McGraw-Hill, 1972), p. 127. This method is used by the U.S. Geological Survey.

4. *Ibid.*, p. 128. Since 1967 this has been the standard method used by the Corps of Engineers.

For a levee this problem is relatively easy. The presence of a levee will alter both the stage-discharge and the stage-damage relations in obvious ways, and this causes no difficulty. The derivations of both the "altered" and the "natural" damage-frequency curves proceed in exactly the same fashion. A dam, on the other hand, is considerably more complicated, because its effect is on the discharge-frequency curve at the damage site and this effect depends on the nature of the storm that produces the flood. Two discharges must be known—at the dam site and at the damage center—and these discharges are not necessarily strongly correlated. In general, the greater the separation between the two sites the smaller the correlation (see, for example, Fig. 6–2).

The result of the calculation described in this section is an estimate of the expected amount of damage that will be prevented by the dam during its lifetime. As seen in Box 6 of Essay 4 (p. 139), this constitutes the greatest part of the flood control benefit of the dam.

IV. NONSTRUCTURAL ALTERNATIVES

Unless a dam is already justified exclusive of its role in flood control, it is not usually an efficient method of achieving the benefits provided by flood control. Addressing exclusively the concern for human lives saved, E. F. Renshaw wrote:

> . . . It would be difficult to find any large scale investment that reasonably can be expected to save as little life per dollar expended as the typical flood control projects, which are inadequate to cope with the rare and particularly disastrous floods.[6]

In the United States, between 1936 and 1970, the average annual death toll from floods was 95,[7] and it has shown no tendency to decrease with time. During this same period more than nine billion dollars has been spent for structural flood control projects,[8] an average of over $250 million per year.

The great majority of flood fatalities occur during flash floods on small, supposedly benign tributaries, two instances of which we have already mentioned: Brodhead Creek in the Delaware Valley in 1955 and Rapid Creek in Rapid City, South Dakota, in 1972. The latter flood killed 235 people even though a massive flood control dam had recently been completed only fifteen miles upstream. The problem in this case was that the storm that produced the flood happened to center over a portion of the basin not protected by the dam, rendering the dam virtually useless. The flood was also made worse by the failure of a smaller dam just upstream from Rapid City. It provides little comfort to the homeless and bereaved survivors of the flood to point out that it was a highly improbable event.[j]

[j]The rainstorm that caused this flood dropped over seven inches of rain in six hours and was tentatively labeled a "100-year" rainstorm by the U.S. Weather

To call a dam "inefficient" as a saver of lives, one must have other alternatives in mind. Among these are zoning regulations, accurate crest prediction capability, and strong emergency relief capability. Although they are probably no less attractive a set of programs in the presence of a dam, in fact they constitute an increasingly respected alternative to a dam. They, along with flood insurance, are known collectively as nonstructural alternatives.

A. Flood Plain Zoning

Of course, the simplest and most direct means of preventing flood damage is to declare the flood plain off limits for all human activities. But the apparent simplicity of this scheme is quite deceptive since the flood plain is not so easy to define precisely. In addition, such a plan would be very wasteful, because a valuable source of human welfare and enjoyment would be lost. An awareness is growing in many a waterfront city (e.g., Pittsburgh, Philadelphia, St. Louis) that the quality of urban life would have been greatly improved if the city had been conscious of the esthetic and recreational value of its rivers and had planned its growth both to preserve and to utilize these values.

Probably the major reason why flood plain zoning has been so slow to develop in the United States is that the responsibility for zoning has been left in the hands of the smallest, least powerful, and most easily influenced units of government: the county and municipal. At this level of government there is generally only a dim awareness of the scope of the flood problem, there is virtually no capability for data acquisition and analysis, and there is no effective means of controlling developments in upstream communities. In addition there is the nearly universal tendency for such local governments to be controlled by business interests, which see the river and flood plain almost entirely in terms of their economic potential, and which tend to assume that they will be taken care of by the state and federal governments should a flood disaster occur. This faith has been amply justified in the past.

Buildings in the flood plain have moderately deleterious effects during a flood, because they present obstruction to the flow of flood waters, which results in the backing up and diversion of water into areas that would not otherwise be flooded. They also can be very destructive when they break loose and wash downstream. Piles of

---

Bureau's local hydrologist. The flood discharge at Rapid City was 28,500 cfs which was over ten times the 2,600 cfs of the previous flood of record! This discharge was eight times as large as the 50-year flood estimated from previous data by the U.S. Geological Survey.

debris, forming into mini-dams and then breaking loose suddenly, worsened the effects of the Rapid City flood. A building, bridge, or dike in the floodway is therefore a kind of public nuisance, and this has been one of the traditional legal justifications for flood plain zoning laws. Our legal system tends to assume that people and companies are not to be compensated for damage they do themselves, but it attempts to protect those who suffer damages resulting from the negligence or errors of others.[9]

In recent years a few states, including Wisconsin, Minnesota, and New Jersey, have instituted flood plain zoning laws, and this concept seems to be gaining popularity. Consider the following, of many possible examples:

- Rapid City, South Dakota, has instituted a new plan for flood plain usage in the wake of the 1972 flood, and certain housing tracts that had been built near Rapid Creek will not be rebuilt. They will be replaced by a park.

- The Corps of Engineers has proposed an entirely nonstructural plan for the Charles River in Massachusetts.[10]

- The people of Littleton, Colorado, on the South Platte River, in response to a proposal of the Corps of Engineers to channelize the river through Littleton (as part of a larger flood control plan for the South Platte), proposed that the money appropriated for channelization be used instead to acquire property in the flood plain that would be converted into a park. The Corps has agreed to support this plan.[11]

- Burlington, N.J., combining urban renewal with flood plain zoning, demolished tenements in the flood plain and replaced them with new housing on higher ground.

The first and most important component of a flood plain zoning plan is an accurate delineation of the flood plain itself. An excellent example of such a study is the report on the Raritan River done by Anderson-Nichols and Company for the New Jersey Division of Water Resources.[12] This study presents a careful and precise survey of the Raritan flood plain and delineates two distinct regions: the floodway and the flood fringe.

The floodway is that portion of the flood plain which is subjected to relatively frequent floods and within which the typical water velocities are large enough to cause serious damage to unprotected structures. The flood fringe is a region in which floods are relatively infrequent and in which water velocities are significantly slower. These descriptions are, of course, far too qualitative to be of much use, but the actual quantitative distinctions are made with the aid of a rather complex, standardized procedure that uses many of the statistical hydrology methods we have described in previous sections. The procedure involves determining a mean annual flood discharge and then multiplying it by appropriate factors to determine the discharge that defines the floodway and the flood fringe. The factors are obtained by statistical analyses of historical flood data and, for example, the outer boundary of the floodway might be defined by the ten-year flood and the flood fringe by the 100-year flood.

Of course, exactly the same kinds of statistical uncertainties are involved in defining the boundary of the flood fringe as in designing a flood control dam. If housing tracts and trailer parks and other vulnerable developments are constructed just outside the flood fringe, a risk is being taken that the public should be aware of. This is where an accompanying insurance program plays an important role, since insurance by its very nature assumes a permanent situation of risk.

The Raritan River study cost the State of New Jersey about one million dollars to delineate 331 miles of flood plain. The greatest portion of this money was spent doing precise surveys to determine the contours of the land and the distribution of structures, so that stage-discharge and stage-damage relations can be made as accurate as possible. Although these costs are large, they are still considerably smaller than those required to erect dams or levees.

The Raritan study makes a number of recommendations, among them: (1) that communities along the river adopt "properly worded land management regulations," (2) that "no fill or structure be permitted within the floodway limits which would alter the natural flood flow," (3) that "all efforts be made to make people aware of the potential dangers associated with the improper use of flood-prone areas," (4) that structural control methods be considered for regions in which they are appropriate, and (5) that flood insurance be obtained under the National Flood Insurance Act of 1968. The building of flood control structures is not excluded, but is recognized as one element of a more comprehensive program.

B. Flood Insurance

By all accounts every past attempt at creating a workable private flood insurance program has been a failure. As we have seen, the major portion of flood damage occurs during the large, rare floods, and it has usually taken only one such major event to wipe out completely whatever insurance reserves had been set aside. The smaller, more common types of floods might be more predictable, but in this case the insurance rates cannot be raised sufficiently high, for occupants of the flood plain have a clear incentive to gamble and carry no insurance: they can count on the federal government to step in with relief measures, grants, and low cost loans in the wake of a flood.

It is not an easy thing to argue against such economic aid to flood victims. The financial losses and the emotional and physical suffering of these unfortunate people are genuinely tragic, and to respond with compassion and aid seems to be the least the rest of us can do for them. The natural tendency is to help the victims replace and rebuild what they have lost and to minimize their dislocation. But we must ask ourselves whether this policy is really helping anyone in the long run. Are we not setting up both the victims and ourselves for a replay of the same scene at some future date? Would it not be more sensible to introduce incentives to relocate out of the flood plain rather than to encourage a return to the precarious situation of the past? Would it not also seem reasonable to demand of those who choose to remain in the flood-prone area that they plan realistically for the possibility that they will experience the same problems again? It is not society's obligation to continue to subsidize clearly unwise and uneconomic choices by some of its members.

There are several ways in which flood insurance can play a role in forcing people to pay the real costs of their occupancy of the flood plain. The government could adopt a policy of refusing to provide aid for flood victims, thereby putting the burden of protection on the flood plain occupants themselves. This would, I believe, be a grossly unfair policy to adopt at this time, given the severe economic inequities that already exist in our society and the fact that most people who now live in flood plains moved there at a time when these questions were not considered worthy of serious consideration.

A more sensible approach would seem to be to accept the fact that society will have to bear the cost of past mistakes, but to insist that any *new* flood plain development and any rebuilding of flood damaged areas be done with the clear understanding that the residents, businesses, and industries that occupy that area are expected to anticipate and make a reasonable effort to pay the costs of any future damages. The best way to do this is with insurance, and this insurance should be mandatory. Mandatory insurance is the only viable alternative to simply turning our backs on the flood victims and saying "we warned you." Human beings do not feel good about themselves when they behave this way. Many states already require auto insurance, and adequate fire insurance is required by all mortgage lenders. A program of compulsory health insurance is considered by many to be a sensible way to handle the country's health care problems. Compulsory flood insurance would fall within this same category and would seem to be in the best interests of both the flood plain residents and the society as a whole.

Of course, as with each of the alternatives considered here, flood insurance by itself is not a complete solution. An intelligent insurance plan would promote zoning and warning systems in order to minimize losses. This is precisely the conception of the National Flood Insurance Act of 1968, in which federal flood insurance is sold only to those communities that meet certain minimum standards for zoning, warning systems and relief capabilities. It seem reasonable to demand that the entire society share the cost of past overdevelopment on the flood plains of our rivers. This concept is embodied in the Flood Insurance Act through federal subsidization of rates, so that present flood plain occupants will be encouraged to purchase the insurance.

The insurance program is being administered by a pool of private companies and the limits of subsidized insurance are $17,500 for a single-family dwelling, $30,000 for two- to four-family structures, and $30,000 for small business properties. An owner who wishes to have extra insurance must pay full actuarial rates. The rate subsidies are seen as a transitory device to ease the readjustment to new land use patterns. New or substantially modified structures pay full actuarial rates. This national insurance plan contains incentives to dedicate the flood plain to parks, beaches, and certain industrial and low intensity residential uses (e.g., properly floodproofed vacation cottages) for which it is economically most suited. Only a small number of communities have so far made the necessary efforts to qualify for this insurance, but one senses a growing awareness and appreciation of this option in many floodprone communities.

C. Flood Warning Systems

Neither flood plain zoning nor insurance presents severe technological problems. When we get to flood warning systems, however, we encounter a fundamentally technological problem that could serve to siphon off some of the creative engineering effort which has traditionally gone into designing flood control structures. The data acquisition and processing problem, the communications problem, the various hydrology and hydraulics problems are all amenable to technological solutions, and depending on how much money one wished to spend, one could conjure up flood warning systems with enough fancy technology to satisfy even the most hardware oriented engineer.

In a flood warning system the most important variable is the time delay between the warning signals and the actual flood. A flood warning system to predict the crest of the Mississippi River at St. Louis should be expected to make predictions several days in advance. For the Delaware River at Trenton one has a time period of the order to ten to twenty hours over which accurate predictions can be made. For flashy tributaries, a time delay of more than a half-hour could cost lives. Clearly the system one designs will be quite different for each of these three cases.

The state of the art of long term crest prediction seems to have reached a reasonably high level. By measuring discharges on major tributaries and using empirical lag times, a crude routing analysis can be done to estimate the height of the crest and its time of arrival at downstream locations. According to an official of the New Jersey Division of Water Resources, the crest at Trenton can be predicted to within one-half foot up to twelve hours in advance. In this official's opinion, there is no excuse for any loss of life in a main-stem flood on the Delaware.

It is on flashy tributaries that rapid early warning systems are necessary. Even when the flood plain of such a tributary has been zoned and its residents insured, a warning system is still required as a hedge against errors in drawing zoning lines. Where it is too late to prevent flood plain development, the warning system is essential so that at the least death and injury and easily preventable property damage can be minimized.

A very simple example of an early warning system has recently been installed on Green Brook near Scotch Plains, N.J. It consists of a device that monitors the gauge height at a certain point upstream, and when this reaches some critical value a warning light flashes in the local police department. This provides an earlier warning that what a local official has called the old "yell and holler system," especially at night.

Areas of the central United States that are subject to tornadoes are familiar with a similar type of early warning system. The sighting of funnel clouds in an area, or even just the appearance of characteristic weather phenomena, are enough to cause tornado warnings to be broadcast urging people to take safe shelter. It is not too difficult to conceive of analogous arrangements for flash floods. Data on the relevant characteristics of a drainage basin (infiltration capacities, lag times, base flows, etc.) could be monitored at frequent intervals and stored in a data bank. Using modern radar and other microwave techniques the location, size, motion and intensity of an approaching storm could be fed into a computer program, which would predict the resulting flood much further in advance than a sensing device ten miles upstream.

There is clearly the possibility for error in predicting flood crests, and the tolerance for error increases as the warning time increases. This presents a rather tricky optimization problem. A warning system should be designed conservatively so that the only result of an error is inconvenience and whatever costs are associated with evacuation procedures. But if the system is too conservative, and people are inconvenienced too many times with no apparent justification, the system is likely to be discredited.[k] Perhaps two signals could be given: first a "yellow light" (possible danger), then a "red light" (imminent danger).

Historically there has been a tendency for communities downstream of a new flood control dam to overestimate the protection it provides. One should expect the same misperception to accompany the introduction of a new warning system. Care must be taken to inform residents of the flood plain both about the threat of flash floods and about the details of the warning system. One way to do this would be to include an easily understandable description of the flood threat and warning system in the documentation accompanying the sale of homes or businesses in the flood plain. Of course, a clear presentation of the flood threat might discourage some people from moving into the area. So much the better!

V. FINAL THOUGHTS

For most of its journey from upper New York State to Trenton, New Jersey, where it begins the transition from an inland river to an estuary, the Delaware flows between fairly steep banks, and its flood plain is narrow. Occasional towns and cities occupy the few reasonably flat areas where the flood plain widens. The Corps of Engineers calculates that, in the 1955 flood of record, about 9,200 acres were flooded between Tocks Island and Trenton, and about 27 million dollars in damage was done.[13] In its benefit calculation the Corps assumed that development on the flood plain would continue at previously experienced rates for the entire basin and that conse-

---

[k]In this connection it would be interesting to find out how effective the tornado warning system is. I am not aware of any sociological studies of the degree to which people actually take the warnings seriously.

quently damage in a future repetition of the 1955 flood would be substantially greater.

This prediction has not been borne out by events in the first fifteen year after H D 522 was written. Burt and Eisel showed that several communities, including Burlington, New Jersey; Easton, Pennsylvania; and Riegelsville, Pennsylvania, have substantially reduced the number of structures on the 1955 flood plain and that the total number of structures on the flood plain in the eight major damage centers has been reduced by over 40 per cent from 2,420 to 1,414.[14]

Thus, nonstructural techniques have already begun making a serious contribution to the prevention of flood damages along the Delaware River, and it would seem that this alternative will be even more important in the future, especially in New Jersey, which has a new flood plain zoning law. Contrary to the assumption in the Corps of Engineers' benefit-cost analysis, expected rates of growth in the Delaware Valley as a whole should not be reliable predictors of rates of growth in the flood plain itself.

It seems clear that the flood control function of the Tocks Island Dam easily passes a benefit-cost test as long as the dam is justifiable anyway for other purposes.[l] But it is most unlikely that a pure flood control dam could be justified. The relatively small damage potential between Tocks Island and Trenton[m] coupled with the high ecological and esthetic value of a freely flowing river and the observed trends toward more judicious use of the flood plain would seem to argue against a Tocks Island flood control dam. It is important that this point be clearly understood by both the public and political leaders, because flood control has continued to act as a powerful emotional impetus behind the promotion of the dam. This impetus has been waning in recent years as the memory of 1955 fades, but it

---

[l]The formal method of judging the merits of adding an additional purpose to a project that is already economically justifiable is to consider the "separable" costs and benefits of this addition. At the time of House Document 522 (1962), the annualized separable costs of providing flood control at Tocks Island Dam were only $207,000. (Largely, this is the annualized cost of making the dam higher above the level of the reservoir than would be warranted by its function for water supply; in effect, the dam is perceived as a wall to contain a flood surge built on top of a wall to store water.) Even allowing for the inflation by more than a factor of two which has overtaken *both* costs and benefits between the analysis in House Document 522 and the analysis reported in Essay 4, this annualized separable cost is far smaller than the annualized benefit from expected reductions in property damage, $3.8 million.

[m]Below Trenton the flooding of the river is dominated by tidal effects in the estuary.

could return to full strength overnight with the occurrence of another major flood on the Delaware. One suspects that if this were to occur, the flood control function of the dam would again become a powerful selling point, independent of the benefit-cost analysis.

Neither a structural nor a nonstructural approach to flood control can provide a perfect guarantee against flood damage, and uncertainties in flood frequency prediction make the long range benefits of a zoning law just as hard to predict as the long range benefits of a dam. Moreover, the magnitude of the impact of a flood on any community depends critically on the effectiveness of the system of emergency relief. It may be that, currently, dollars and effort spent on simplifying the relief system—which now confronts the flood victim with a bewildering array of public and private agencies having overlapping responsibilities—would yield the largest return, in terms of reduced anguish in the flood plain. Clearly, the choice of approach to flood control involves esthetic and moral judgments as much as economic and technical judgments.

We are now presented in part with a choice between two fundamentally opposed views of the proper relationship of human beings to nature. A dam or a levee symbolizes humanity's desire to dominate and control nature, and thereby to provide new options for development. A flood plain zoning law, a flood warning program, and a flood relief program symbolize a desire to adapt to nature and to confine humanity's options within the limits imposed by natural phenomena, thereby preserving the natural environment. Both seek to enhance the general quality of life.

Underlying the conservationist's clear preference for a nonstructural approach is the belief that "nature knows best" and that man is too stupid and clumsy to be able to grasp the subtleties of nature's mechanisms and manipulate them without risking irreparable damage. But this characterization is too negative by itself. There is also the positive reverence for nature in both her benign and violent moods, and a strong tendency to equate beauty with virginity. To the naturalist, beauty can be found in widely diverse places: a barren desert populated chiefly by dry mesquite and lizards, a high mountain pass covered with snow, a coral reef teeming with aquatic life, or a lonely stretch of wild river lined with green forests and rushing over rapids and falls. The only feature these various scenes have in common is their isolation from man and the fact that they have existed substantially as we view them now for millions of years without change, and that they will continue to exist for millions more if only they are left alone.

Theodore Roosevelt captured the essence of this esthetic in his preface to a collection of hunting stories:

There are no words that can tell of the hidden spirit of the wilderness, that can reveal its mystery, its melancholy, and its charm. There is delight in the hardy life of the open, in long rides, rifle in hand, in the thrill of the fight with dangerous game. . . . [We need] the silent places . . . the wide waste places of the earth, unworn by man, and changed only by the slow change of the ages through time everlasting.[15]

Aside from the references to hunting, this might very well serve as the credo of the modern day Sierra Club. The reader is urged to compare this quote with that of Allan H. Cullen in section I of this essay. These two quotes give an accurate measure of the philosophical gulf separating the conservationists from the technologists.

Most of us, including this author, can identify to some degree with the sentiments expressed by both writers. There may be some engineers who will not be content until every stream more than five feet wide is dammed, and there may be some conservationists who will not be content until we all return to living in caves, but for most of us it is extremely difficult to form a firm ideological commitment to one side or the other. We can, however, make one statement about attitudes toward flood problems with which most people would agree. It does seem that on too many occasions in the past the choice that has been examined has been between controlling floods by structural means or doing nothing at all. The adaptive alternative has been, with few exceptions, ignored. The right choice is between control and adaptation rather than between control and inaction.

Although in most cases I would prefer a combination of control and adaptation, I incline toward adaptation. Adaptive approaches are inherently more flexible than control approaches. Zoning lines can be redrawn or insurance rates can be changed as new information becomes available, but a 160-foot-high, 3,200-foot-wide dam will be around for a long, long time to come. One does not casually move aside three-and-one-half million cubic yards of earth and rock if one has second thoughts on the matter.

This flexibility is critical in the face of uncertainty. It is not possible for human beings, even with the most careful and objective analysis, to foresee all the ecological consequences of a major project. In the case of the Tocks Island Dam, even if it were determined that the lake would not eutrophy and that the shad would be able to climb the fish ladders to spawn, there could still be any number of serious, even disastrous, ecological effects which, if we had been able to predict them in advance, would have caused us to abandon the dam.

It is often argued that if everyone thought this way nothing would ever get done. I would state this in the slightly weaker form that if more people thought this way, a lot less would get done. That would almost certainly be a good thing, especially with regard to massive projects such as the Tocks Island Dam.

APPENDIX A

The hydrograph in Figure 6-3 has two critical features: (1) a peak discharge, which is related to how high the water will rise at the crest of the flood, and (2) a lag time, which expresses how long after the start of the storm the crest of the flood arrives at the mouth of the basin. Both of these features can be understood quantitatively using the geometrical model in Figure 6A-1. In this figure, runoff is assumed to flow in a straight line. In each of the situations in Figure 6A-1, the shaded area shows where rain can fall in the basin such that it arrives at the mouth of the basin at a single time.

Runoff from rain falling at the left-hand edge of each shaded region at the beginning of a storm and runoff from rain falling at the right-hand edge at the end of the storm will drain across the basin together. The width of the shaded region is the distance that runoff will flow, moving at the basin's average velocity (v) during the duration of the storm (T). In the case where v is constant everywhere in the basin, the boundaries of the shaded region are fractions of circles centered at the mouth of the basin. If the rain starts suddenly, falls uniformly over time, and then stops suddenly, the shaded area is proportional to the discharge which will eventually appear at the mouth. The hydrograph, therefore, is generated by calculating the shaded area as the shaded area sweeps to the left.

Elementary calculus is required to calculate the areas in Figure 6A-1, and thereby the full hydrograph. But the peak discharge can be estimated using only geometry. The peak discharge corresponds to that particular shaded area of width vT that is centered on the diameter of the circle, as in the middle drawing. Given that the radius of the basin is R, the radius of the circle passing through the middle of the shaded region corresponding to the peak discharge is $R\sqrt{2}$, since such a radius is a chord traversing 90 degrees of the circle. If the thickness of the shaded area, vT, is much less than the radius of the basin, R, then, *approximately* (1) the inner radius of the shaded region is $R\sqrt{2} - vT/2$, and (2) the outer radius is $R\sqrt{2} + vT/2$, and

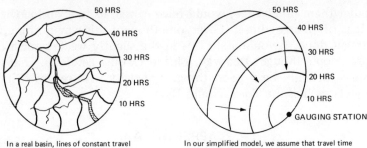

In a real basin, lines of constant travel time are irregular.

In our simplified model, we assume that travel time is proportional to bee-line distance.

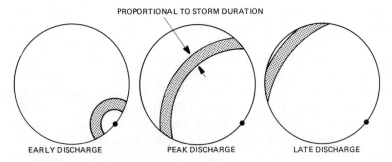

All the water reaching the gauging station at a given moment originated within a band whose width is proportional to the storm's duration. If the rain is uniform, then the discharge at any moment is proportional to the area of the corresponding band.

Figure 6A-1. Progress of Storm Runoff

(3) the shaded area (one-quarter of a thin ring) is $(\pi/2) (R \sqrt{2}) (vT)$.

The lag time, T_L, is defined as the time from the start of the storm to the peak discharge. Thus, it is the time for runoff to flow from the outer radius to the mouth of the basin:

$$T_L = \frac{1}{v} [R\sqrt{2} + \frac{vT}{2}] = \frac{R}{v} \sqrt{2} + \frac{T}{2} \qquad \text{(A1)}$$

The peak discharge, D_{max}, is the product of the intensity of the runoff produced by the storm (P) (measured, for example, in inches per hour) times the shaded area, which is one-fourth of a thin ring:

$$D_{max} = P\frac{\pi}{2}(R\sqrt{2})\,vT \qquad (A2)$$

If we use precise data for our model storm, R = 17.8 miles, v = 0.89 mph, T = 5 hours, P = 0.65 inches per hour, we find that the lag time is 31 hours and the peak discharge is 74,000 cubic feet per second.

If a storm is of long enough duration to invalidate the assumption that vT is much less than R, then the approximate formulas written above will be inaccurate. If one must analyze a storm of long duration, it may be convenient to treat the storm as a series of short storms and sum the hydrograph corresponding to each short storm.

We can reexpress the formula for the peak discharge by introducing a quantity, Q, the total runoff produced by the storm. Since $Q = P\pi R^2 T$, we may write:

$$D_{max} = Qv/R\sqrt{2} \qquad (A3)$$

or, including the lag time as well:

$$D_{max} = Q/(T_L - T/2). \qquad (A4)$$

Since the lag time is much longer than the duration of the storm, we thus have the nice result that the total runoff from the storm is approximately the product of the peak discharge and the lag time.

The exact formulas for the shaded areas in the general case are not given here but were used to generate the hydrograph in Figure 6-3.[a] It must be remembered that, unless the stream bed is initially dry, the flows we are calculating should be added to the flow already present (called the base flow). Here, too, conditions existing prior to the storm (the magnitude of the base flow) can be crucial in determining whether or not a flood occurs.

We may try to apply these formulas to the basin above the site of the proposed Tocks Island Dam. The area of that basin is 3,827 square miles. Assuming the drainage basin is circular (a rather poor assumption in this case), its radius would be 35 miles. The Corps reports in H D 522 that the design storm, with a total runoff of 586,000 acre feet, would produce a peak discharge of 211,000 cfs at

---

[a]The exact formula for the peak discharge yields a value of 75,000 cfs for our model storm, only one percent different from what we have found here using an approximation.

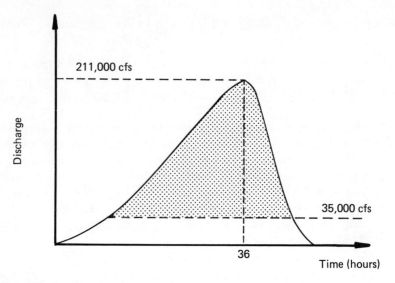

Figure 6A-2.   Approximate Hydrograph for Tocks Dam Site.

the dam site in the absence of the dam.[b] The corresponding storm duration is not specified, but it would be short; let us assume it is four hours. Using equation (A4) to solve for the lag time (since T, D_{max}, and Q are specified), one finds that T_L = 36 hours.

Using equation (A1) to solve for the average runoff velocity (since R, T, and now T_L are known), one finds that $v = 1.6$ miles per hour. Evidently, the basin above Tocks Island is relatively flashy, presumably because it is largely mountainous and the water runs off steeply sloped land.

The dam is designed to discharge at 35,000 cfs for most of the natural hydrograph period. To obtain a rough estimate of the needed storage in the design storm, I have drawn Figure 6A-2, a very crude hydrograph, but arranged to have the lag time and the peak discharge just calculated. A very rough graphical estimate of the shaded area in the figure gives a short term storage of 287,000 acre feet, which compares remarkably well with the figure of 275,000 acre feet given by the Corps in H D 522.

---

[b]One acre foot = 43,560 cubic feet. The total basin runoff corresponds to 2.87 inches of runoff (rainfall minus infiltration) when averaged over the whole basin.

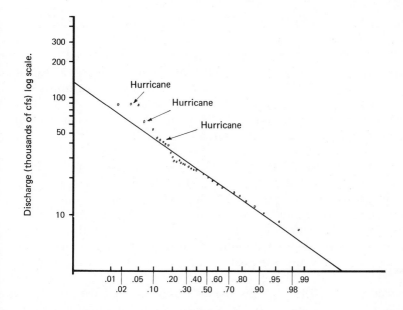

Exceedence Frequency
(probability that a flood of given discharge will recur within a year)

Figure 6B-1. Discharge-Frequency Curve for the Lehigh River at Bethlehem, Pa.
The distorted horizontal axis is characteristic of "probability paper."
Note: Some points have been deleted for clarity in the portion of the curve above 40 percent exceedence frequency.

APPENDIX B

The Corps begins its analysis with stream runoff data which is gathered by the U.S. Geological Survey from 108 stream gauging stations in the Delaware Basin. Most of these are equipped to convert the stage (level) of the stream into a discharge (cfs) figure. The yearly peak discharges are used in a flood analysis. In a statistical analysis of droughts, one would use the yearly minimum discharges.

The annual peak discharges for the N year period of record (typically $N = 40$–50 years) are next rank ordered according to their magnitudes, the largest being numbered one and the smallest, N. The recurrence interval of a given discharge is then given by N/m where m is the rank order of the given discharge.[c] For example, the

[c]The Corps actually used a slightly different method, called the Beard method, which tends to assign longer recurrence intervals to the very rare floods. However, it is quite similar in principle to the simple method we use here.

second largest peak discharge in a 40-year record would be called a 20-year flood.

The logarithms of the peak discharges are then plotted against the exceedence frequencies[d] on special probability paper, as shown in Figure 6B-1. This paper is designed so that if the logarithms of the peak discharges are normally distributed then the points will form a straight line, with the mean discharge at 50 percent exceedence frequency and the slope of the line equal to the standard deviation of the distribution.

If peak discharges are in fact log-normally distributed, this must ultimately be related to the fact that the peak discharge in any year is determined by a number of independently varying multiplicative factors that are more or less randomly distributed. One thinks immediately of storm intensity, storm location, infiltration capacity, previous stream depths, amount of snow cover, etc., as variables that would help determine the peak runoff.

The Corps of Engineers found that the assumption of a log-normal distribution for the peak discharges was a poor one for the Delaware Valley. There seem to be two quite distinct populations of peak discharges: those caused by ordinary storms and those caused by hurricanes. The hurricane-created discharges are rarer but tend to be considerably more severe than would be predicted by fitting the annual data to a single log-normal distribution. Accordingly, the smaller peak discharges are not much help in predicting the recurrence frequencies of the rarest and most devastating floods. In a 40-year record there are at most thirteen or fourteen hurricane discharges. This is statistically equivalent to having only a fourteen-year record of annual peaks, an awfully short record from which to estimate future recurrence intervals with much confidence.

This procedure was followed in generating a discharge-frequency record for each of the 108 gauging stations in the basin. The Corps found that, given the area drained by each stream and the average slope of the stream bed (e.g., in feet of descent per mile of run), the main features of the record of each stream could be reasonably well predicted. This enabled the Corps to estimate the discharge-frequency record for the many streams within the Delaware Basin which have no gauges. At this point in the analysis the Corps had a discharge-frequency curve for any point in the basin at which flood damage might occur. Wherever the stage-discharge relation for a location is known, relating height of a stream to its rate of flow, it

[d]Exceedence frequency is the inverse of the recurrence interval. A twenty-year discharge would have a 5 percent exceedence frequency—i.e., a probability of .05 that it would be exceeded in any given year.

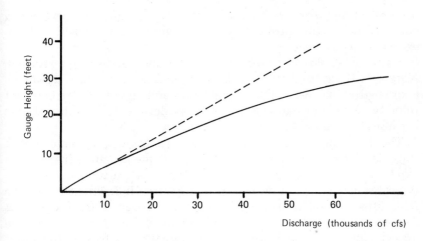

Figure 6B-2. Typical Stage-Discharge curve
Doubling the discharge less than doubles the height of the river, because the river spills over its banks.

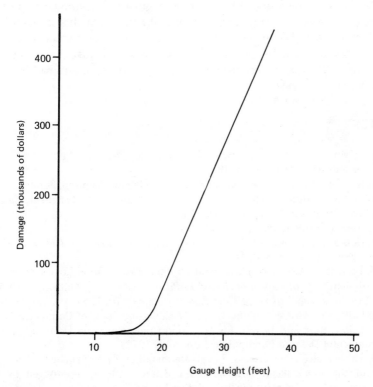

Figure 6B-3. Typical Stage-Damage curve

becomes straightforward to construct a stage-frequency curve, i.e., a curve showing the probability that a given gauge height will be exceeded in any year.

Figure 6B-2 shows a more or less typical stage-discharge relation. Note that the dotted straight line corresponds to the discharge being contained within perfectly vertical banks and moving with a constant velocity. Most stage-discharge relations deviate from this extreme because the channel has a sloping boundary.

The final step is to combine the stage-frequency curve with a stage-damage curve to produce a damage-frequency curve from which expected annual damages (in dollars) can be calculated. A fairly typical stage-damage curve is shown in Figure 6B-3. Note that for the first fifteen feet in gauge height little damage is done but that damage rises rapidly for stages higher than this. This is what one expects intuitively and we might denote fifteen feet as the flood stage at this particular location since a "flood" occurs only if the stage is exceeded.

The results of combining the three graphs in this Appendix is the damage-frequency curve in the text, Figure 6-7. Damage is plotted against exceedence frequency (probability per year that a given level of damage will be exceeded), because in that form the expected annual damage can be estimated graphically: it is just the area under this curve. The expected annual damage, in turn, is entered into the cost-benefit analysis.

NOTES

1. Calvin Kentfield, "The River Did Not Stay Away," *New York Times Magazine* July 15, 1973, pp. 14–19.

2. Allan H. Cullen, *Rivers in Harness*, (Philadelphia: Chilton Books, 1962).

3. For some other examples see W. G. Hoyt and W. B. Langbein, *Floods*, (Princeton: Princeton University Press, 1955), p. 3.

4. Allan H. Cullen, *op. cit.*, p. 57.

5. House Document 522, *U.S. Army Corps of Engineers Delaware River Basin Report*, vol. I, 1958, p. 48.

6. Edward F. Renshaw, "The Relationship between Flood Losses and Flood Control Benefits" in *Papers on Flood Problems*, Gilbert F. White (ed.) University of Chicago, Dept. of Geography Research Paper #70, 1961.

7. *Statistical Abstract of the U. S.*, (Washington: Dept. of Commerce 1972)

8. Laurie Burt and Leo M. Eisel, "Flood Control and the Delaware River," Environmental Defense Fund publication, April 1973.

9. These matters are discussed in greater detail by E. W. Beuchet in "A Legal View of the Flood Plain," Harvard Law School (1961), reproduced by the Tennessee Valley Authority for limited distribution.

10. Laurie Burt and Leo M. Eisel, *op. cit.*

11. The Corps' position is stated by Harry A. Dolphin, Chief, Public Affairs Office, Missouri River Division, Omaha, Nebraska in a letter to the editor of "Not Man Apart," the magazine published by Friends of the Earth.

12. Flood Hazard Report No. 2, "Delineation of Flood Hazard Areas, Raritan River Basin," Anderson-Nichols & Co., Inc. as consultants for the State of New Jersey, Dept. of Environmental Protection, Division of Water Resources, March 1972.

13. H D 522, Appendix D, Tables 2 and 4.

14. Laurie Burt and Leo M. Eisel, *op. cit.*

15. *African Game Trails, Works*, vol. 5, xxvii, quoted in Roderick Nash, *Wilderness and the American Mind*, (New Haven: Yale University Press, 1967), p. 150.

✳ *Chapter 7*

Electric Power on the Delaware

Thomas F. Schrader and Robert H. Socolow

I. INTRODUCTION

The electric utilities that serve the Delaware Valley and neighboring regions once included in their vision of the future a 1,300-megawatt pumped-storage facility that would depend on the Tocks Island reservoir as a lower pool, and a 33,000-megawatt network of steam-electric generating plants that would evaporate tremendous amounts of cooling water from the Delaware River. Without the Tocks Island Dam, pumped storage will probably not be built, and, under the present policies of the Delaware River Basin Commission (DRBC), neither will most of the downstream power plants—at least at the sites the utilities originally suggested. Not surprisingly, electric power looms as a significant issue in the debate over constructing the dam.

The power companies speak in threatening terms about the consequences of the demand for electricity outgrowing their generating capacity. They predict that rationing of electricity, reduced industrial growth, and severe unemployment will result if their schedule for constructing new power facilities is not met. The DRBC, which is responsible for planning and managing the region's water resources, has tied the fate of many of the utilities' power plants to the Tocks Island project. The Commission staff projections assert that, without the Tocks Island project, the Delaware's flow is not adequate to meet the future water demands of the power plants, as well as those of industries and cities in the region, and that unless the Tocks Island Dam is built, even the water supply for plants now under construction may be in jeopardy by 1980. They conclude that the utilities would either have to bolster the flow with their own offstream dams and reservoirs or shut down during the late summer periods of low flow.

The projections of the utilities and the DRBC are supported by detailed quantitative studies, which thwart casual criticism. However, like all projections, theirs embody crucial assumptions, which are open to question. Both the utilities and the DRBC have perceived their responsibilities entirely in terms of assuring an adequate supply. The utilities are the energy providers; the DRBC, in spite of a mandate that would permit a broad role in regional planning, perceives itself primarily as a water provider. Neither considers any attempt to *control* demand as within its prerogatives. Thus, the projections of both the DRBC and the utilities are based on the conventional model of indefinite exponential growth. If energy conservation becomes an effective national policy, then, of course, all such projections may need fundamental revision.

Moreover, as the utilities are primarily concerned with minimizing the dollar cost of providing the power, they generally postulate the lowest cost means of cooling. At some additional cost, the utilities could adopt less water consumptive means of cooling. When such options are assumed in a forecast, the projections of water consumption associated with a given projection of energy consumption are reduced substantially.

This essay reviews the analyses of demands for energy and water in the Delaware River Basin and the strategies for meeting these demands developed by the utilities and the DRBC. Section II describes the forecasting of new electric generating capacity. Section III explains why growth in electric power consumption need not necessarily require growth in fresh water consumption to the same extent. Sections IV and V discuss how the Tocks Island Dam decision is linked to electric power supply: at stake are the expansion of downstream generating capacity (section IV) and the expansion of pumped storage (section V).

II. THE EXPANSION OF ELECTRIC GENERATING FACILITIES

Demand Projections by the Utilities

The total service area of the nine power companies which operate in the Delaware Valley includes all of New Jersey and Delaware, most of Pennsylvania and parts of Maryland and New York (see Fig. 7-1). The population of this region, approximately 50 million people, is serviced (1974) by more than 30,000 megawatts of electric

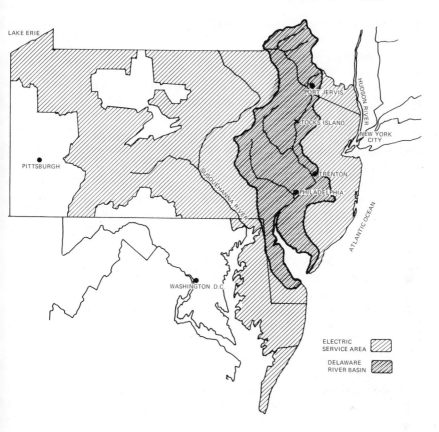

Figure 7-1. Total Electric Service Area

The electric service area supplied by the electric companies which presently own and operate, or propose to install, major generating facilities within the Delaware River Basin.

power plant capacity. (1,000 megawatts is a typical size for the major fossil fuel fired and nuclear power plants under construction today; earlier power plants tend to be much smaller.) This installed capacity exceeds by about 20 percent the "peak demand," which occurs during the afternoon of a hot summer weekday.[a]

It is this peak demand that is the subject of the demand projections performed by the electric utilities, for they must have the power plants built and functioning (or must be able to borrow the power) when the peak demand occurs, and they must allow for

[a]This is true all over the eastern seaboard; annual peaks still tend to occur in winter in some inland areas (central Pennsylvania is an example) where winter is more severe and summer air conditioning is not as widely adopted.

inevitable breakdowns and repairs. Peak electric demand is also the appropriate subject of attention of the water professionals (rather than, for example, demand averaged over the year, which is typically about half as large) for a different reason: the yearly peak occurs in the summer, when the river flow is lowest and the allocation of scarce water resources is most rigorously constrained.

The electric utilities have not ordinarily made public their plans for the construction of power plants until the time when permissions and approvals had to be sought, rarely more than ten years before the plant would be producing electric power. On the other hand, those responsible for the planning of water allocations, in a basin for which a dam with a 50-year or 100-year "project life" is slated, are driven to consider more distant horizons. The Delaware River Basin Commission, faced with requests for approvals of power plants, one at a time, demanded in 1971 that the Basin's utilities prepare a fifteen-year, Basinwide plan for power plant construction.[1] The result was a 1971 Master Siting Study,[2] and, approximately two and one-half years later, a 1974 Master Siting Study,[3] a modest but significant revision of the earlier study. These two documents are the subject of brief discussion in the remainder of this section, and again in section IV.

The Master Siting Studies take the reader through a three-step argument. First, peak demand is projected for the entire service area of Figure 7–1, an area four times larger than the area of the Delaware River Basin. Second, the additional capacity required to meet this demand year by year is displayed. Third, the particular power plants that the utilities wish to construct to meet that demand, and the scheduled times of completion, are itemized. As will be seen, in the two Master Siting Studies this third step was confined to plants in the Delaware River Basin.

In Figure 7–2, graphs from MSS-74 for the first two steps in the argument are reproduced. The projection of peak demand is a smooth curve, representing exponential growth from 27.2 megawatts in 1974 to 67.1 megawatts in 1988, an average rate of growth of 6.66 percent per year, corresponding to a doubling time of 10.8 years.[b] The projection of installed capacity is a bumpy curve, reflecting the large size of the individual power plants that are planned.

Relative to MSS-71, the projected rate of exponential growth of peak demand in MSS-74 is about one percentage point per year *less*.

[b]Close inspection of Figure 7–2 suggests that the rate of exponential growth is somewhat higher than this average in the first few years of the period and somewhat lower in the last few years.

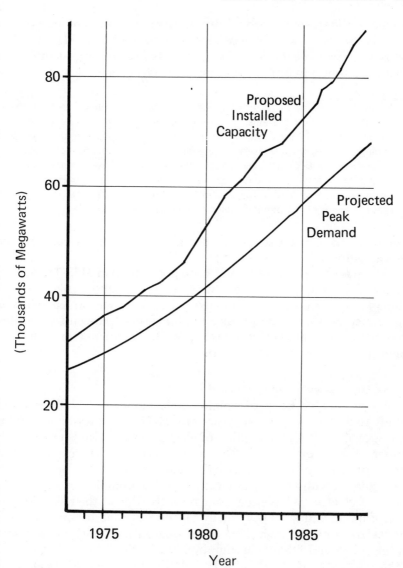

Figure 7-2. Projected Peak Electric Demand and Proposed Installed Capacity for the Service Area of Figure 7-1, May 1974
Source: MSS-74, Figure No. 1.

A clue to the reasoning behind this downward revision of growth rate is to be found in the few new sentences found in the "Growth and Capacity" sections of MSS-74. (The two reports are identical for pages at a time.) In MSS-74, but not in MSS-71, one finds:

> Existing programs by utilities to conserve basic resources used in the operation of their systems, and programs to promote conservation of energy among their customers are becoming effective, changing to some extent the historical pattern. Long-range forecasts of needed electric generation will take into account this change in use. These companies have recognized the need for conservation of basic energy resources and also recognize their obligation to plan for the future demands for electricity so that the needs of the public for electrical energy can be met.[4]

For two and one-half sentences, the concept of energy conservation gets an airing.

The word "conservation" did not appear at all in MSS-71. And, as Figure 7–2 shows, at the time of MSS-74 the utilities' planners still clung to the vision of indefinite exponential growth, which had been confirmed as a method of projection for several consecutive decades; "conservation" merely stretched out the predicted growth over time—and not by very much, at that.

B. Other Views of Future Demand

A considerable body of opinion is developing at this time which holds that the next fifteen years are likely to witness considerably less growth in the consumption of electric power than is projected in either MSS-71 or MSS-74. The critical variable is the change in the price of electricity: after years of falling prices (representing, in particular, technological innovation and economies of scale), the price of electricity has been rising recently (due to the rising costs of fuel, capital, and labor). Virtually all those willing to predict expect prices to continue rising for some time. The connection between rising prices and falling consumption is quantified through studies of "the elasticity of demand." (The elasticity of demand is approximately the percent change in demand divided by the percent change in price.) Estimations of elasticities require the statistical treatment of data and are notoriously difficult. During the long period when prices were falling at nearly a constant rate, and were expected to continue to do so, studies of elasticity were superfluous. It is when price trends change that elasticities become crucial to the projection business.

To show the significance of price elasticity, we borrow on the results of a widely cited study by Chapman, Tyrrell, and Mount,[5] who fit an algebraic model to data on energy prices, electricity consumption, and per capita regional income for eight regions of the country over the years 1945–1970. When they inserted into their model the 1970 Federal Power Commission projections[6] for the growth in national annual electric power consumption, they concluded that implicit in the FPC projections is an assumption that the price of electricity, in constant dollars, will *fall* continuously (dropping by 24 percent from 1970 to 1980 and by 39 percent from 1970 to 1990). Inserting into their model the FPC's predictions of gradually *rising* prices (19 percent from 1970 to 2000) presented in the 1970 National Power Survey, and holding all other factors constant, they find a much slower rate of growth than the FPC's own projection in the same survey: consumption is down 22 percent in 1980 and 47 percent in 1990 relative to the FPC projections. Finally, inserting more rapidly rising prices (a doubling of the price of electricity between 1970 and 2000), and holding all other factors constant, they find a still slower growth rate: down 32 percent in 1980 and 63 percent in 1990, again relative to the FPC projections.

The projections of growth of regional peak demand in MSS-71 are contemporaneous with the projections of total national consumption in the FPC's 1970 National Power Survey, and a close inspection shows ten-year doubling to be characteristic of both. How rising prices might reduce the growth projected in MSS-71 is shown in Figure 7–3, where the "correction factors" derived in CTM are used to "correct" the 1980 and 1990 peak demand values found in MSS-71. The demand projections are dramatically reduced.

Two other recent studies of future energy supply and demand, one by the Ford Foundation[7] and one by the Federal Energy Agency,[8] have confirmed the likelihood of rising prices and reduced demand. These reports go further in arguing that reductions in rates of growth and energy consumption (including electricity consumption) need not have deleterious effects on the national economy. The Ford Foundation report calls particular attention to the ways in which the deployment of energy conserving technology will stimulate the economy. Time will tell.

C. The Location of New Capacity

The projection of new capacity in the Service Area of Figure 7–1 was not revised downward anywhere near as much as the projection of peak demand, between MSS-71 and MSS-74. As a result (as can be

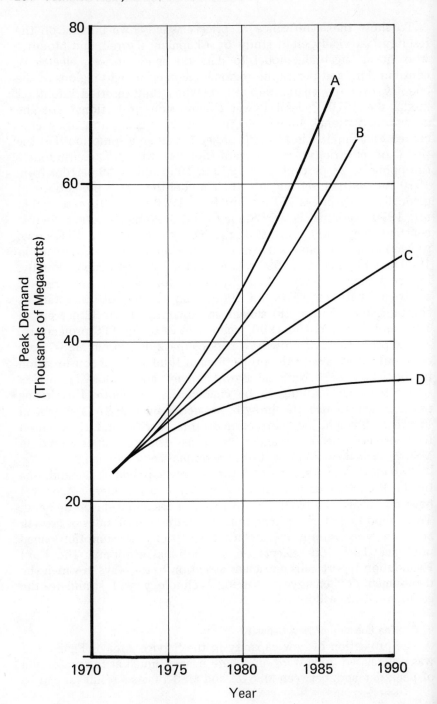

Table 7-1. Comparison of the 1971 and 1974 Master Siting Studies. (All figures are in thousands of megawatts.)

	MSS-71 (1971 to 1986)		MSS-74 (1973 to 1988)	
Capacity installed at start of study period				
Total service area	27.2		33.5	
Delaware River Basin	6.3		6.8	
(percent in Basin)		(23.2%)		(20.3%)
Capacity added in next fifteen years				
Total service area	59.7		54.2	
Delaware River Basin	34.4		22.5	
(percent in Basin)		(57.6%)		(41.5%)
Total capacity installed at end of study period				
Total service area	86.9		87.7	
Delaware River Basin	40.7		29.3	
(percent in Basin)		(46.8%)		(33.4%)

seen in Figure 7–2), MSS-74 calls for a 30 percent reserve capacity in 1988, compared to 20 percent reserve in 1973 (MSS-71 had kept the reserve under 25 percent throughout.) Apparently, the authors of the Master Siting Studies were more prepared to revise the rate of growth of demand than to revise the rate of growth of capacity to meet that demand. However, as Table 7–1 shows, 12,000 megawatts of new power plant capacity were shifted out of the Delaware River Basin.

The geographical distribution of the new power plants in the Service Area of Figure 7–1 was altered between MSS-71 and MSS-74 in two ways. Not only was a smaller fraction of the new power plants assigned to the Delaware River Basin, but also, within the Delaware River Basin, there was much more of a cutback in fresh water power plants than in salt water power plants. Figures 7—4 and 7—5 show

Figure 7-3. Published and Modified Projections for Peak Electricity Demand for the Service Area of Figure 7-1.

A. 1971 Master Siting Study. Published curve.

B. 1974 Master Siting Study. Published curve.

C. Modification of curve A, using "correction factors" for 1980 (2.38/3.05 = 0.78) and 1990 (3.01/5.66 = 0.53) calculated in CTM for electricity prices rising 19 percent by the year 2000. See Table 3 in CTM.

D. Modification of curve A, using "correction factors" for 1980 (2.07/3.05 = 0.68) and 1990 (2.11/5.66 = 0.37) calculated in CTM for electricity prices doubling by the year 2000. See Table 3 in CTM.

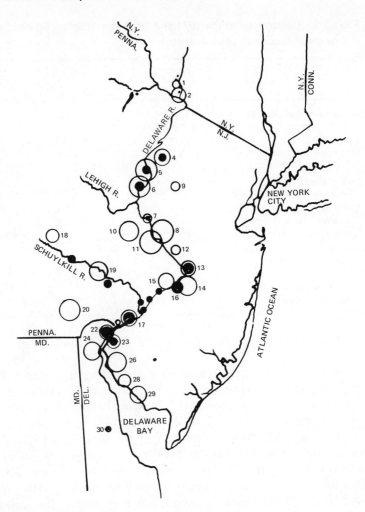

Figure 7–4. Power Plants, 1971 Master Siting Study

⊘ Existing plants in 1971

○ Proposed plants to 1986

Areas of circles are proportional to plant capacities. Numbers identify plants.
See Table 7–2.

the power plants currently in place in the Basin, slated for construction in MSS-71, and slated for construction in MSS-74. Table 7–2 gives the schedule of construction of all of the principal plants discussed in the two Master Siting Studies.

A simple explanation for both these alterations is that the uncertainty about the date of completion of the Tocks Island Dam

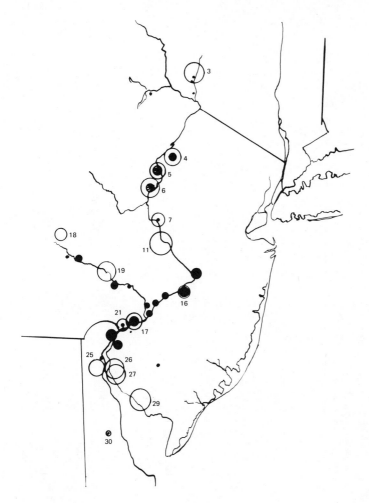

Figure 7-5. Power Plants, 1974 Master Siting Study

🌐 Existing plants in 1974

◯ Proposed plants to 1988

Areas of circles are proportional to plant capacities. Numbers identify plants.
See Table 7-2.

led the utilities to postpone several of the large power plants
scheduled for the region between the dam site and Trenton, where
water for cooling would be in short supply without the dam, and to
advance the planned time of construction of those power plants
elsewhere in their territories that had no equivalent pressures upon
them. A closely related explanation is that the utilities came to

Table 7-2.   Schedule of Construction of Major Generating Plants
N nuclear; F fossil; CC combined cycle; PS pumped storage.

	1971 Master Siting Study			1974 Master Siting Study		
Generating Plant	Capacity (mw)	Avg. Water Use (cfs)[a]	Year in Operation[b]	Capacity (mw)	Avg. Water Use (cfs)[a]	Year in Operation[b]
A.	*Above Trenton*					
1 Lumberland (Metauque), PS	300	c	80,81	—	—	—
2 Lumberland (Delaware), F	1200	20.4	82,85	2400	70.0	86,88
3 Lumberland (Cliff), N	—	—	—	1300	c	82
4 Kittatinny, PS	1300	c	76,79	1120	28.0	84
5 Portland, N	2400	56.0	81,83	1600	27.4	75,77
6 Martins Creek, F	2400	41.0	75,77,81	926	16.0	76,80
7 Gilbert, CC	320	2.0	73,74	—	—	—
8 Frenchtown, N	3000	73.2	83,84	—	—	—
9 North Jersey, CC	316	2.0	85	—	—	—
10 Lower Lehigh, N	2240	50.0	83,85	—	—	—
11 Upper Delaware River, N	3000	80.0	83,85	3000	80.0	86,88
12 Thuerk, CC	316	2.0	80	—	—	—
Totals	16792	326.7		10346	221.4	
B.	*Trenton to Wilmington*					
13 Mercer, F	400	1.6	85	relocated to Hope Creek		—
14 Newbold Island, N	2200	54.2	78,79	—	—	—
15 Croydon, F	1500	28.0	86	—	—	—
16 Burlington, CC	40	0.1[d]	73	40	0.1[d]	74
17 Eddystone, F	800	4.6	74,75	800	4.6	74,75
18 Berne, N	1200	28.0	85	800	14.0	86
19 Limerick, N	2100	54.0	76,77	2110	54.0	80,81
20 Mid-County, N	2320	e	79,81	600	8.8	78
21 Chester, F	—		—	—	—	—
Totals	10570	170.4		4350	81.4	

Table 7-2 continued

C.

	Below Wilmington						
22	Edge Moor, F	400	3.2	73	installed		80,82
23	Deep Water, F	700	3.2	78,81	—		76,77
24	Red Lion, N	1600	23.8	79,82	relocated to Summit		81,82
25	Summit, N	—	—		1540	19.8	80,82
26	Salem, N	2205	28.0	75	2205	28.0	76,77
27	Hope Creek, N	—	—		2200	53.2	81,82
28	Bayside, F	900	4.1	84,86	—	—	85,86
29	Delaware Bay, N	1500	19.1	86	2300	30.6	74
30	Dover, F	110	f	74	110	f	74
	Totals	7415	81.4g		8355	131.6g	

[a] See Figure 7-6 (p. 280) for a graphic representation of the cumulative average consumptive water use for the power plants proposed in both siting studies.

[b] Some power plants have two or three separate units, expected to go into operation in different years.

[c] Pumped-storage plant (see section V).

[d] Air cooled capacity of 528 mw also to be added.

[e] Mid-County was to import cooling water from the Susquehanna River Basin.

[f] Uses municipal water, which was not included (!).

[g] As discussed in section III, only a portion of the water consumed in the saline reaches of the River needs to be replenished with fresh water.

perceive that even with the Tocks Island Dam in place the competition for water in that reach of the Delaware was likely to be formidable, and the Delaware River Basin Commission was likely to impose a tough set of regulations on the utilities. The types of constraints the DRBC is able to put on power plant operations, among them requirements for the maintenance of stand-by supplies of cooling water, are discussed in some detail in the next section.

There remains the question of where new power plants *should* be located. Is the "fair share" of the Basin relative to the whole service area to be found by calculating its share of the electric power consumption (presumably, approximately the same as its share of the population, which is 40 percent), or by its share of environmental carrying capacity (measured crudely by its share of the area, which is 27 percent), or how? There has been a continuing thrust by the electric utilities to generate their power requirements within their own service areas. As transmission costs have dropped relative to production costs, however, two trends can be discerned: (1) the tying together of more and more generating capacity via regional grids,c thus freeing a utility from the necessity of building all its capacity within its territory; and (2) the creation of consortia to develop special generation sites, such as sites near coal mines, sites in the ocean, and (as discussed in section IV below) sites amenable to pumped storage.

Alternatives to power development on the Delaware include floating nuclear power plants in the Atlantic, generating stations in the Susquehanna River Basin, and plants in western Pennsylvania. Each alternative possesses its own set of economic, political, and environmental trade-offs that need to be evaluated before adopting policies for the Delaware River Basin. Care needs to be taken to assure that policies designed to limit exploitation of the Delaware do not impose even greater damages elsewhere. Miles of high voltage transmission lines to tie out-of-Basin power facilities to demand centers, the remote threat of nuclear contamination of coastal waters, and/or extensive power development on the Susquehanna may be unacceptable trade-offs for a free flowing Delaware.

A comparison of the sites in the Delaware River Basin postponed or abandoned by the utilities with the sites outside the Basin promoted to an earlier construction date would be instructive, and

---

cOne example is the Pennsylvania-New Jersey-Maryland ("PJM") Interconnection, which ties together a territory slightly larger than the Service Area shown in Fig. 7–1.

might be undertaken using various social and environmental indices. Such a study can now be done: the schedule for construction of sites outside the Basin, which was not contained in the first two Master Siting Studies, has finally appeared in the public record.[d] A comparison of upstream and downstream sites *within* the Basin is itself instructive; it is our central concern in the next two sections of this essay.

III. WATER DEMANDS FOR COOLING

Almost all the power development proposed in the 1971 and 1974 Master Siting Studies consists of major steam-electric generating stations. The fresh water impact will be largely determined by the quantity of heat they reject, their cooling method, and their location within the Basin. The quantitative details are found in Box 1.

Ordinarily, the heat rejected by a power plant is simply dispersed to the environment, and is referred to as waste heat. The heat does not *have* to be "wasted." It could become someone else's useful heat. The pairing of generating stations with industrial plants, to form so-called "total energy systems," can keep the heat from dispersing into the environment until it is used in a manufacturing process or in driving a building heating and cooling system. Not only is energy saved, but also water, since the rejected heat eventually gets dissipated to the atmosphere, without the help of a special cooling system. However, this scheme is rarely adopted. There are problems in matching heat requirements with electricity generating schedules, and these are exacerbated by the regulatory processes of the state public utility commissions. In virtually every power plant, the rejected heat is carried away unused.

A. Cooling the Coolant

What happens to the heat carried away by the coolant? It is dissipated through a cooling system in one or more of three ways: conductance to the ground, radiation and convection to the atmosphere, and evaporation. Cooling systems differ considerably in the relative importance of these three processes. Since of the three only evaporation involves a consumptive loss of water, the type of

---

[d]One of the accomplishments of the 1975 consultants' report (see Essay 3, sections V and VI) was to extract these plans from the utilities.

Box 1 Quantitative Estimates of the
Consumptive Use of Water for Cooling

When one cubic foot of water evaporates, at ambient temperatures, it entrains about 65,000 btu of heat. The corresponding statement in different units is: Heat can be removed at a rate of 1,000 megawatts (thermal energy) by the evaporation of water at a rate of 15 cubic feet per second (cfs). In a practical calculation of consumptive use of water from a power plant, one must use this fact of nature together with (a) the electric efficiency of the power plant; (b) the fraction of the rejected heat that is dissipated directly to the atmosphere, instead of being rejected at the power plant's condensers; and (c) if water is used to cool the condensers, the fraction of the cooling done by evaporation instead of by temperature rise in the liquid state.

Finally, as is discussed in the text, the significance of a given level of consumptive use of water depends critically on where the plant is located. In particular, for a site in an estuary or bay, it is possible (though difficult) to estimate a fraction that gives the relative impact of consumptive use on, for example, the salt front of the river, relative to the impact of the same consumptive use occurring in the fresh water portion of the river. The fraction will be less than one.

Electric Efficiency. The Second Law of Thermodynamics states that disordered energy (heat) cannot be converted to ordered energy (electricity) with 100 percent efficiency. As a consequence, when electrical energy is produced from a chemical or nuclear fuel through the intermediate step of hot steam, more fuel must be consumed than emerges as electrical energy. More precisely, the efficiency of such a conversion cannot be greater than $(T_1 - T_2)/T_1$, where T_1 and T_2 are the intake and outlet temperatures of the conversion engine, measured on an absolute temperature scale. Practical power plants come within about a factor of two of that ideal efficiency.

The rate at which electrical energy is produced, divided by the rate at which chemical or nuclear energy is consumed, the "efficiency," is about 40 percent for large fossil fuel plants and it is about 33 percent for current nuclear plants (which, for reasons related to safety, operate with lower

---

cooling system adopted can significantly influence the water quantity accounts in a river basin.

There are essentially four methods of cooling: (1) once-through cooling, (2) cooling ponds, (3) wet cooling towers, and (4) dry cooling towers. In once-through cooling, water is simply drawn from a river, passed through the power plant condensers (where it absorbs the rejected heat), and discharged back to the river. Because a substantial fraction of the heat in the discharged water is removed from

temperature steam than fossil fuel plants). The remaining 60 percent for a fossil fuel plant or 67 percent for a nuclear plant is rejected in the form of heat at the power plant.

Losses to the Atmosphere. Of the heat rejected at the power plant, a fraction is lost directly to the atmosphere, rather than appearing at the condensers. For a fossil fuel plant, which must exhaust hot gases up a flue, the fraction is about 25 percent; for nuclear plants it is about 7 percent. Combining this characteristic with the previous one, the reader will find that when electric power is produced at a rate of 1,000 megawatts at a fossil fuel plant, heat is produced at the condensers at a rate of 1,000 (60/40) (0.75) = 1,100 megawatts; whereas when electric power is produced at a rate of 1,000 megawatts at a current nuclear plant, heat is produced at the condensers at a rate of 1,000 (67/33) (0.93) = 1,900 megawatts. Thus current nuclear plants generate almost twice as much heat at the condensers as fossil fuel plants delivering the same electric output.

Role of Evaporation (Consumptive Use) in Cooling. In wet cooling towers and in cooling ponds, essentially all the removal of heat from the condensers occurs by means of evaporation. In "once-through" cooling, evaporation still occurs, because the river, warmed by the heated water returning from the condensers, cools down not only by convection and radiation to the atmosphere but also by evaporation to the atmosphere. A typical fraction of the heat loss ultimately associated with evaporation is 0.6. In dry cooling towers, there is no loss by evaporation—there is no water! All the heat is removed from the condensers by convection and radiation to the atmosphere. Thus, the rate of water consumption we estimate here for 1,000-megawatt fossil fuel plants is 17 cfs, 10 cfs, and 0 cfs, and for a 1,000-megawatt nuclear plant is 28 cfs, 17 cfs, and 0 cfs, for wet cooling towers, once-through cooling, and dry cooling towers, respectively. These values are in rough agreement with those quoted in Table 7-3 below. Among the effects we have not included, one important one is the carrying away of droplets in liquid form from a cooling tower (called "drift"). These droplets evaporate, and add to the consumptive use.

the river by convection, conduction, and radiation, the once-through system does not typically lead to as large an evaporative loss of water as other methods of cooling.

Once-through cooling has been the most common method of cooling in most parts of the world. From an environmental standpoint, it has a major drawback: the heated water disrupts the local aquatic ecology, killing or driving away cold water species of fish and other aquatic life and attracting warm water species. Even the latter may be killed if suddenly the plant is shut down for repairs. These environmental problems have led to regulations on discharges of heated water (so-called thermal pollution) in the United States, forcing the utilities to employ other cooling systems. Only three of the power facilities proposed in MSS-74 (Summit, Salem, and Delaware Bay) use once-through cooling. All three are located in the estuary or Bay, where large quantities of water are available to dissipate the rejected heat.

Cooling ponds and spray ponds cool the heated water by circulating it between the power plant and an artificial pond. Cooling ponds require an acre or two for each megawatt of capacity; thus, a 1,000-MW plant requires more than a square mile. Cooling ponds transfer most of the waste heat to the air by evaporation from the pond's surface, and hence have a large rate of consumptive use of water. Spray ponds, on the other hand, can be significantly smaller, and will consume less water since there is radiative and convective heat transfer from the spray to the air. Spray ponds, however, sometimes cause local fogging and icing. Because large amounts of land are not available and because the topography is generally unfavorable in the Delaware Basin, the utilities do not plan to use either cooling or spray ponds with any of the proposed power plants.

Wet cooling towers also work by evaporating water. In the tower, hot water from the steam condenser splashes down over the fill, or packing, breaking into small droplets that evaporatively cool themselves in the air flowing through the tower. The cooled water is collected under the fill and recirculated through the power plant. In addition to water lost to evaporation, some water is lost in droplets that are not recollected but are blown out with the air current. Water consumption is about twice that of once-through cooling. Not surprisingly, wet cooling towers can contribute to local fogging and icing.

The air flow through a cooling tower may either be provided by natural convection or by mechanical means. Natural draft cooling towers must be huge structures, often 300 to 400 feet high and 200 to 300 feet in diameter at their bases. The initial construction costs are two to three times the costs for once-through cooling. Mechanical draft wet cooling towers are less costly to build but more costly to operate. Much smaller, they use motor driven fans to drive air through the tower. The utilities in the Delaware River Basin currently plan to use natural draft cooling at most of their new power plants.

Dry cooling towers have no evaporative losses. Cooling water is circulated through finned tube bundles in the base of the tower, and waste heat is rejected directly to the air by conduction and convection. Because there is no evaporation, dry cooling towers require large air flow rates and large heat exchange surface areas. Their performance is sensitive to the ambient air temperatures; they function most poorly in hot weather, just when generating capacity is most needed to supply peak electric demands.

The use of dry cooling towers is presently limited to generating units of relatively low capacity. The large surface area and large air flow rates make dry towers substantially more expensive than wet cooling towers. Dry cooling towers can increase the capital cost of a power plant by 25 percent. This higher investment cost, however, can be partially offset by savings in transmission costs. This will be the case when load centers are far from substantial water supplies, as in the arid southwest of the United States; an air cooled power plant sited close to the load may compete favorably with a water cooled power plant hundreds of miles away. The relative costs of dry cooling may come down, as heat exchangers and turbines are improved, in which case wet and dry cooling towers may compete everywhere.

A summary comparison of the four methods of cooling is presented in Table 7–3.

B. Siting and Water Use

Ultimately, the magnitude of a water use must be measured by its effects on competing water uses. The quantity of water evaporated by a power plant may by itself be an insufficient measure of use since a gallon taken from one place may affect other uses more strongly than a gallon taken from another place. This is in fact the case on the Delaware River. Cooling water evaporated from the fresh water reaches of the river has a greater aggravating effect on salt intrusion than an equal quantity of water evaporated from the saline estuary.

A convenient way to quantify this difference is to translate it into demand for reservoir storage: thus the burden of a power plant upon the river may be measured by the amount of additional reservoir storage its presence requires to leave the degree of salt intrusion unchanged. By this measure, plants on the fresh water part of the river are substantially more burdensome than plants on the middle or lower estuary. According to a recent study, consumptive use near the Chesapeake and Delaware Canal, where Delmarva's Summit Power Station is proposed, requires only about 33 percent of the storage required by a fresh water plant. Use near Artificial Island, where the Salem plant is under construction and the Hope Creek Station is proposed, was shown to require only 20 percent storage, and use

Table 7-3. Comparative Costs and Advantages of Cooling Water Systems

Cooling Type	Water Consumption[a] (cfs/1000Mw) Fossil Fuel	Nuclear Fuel	Investment Cost[b] ($/kw) Fossil Fuel	Nuclear Fuel	First Cost	Water Consumption	Thermal Discharge to Rivers	Other Difficulties
Once-through	10-15 (11.5)	15-20 (17)	2-3	3-5	Low	Low	Yes	Large withdrawal requirements
Cooling ponds	15-30	25-40	4-6	6-9	High	High	No	Large land requirements; local fogging and icing.
Wet cooling towers	18-30 (20)	27-40 (29)			High	High	No	Vapor plumes contribute to fogging and cloud cover
Natural draft			6-9	9-13				
Mechanical draft			5-8	8-11				Mechanical draft towers are noisy
Dry cooling towers	0	0			High	None	No	Large size, penalties in lost capacity in warm weather, but flexible siting
Natural draft			20-24	28-32				
Mechanical draft			18-20	26-28				

[a]Adapted from *The 1970 National Power Survey*, p. 1-10-8, or (for values in parentheses) a weighted average of the maximum rates of consumptive use for all facilities of each kind proposed for the Delaware Basin in the 1974 Master Siting Survey.
[b]*The 1970 National Power Survey*, p. 1-10-17. Relative costs probably remain reliable even though the costs for each method have risen considerably.

below the Cohansey River, where the Delaware Bay plant is proposed, was shown to need no storage.[9]

C. Factors Determining Water Use

To summarize: several significant factors intervene between the
demand for electricity in the service area and the resulting demand
for reservoir storage in the Delaware Basin. These are:

1. *The fraction of demand in the entire Service Area that is to be
met by plants located in the Delaware Basin.* This is a complex
matter of environmental cost, economic efficiency, and social equity.
Among the elements to be considered are the relative population,
area, runoff, and existing power capacity of the Basin, as well as
economic trade-offs among cooling costs, transmission costs, and fuel
transportation costs.

2. *Type of plant.* Present nuclear plants, for example, add almost
twice as much waste heat to the cooling water, per kilowatt hour of
electricity, as present fossil plants.

3. *Type of cooling.* Wet towers, required on the fresh water part
of the river to protect aquatic life, evaporate more than one-and-
one-half times as much water per btu of rejected heat as once-
through systems. Dry cooling towers, though presently expensive,
would make this factor close to zero.

4. *Location within the basin.* A gallon of water evaporated from
the saline estuary requires substantially less compensating reservoir
storage than a gallon evaporated from the fresh water reaches of the
river. At locations on the estuary currently proposed for power
plants, this factor varies from one-third to zero.

When these four factors are multiplied together, they translate kilowatt hours of electric demand in the Service Area .into storage
capacity (or cubic-feet-per-second of safe yield) in the Delaware
Basin.

The relevant kilowatt-hours of demand are those that occur
during periods of low river flow; all calculations are based, in fact, on
severe drought conditions. Implicit, therefore, is a judgment about
the price we are willing to pay to avoid a shortfall of power on rare
occasions. Since low flow episodes are almost certain to occur during
the summer air conditioning season, one may speculate that the main
consequence of at least a moderate shortfall would be a forfeiture of
some air conditioning. How much are we willing to pay to prevent
such a forfeiture on rare occasions? Today's planners do not pose the
problem of costs in this form. The possibility of any shortfall,

though it always exists at some probability level, is considered unthinkable.[e]

All the four factors listed above can be varied substantially by planning decisions. This will be appreciated as we now consider how the changes in plans for power plant siting between the 1971 and 1974 Master Siting Studies for the Delaware River Basin (introduced in section II) affected the safe yield projections for the Basin's water supply.

IV. PROJECTIONS OF WATER FOR COOLING IN THE DELAWARE BASIN

The two Master Siting Studies present an interesting comparison of utility planning under different regulatory policies. The 1971 Master Siting Study reflects the absence of specific policies regulating the utilities' use of Delaware River water. Consequently, it could be considered as an indication of the power plants the utilities would develop if allowed unconstrained water use.

In the 1971 Study, the rate of consumptive use of water associated with the power plants installed between 1971 and 1986 had a maximum value of 700 cfs and an average value of 560 cfs.[f] The utilities retained the consulting firm, Tippetts, Abbett, McCarthy, and Stratton (TAMS), to examine the consequence of such consumptive losses for the water resources of the Basin. Using a modified version of the HEC-3 computer model of the Corps of Engineers,[10] and making the important assumption that all the DRBC Comprehensive Plan reservoirs including Tocks Island would be in operation, the TAMS study (March 1972) concluded:

> If the drought of the 60's were to recur when non-power consumptive uses in the Delaware River Basin have grown to levels projected in this study for 1986:
>
> a. Freshwater flow to the estuary would exceed the Delaware River Basin Commission flow goal of 3000 cubic feet per second by about 10 percent, and
>
> b. DRBC salinity limits would not be exceeded.[11]

However, if the Tocks Island Dam were not built, but all other Basin

---

[e]The problem of power shortfall due to drought is closely analogous to that of water shortfall. The latter is discussed in some detail in Essay 5.

[f]Both Master Siting Studies have chosen to emphasize the average, rather than the maximum rate of consumptive use of water. The average rate is about 80 percent of the maximum rate, and the choice of the average rate amounts to the judgment that even during the months of peak consumption, about 20 percent of the capacity will not be available.

reservoirs were built, the TAMS study concluded, "the minimum flow at Trenton will be reduced to 2,409 cfs."[12]

When the 1971 Master Siting Study became public in January 1972, the dependence of the proposed power plants on the Tocks Island Dam immediately became an issue. Proponents of the dam gained a significant argument in their favor, because of the shortage of electricity and the apprehension about future supply. Critics questioned the need for such an extensive proliferation of power plants and challenged the propriety of the federal government constructing the Tocks Island Dam to provide water to the power companies.[g]

The DRBC, too, was disturbed by the utilities' Master Siting Study. The DRBC appeared not to have expected water consumption associated with electric power plant cooling to grow to the level that the utilities proposed for 1986 until after the year 2000. Figure 7–6 shows the tremendous difference in the projected water consumption between the power companies' December 1971 Master Siting Study and the DRBC's November 1971 staff paper on water demands.[h] The DRBC's reaction to the 1971 Master Siting Study was that the Commission "by no means" would allow the amount of water for electric power generation to approach the utilities' stated requirements.[13]

Before the 1971 Master Siting Study was completed, the utilities had filed with the DRBC and the AEC a statement of intent to construct two 2200-MW nuclear power plants, one at Newbold Island and one at Limerick.[i] For a long time, the DRBC, presuming the Tocks Island Dam would be available to provide cooling water for these plants, did not consider what it would require of the utilities if the dam were not ready. Only when the DRBC was pressed by the Philadelphia Electric Company and the AEC in late 1972 did the DRBC confront that issue. Concerning the Limerick station, the AEC Safety and Licensing Board staff concluded that the AEC should not assume that the large quantities of water required by Limerick's wet cooling towers would be provided in periods of low flow by releases from the Tocks Island reservoir. Accordingly, the AEC directed Philadelphia Electric

> ... to furnish evidence of a firm commitment, not contingent on the approval of the Tocks Island project, from the Delaware River Basin

[g]The TAMS study (p. IX-6) estimates that it would cost the utilities about 30,000 dollars per year for each cfs of consumptive use, if small offstream reservoirs were used.

[h]The DRBC study is discussed in more detail in Essay 5 on water supply.

[i]Newbold Island is on the Delaware between Trenton and Philadelphia. Limerick is on the Schuykill River above Philadelphia (see Figs. 7–4 and 7–5).

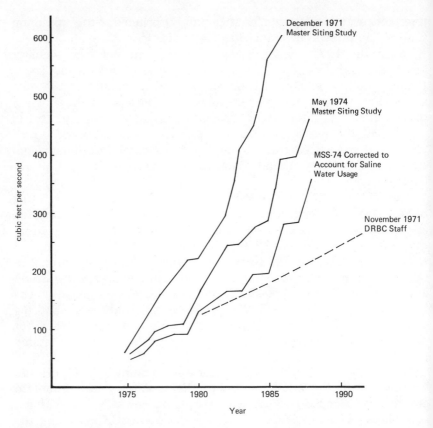

Figure 7-6. Projections of Average Consumptive Water Use by Electric Generating Plants Proposed in the Delaware Basin

The DRBC-71 curve figures importantly in the discussion of the DRBC water projections in Essay 5. The DRBC evidently anticipated a much smaller growth of power plant capacity in the Basin than the utilities.

Commission to allocate the required amount of water for plant operation.[14]

In March 1973 the DRBC conditionally approved Limerick's water supply, setting a precedent for Newbold Island and the other proposed power plants. Among the constraints imposed by the DRBC were two that had significant repercussions on the utilities' planning. First, whenever flow in the river at Trenton fell below the 3,000 cfs standard, the generating stations could be operated "only at such percentages of full load as the available water supply allows, as determined by the Commission."[15] This could mean the loss of generating capacity during periods of low flow, which (as we have said) occur in late summer during the air conditioning peak. Second, the DRBC insisted on a mechanism to avoid the imposition of such cutbacks.

> Prior to January 1, 1977, the Commission will, in its sole discretion, determine the adequacy of the then existing storage facilities on the Delaware River or its tributaries together with additional storage to be built to supply all needs (including the applicant's) for water supply from that source by the year 1980. If the Commission then determines that the storage will not be adequate for all projected needs of the basin, the applicant will build or cause to be built, at its own expense, at a location approved by the Commission, for service in 1980, a reservoir of sufficient storage capacity to assure the water supply needed for consumptive use by the Limerick plant, during periods when such use would reduce the flow in the Delaware River at Trenton gage below 3000 cfs. Storage and release of water in such facility will be under the Commission's regulation, at the expense of the applicant.[16]

Within this framework, the DRBC stated that *if* Tocks Island or an alternative were not available by 1980, both the Limerick and Newbold Island power plants would be required to provide their own water storage.[17]

The effect of these policies was to tie the utilities' planning directly to the Tocks Island project. As a result, the power companies had a strong interest in the construction of the dam. Separately and in groups the utilities testified on behalf of the dam before Senate and House Appropriations Committee hearings. But they only briefly mentioned their own need for Tocks water; instead they argued that Tocks was a "sorely needed" multipurpose project.[18] In the same period, the Philadelphia Power and Light Company made preparations to provide backup water storage for the Limerick Power plant. Public Service Electric and Gas acceded to the request of the AEC that it move the Newbold Island plant into Delaware Bay, to a location ("Hope Creek") alongside the Salem plant, which was already under construction.[j] And all the Basin's utilities set about revising their Master Siting Study.

---

[j]The principal reasons for the AEC request were more related to safety than to water supply. One of the ironies of the move is that, at least in current plans the plant is to be moved lock, stock and cooling tower. The cooling towers have a far less obvious justification at a site on the Bay than at a site where the river is narrow, and, moreover, salt water cooling towers have special problems, associated with the salt. The decision to retain a possibly unnecessarily costly cooling system apparently stems from a hope to avoid further delays in the licensing process.

In the 1974 Master Siting Study, the proposed total increase in steam-electric generating capacity in the Delaware River Basin by 1988 is 21,670 megawatts, more than 12,000 megawatts less than the construction proposed in the 1971 Study. Moreover, only one-fourth is to be in operation by 1980. On the average, water consumption is 25 percent less than projected in 1971 and is delayed three to four years, reaching 420 cfs in 1988. Although significantly less than the water needs claimed in the 1971 Master Siting Study, the revised needs still total over twice those projected by the DRBC in their November 1971 staff paper. The water consumption associated with new capacity is shown in Figure 7–6 (above).

The delay in construction and the drop in capacity are particularly striking for the two regions above Wilmington, as seen in Table 7–2 (section II). Below Wilmington, the previously planned power expansion is delayed only a year due to snags in construction, and the relocation of the Newbold Island plant to Hope Creek actually increases the total consumptive use of saline water.

For some time the DRBC refused to recognize the lesser impact of cooling water taken from saline parts of the estuary. The 1974 Master Siting Study also makes no allowance for this. But the DRBC's decision to require the utilities to provide their own water storage in the absence of Tocks led two utilities to sponsor the United Engineers study (mentioned earlier in this section)[19] to persuade the Commission that its policy of full compensation is unwarranted when the cooling water is taken from the saline estuary. The DRBC's latest plan for water supply indicates that they now accept the United Engineers' argument.[20]

In Figure 7–6, we show the results of a calculation of the "effective" consumptive losses of water when the United Engineers' adjustment factors are imposed on the MSS-74 projections. The adjustment for brackish water consumption dramatically reduces the MSS-74 projections of water needs. The adjusted consumptive losses of water associated with MSS-74 power plants are seen to be roughly half as large as the unadjusted consumptive losses associated with MSS-71 power plants. Of the 600 cfs water loss rate projected for 1985 in MSS-71, 200 cfs has been eliminated by the delay of power plants or their relocation out of the Basin, and 100 cfs has been eliminated by the United Engineers' reappraisal of the relatively small effect of the consumption of saline water on fresh water storage requirements.

The argument that the Tocks Island Dam is needed to provide water for the cooling of nuclear power plants on the fresh water reaches of the Delaware, after all, permits counterargument. The rate

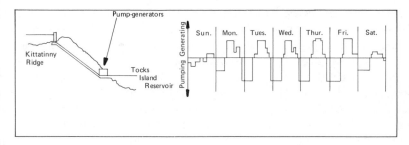

Figure 7-7. Sketch of Pumped-Storage Scheme and Pumping-Generating Cycle (From Corps of Engineers, "A Comprehensive Evaluation of Environmental Quality," 1971)

of growth of demand for electrical energy may be exaggerated. The Delaware Basin may not be the best place to put the plants. It may make sense to locate the Delaware Basin plants in the brackish Bay, and to choose fossil fuel plants. Perhaps through taxes related to the flow of the river, it may make sense to restrict electric consumption in the rare periods of very low water flow.

V. POWER AT TOCKS ISLAND

A. Pumped Storage

The Tocks Island Dam is linked to electric power generation in two distinct ways: first (as we have just seen), it could provide cooling water for the big downstream plants in time of drought; and second, it could be an element in a pumped-storage system, whose purpose is to match the steady output of the big plants to the daily fluctuations of demand. The pumped-storage system would work as follows. At night or on weekends, when the demand is at its lowest, power would be transmitted to Tocks Island to pump water from the Tocks reservoir to another reservoir on top of Kittatinny Ridge. Then, during the day, when electric demand is at a peak, the stored water would be released to spin turbines and regenerate part of the original power. Figure 7-7 illustrates the facility and the pumping-generating cycle.

While the arrangement consumes about three kilowatt hours for every two it produces, its potential economic advantage comes from converting low value off-peak energy into high value on-peak energy. The energy losses inherent in pumped storage can only be justified economically if the fuel cost of electric generation is low, as it has been for nuclear plants. Until nuclear plants were imminent, few pumped-storage systems were built. Despite their inefficiency, the utilities argue, "pumped storage is an ideal solution to the problem of providing peaking power" and is "essential to the continuing health, welfare and long term productivity" of the region.[21]

Prior to 1960, pumped storage was a relatively untried idea. Public Service had looked into the concept as early as 1947, but it was not until the mid 1950s that reversible pump-turbine development made pumped storage economically attractive and technically feasible. In 1956, New Jersey Power and Light began an investigation of pumped-storage possibilities on both sides of Kittatinny Mountain. One project consisted of a lower reservoir formed by a dam across Yards Creek and an upper reservoir constructed on top of Kittatinny Mountain about a mile from the Tocks Island dam site and a half-mile from Sunfish Pond.[22] This project was built in 1967 and is now in operation. New Jersey Power and Light also investigated a second pumped-storage facility that used the north side of Kittatinny Mountain and the Delaware River. Conceived before the Tocks project, this plan did not depend on the Tocks Island Dam. Rather, a lower pool was to be created by constructing a low weir across the Delaware River. The upper reservoir was again to be on Kittatinny Mountain, located between the Yards Creek reservoir and Sunfish Pond.[23]

The Tocks Island Dam project, as authorized by Congress in 1962, provided continuous hydroelectric power at the dam site (about 70 megawatts), where the water would fall about 100 feet from the lake behind the dam to the riverbed on the downstream side. This isn't very much power nowadays, when new power plants come on line 1,000 megawatts at a time. But this power had symbolic value for those in Congress and in the utilities who were veterans of the historic public-versus-private power controversies. Perhaps in part to remove public power from the scene, the utilities proposed to build and operate a facility that combined the hydroelectric plant and the pumped-storage plant, a Y-shaped unit that could direct the water from the mountaintop reservoir either back to the lake or down to the riverbed. There were substantial cost savings as well, relative to separate hydroelectric and pumped-storage facilities, and the proposal was incorporated in the Corps of Engineers' overall plans for the environs of the dam.

The utilities, in one version of their plans, shifted the location of the upper reservoir of the pumped-storage system to the natural lake known as Sunfish Pond. There followed an outbreak of "Save Sunfish Pond" bumper stickers and the first politically significant opposition by environmental groups. As described in more detail in

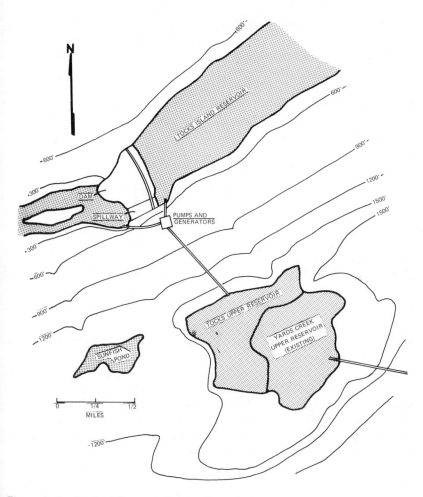

Figure 7-8. Revised Pumped–Storage Plan, 1971.

Essay 2, the utilities finally agreed to revise their plans again, and to build an upper reservoir separate from Sunfish Pond. The revised schematic plan for that facility is shown in Figure 7-8. It would expand the Yards Creek upper reservoir and connect this to the Tocks Island reservoir through underground conduits. The peak power that could be generated by this system would be 1,300 mega-watts, a rate that would be sustained for about six hours per day. The daily shift of water would cause a 100-foot fluctuation in the level of the upper reservoir and about a one-foot fluctuation in the lower one.

There is considerable doubt about whether this compromise plan really protects Sunfish Pond. The proposed new upper reservoir would cover 16 percent of Sunfish Pond's watershed, and its waters might well leak into the Pond. There is also controversy about the cost effectiveness of pumped storage at Tocks Island. Especially with the future of nuclear power in the Basin somewhat uncertain, there may now be alternative storage schemes both economically and environmentally superior.

B. The Alternatives to Pumped Storage

Pumped storage is one of several approaches to peak power generation. In general, currently available and proposed peaking units can be divided into two broad categories: (1) those, like pumped storage, that draw their energy from other power plants during off-peak night hours, store it, and release it during the day; and (2) those that use "raw" fuels to generate power directly as needed to meet the variable daytime load pattern. Tables 7–4 and 7–5, respectively, list devices of the two types. The potential economic advantage of pumped storage stems from its low capital cost, long life, and low maintenance costs. Since pumped storage is intended to supply peak electric demands that occur for only four to eight hours each day, its low investment cost for every kilowatt of capacity is particularly important, while relatively high operating costs for each kilowatt hour produced may be acceptable.

The investment costs of the utilities' proposed Kittatinny Mountain project would clearly be greatly reduced if the government were to construct the Tocks Island Dam. Also, although the advantages of some pumped-storage facilities are offset by the expense of high capacity transmission lines to and from the project, the proposed Kittatinny Mountain development requires only the upgrading of the existing Yards Creek transmission facilities. Excluding land and transmission costs, the capital cost of the Kittatinny Mountain pumped-storage project was estimated to be just under $100 per kw of capacity in the utilities' 1969 analysis.[24] This cost is probably near $150/kw at current prices and will continue to climb each year with construction costs.

The relative operating costs of pumped storage and other storage devices are highly dependent on the availability of base load generating stations that would otherwise be idle. Any estimate of the cost of energy from pumped storage necessarily has to assume a schedule for introducing new base load power plants. Indeed, a great deal of the utilities' optimism about pumped storage results from the anticipated installation of relatively high efficiency base load steam-electric units, which are designed for continuous operation. Particularly, the planned rapid expansion of nuclear power capacity, with its low incremental cost per kilowatt hour, enhances the economics of pumped and other types of energy storage. Their advantages, however, may be reduced if recent nuclear construction delays, soaring construction costs, and questions about nuclear safeguards persist.

Storage techniques other than pumped storage are relatively untried, but recent advances in materials and design could make several techniques viable by 1980 or earlier. Flywheel storage, in particular, seems to be a promising alternative. Attractive energy-to-weight ratios have been made possible by fiber composite materials initially developed for aerospace uses. A 15-foot diameter flywheel can store over 10,000 kwh with 93-95 percent efficiency. Costs per kilowatt of installed capacity in one estimate were near $110 at 1973 prices. They can be expected to fall as new and better fibers are brought into large scale production. Flywheels have the further advantage of easy local siting near load centers, cutting the transmission costs and friction losses associated with pumped storage.[25] The other storage types of peaking units listed in Table 7-4 appear less attractive, although they are all being actively investigated.

The generating types of peaking units listed in Table 7-5 are different from the storage devices in that they produce electricity directly from fuels and are decoupled from the base load plants. Their attractiveness is highly dependent on the future availability of clean fuels, which in turn depends on the development of supplies of low btu or other synthetic gases produced from coal. Again, because of low capital costs, the higher fuel costs of these units may be acceptable.

Combustion turbines and combined-cycle plants appear especially attractive schemes of the generating type. Combustion turbines are simple cycle turbines and are, essentially, aircraft engines adapted to ground use. In the past they have had low efficiency and have placed high demands on the clean fuels they burn. With higher inlet temperatures, efficiencies are expected to improve to 35 percent by 1980 and reach nearly 40 percent by 1990. Combined-cycle plants couple combustion turbines with steam turbines. By capturing the heat from the exhaust jet of a combustion turbine and using it to help fire a steam-electric plant, the combined-cycle plant makes better use of the fuel's energy. Higher operating temperatures are expected to push efficiencies to 50 percent by 1980 and 55 percent by 1990.[26]

Because of this high efficiency, the use of high quality fuels in combined-cycle plants may not be unduly wasteful. Both kinds of

Table 7-4.   Storage Devices for Peaking Power

Device	Projected Device Efficiency (%)[a]	General Advantages independent of oil and gas		General Disadvantages fuel and pollution penalty due to inefficiencies running time limited by storage capability	
		Specific Additional Advantages		Specific Additional Disadvantages	
Pumped storage (river to mountain top or river to below-ground cave)	67	low outages low maintenance costs long life low capital cost		land requirements remote location from demand centers	
Flywheel	95	easy location near demand centers small land requirements low capital cost		—	
Fuel cell (with hydrogen storage)	60	easy location near demand centers		low unit capacity	
Storage battery	70–80	easy location near demand centers		low power and energy density low unit capacity short life	
Compressed air storage	80–90	flexible siting possible near present generating stations or near demand centers		requires sizeable storage tank or cavern	

[a]The listed efficiency is that of electricity storage and regeneration. The overall energy efficiency of storage schemes, including original electric generation and transmission energy losses, would be about one-third of the device efficiency.

Table 7-5. Generators for Peaking Power

Device	Projected Efficiency (%)	Specific Additional Advantages	Specific Additional Disadvantages
		General Advantages easy location near demand centers can operate for extended periods if necessary low pollution	*General Disadvantages* dependent on oil and gas until coal conversion technologies are commercialized
Combustion turbine	35	—	loss of efficiency at part load costly maintenance NO_x formation
Combined cycle	50	—	—
Fuel cell	40	improved efficiency at part load	moderate life low unit capacity
Steam peaking	30	—	requires cooling water
Diesel	25-30	—	low unit capacity

plants are clean burning devices that are suited for local siting near load centers. Also, because they are factory fabricated, packaged systems, they can be installed at competitive costs, near $100 to $150 per kw at 1973 prices.

Other generating types of devices also hold promise. For example, fuel cells using hydrocarbon fuels are expected to achieve efficiencies near 40 percent in small units (25 megawatts) by 1980, and Public Service has already scheduled installation of several fuel cell units by 1982. Aside from high efficiency, fuel cells have the advantage of clean operation and they are usually air cooled, rather than water cooled.

There is also a nondevice alternative to pumped storage. As we noted in section II, modifications in the price of electricity can affect demand. Rates that penalize daytime use and encourage nighttime use could broaden the daily peaks, allowing the more efficient application of fewer peaking units.

C. Current Status

The Tocks Island Dam now (as of November 1975) seems likely to be deferred, perhaps indefinitely, and the utilities must decide what to do. As long as the construction of pumped storage was linked to the construction of the dam, the utilities presented a small target to environmentalist critics. In principle, the utilities could now revive their old plan for a weir in the river (that is, for pumped storage without a major dam); politically, this would almost surely be a mistake. The utilities must now, with new vigor, turn to alternative ways of providing storage and peaking power.

Perhaps, this time around, the utilities will make more of their analyses public, and will document them fully. Only two years ago, a utility executive told us that "the utilities have made the decision to undertake pumped storage and are running with it," and that was that! Well, they seem to have been tackled. The choices among peak pricing programs, storage systems, and peak period generating systems ought to be public choices. The external costs of each of these alternatives can only be properly evaluated through open and substantive public discussion.

NOTES

1. Delaware River Basin Commission Resolution No. 71–3, adopted April 7, 1971.

2. *Master Siting Study: Major Electric Generating Projects, Delaware River Basin, 1972–1986*, report to the Delaware River Basin Commission by the Delaware River Basin Electric Utilities Group, December 1971 (hereafter, MSS-71).

3. *Master Siting Study: Major Electric Generating Projects, Delaware River*

Basin, 1974–1988, report to the Delaware River Basin Commission by the Delaware River Basin Electric Utilities Group, May 1974 (hereafter, MSS-74).

4. MSS-74, p. 3.

5. Duane Chapman, Timothy Tyrrell, and Timothy Mount, "Electricity Demand Growth and the Energy Crisis," *Science* 178 (1972): 703–708 (hereafter, CTM). In CTM, annual electric power consumption (not, incidentally, peak demand) is studied in a model that also incorporates regional population, price of natural gas, and regional per capita income. Short run and long run elasticities are distinguished, as are three classes of consumers (residential, commercial, and industrial).

6. U.S. Federal Power Commission, *The 1970 National Power Survey* (Washington, D.C.: U.S. Government Printing Office, 1971).

7. *A Time to Choose: America's Energy Future,* Final Report by the Energy Policy Project of the Ford Foundation (Cambridge, Mass.: Ballinger, 1974).

8. U.S. Federal Energy Administration, *Project Independence Report* (Washington, D.C.: U.S. Government Printing Office, 1971).

9. G.A. Englesson and R.H. Anderson, *Delmarva Power and Light Company Summit Power Station Units 1 and 2: The Impact of Consumptive Use of Water on the Salinity Distribution in the Delaware Estuary,* (Philadelphia: United Engineers and Constructors Inc., 1974).

10. Generalized Computer Program HEC-3, developed by the Hydrologic Engineering Center of the U.S. Army Corps of Engineers, Davis, California.

11. Tippetts-Abbett-McCarthy-Stratton, *Water Resources Study for Power Systems,* March 1972, p. 1.

12. *Ibid.,* p. VIII. 12.

13. Letter to Commissioner Maurice K. Goddard from James F. Wright, Director of the DRBC, July 24, 1972.

14. As quoted in Delaware River Basin Commission, *Docket No. D-69-210CP,* March 29, 1973. p. 3.

15. Delaware River Basin Commission, *Docket No. D-69-210CP,* March 29, 1973, p. 7.

16. *Ibid.*

17. DRBC, *Supplemental Comments on Limerick and Newbold Nuclear Generating Stations, Delaware River Basin,* enclosure with letter to Daniel R. Mueller Directorate of Licensing, U.S. Atomic Energy Commission, June 6, 1973, p. 6. (The emphasis on "if" is the DRBC's.)

18. See, for example, U.S. Congress, House of Representatives, Committee on Appropriations, *Public Works for Water and Power Development and Atomic Energy Commission Appropriations, 1975,* 93rd Congress, 2nd Session, April 1974, pp. 444–451, 458–460, 474–476.

19. G.A. Englesson and R.H. Anderson, *op. cit.*

20. DRBC, Resolution No. 74-6, Adopted May 22, 1974, Section 5-3.3.

21. Jersey Central Power and Light and Public Service Electric and Gas, *Yards Creek Pumped Storage Electric Generating Station* (undated pamphlet).

22. U.S. Army Corps of Engineers, *Delaware River Basin Report,* December 1960, Appendix T, p. T-52.

23. *Ibid.,* p. T-53.

24. Jersey Central Power and Light Company, New Jersey Power and Light

Company, and Public Service Electric and Gas Company, *Third Amendment and Supplement to Application Approved August 1962, DRBC Docket No. D-62-2, for Approval of Kittatinny Mountain Project*, March 1971, Exhibit 2-3.8(a)(7).

25. Richard F. Post and Stephen F. Post, "Flywheels," *Scientific American* 229, (6) (December 1973): 17–23.

26. U.S. Federal Power Commission, *The National Power Survey*, Advisory Committee Report: Energy Conservation (Washington, U.S. Government Printing Office, 1974): 96–98.

Part 4

Nature and the Computer

Computers have greatly extended man's capacity to do both sensible and silly things. They have also complicated the task of finding out which kind of effort has been done. The best that can be done with a computer may or may not be better than no effort at all. A computer model can do a lot of harm if its audience loses track of the model's limitations.

The two essays in this section present a broad critique of mathematical models of water resources, from two complementary perspectives. Robert Cleary, a water resources engineer, has the highest hopes for them; Daniel Goodman, an ecologist, is made nervous by them. Each devotes a considerable portion of his essay to a single model, LAKECO, which has played a prominent role in the Tocks Island Dam controversy. The model claims to shed light on whether the lake behind the dam will eutrophy at a given rate of inflow of various nutrients. Were it reliable, it could help disentangle one of the most perplexing issues that have stalled the Tocks project. It could, for example, assist the planners who have to design the recreation facilities around the lake, allowing them to anticipate which coves along the lake shore are likely to be filled with noxious weeds in which seasons of the year.

Both authors make it clear that LAKECO cannot do this. It is beyond repair in two critical respects: it is one-dimensional, which makes it unable to reflect any spatial variations other than with depth; and it is simplistic in its treatment of the biological reactions that govern the growth of algae. According to Goodman, spending money to make the model more elaborate is ill advised—the science of ecology is at far too primitive a stage to be reduced to mathematical expressions of the kind such models require. Leaving the biology aside, says Cleary, models in their place are an invaluable tool in allowing the decision maker to assess the consequences of a wide range of alternatives.

Goodman is persuasive that biological systems will be especially refractory to model, because evolution has put a premium on being unpredictable. However, some would argue that every scientific frontier appears chaotic to those who work there, and that generalizations of use *are* being drawn from ecology at this time. Some pollutants do more harm than others, some components of ecosystems are more vulnerable to shock than others, some minimal size habitat is needed to sustain a population above extinction. As ecologists learn the principles that clarify issues such as these, and as the truths that emerge are given public expression, rational decision making, conceivably, could be the better for it.

✳ *Chapter 8*

Mathematical Models

Robert Cleary

I. INTRODUCTION

The application of mathematical models in water resources decision making has now become a fairly common and accepted practice. Many factors have contributed to this widespread use of models including: the enormous complexity of current water resource projects, the availability of computers, and more refined and proved systems analysis techniques. Despite this growth in the use of operational models and the frequent appearance of new models, there is little written for the layman on the philosophy, internal structure, and proper application of these models.

Mathematical modeling in water resources has become, and continues to become, such an esoteric and guarded art that only a small number of people in the country are qualified to interpret the results and inner workings of current models; and an even smaller group is able to develop new models, particularly those involving biological variables. These gurus of mathematical modeling are the experts who must be relied upon and consulted (often for considerable fees) by local, state, and federal agencies around the country who believe models will help solve their problems. This concentration of tools of analysis in the hands of so few is most unfortunate, for familiarity with these tools could be valuable to at least two large and important groups of people: (1) the decision makers themselves, and (2) concerned citizens who are directly affected by these decisions.

This essay is a modest attempt to explain mathematical modeling and the role of simulation, in terms the concerned layman can understand and apply. The Tocks Island Dam controversy is used as an illustrative example of the current use of mathematical modeling in water resources decision making. The role of a currently popular ecosystem simulation model in that controversy should serve as an interesting case history of the application of a major digital computer simulation model.

II. WATER RESOURCES MODELING

A. Evolution of Water Resources Modeling

Mathematical modeling of water resources dates back at least to 1925, when the classical Streeter-Phelps "oxygen sag" equation was first published.[1] It was a simple effort designed to simulate mathematically the dissolved oxygen concentration in a river downstream of a source of pollution. Although the mathematics used were unsophisticated and many factors affecting dissolved oxygen (DO) were not considered, the results were quite remarkable in how closely they simulated measured DO values. In fact, many present-day water resources studies[2,3] have used DO models principally based on this original oxygen sag equation, modified to handle additional DO factors.

From 1925 until the early sixties, most mathematical models were solved analytically, and environmental problems were studied largely by "hand calculations." This naturally limited the scope of the studies. However, starting in the early sixties, computers began to become larger, faster, and more accesible, and large mathematical modeling efforts became feasible. Problems that previously were too complex to solve by hand could now be approached. One of the first large scale water quality modeling efforts was the Delaware Estuary Comprehensive Study (DECS), which began in 1962 and ran for four years.[4] It focused on the Delaware DO distribution and has served as a basis for many subsequent modeling efforts.[5,6,7]

The use of mathematical models in water resources analysis and decision making can be of considerable importance to the ultimate disposition of a large water resources project. However, as with all evolving engineering tools of analysis, models have inherent constraints that determine the boundaries of analysis within which they may be properly applied. These constraints may take many shapes, but the principal concerns are the limitations associated with spatial dimensionality, time "dimensionality," and variables that measure the biological activity of the water. A firm understanding of a model's limitations is critical in assessing what questions a model can answer reliably and accurately. Misapplication of water resource models is commonplace, but so is underapplication: the failure to develop or use a model in a situation where the model would have been helpful.

B. Mathematical Models in General

In simple terms, mathematical modeling is a process that attempts to describe a dynamic, physical phenomenon by mathematical relationships which, when combined with accurate input data, imitate the real system. For example, if one considers a stagnant swimming pool, a differential equation could be written that equates the rate of temperature change in the pool to the net rate of evaporation, radiation, and convection occurring at the pool surface. After some simplifying assumptions, this equation could be solved, giving an algebraic expression that relates the time dependence of the temperature (the response) to the time dependence of some system disturbances, e.g., the ambient air temperature.

The advantages of using mathematical models to study a physical phenomenon are many. The given system may be studied as thoroughly as one wishes; i.e., any number of hypothetical alternative configurations may be probed, usually with a minimum of effort on the investigator's part. The investigator learns which variables are modeled easily and which need to be studied closely, leading to significant increases in overall project efficiency. In the swimming pool example, one could sit at the pool and measure the temperature for many months under diverse atmospheric conditions and plot such results on a multitude of graphs, each corresponding to different environmental conditions. This would take a great deal of time and the applicability of the results would be limited. The results would be contained in a mound of graphs; and because of the capriciousness of the weather, not all conditions would have been empirically studied. With a mathematical model and a computer, however, one could simulate an annual twelve-month weather cycle, through computer programmed meteorological relationships, and produce an output of temperature versus time for any period of the year and any specified environmental conditions. The savings in time and money, in addition to increased efficiency, are obvious.

In a water context, mathematical modeling is commonly used for water resources planning, management and decision making. Properly constructed models help our understanding of environmental behavior and broaden our information base, and thus they serve as invaluable tools in informed environmental decision making. Models are often used to predict the consequences of several viable alternative water resource plans that have a common data base and mathematical structure, but that differ in operational procedures.

C. Deterministic vs. Stochastic (Probabilistic) Models

The modeler who wishes to construct a mathematical model of a water quality variable, e.g., the temperature in a river, may use either of two approaches: deterministic or stochastic. (Occasionally a combination of both approaches is used, but this is a rare exception.) A deterministic model is one in which each variable and each parameter can be assigned a definite fixed number, or a series of fixed numbers, for any given set of conditions. In contrast, a stochastic model has uncertainty built into it: variables or parameters used to describe the input-output relationships and the constraints are not specified precisely.[8] Statistical techniques are used and results are expressed in language such as: "the value of dissolved oxygen will be 4 ± 1 mg/1 with 95 percent probability," meaning that in the long run the dissolved oxygen will be greater than 5 mg/1 or less than 3 mg/1 only 5 percent of the time.

Virtually all the large digital simulation models of water quality at present are deterministic in structure. Stochastic models are principally found in water quantity modeling, such as rainfall-runoff predictions and stream flow forecasting. The principles of deterministic modeling date back hundreds of years. By contrast, stochastic theory is relatively new, with most of the applications to water resources research appearing in the last fifteen years. For the foreseeable future, it appears that deterministic modeling will dominate water quality modeling. There are several reasons for this. Accurate and reliable stochastic models require extensive, precise and continuous records of data. Such data are rare; if a model of a future water resource, like a new lake, is desired, no such data *can* exist. The theoretical foundations for stochastic modeling are still being developed. And deterministic models have a track record: many water systems have been deterministically studied in a thorough and extensive manner, and several fundamental equations and relationships, such as the Streeter-Phelps equation, have been verified.

D. Modeling Variables and Transport Dynamics

In the simulation of water problems, the first choice is which water quality variables (responses or outputs) to model. The selection should reflect the questions being posed by the decision makers.

The most common variables used in water quality modeling are: dissolved oxygen (DO), biochemical oxygen demand (BOD, a measure of the strength of DO consuming wastes), temperature, and nutrients (typically phosphorous and nitrogen). Some other water quality indicators are turbidity, pH, conductivity, trace metal constituents, algal crop, total dissolved solids, bacteria concentration (particularly coliforms), and fish crop.

Complex and little understood chemical interactions and reactions, as well as gaps in the empirical data, make some variables more difficult to model mathematically than others. Thus the most pertinent parameter may not be modeled and environmental analysis may be based on how a secondary variable behaves. For example, most of the models of water quality in rivers have focused on predicting the concentration of dissolved oxygen along the length of the river. Two reasons for this focus are (1) we have had the most experience and success with this variable, and (2) an adequate DO concentration is a necessary condition for satisfactory water quality.

To be sure, in some rivers, the concentration of a particular toxic chemical would be much more pertinent to model than DO. However, because of a lack of understanding of how this chemical interacts, it may not be modeled, and instead the general health of the river may be measured only by its DO level. Unfortunately DO is not a sufficient condition for satisfactory river water quality; the river may be saturated with DO but unfit to bathe in due to high concentrations of toxic wastes.

Up until a few years ago, all the water quality variables used in models were "dead"—i.e., they did not describe organisms. The variables either acted like "good" chemicals, having fixed and well known kinetics or stoichiometric relationships (such as the DO used in satisfying a biochemical oxygen demand), or else were physical variables such as temperature. "Dead" variables are the most desirable to deal with (from an ease of modeling viewpoint) because they can be described by well known laws of physics and chemistry or by proved empirical relationships; and, in general, they obey these relationships regardless of the changing ambient conditions.

On the other hand, "live" variables, which have begun to appear in recent environmental modeling, are very difficult to simulate because we have not been able to define their behavior fully. One example of a live variable is phytoplankton, which has appeared in recent eutrophication models.[9] There are some empirical relationships that are being used to describe such live variables as phytoplankton, but often the description is crude, incomplete, or in partial error over a given time frame. The magnitude of the task of developing adequate models of live variables is described vividly in Daniel Goodman's essay, following. How much of that task can be accomplished as engineers and biologists begin to develop new working relationships remains to be seen.

All water bodies have characteristic hydrodynamic qualities. All reaches of rivers are marked by the presence of bulk advective flows, including estuaries, the portions of rivers influenced by tidal currents. In most rivers the primary advective flow is along the longitudinal axis, toward the ocean; this is the flow that is usually measured by a gauging station. In most estuaries two flows are occurring simultaneously: the fresh water current and the tidal current. The fresh water flow is continuous and is always toward the ocean; on the other hand, the tidal current is sometimes against the fresh water flow and sometimes with the flow, depending on whether flood tide or ebb tide conditions are operating. In rivers, when a pollutant is discharged, it is carried away downstream, never to be seen again. Estuaries, by contrast, transport the pollutant downstream on the ebb tide but return some of the waste on the flood tide; thus the pollutant moves back and forth in an oscillatory fashion, slowly making its way to the ocean because of the positive fresh water current. Lakes and reservoirs, in contrast, generally do not have a characteristic advective flow. Mixing and transport of material in such bodies of water is primarily caused by wind action, density effects, and concentration gradients.

An example of density influenced transport is the temperature stratification that occurs in all deep lakes. In general, a lake has a constant temperature in the early spring. As summer approaches, the upper layers (epilimnion) warm up, primarily through absorption of solar radiation. These layers, being at a higher temperature than the lower layers (hypolimnion), are less dense and tend to remain on top, producing a temperature stratification throughout the water body. In the fall the upper layers cool off, become more dense, and begin to sink. This causes a phenomenon known as the fall overturn; the entire lake may be mixed in the process. This can sometimes cause temporary water quality problems, when the lower quality water (low in DO and high in organic matter) in the hypolimnion mixes with the higher quality water in the epilimnion.

A mathematical model will trace the concentration of each of the water quality variables as it is advected either vertically or horizontally, as it diffuses (by molecular or turbulent transport) from regions of high concentrations to regions of low concentrations, and (if it is a "nonconservative" variable) as it undergoes chemical or biological reactions. The advective flows, diffusive transport, and chemical and biological reaction mechanisms are modeled by equations involving a few phenomenological parameters.

E. Space and Time

Space Dimensions. The present state of the art of large, operational, digital simulation models is rather elementary, in the sense that most models are one-dimensional in structure. This means that spatial variations of a given water quality parameter occur only in one direction, with homogeneity assumed for the remaining two dimensions. These models are therefore severely limited in the situations they represent accurately; however, they are often applied as a first approximation in a wide range of problems.

There are several reasons why substantial progress has not been made in developing two- and three-dimensional models. One reason is that real water resources problems are extremely complex, and our knowledge of internal processes (particularly hydrodynamic phenomena) is so incomplete that progressing beyond one dimension is thought by many to be unjustified, considering the many assumptions that would have to be made. Another reason is that two- and three-dimensional data bases are not available in sufficient quantity or quality, and thus model coefficients could not be calculated nor could such advanced models be fully verified. A third reason is the enormous demands on computer memory and time associated with two- and particularly three-dimensional numerical models, which greatly reduces their potential usefulness.

A final reason is that, in many cases, the questions being asked by decision makers are such that the approximate accuracy provided by a one-dimensional model is adequate for their purposes. For example, many rivers exhibit cross-sectional homogeneity (that is, pollutant concentrations vary only along the length of the river but neither across the river nor as a function of depth); in these cases, a one-dimensional model would be most suitable. One-dimensional models have also been demonstrated to be satisfactory for predicting the vertical variation of temperature in stratified lakes and reservoirs. [10,11]

Suppose a one-dimensional model is used to describe a nuclear power plant discharging hot water into a river. As represented in Figure 8-1, when a one-dimensional energy transport model is used to simulate the downstream temperature distribution, temperature variations in the Y and Z directions are assumed to be negligible, with temperature attenuation occurring only along the longitudinal or X axis (the downstream direction). This means that at any point, X_1,

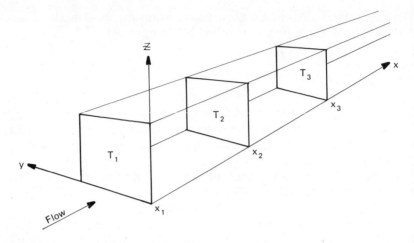

Figure 8-1. Temperature in a One-Dimensional Model

in the river, the temperatures at the top, middle, bottom, and sides of the river are the same, let us say T_1 (Fig. 8-1). At another point further downstream, X_2, the temperatures at the top, middle, bottom, and sides of the river are the same and equal to T_2; T_2 is numerically lower, however, than T_1. In effect, when a one-dimensional model is used, one is assuming that the modeled water quality variable, e.g., DO, BOD, or temperature, is homogeneous throughout the planes formed by the remaining two dimensions.

A two-dimensional model assumes variations occur in only two directions, with homogeneity in the third dimension. For example, let us again consider the modeling of temperature in a river. When hot water is discharged to a river it tends to remain in the upper layers due to density effects. This causes a vertical stratification with the hottest water on top and the coolest water at the bottom. As the water moves downstream, energy is lost to the ultimate sink: the atmosphere. As energy is lost, the temperature decreases in the longitudinal direction. Figure 8-2 illustrates how temperature varies in a two-dimensional model.

At X_1 in Figure 8-2, the surface temperature throughout the entire Y direction is T_1; however, the temperature decreases with depth, where T_1 is greater than T_1', which is greater than T_1''. At any fixed depth there is no lateral variation, i.e., the temperature is the same as one transverses the river from one bank to the other. At X_2 and X_3 a similar temperature structure is found, with the exception that the temperature is attenuated (by energy losses to the

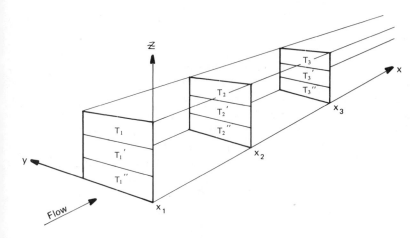

Figure 8-2. Temperature in a Two-Dimensional Model

atmosphere) at every depth, i.e., T_1 is greater than T_2, T_1' is greater than T_2' and so on.

A three-dimensional model is the most realistic possible, as variations in the longitudinal, vertical, *and* lateral directions are accounted for. In the example used previously, a three-dimensional model would predict temperature variations along the length of the river from the top of the river to the bottom, and from one bank to the other.

To take another example, consider the case of a single pipeline discharging secondary treated sewage into a river. After the waste enters the stream, it mixes vertically and laterally as it moves longitudinally downstream. Usually the depth of the stream is smaller than the width, and the waste will first become well mixed or homogeneous with respect to the depth dimension. Further downstream, the waste will continue to spread laterally until it contacts the banks, at which point it is laterally and vertically homogeneous. Below this point in the river (whose exact location depends, among other things, on the river dimensions and turbulence characteristics) the one-dimensional model may be applied to predict how the waste concentration will decay with distance. The model is not applicable above this point, although it is highly probable that one-dimensional models have been misused in this way. Because it may be a significant distance downstream before the one-dimensional model is appropriate, in many cases the waste (or temperature, in the case of thermal pollution) has had a chance to decay to a point where the concentration is essentially innocuous and there is not real point in modeling any additional decay.[a]

Most of the comprehensive, operational water resource models are one-dimensional. As environmental concerns increase and our questions become more complex, the demand for and use of more advanced, multidimensional models will also increase. There are many water resource problems that may be suitably approximated with a two-dimensional model. In rivers, because depths are relatively small, vertical mixing occurs rapidly and for many problems a two-dimensional model (lateral and longitudinal) is appropriate. For thermal pollution modeling, the vertical dimension cannot be neglected, because energy losses to the atmosphere result in vertical temperature stratification. For narrow rivers, however, a two-dimensional model is often suitable, in which variations in the lateral dimension are ignored. The development of comprehensive two-and three-dimensional water resources models is currently an area of active research, and significant advances can be expected over the next five years.

The Time Dimension.   A steady state model is one in which there are no variations with time of the variables being modeled (e.g., DO) nor of any model parameters e.g., the river velocity or waste discharge rate. An unsteady state model, on the other hand, allows for variations with time. Unsteady state models are more complex and difficult to solve but they are evidently more realistic and comprehensive.

A steady state model may sometimes be used, even though in water resources problems very few processes are time invariant. Consider a model of the DO distribution in a river that has several industrial plants and combined sewer overflows discharging into it. During certain seasons, if the plants are operating at a constant rate of production and if there are no rain storms, the steady state DO models might be appropriate. However, if it suddenly rains and the combined sewers overflow into the river, or if the plants begin to operate irregularly, the steady state model cannot handle the resulting situation.[b]

---

[a]Y.L. Lau has demonstrated that one-dimensional temperature models are not very useful because by the time they are applicable, most of the serious temperature dissipation has taken place. He has presented an analytical two-dimensional model to improve on this situation.[12]

[b]Ackerman and Sawyer[13] were critical, and rightfully so, of the DECS DO model because it was steady state and could not properly account for the many time varying phenomena which occur in the Delaware estuary.

If a steady state model is used under unsteady state conditions, the results will certainly be in error, the magnitude of which will depend on the particular circumstances. The point for the nonexpert to remember is that a steady state model cannot account for any processes or effects that vary with time; if these time varying processes are a major input to the water resource system, then the results of using a steady state model should be vigorously scrutinized and used with caution.

III. MATHEMATICAL MODELS AND THE DECISION MAKER

Decision making in water resource problems involves choosing the best strategy from among several alternative courses of action. Because of the complex hydrological, ecological, and economic interactions and consequences, it is not an easy task, even for simple systems. However, if the decision maker has a mathematical model that simulates the behavior of the real water system, his task is made considerably easier. For, when this model is implemented on a high speed digital computer, an enormous number of alternative plans may be simulated and the consequences of each compared and contrasted. Models are invaluable tools for achieving intelligent planning, decision making and eventual management of a water resource. Without models, it is virtually impossible to arrive at informed environmental decisions for many of the comprehensive water resource problems facing federal and state agencies today.

The rules by which alternatives are compared must be specified, and this is usually not done by the modeler but by his client, a "decision maker." Models may be used to test alternatives but they do not choose which alternative is best for public policy. Modeling provides pertinent information and makes comparisons; the decision maker chooses the strategy. He must consider not only the results of his modeling effort but the implementability of each alternative. The most technically sound solution may not be the most politically sound. For example, if there were a number of industrial plants dumping wastes along a 50-mile stretch of a river, it is possible that the optimum solution, which achieves minimum pollution impact at a fixed total cleanup cost, will have 25 per cent of them using no waste treatment, 25 per cent using 60 per cent BOD removal and the remainder removing 95 per cent of their BOD. Although the solution is technically sound and economically optimal, it is probably impossible to implement, and other alternatives will have to be considered by the decision makers.

Although there is no question that mathematical models could be invaluable tools for the water resource decision maker or manager, they appear to me to be underused. There are many reasons for this unfortunate situation. Beginning in the early sixties, the term "systems analysis" became fashionable in all fields of engineering. Many of the early practitioners, excited about their new tools, developed boundless optimism for this sophisticated approach. In their exuberance, they convinced senior management personnel (who were trained long before the age of computers) to invest a great deal of time and money in their projects, with the promise that these new techniques would solve all the complex water resource problems imaginable. Not surprisingly, very few breakthroughs were made. In many cases substantial resources were wasted, and senior officials developed a hearty skepticism for any project or management tool with the word "model" or "systems" in it.

Many of the early modeling projects failed because the researchers were either unskilled in systems analysis techniques or did not have the water resources background to direct and apply these new methods properly; in other cases too much was promised or the models were misused. Over the last five years or so, slowly but steadily, more people have become skilled in both systems techniques and the fundamentals of water resource and environmental engineering problems. Concurrently, digital simulation models have been improved to the point where they are of considerable usefulness in a variety of water resource problems.

Modelers now are seeking to change the poor image early modeling efforts earned and to get models widely applied. They are beginning to take some of the mystery and "black box aura" out of modeling, writing user manuals so that the nonexpert can understand how the model was built and how to use it. The assumption is that when the decision makers are involved in the development, operation, and feedback improvement of the models, they will better appreciate the strengths and weaknesses of models, and much of the present skepticism will fade. If operational models for water resource decision making were located in widely accessible locations such as designated universities or federal agencies, where anyone could study and use them, this might help further. It is still true that certain important models are held by a handful of experts who charge for their services and whose findings cannot be independently checked.

An adequate awareness of the uncertainties in the output of mathematical models invariably disappears in the communication of results from modeler to decision maker. These uncertainties are not the least bit mysterious; they enter when our knowledge is either incomplete, unquantifiable, or not useful in an engineering sense.

Even when we are fortunate enough to know a great deal about a physical phenomenon, the mathematical formulation in its most complete form may be impossible to solve or perhaps too costly to solve in terms of computer time and memory. Therefore, in almost all modeling situations, assumptions and simplifications must be made that place bounds on the range of validity for the model.

The field of water resource management is replete with examples where numerical output of a model was treated as though the degree of uncertainty was zero. To try to flag this problem, a major ecosystem modeling study for the Office of Water Resources Research contained the following caveat at the end of the report: "The risk we run is that one may believe too strongly in the model *per se* and place too great an emphasis on absolute values to the detriment of the model's greatest capability—to compare choices."[14] Unfortunately, the sentiment expressed by this quote is too often not appreciated by those responsible for making decisions.

Uncertainty in water resource decision making is not pleasant to deal with. It would be nice if models produced results that could be depended upon with 100 percent certainty. But they never do. The fate of multimillion dollar projects may depend on how the non-technically trained decision makers handle this uncertainty.

IV. MATHEMATICAL MODELING AND THE TOCKS ISLAND DAM CONTROVERSY

A. The McCormick Report: Eutrophication Is The Major Issue

The water resource decision making leading to the U.S. Corps of Engineers' Tocks Island Dam proposal occurred in the late 1950s, before large scale, operational mathematical models of water systems were available. Indeed, in those years very little consideration was given to the environmental and ecological consequences of damming a large river; had ecosystem models been available, they probably would not have been used.

In recent years there has been much opposition to the dam for a variety of reasons. One key issue, however, has been eutrophication. In 1971, McCormick and Associates,[15] under a contract from the Corps, predicted that accelerated cultural eutrophication would occur if the proposed impoundment were built.[c] They also concluded that if the river were dammed and no sewage effluents were allowed into the lake, i.e., current background conditions were

---

[c]Eutrophication means various things in various contexts, as described in the following essay. Here, the development of excessive plant growth of a noxious character is at issue.

perpetuated, the impoundment would undergo relatively slow natural eutrophication. The McCormick Report was based on very limited data and on some observations of other reservoirs (notably Cannonsville and Pepacton) in the region. Mathematical modeling of potential eutrophication was not done; indeed, the report concluded that "no existing model (September 1971) can describe or predict the complex interrelationships between physical, chemical, and biological parameters." Furthermore, McCormick and Associates felt that to develop such a model would take a "large commitment of funds" and a "truly national effort." Actually, at the time of their study, an attempt at such a model was in progress, but McCormick and Associates chose to dismiss it. Chen and Orlob, of the well known water resource consulting firm Water Resources Engineers (WRE), reported their initial ecologic modeling efforts to the Federal Water Quality Administration in 1968.[16] In October 1970, Chen published a paper[17] in a widely read technical journal that outlined an ecologic model applicable to rivers and impoundments; the model was "based on fundamental principles of biology, chemistry, and physics."

When the McCormick Report was received by the Corps, it undoubtedly caused considerable consternation. The report was very damaging in its eutrophication estimate; what's more, it seemed to leave the Corps with no recourse: without a model to attempt a second credible look at the question, the report and its damning conclusions appeared to lie unchallengable. However, fate was on the side of the Corps. Shortly after receiving the report, Dr. John Burnes, the chief of the environmental branch of the Philadelphia District of the Corps, attended an international conference at which Chen presented a paper on his ecologic modeling efforts and their application to impoundments. Burnes was quite surprised to learn of this model, since he had understood the McCormick Report to say that no such model existed. He also was quite delighted, for this model gave the Corps a viable alternative approach to eutrophication assessment; the worst that could possibly happen would be that the model would confirm the predictions of cultural eutrophication problems, and there was always the chance that results would be predicted in support of the Corps' position.

The Corps contracted with WRE to adapt their general lake ecologic model to the Tocks Island case, and in February 1973 WRE submitted its report to the Corps.[18] WRE concluded that Tocks Island Lake (the report is careful rarely to mention the word *dam*) "appears capable of supporting a well balanced ecosystem without undesirable quality changes as long as careful attention is given to the nature and magnitude of nutrient loading." It included in what it considered "careful attention," the application of advanced waste treatment, including 95 per cent phosphorous reduction relative to secondary treated effluent.

B. LAKECO: An Ecosystem Simulation Model

WRE's lake eutrophication model, known as LAKECO, is perhaps the best state of the art, operational ecologic simulation model for reservoirs in the world today. It has been adopted by the U.S. Corps of Engineers and is presently available to all Corps offices through the Corps' Hydrologic Engineering Center (HEC) in Davis, California. Since WRE's Tocks Island ecologic simulation study concludes that eutrophication will not be a major problem, provided advanced waste treatment is practiced, it would appear to nullify a major objection to building the dam. But the report has not had this effect. There are many private doubts at the Corps and the DRBC about LAKECO's predictive capabilities. These doubts have evidently permeated the decision making processes in several quarters, and the eutrophication issue still remains very much alive.

LAKECO has been the major mathematical model involved in Tocks Island decision making to date, and WRE's conclusions are favorable to dam proponents. Many feel secure, perhaps even smug, in their position, because they are backed by a sophisticated technological tool and recognized modeling experts, and because opponents of the dam have no comparable technological support. Since LAKECO not only is important to the Tocks Island controversy but no doubt will also be used in eutrophication disputes and decision making throughout the country (HEC plans to distribute user manuals to Corps offices), it is important to understand LAKECO's internal structure, capabilities, limitations, and credibility. Such understanding should help to put LAKECO in a reasonable perspective and aid in its proper application and interpretation.

The History of LAKECO. Water Resources Engineers is over ten years old, making it one of the oldest consulting firms of its type in the United States. Its first major effort was a series of water quality models of San Francisco Bay and Delta. Then, in 1967, the firm began to develop and refine a one-dimensional temperature model for streams and reservoirs, supported first by the State of California's Department of Fish and Game, then by the Federal Water Pollution Control Administration (now the Environmental Protection Agency), the United States Army Corps of Engineers, and the State of Washington's Pollution Control Commission. The WRE temperature model, which forms the basis for LAKECO, has had some difficulties in application and is regarded with caution by workers in the field.[d]

In 1968, WRE submitted a report to the Southwest Region of EPA entitled: "A Proposed Ecologic Model for Eutrophying Environment." This was the initial phase in the development of LAKECO. In 1970, Chen published a paper outlining WRE's ecologic simulation model for rivers and reservoirs, and preliminary tests of the model were reported for a one-dimensional, segmented river. In July 1970, the Office of Water Resources Research (OWRR) gave a two-year contract to WRE to develop a general purpose model for the simulation of aquatic ecosystem behavior. In December 1972, WRE submitted their final report to OWRR. As they had done several times previously, WRE refused to provide a program listing for public use, despite being funded by public funds.

The model became available to the public only as a result of the efforts of the Corps of Engineers, whose contract required WRE to supply the model as well as to advise and train the Corps in operating it. It is now a major model in the Corps' arsenal of water quality simulation models. I expect it to be used frequently, for the eutrophication issue has been such a successful weapon for environmentalists who oppose the Tocks Island Dam that it will no doubt be cited by other environmental groups who oppose dam projects throughout the country.

At first acquaintance, LAKECO appears formidable. It simultaneously simulates 22 variables including: DO, BOD, pH, temperature, phosphorous, nitrogen (3 forms), algae (3 types), fish (3 types), zooplankton, and benthic animals. In a typical simulation each variable has its own distinct differential equation, which is also subscripted with a designation of the specific slice in the vertical direction. Thus, when ten variables are being simulated and a reservoir 150 meters deep is divided into two-meter slices, 750 differential equations must be considered. In addition there are hydrodynamic equations that describe how flows move in the system. Many of these equations are coupled, because many of the concentrations affect one another. In spite of all this complexity, the equations can in fact be handled with no great difficulty on a modern computer. The most significant problems associated with LAKECO lie elsewhere: in its hydrodynamics, considered below, and in its biology, considered in the next essay.

[d]Specifically, I am familiar with one experience where Battelle Northwest (Richland, Washington) found they had to rewrite the program completely.

Hydrodynamic Simulation in LAKECO. The hydrodynamic scheme in LAKECO is rather simple in concept. The underlying philosophy is that water seeks its own density layer. Water flowing into the reservoir has a certain density based primarily on its temperature: it enters the layer in the lake that has the same temperature, and then *instantaneously* mixes through the volume of that layer. Since water is assumed incompressible, the inflowing water to a layer displaces water from that layer, which causes a net advective flow along the vertical axis. Outflow from the reservoir may occur from one or more of the outlets at various depths, depending on the particular discharge pattern desired. It is assumed that the outlet may be modeled as a slit having the same width as the reservoir dam at that level. Outflowing water comes from the layer at that elevation and from layers just above and below, in accordance with density based criteria. If the flow into the lake is not equal to the flow out, this net advective vertical flow results in a change in the surface level of the lake.

LAKECO, as a one-dimensional model, is composed of vertically stacked, continuously stirred tank reactors (CSTR's), in each of which physical, chemical, and biological phenomena can occur. The concentration of abiotic and biotic constituents and the temperature in each tank may change with time but never with spatial position within the tank. A tank typically represents a slice of reservoir two meters thick; the thinner the tanks, the more accurate the model, but the higher the cost in computer time. Since the tanks are vertically arranged, LAKECO is strictly applicable to a longitudinally and laterally well mixed reservoir where variations in concentration are significant only along the vertical direction. Figure 8-3 illustrates the spatial segmentation required by the model.

However, the cost of such simplification is a loss in accuracy and realism. By definition, the flow entering any CSTR instantaneously mixes with the entire volume of the tank. In the case of Tocks Island Lake, this means that if one pound of phosphorous is dumped in at the upstream end of the lake, it instantaneously mixes over the entire length of the lake (a distance of 37 miles), over the entire width, and over the depth of the stirred tank slice. Such incredible mixing would predict a tremendous and misleading dilution effect on any nutrients entering the lake. One doesn't have to be a mathematical modeler to be justifiably skeptical of the results predicted by a model that instantaneously mixes nutrients throughout a volume of water 37 miles long, up to 3,000 feet wide and approximately six feet deep. Thirty-seven miles of water can neutralize the effect of almost any

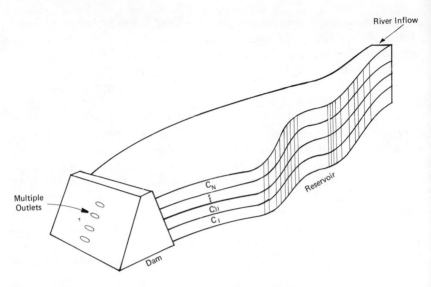

Figure 8-3. Horizontal Reservoir Slices used in LAKECO.

contaminant. Such dilution power has long been the dream of many an industrial water manager!

WRE justifies its one-dimensional model by the following interesting quote:[18]

> Orlob and Selna[e] have shown by comparison of simulated and observed behavior that the one-dimensional representation is satisfactory for reservoirs and lakes that exhibit pronounced annual cycles of thermal stratification.

This statement is patently misleading, for while Orlob and Selna (as well as others) have shown that for many reservoirs a one-dimensional temperature representation is adequate, the WRE statement implies that for stratified reservoirs, *all* water quality variables (notice they do not distinguish any particular water quality variable) may be adequately represented by one-dimensional models.

Because temperature varies directly with density, and because perturbations of temperature by sun and wind are driven primarily in the vertical direction, it is not surprising that in many reservoirs, temperature varies almost exclusively in the vertical direction. However, in the case of such water quality variables as nitrogen, phosphorous, and BOD, perturbations occur along the longitudinal axis,

---

[e]The work under discussion by Orlob and Selna is our note 10.

i.e., in the direction of the river flow, and therefore one would expect concentration variations to occur at least along this axis.

In any dammed-up river, the resulting lake tends to be elongated, with water quality variations occuring along the length of the lake. For example, because of phosphorous' tenacity in attaching itself to soil particles, one would expect the upstream end of a reservoir to have higher concentrations of phosphorous than the area near the dam (the heavier soil particles would tend to settle out at the upstream end). Therefore one might expect to find local algal blooms at the upstream end whose effect would gradually move towards the dam.

LAKECO cannot predict this local, longitudinal effect. It instantaneously mixes the phosphorous and soil particles throughout the volume of the layer nearest the inflow density, and thus dilutes the effect of phosphorous to an inconsequential level. Conversely, in the case of a discharge of sewage effluent at a point near the downstream end of the reservoir, the effluent might actually pass rapidly through the outlet with negligible effect on the lake. However, LAKECO would instantaneously mix this discharge throughout the volume of its discharge layer, thus making nutrients available to every chunk of fluid in the layer volume, and might conceivably predict an algal bloom when in reality there could be none.

In summary, LAKECO is inherently capable of simulating only longitudinally and laterally well mixed reservoirs and lakes. It is highly limited in its applicability to long reservoirs (such as the one that would be formed by the Tocks Island Dam, or a dam on almost any river), since significant concentration variations will generally occur along the length of the reservoir; the errors introduced increase with the length of the reservoir. In the case of a lake as long as Tocks Island Lake, the errors would be expected to be of such magnitude as to preclude any definitive analysis by LAKECO, and at least a two-dimensional (longitudinal and vertical) model would appear to be required. Unfortunately, two-dimensional, comprehensive eutrophication models are not presently available.[f]

V. CONCLUSION

LAKECO has certainly contributed to the advancement of the state of the art of a field still in its infancy, and for this WRE will be remembered. Before LAKECO, "advanced" ecosystem models generally assumed complete mixing and contained no hydrodynamic

[f]This section benefitted from several analyses of LAKECO done by Douglas Zaeh, a Princeton undergraduate.

subroutines. As most of these early studies dealt with small, shallow ocean bays or small ponds, the assumption of complete mixing could be lived with. LAKECO now allows us to extend these early efforts to deep water bodies where vertical concentration variations may be modeled by a series of stacked stirred tanks. But for many applications LAKECO and its next several successors are likely to be inadequate, and water resources decision makers who consult these models to broaden their information base must be kept aware of their shortcomings and questionable assumptions.

In the particular case of Tocks Island, the application of LAKECO has clearly not resulted in a clarification of the eutrophication issue; indeed, it may have contributed to even more clouding of the question. Because of the length of the Tocks reservoir, important longitudinal concentration variations are certain to occur, and LAKECO is completely incapable of predicting these changes. In addition to inherent hydrodynamic limitations, the 365-day Tocks simulation was based on only 24 daily grab samples of nitrate data and 20 daily grab samples of phosphate data. These data were massaged by a special "data generator" program, which precedes LAKECO, into 365 days of nitrate and phosphorous data.

The McCormick Report was most emphatic on the lack of input water quality data, and its recommendation that more data be collected was not carried out in time for the WRE simulation. Hence, even if the model were perfect, the data base used is so pathetically small (and the numerical values in some cases so questionable) that accurate model predictions are most certainly precluded. In addition to the lack of water quality data, the weather data used to model the reservoir temperature also is somewhat limited, and in the case of solar radiation was taken from New York City, some 60 miles away.

In summary, the very poor data base, combined with the inherent one-dimensional character of LAKECO, makes the WRE eutrophication conclusions highly suspect. It is recommended that these LAKECO derived conclusions be excluded completely in future Tocks Island decision making.

NOTES

1. H.W. Streeter and E.B. Phelps, "A Study of the Pollution and Natural Purification of the Ohio River", Part III, "Factors Concerned in the Phenomena of Oxidation and Reaeration," U.S. Public Health Service, Public Health Bulletin No. 146, 1925.

2. Texas Water Development Board, "Simulation of Water Quality in Streams and Canals:" DOSAG-I, 1970.

3. Hydroscience, Inc., report prepared for the Delaware River Basin Commission, "Water Quality Analysis of the Upper Delaware River: Easton to Trenton," 1971.

4. U.S. Department of the Interior, FWPCA, "Delaware Estuary Comprehensive Study: Preliminary Report and Findings," Philadelphia, Pennsylvania, 1966.

5. Texas Water Development Board, "Simulation of Water Quality in Streams and Canals: QUAL-I, 1971.

6. General Electric, report prepared for U.S. Dept. of the Interior, FWPCA, Philadelphia, Pa., "DECS III, Mathematical Simulation of the Estuarine Behavior," revised version, 1967.

7. Water Resources Engineers, Inc., report prepared for the Dept. of Fish and Game, State of California, "Prediction of Thermal Energy Distribution in Streams and Reservoirs," 1967.

8. D.M. Himmelblau, "Process Analysis by Statistical Methods" (New York: John Wiley, 1969).

9. E.J. Middlebrooks, D.H. Falkenborg, and T.E. Maloney (eds.), "Modeling the Eutrophication Process" (Ann Arbor, Mich.: Ann Arbor Science Publishers, 1974).

10. G.T. Orlob and L.G. Selna, "Temperature Variations in Deep Reservoirs," *J. Hydraulics Div.*, ASCE, vol. 96, no. HY2, 1970.

11. P.J. Ryan and D.R.F. Harleman, "Prediction of the Annual Cycle of Temperature Changes in a Stratified Lake or Reservoir: Mathematical Model and User's Manual," Parsons Lab. Report No. 137, M.I.T., 1971.

12. Y.L. Lau, "Temperature Distribution Due to the Release of Heated Effluents into Channel Flow", Dept. of the Environment, Inland Waters Branch Canada, Tech. Bulletin No. 55.

13. B. Ackerman and J. Sawyer, "The Uncertain Search for Environmental Policy: Scientific Factfinding and Rational Decisionmaking along the Delaware River" University of Pennsylvania Law Review (January 1972).

14. Water Resources Engineers, Inc., report prepared for the Office of Water Resources Research, U.S. Dept. of the Interior, "Ecologic Simulation for Aquatic Environments," 1972.

15. J. McCormick and Associates, "An Appraisal of the Potential for Cultural Eutrophication of Tocks Island Lake," prepared for the Dept. of the Army, Philadelphia District, 1971.

16. C.W. Chen and G.T. Orlob, "A Proposed Ecologic Model for a Eutrophying Environment", report to the U.S. Dept. of the Interior, FWQA, Southwest region, Water Resources Engineers, Inc., 1968.

17. C.W. Chen, "Concepts and Utilities of Ecologic Models", *J. San. Eng. Div.*, ASCE, vol. 96, no. SA5, 1970.

18. Water Resources Engineers, Inc., "Ecologic Simulation: Tocks Island Lake," prepared for the U.S. Army Corps of Engineers, Philadelphia, Pennsylvania, 1973.

Chapter 9

Ecological Expertise

Daniel Goodman

I. WHO SPEAKS FOR THE ANIMALS?

I remember a scene from a science fiction movie in which a solemn council was deliberating the declaration of war on a neighboring planet. This film, by now, is quite dated—all the men around the table sported Smith Brothers beards and Flash Gordon dentist smocks. But in one respect the scene still might be an eye-opener, for the council was an absolute model of pluralism. Listening to the representatives vote in turn, one could not help but be impressed when, for example, a man intoned, "The animals say war."

Provided we believed them, it surely would be nice to have nature's representatives speaking with such authority on environmental decisions. Instead, we get ecologists.

A "pluralist" justification for having nature and her creatures represented in our decisions, on the grounds that their wishes have some right to a proper hearing, is difficult to propound in such a manner as to be persuasive in our culture. To begin with, the notion of rights attaching to other than human beings strikes most of us as something of an incongruity. The nearest we generally come to admitting such a possibility is when we manifest an aversion to excessive physical cruelty toward those among the higher vertebrates with which we occasionally empathize. Even these creatures are not generally thought to have such minimal rights as a right to life, as individuals, except that their death, especially if intentional, ought to be painless. Admittedly, it is humanly possible to believe otherwise.

We are constantly told, for example, of the contrary sentiments of the American Indian; but, by and large, such sentiments do not speak to the spirit of our times.

A second difficulty is that nature's representative at our councils would be a human, raising problems of conflict of interest, at the very least. How does he know what nature wants? And why should we believe him? King Solomon's ring would be very handy at this juncture. Our best scientists could very well ask a bee where that morning's supply of nectar and pollen came from, and get an answer; but that is about the limit to the subtlety of our present ability to communicate directly with fellow species. This seems rather distant from such grave matters as interplanetary war, or even damming a small river.

If we abandon dialogue in favor of evolutionary exegesis, we may ask Darwin's successors just what it is that nature's minions want. The reply is terrible and uncompromising: "... to multiply and inherit the earth, each and every one of them." The reply is also unhelpful, for we know, just as Malthus knew, and Darwin after him, that they can't *all* inherit the earth; even if the last human were gone, they couldn't. Whether it makes any moral difference that we interfere (for totally selfish reasons, at that), rather than let them bloody tooth and claw on their own, is not at all clear.

We will move closer to a form of argument consonant with political thinking distinctive of the last few centuries by adopting a trick of Rousseau's. Let us try to imagine a situation that, if it had existed, would account figuratively for some reciprocity of obligation between ourselves and nature, an ecological contract if you will. Mankind's part of the agreement, evidently, would be to restrain its innate rapacity, and forbear unlimited exploitation of nature. In return, nature would promise continued sustenance, and some level of security from those plagues she has in ample store. If we overstep the bounds of the contract, the deal is off and we reap the whirlwind—very good reason for admitting nature's representative to our council.

Exactly which activities exceed our rightful "claims" on nature are not determined by our little parable. This question we must settle among ourselves, probably on a case-by-case basis, with constant reference to our best understanding of the underlying reality which gives substance to the contract metaphor. Holy men or poets will not satisfy us that they can provide this understanding, for we think it a technical, scientific matter. And so it is that, when the question "Who speaks for the animals?" is asked, one answer is, "The ecological expert."

Ecology and Environment

At this point it will be useful to try to differentiate *ecological* from *environmental*. Recent use of the terms, "the environment," "environmentalist," "environmental hazard," etc., allows *environmental* to describe a wide range of issues, including issues that fall in the older domains of conservation and the esthetics of nature, as well as public health matters involving pollution and crowding, global bookkeeping in matters such as weather, food, and population, and an amalgam of natural resource management and civil engineering that bears on the prerequisites for, and consequences of, various styles of civilization. I will follow this broad usage.

The term ecological, as used in such phrases as ecological issue, will refer to that subset of environmental matters that may reasonably be construed as falling under the purview of specialists trained in the field of academic ecology. This would mainly involve interactions of living things among themselves and with aspects of their surroundings. Thus a concern such as whether air pollution will lead to another ice age is an environmental issue that, according to this usage, is not strictly ecological, since the real question is whether this climatic change will result: we all know that, if it does, it will be bad for peregrine falcons, and redwoods, and people. On the other hand, a concern over air pollution's reducing the growth rates of plants is ecological, in the sense I propose. This distinction will help narrow the focus of my discussion of "ecological expertise."[a]

II. WHAT DID THE EXPERTS KNOW?

If we consider only the ecological expertise that has been brought to bear on the Tocks controversy, and ask, "What have the experts shown that they know?" or more particularly, "What have they shown that they know about the *scientific* questions that were put to them?" the most honest short answer would have to be, "Not much."

[a]The matter is blurred somewhat by real people and events. For example, Paul Ehrlich is recognized as a first-rate academic ecologist, yet the "population bomb" popularizations for which he is famous seem to me environmental rather than ecological. Conversely, some of the ecologists who are involved in such activities as preparing Environmental Impact Statements have become perturbed at the ease with which engineers, promoters, and possibly even charlatans can label themselves ecologists; and so the Ecological Society of America's journal, *Ecology*, and quarterly *Bulletin* have become, of late, forums for editorials, letters, and articles debating the merits of a professional code of ethics and a certification program for ecologists, even though the Society is academically based and its journal is one of the principal vehicles for publication in "pure" academic ecology.

The major environmental issues in the Tocks controversy have been the loss of a "natural system," interference with the shad migration, damage to the oyster industry in the Delaware estuary, and eutrophication of the reservoir. It is not certain that the "natural system" issue is strictly a scientific question. This matter will be explored later. Here we will concern ourselves with the three other issues, as these seem to have a clear factual basis.

The shad fishery may indeed be jeopardized by the project, as both the dam and the still water of the 37-mile-long lake will pose obstacles to the fishes' reproductive migration. Spokesmen for interested parties have variously claimed that the shad will or will not survive the project and that remedial measures such as fish ladders will or will not solve the problem. It is the recent experience of the Bureau of Sport Fisheries and Wildlife that adult shad will successfully negotiate certain kinds of fish ladders on their spawning run,[1] and as of 1971 there was a joint commitment of the Fish and Wildlife Service and the Corps of Engineers to build such facilities. (Earlier, the Corps was reluctant to incur such expenses for the benefit of fish.) There was talk of providing temporary fish passage facilities for the eight-year construction period, but no specific plan was ever adopted. The present life cycle of the Delaware shad is so short that a complete blockage for a few years could virtually exterminate the upstream spawning population.

Similarly, plans for screening various intakes to protect migrating fish from entrainment in the primary hydroelectric or possible pumped-storage flows were never made definite. The Bureau agreed that something of the sort would be needed, but this matter wasn't even mentioned in the Corps of Engineers' 1971 Environmental Impact Statement for Tocks Island Lake or in the New Jersey Electric Utilities' environmental statement to the DRBC. The Corps' "Comprehensive Evaluation of Environmental Quality" claimed that fish could pass through appropriately designed turbines without excessive injury.[2] The Corps cited a study of fish protective devices at the Muddy Run Pumped-Storage Project on the Susquehanna River, where it was concluded that "there is no need to provide protective facilities for the resident fisheries or other organisms now present at the site."[3] This study, however, did not concern migratory fish, so actually it is irrelevant to the shad question at Tocks. In fact, the report specifically states that if a migratory fish, such as the shad, were to be established in the waters in question, it would be a whole new ball game. Fisheries biologists at the Bureau of Sport Fisheries and Wildlife estimate that at the peak of the spawning run, 45,000 adult shad will pass Tocks Island in one day. The report of a Bureau hydraulic engineer points out that the diurnal cycle of a pumped-storage operation will cause migrating fish to be entrained a number of times before they are past it, with multiple opportunities both for injury and for confusion of migratory behavior.[4]

No one had an evidentiary basis for predicting that adult shad, once past the dam, would continue their upstream migration through the reservoir, or that young shad, which seem to drift with currents, would successfully pass through the reservoir in their downstream migration.[5] So the root question of whether the shad will survive the project in significant numbers never was answered authoritatively.

The question of possible damage to the oyster beds in the Delaware estuary is in a similar state. Some opponents of the dam worried that reduced springtime flow will cause the salinity in the estuary to increase, allowing the oyster drill, which normally is barred by its lower tolerance for fresh water, to migrate upstream, greatly increasing its depredation on the oysters. The Corps has indicated that the release schedule of the dam could be adjusted to keep the flow rate high enough during the critical spring period to keep the oyster drill damage to a minimum. Indeed, in its "Comprehensive Evaluation of Environmental Quality" the Corps went so far as to suggest that the release schedule might even be arranged for higher than normal spring flows so that the oyster fishery would be improved by the project.

Sooner or later the water managers will find their water sorely overcommitted. Temperature, oxygen tension, and flow rate of the release water will be important to upstream migrating adult shad in the spring, and downstream migrating juvenile shad in the fall; flow rates will affect the severity of the summer oxygen depletion in the pollution block at Philadelphia.[b] There is brave talk of using reservoir drawdowns as a fisheries "management" technique.[7] The depths from which water is withdrawn or returned to the reservoir, and the rates, will affect water condition in the reservoir with implications for management of eutrophication[c] and lake fisheries;[d] selective

[b]The present Delaware River shad fishery represents just a fraction of 1 percent of the annual catch at the turn of the century. The primary cause of the decline of this population has been the stretch of badly polluted water, near Philadelphia, which the migrating fish must pass. This pollution barrier is essentially impassable for much of the summer, due to an insufficiency of dissolved oxygen, exacting a heavy toll on returning adults and downstream migrating juveniles. These matters are discussed in a well documented report.[6] Conceivably, appropriate water releases from the reservoir during periods of low flow could mitigate the Philadelphia pollution block.

[c]Computer modeling of the relation between water conditions and the mode of release at the dam was undertaken by a consulting firm, Water Resources Engineering.

[d]For example, the "two-story" fishery touted by the Corps in its impact statement, and described in some of the Fish and Wildlife memos (e.g., Jenkins[7]), require that the lower levels of the lake be cold but well oxygenated.

withdrawal will similarly determine the nature of river fisheries directly downstream of the dam. The Delaware conservation department was worried that a higher flow rate would simply move the Philadelphia pollution block downstream into Delaware waters, and possibly further pollute the oyster beds![8] Clearly, the systems engineers will have their hands full long after the biological facts are secured.

The Fish and Wildlife Service claims to have data indicating the correlation between salinities over the oyster beds and flow rates in the Delaware River, and they seem confident that salinity is the determining factor in controlling the oyster drill. However, nothing much seems to be known about a protozoan infection that has been making severe inroads in the Delaware oyster beds since the mid 1950s, so there is no telling whether the oyster fishery will improve or decline with or without the dam.[e]

These two issues, the shad and the oysters, were handled very casually. With the exception of the Fish and Wildlife Service's involvement in the design of a fish ladder, there was no concerted application of expertise to answer the factual questions raised in these controversies. Instead, the major parties in the debate simply asserted that one outcome or another would or would not occur, or they off-handedly quoted someone to such effect. We might easily believe that appropriate ecological expertise was underemployed in these issues. This seems all the more likely when we consider that the shad and oyster issues in themselves were not politically significant in the debate—they were mostly used as symbols, and the symbols did not excite much response.

The eutrophication issue, on the other hand, has been politically significant. It certainly has delayed project approval, and in time it may decide the matter. The eutrophication issue has proved more important than the shad and oysters, in part because people were more ready to accept that "eutrophication" is evidence of environmental deterioration of some sort. Perhaps this acceptance was conditioned by familiarity with eutrophication as an issue in other, not necessarily local, controversies—phosphate detergents, sewage

---

[e]The oyster catch in recent years has been about one-tenth that of the previous few decades, and even less than earlier in the century. While some upstream migration of the oyster drill has been noted, the primary cause for the recent decline of the oyster fishery seems to be the protozoan disease, which may or may not have some connection with salinites or pollution. Various bits and pieces of information on the biology of the oyster problem are summarized in the Bureau of Sport Fisheries and Wildlife memorandum by Massman.[6]

treatment, agricultural fertilizers, etc.—and by the fact that the feared outcome has a high visibility.[f]

Almost everyone will agree that a reservoir suffering algal blooms looks weird and smells bad. Because of this, the project promoters and the politicians responsible for making a decision on the project are sensitive to the possibility of eutrophication: if the lake goes sour, it will stand as a public monument to a seamy side of their decision.

The dollar cost of eutrophication is not quite so clear. If the lake becomes outrageously foul, the recreation value of the project will diminish significantly. However, many recreation activities are compatible with at least some level of eutrophication; and I don't suppose that terribly objectionable conditions will persist year round. That is, if there were no special commitment to preventing or remedying anticipatable eutrophication, the dollar cost of its occurrence would not loom large in a conventional benefit-cost analysis. Given a commitment to prevent eutrophication in the lake, the costs of appropriate effluent control programs (necessary in the entire upriver drainage basin, as well as in the immediate Tocks area) can be awesome.[10]

It is one of the ironies of the Tocks controversy that in the matter of "eutrophication"—the only environmental issue that clearly has been perceived as more than an irritant at the decision maker's level—it is quite evident that ecological expertise, as employed, was not effective in resolving the question, "Will the lake become eutrophic?" The Weston study[10] included a rough phosphorus budget of the Delaware and concluded that "the reservoir will be threatened with an increased rate of eutrophication." McCormick Associates

---

[f]Part of the Bureau of Sport Fisheries and Wildlife's interest in the fish ladder to mitigate blockage of the shad migration at the dam seems to be motivated by recognition of the "visibility" of this impact. In their memo we find:

> It is inconceivable in this enlightened environmental age that hundreds of thousands of adult shad can be blocked at the dam without provision for their upstream passage, and we are certain this situation will not occur. . . ."
> We believe it prudent to provide a fishway to assure preservation of gene pool of the upstream races against future habitat losses downstream. It is also realistic, since the public would not likely countenance blockage at the dam if it resulted in obvious fish kills.[9]

It is tempting to conclude from this that the question of loss of shad, as adults or young, *in* the reservoir is of lower priority simply because the outcome is of lower visibility—the fish would simply disappear.

found the data base insufficient, but concluded that eutrophication seemed probable.[11] A transparently absurd computer model used by Water Resources Engineering predicted that the reservoir would not eutrophy if the present level of nutrient input were maintained.[12]

The question, "Will the lake be eutrophic?" actually encompasses several quite different possible questions, depending on the intended meaning of eutrophic. The ambiguity of the term has, of course, added to the confusion of the public debates, for project opponents use "eutrophic" to designate a truly abominable stagnation, while apologists speak of "eutrophication" as a slight enrichment which may even be somewhat beneficial to the fisheries.[g]

The Environmental Protection Agency never was satisfied with the treatment of the eutrophication problem in the documents it received,[h] and the Council on Environmental Quality refused to commit itself to a prediction on eutrophication at Tocks, given the uncertainty of the data and the calculations. All in all, the most

---

[g]Compare, for example:

> Among the environmental dangers, perhaps the most serious is that, if the waters are impounded in a reservoir, as presently planned, "eutrophic conditions would develop rather rapidly." The oxygen would be virtually exhausted and the lake would be dead. . . Eutrophication of the reservoir would rule out its use for recreational purposes. Fish would not live in it and its stench would be intolerable. . . (letter from Senator Case [R-NJ] to CEQ, January 14, 1972).

And:

> Blooms of algae can be expected to occur on the reservoir, but these will not pose problems to fish production or fishing (Slater, et al., Bureau of Sport Fisheries and Wildlife memo, *op. cit.*).

Or:

> Eutrophication is the process of aging experienced by all lakes in which plant growth—algae—occurs. Such growth is accelerated when abundant nutrients, especially phosphates, are available (DRBC statement in "The Keystone Project, Tocks Island Revisited," *Delaware Basin Bulletin*, 10, Sept/Oct 1971).

[h]The Environmental Protection Agency, in its review of the Corps' 1971 Impact Statement (this was the third draft received by EPA), wrote:

> Our principal concern is the still unresolved issue of water quality in the reservoir, particularly the risk of rapid eutrophication. . . .
> There is a division of opinion among EPA offices which have reviewed the statement as to whether the risk of eutrophication is controllable by careful management plans or whether probable waste loads will be too great to permit maintenance of high water quality in the reservoir by management at the site. We do not have enough information to resolve this question at the present time (letter appended to the Impact Statement).

The EPA response to the revised Impact Statement, which was accompanied by the "Comprehensive Evaluation of Water Quality" and a consultants' study

persuasive argument that has been brought to bear on this question is the homely observation that a nearby reservoir, which in many ways is similar to the one planned for Tocks, has in fact become disagreeably eutrophic. Thus, where ecological experts were systematically employed in the Tocks Island Dam controversy, they were ineffectual.

The failure of ecological experts to deliver the goods when asked to make a practical and specific prediction is not a peculiarity restricted to the Tocks case. Many environmental controversies involving seemingly straightforward factual questions go unresolved. Why this should be so is explored next.

III. WHAT MIGHT THE EXPERTS KNOW?

We have gained the impression that ecology is not, at present, very effective as a predictive science. This is not necessarily a dishonor, for it is quite conceivable that the phenomena that comprise the domain of "macrobiology" are refractory to the sorts of simplifying insights that have made physics and chemistry, as we know them, possible. In other words, there might be some peculiarities of the biological world that, when considered at the level of whole organisms, populations, communities, and ecosystems, make the scientific questions we want to ask of the ecological experts extraordinarily difficult—so difficult that it is too much to hope that the answers be anywhere near as reliable as the answers that could be expected of, for example, a competent chemical engineer operating within the scope of his expertise. I will argue that this is the case.

Six distinguishable features of the biological world mitigate against a predictive ecology. Three of these are simply observed facts: that there are many species; that organisms exhibit "homeostasis" in their internal milieu; and that many (perhaps most) of the species populations found living at a particular site seem to affect one another. The other three features are not direct observations but, instead, are abstract principles inferred by evolutionary logic from a few observations: that each species is in some functionally important way different from every other; that organisms do not respond in simple, generalizable ways to the factors that are important to their survival; and that whatever balance does exist in a natural system is in part a

---

of the eutrophication problem, was more definite: "EPA's conclusion is that a eutrophication hazard exists for the proposed Tocks Island Lake under existing waste treatment conditions in the Upper Delaware Basin. We should point out that the eutrophication problem is a result of the impoundment. . ." This letter to the Corps then requested more specific plans for waste treatment.

consequence of its history. These facts and principles will be discussed in alternating order.

A. The Multitude of Species

One of the most striking aspects of the biological world is the vast numbers of different kinds of organisms. One attempt at compilation of the numbers of described species of various groups of animals[13] is reproduced in Table 9-1. We must add another 200,000 or so species of plants. For some of these groups the listing probably is near complete. For example, this is thought to be true for birds, on account of several kinds of evidence: it is felt that the world's bird fauna have been well researched, most of the places that birds could inhabit have been visited by naturalists, birds are readily visible to the naked eye and are not especially secretive in their habits, and, finally, the rate at which new bird species are being described is quite low. By comparison, we can see that these kinds of reasons do not apply so obviously to groups such as insects, and indeed it is thought that there may be at least as many undescribed insect species as are now known. One estimate, based on observations regarding the relative commonness and rarity of insect species, sets the total number at three million.[14]

Not only are there very many species in the world, there often are very many species in lesser geographic areas. As examples of the numbers of species that may be found in a given region or sample, one might find the following instructive: 1,395 bird species are known from Colombia;[15] about 2,500 species of flowering plants are known from Florida;[16] 134 species of ants have been found on the island of Trinidad;[17] over 300 species of shrimplike creatures of the genus *Gammarus* have been described from Lake Baikal;[18] about 300 species of the fruit fly (*Drosophila*) found in the Hawaiian Islands are found nowhere else;[19] a series of quarter acre sample plots in deciduous cove forest in the Great Smoky Mountains each encompassed 46 to 68 species of vascular plants;[20] a single block of soil eight inches square and one inch deep yielded 25 species of nonpredaceous mites;[21] and a single light trap operating in Maine for four years caught 349 species of moths.[22]

The Park Service prepared a checklist of biota of the Tocks Island Recreation Area, which is summarized in Table 9-2.[23] We note that the numbers are impressive, even though entire phyla have been omitted.

B. Every Species Is Different

It has long been recognized that organisms have a capacity for geometric increase. Only because of high mortality does this increase

Table 9-1. Estimated Number of Known Species of Recent Animals

Protozoa	30,000	Linguatula	70
Mesozoa	50	Chelicerata	35,000
Porifera	4,500	Crustacea	25,000
Coelenterata	9,000	Other arthropods (excl. insects)	13,000
Ctenophora	90	Insecta	850,000
Platyhelminthes	6,000	Mollusca	80,000
Acanthocephala	300	Pogonophora	1
Rotifera	1,500	Bryozoa	3,300
Gastrotricha	175	Brachiopoda	250
Kinorhyncha	100	Echinodermata	4,000
Nematomorpha	100	Phoronidea	4
Nematoda	10,000	Chaetognatha	30
Priapulida	5	Hemichordata	80
Nemertina	750	Tunicata	1,600
Entoprocta	60	Fishes	20,000
Annelida	7,000	Reptiles and amphibians	6,000
Echiuroida	60	Birds	8,590
Sipunculoidea	250	Mammals	3,200
Tardigrada	180		
Onychophora	65	Total	1,120,510

E. Mayr, E.G. Linsley, and R.L. Usinger, Methods and principles of systematic zoology 1953. (New York: McGraw-Hill, 1953)

Table 9-2. Numbers of Species in Tocks Island Region

Numbers of species of various groups expected in the Tocks Island region on the basis of collections, sightings, or overlap with known range:

Vascular Plants	1,129
Fish	46
Reptiles and Amphibians	52
Birds	250
Mammals	53

NOTE: No attempt was made at exhaustive listing of algae, fungi, mosses or invertebrate animals.

National Park Service, "A Natural History Survey of the Proposed Tocks Island Reservoir National Recreation Area", unpublished.

fail to materialize. In Darwin's words, ". . . as more individuals are produced than can possibly survive, there must in every case be a struggle for existence, either one individual with another of the same species, or with the individuals of distinct species, or with the physical conditions of life."[24] If the world is such a harshly competitive place, the continued existence of so many species raises unsettling questions: How can so many species, locked in bitter struggle, directly or indirectly, avoid exterminating one another? Why is not the world's biota reduced to the few most "competitive" species? Evidently, every species must have some ability, figuratively, to stay out of the way of most other species; and among those species that are in more or less direct competition, each must in some essential way be *different*, so that there is some season and some place where each species is more effective than its rivals in the struggle for existence. That each species is best at something different—something that is its "business" in life—is at the core of the ecological concept of a species' niche. There have been many attempts at giving formal mathematical expression to these ideas. Some of the more promising models have implied that for species to coexist, each, when very abundant, must be deterred from further increase by a different limiting factor.[25] These models are in accord with the naturalist's intuitions, but they are not directly applicable as scientific "laws," because simplifying assumptions upon which the proofs rest are too restrictive.

C. "Homeostasis"

Organisms do not behave as simple physicochemical systems, although as far as we know they *do* obey the laws of physics and chemistry. The difference lies in the remarkable degree of integration and regulation of the physical and chemical processes within the organism. Much of the regulation of internal processes seems directed at the maintenance of some constancy of the internal milieu. Such regulation is called "homeostasis." A simple nonbiological example might be a buffered solution, which maintains a fairly constant pH despite the addition of moderate amounts of acid or base. In the metabolism of living things, this kind of behavior is the rule rather than the exception.

Osmoregulation is one class of well documented examples of biological homeostasis: it consists in the maintenance of fairly constant concentrations of many organic and inorganic solutes inside the cell—and in some of the body fluids of multicellular organisms—despite considerable variation in the concentrations of these solutes in the surrounding medium.[26] A second, commonly observed class of examples is temperature acclimation. The rates of individual biochemical reactions are related to temperature according to the usual Arrhenius equation of physical chemistry.[i] Gross metabolic rates, such as oxygen uptake, indices of the combined activities of many individual biochemical reactions, exhibit the same kind of dependence on temperature in the short run. Thus we can predict the change in the rate of oxygen uptake as temperature changes by a simple analogy from physical chemistry. However, after a period of acclimation to the new temperature, lasting a few hours to a few days, the organism's rate of oxygen uptake generally readjusts to a rate that is closer to its original rate. This homeostatic regulation of the rate of a biological process clearly is not predicted by application of the Arrhenius equation. Warm-blooded animals, of course, maintain a constant internal temperature despite considerable variations in the temperatures of their surroundings; and many cold-blooded animals do a fair job of reducing fluctuations of their internal temperature by moving in and out of the shade and orienting themselves appropriately relative to the wind and sun, as the ambient temperature changes.

To be sure, not everything about an organism will remain constant (or more or less constant), for *some* processes must work at exceedingly variable rates in order to achieve the homeostasis we observe in other processes. For example, considerable variation in energy expenditure will at times be required for some kinds of compensation for environmental fluctuation.

We see from this that a prediction of biological responses to

---

[i]The logarithm of the rate constant is equal to a constant minus a term that is proportional to inverse of the absolute temperature, approximately implying that the logarithm of the rate of the reaction will be linearly related to the centigrade temperature for small temperature changes. This phenomenon, and acclimation, are explained in Prosser and Brown.[26]

environmental conditions that rests on physicochemical analogy is very likely to be incorrect and will consistently underestimate a very fundamental complexity of the system under study.

D. Nongeneralizable Adaptations

If living things had only to contend with the problems of physical and chemical degradation, they could all adopt much the same strategy for survival—a tuning of their biochemical machinery to best advantage against the second law of thermodynamics. In fact, at a very basic subcellular level—the metabolic pathways—the basic chemical machinery of almost all organisms is very similar. At this level of chemical building blocks, organisms are using the same strategy.

Whole organisms, however, have another level of problem to contend with, rooted in the fact of competition. Above the level of chemical building blocks, organisms have to contend with *each other* in the struggle for existence. Since all the combatants in this arena are evolving, there will be a complementarity, or reciprocal evolution, to all generalizable strategies: as the prey become more fleet, so do the predators; as the hunted becomes more elusive, the hunter becomes more meticulous; as armor becomes thicker, the weapons of assault become more penetrating; as chemical defenses become more potent, the mechanisms of detoxification become more effective, and so forth. Every new evolutionary development that gives one species a temporary advantage becomes itself the source of a selection pressure, driving this species' opponents to evolve means of nullifying that advantage—move and countermove.[27]

We may assume, therefore, that all the generalizable strategies were adopted, and their reciprocal effects cancelled, very early in the history of any biotic interaction. The subsequent history, then, may be viewed as a search for nongeneralizable *tactics*; and each species, as a consequence, has become a bag of tricks rather than an easily predictable strategist.[28] In fact, the whole point of the evolutionary game is to find tactics so outlandish that the probabilities of their respective countertactics are minimal, and to deploy these capabilities as deceptively as possible.[29] The more discontinuity that an organism can display in this kind of adaptive behavior, the harder it is for his opponents to track him, and the less opportunity they have to evolve the neutralizing response.

In our recent experiences with some antibiotics and pesticides, we can see a nutshell lesson in this kind of strategy. Used intermittently, the "wonder drugs" and chemical weapons in the war against insects were devastating. Used continuously, the target species developed resistance, until the new-found arsenal, in some instances, proved all but useless. The optimal strategy, it seems, would be to use these tricks only in times of greatest need. An adaptive trick should be played often enough to derive some benefit, but seldom enough so that one's opponents do not catch on. A trick that no longer appears improbable will not fool anyone. So, not only are species different in their responses to critical factors; the *ways* in which they are different involve improbable and discontinuous behavior.

Of course, we are aware of highly visible examples of such behavior: sea turtles live in the water, but breed on land, toads live on land, but breed in water; salmon live in the sea, but breed and die in fresh water; caterpillars become butterflies; some parasitic flatworms have three successive obligate hosts. We see huge annual migrations of some large herbivores, massive irregular population eruptions of locusts, and exquisitely regular synchronization of life cycles more than a decade long in cicadas. Water fleas go through cycles of generations with altered morphology during the course of one season; rotifers may reproduce parthenogenetically or sexually, depending on environmental conditions. Tardigrades can form a drought resistant cyst that remains dormant until it is moistened; slime molds can live as single-celled, amoebalike creatures or can temporarily aggregate into a motile syncytium, and so forth.

These dramatic, visible examples are the stuff of Disney's nature movies, perhaps trivial-looking biological curialia, but this is only the tip of a very important iceberg—the obvious, unmistakable tricks some organisms play for survival just give us a hint at the diversity of tactics that might not so catch our attention but that nevertheless may be critical components of biological interaction.

E. Everything Is Connected

If, in some sense, all organisms are jostling for a slice of the same pie, it stands to reason that any change in one species population will affect other species populations. After all, one species may be host to several parasites, prey to several predators, a predator on other prey, and rival for food and space with several competitors; and these in turn, interact with their parasites, predators, prey, and competitors, till one cannot pick a flower but "trouble a star." This does not tell us, though, how much the star was troubled.

From what was said in the prior sections concerning complexity, we can guess that the intensity of effects propagated through a biological community, after perturbation, will not be predictable, a priori. Some disturbances will damp out after affecting a few populations; others will be amplified in transmission, with the effect increasing as it is passed from population to population, as in food-chain concentration of some pollutants.[30]

The eco-crisis literature is by now replete with cautionary tales of snowballing side effects, such as the story of DDT being sprayed on an Asian village in an attempt to control malaria, with the result that there was a rat epidemic and a housing disaster! According to the story, the DDT was absorbed by insects, and then concentrated by some insect-eating lizards that lived in and around the thatched huts of the village. The village cats ate the DDT-contaminated lizards and were poisoned, thus letting the rat population explode. The lizards, it seems, had been instrumental in controlling some caterpillars that specialized in eating the local roofing thatch. With the demise of the lizards, a plague of caterpillars riddled the roofs to the point of collapse.[31]

F. The Importance of History

The genetic composition of a population, relative to its initial composition, is in large part a consequence of the past selection pressures to which the population was exposed. In other words, the present adaptations represent a compendium of past successes fixed by the "memory" of natural selection.[32] This implies that whatever degree of stability may be found in an ecological interaction is a reflection of a history of past interaction. Present stability, therefore, gives no assurance of future stability under altered interactions or novel conditions. Unprecedented types of perturbation of a community seem almost certain to elicit reactions that will be qualitatively different from the stabilizing behavior that is a result of mutual adjustment in evolutionary time. This sort of theorizing does not lead to a clear picture of what the detailed reaction will be, but it does provide a strong suggestion that the reaction will be undesirable, if only by analogy with haphazard tinkering in a finely tuned mechanism.

Taken together, these six features of biology cast a pall over the prospects for a predictive science of ecology. It is as if chemistry found itself faced with a periodic chart of *millions* of elements, thousands of which may be present in any reaction, all of which are bizarrely different from one another, all of which are badly behaved from a statistical standpoint, and all of whose properties may change with history. This is an extraordinarily difficult situation for a developing science.

What little we do know of evolutionary macrobiology that stands comparison with the "hard" sciences is the legacy of men who not only were brilliant scientists but must also be ranked among history's most creative applied mathematicians. So it is not as if first rate scientists have not been trying to develop this aspect of biology: they have tried and are trying, and have achieved some limited success, but it must be understood that the inherent difficulties of a predictive biology are far greater than those that had to be resolved in order to get physics and chemistry started in their modern direction. In moments of self-pity, the biologist may feel sure that the living world evolved expressly in order to defy analysis; and from our discussion of the peculiarities of this living world, we see that in a way it has.

In the absence of predictive theory, and in the presence of fundamental obstacles to predictive theory, it is not possible to draw upon the capital of scientific expertise in the usual manner. The scientific *method* still applies, so it is worthwhile employing competent ecologists for empirical resolution of relevant questions; and the experience of the trained naturalist will be invaluable in properly phrasing the questions that are put to empirical test. But it seems exceedingly unlikely that we could profitably employ armchair expertise. We should not at present hope to find an ecological expert who can pull half a dozen key equations out of a college text, refer to the CRC handbook for the values of critical coefficients, look at the blueprints for a proposed project, and then make reliable predictions of ecological consequences.

IV. WHAT DOES THE COMPUTER KNOW?

We shall next consider what happens in this realm of complex phenomena, for which there is no adequate analytical theory, when the rococo temptations of computer modeling are present. The conventional wisdom of the day—"garbage in, garbage out"—has it that the computer can't know any more than the experts. In ecology this can be taken to mean that computer models at present generally are not much help as predictive devices. The one major ecological model employed in the Tocks case was the attempt by Water Resources Engineering at predicting eutrophication.[33] The hydrological nuts and bolts of this model are treated in the preceding essay. Here we will try to assess the biological side of the model.

The developers of this model state in the conclusions of their report that under present nutrient loads, the proposed reservoir "would not experience either algal blooms or anaerobic conditions," nor would it under the projected load for the year 2000, given "advanced" waste water treatment. Less advanced, "secondary" treatment of the projected load, it is claimed, would result in "nuisance algal conditions," but still would not create "anaerobic conditions."[34] Now the ecological question that prompted this model concerned "eutrophication." Thus, our first worry has nothing to do with the model, per se, but merely asks about the vocabulary of the questions that motivated it.[35] This is a complicated worry, for the word eutrophication is ambiguous. In general and scientific usage, we find four different but interrelated meanings of eutrophication. It may designate:

1. An *index* to the nutrient level, or nutrient load, of a body of water, most often specified in terms of phosphorous, nitrogen, carbon, or silicon, in some combination, but other elements sometimes are included.
2. An *index* to the level of organic productivity in a body of water, usually expressed as a rate, in mass or energy units, of photosynthesis per unit area or volume, but other kinds of production such as fish, may be cited.
3. A *process* in the successive chronological development of a lake, as both a biological and a physical unit, usually referred to, metaphorically, as "aging".
4. A *state* of ecological degradation of a body of water, characterized by one or more symptoms such as marked algal blooms, unpleasant odors or unpleasant flavors of algal or bacterial origin, and fish kills caused by oxygen depletion or, possibly, algal toxins.

According to usage 1, a eutrophic lake is one with a relatively high nutrient load or nutrient concentration, while according to usage 2 it would be a lake with a relatively high rate of biological production. Inasmuch as nutrients are necessary for biological production, and some are often in short supply (limiting), it is almost inevitable that the two indices, 1 and 2, will be positively correlated; but they are not identical.

The undesirable properties of a eutrophic lake in sense 4 are consequences of extreme rates of growth of certain algae or bacteria relative to the lake's capacity for reaeration, mixing and flushing, so that incidence of this state will be related to both the indices 1 and 2.

As a lake fills in with sediment, the relationships among some of the lake parameters (depth, area, volume, inflow) change so as to increase nutrient load per unit volume and (neglecting turbidity) the average light exposure, leading to increased productivity, which may in turn cause reducing conditions in the lower water strata, permitting regeneration of nutrients from the sediments, leading to further increase in the nutrient load, etc. So the aging process of the lake corresponds to a progressive increase in the "eutrophication" indices 1 and 2, and the increase, in time, may possibly exceed the threshold for the eutrophication state, 4. In the meantime, the increased production causes an increase in the rate of sedimentation, thereby accelerating one of the initiating factors in the aging. Thus it is possible to speak of the artificial fertilization of a lake as accelerating its rate of aging. This, in recent years, has culminated in loose talk about "killing" lakes through nutrient pollution; but, as the rate of total biological production in a lake usually increases with age, the metaphor is inappropriately mixed. The virtual "death" through aging of a lake occurs only when the lake has finally been completely filled in. Admittedly the changes in species composition that accompany trophic age may not suit our tastes, but that constitutes the "death" of some favored species—hardly the "death" of the lake.

Usage 4, the description of a noxious state, is the only one that invariably implies a lessening of the lake's utility for human purposes. The other usages refer to indices and processes that only correlate with the undesirable state, and only for extreme values at that. Thus, perception of eutrophication as a problem should explicitly invoke meaning 4. In this regard, the words "algal bloom" and "nuisance algal conditions" in the model report look appropriate, but examination of the model's actual output shows that what was modeled was aggregate algal mass, without reference to the type of algae, and with no special criterion for blooms.

The modelers used the number, one milligram of algae per liter of water, as the threshold criterion for a "nuisance condition."[36] This probably represents their guess at a visibility threshold. When we consider that only certain species of algae are responsible for the objectionable tastes, odors and toxins of the eutrophic state (4), and for that matter that only certain species of algae are present in large numbers in massive algae eruptions (owing to their tolerance of certain environmental conditions and their unpalatibility to the animals that usually graze on algae), the model's output (biomass) does not speak exactly to the problem of eutrophication. The oxygen balance output, if correct, is more to the point.

Our second worry is about the workings of the model. Whatever the output does represent, is it a reliable prediction, and how can we tell? There are two quite different approaches to predictive modeling. A model may be a probabilistic assessment of purely empirical observations, largely divorced from causal interpretation; or it may be an analytical model, a coupled system of mathematized relations which individually are descriptions of causal mechanisms

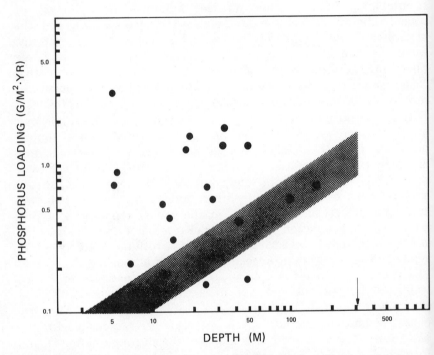

Figure 9-1. Phosphorus Input vs. Mean Depth for a Number of Lakes

Lakes above the shaded band were eutrophic, lakes below the band were not. Lakes in the band showed signs of incipient eutrophication. Lake Tahoe fell off scale in the direction indicated by the arrow. (Redrawn from Vollenweider.[37])

grounded in scientific law. Of course, models do not necessarily exist as pure types. For example, some parameters in a model incorporating causal representations may require empirical determination. The important difference between the two types is that they are justified in different ways. The information that legitimates an empirical model is strictly in the data; while the information that legitimates a causal model is derived from general scientific laws.

We might best understand empirical modeling by examination of a bare-bones model of this sort, which is so simple it does not require either a computer or explicit mathematics. Figure 9–1, redrawn from work by Vollenweider,[37] shows a two-dimensional space, a coordinate system in which each body of water is assigned a point on the basis of its average depth and its phosphorus input. When Vollenweider did this for a number of lakes, he observed that the lakes he knew to be eutrophic and those he knew not to be eutrophic fell in different parts of the "space." Moreover, when logarithmic scales were employed for the two axes, the boundary between the eutrophic and noneutrophic "phases" in the space gave the appearance of a straight band. On either side of the band trophic state seemed determinate. Lakes falling in the bank were "threatened" with eutrophication. With a healthy dose of optimism, we might use this diagram for predictions—to find out whether a lake with a given mean depth and phosphorus input will be eutrophic, locate the corresponding point in the diagram, and see which phase it falls in. (We could carry out an equivalent exercise algebraically without recourse to graphs.)

Ignoring the question of experimental error (i.e., the reliability of the empirical determinations of depth, phosphorus load, and eutrophy), how reliable are the predictions of this sort of model? If the data on which Figure 9–1 was based were exhaustive—every lake in the world being included as preliminary data—we should feel very confident about it indeed, but of course, except for newly created lakes, the model, then, would not be a predictive device at all, but rather a mnemonic device, conveniently storing certain facts for later use. Vollenweider actually used data from nineteen lakes, so we don't feel nearly so confident about the diagram as we might. On the basis of a few scattered points, how can we tell that the shape of the border is straight, and how can we tell that the two "pure" phase regions really are pure? We can't. We don't know that the twentieth lake would not alter the shape or the position of the border, or appear as a eutrophic "island" inside the noneutrophic region, or vice versa. And after the twentieth lake we would not know about the twenty-first.

What we do know is that the same model with more data surely would be more persuasive. If, say, two hundred lakes were plotted, and we found that they fit the pattern, then we might start feeling comfortable with use of this model in prediction. Also, the more thoroughly the data covered a particular region of the diagram, the more confident we would feel about predictions concerning lakes whose depth and phosphorus load corresponded to points in that region. Thus, if a dozen known lakes fell appropriately near both sides of the phase border in the lower left part of the diagram, but none was plotted near the phase border in the upper right, we should think the former part of the border reasonably justified, but we would have to admit that the latter part was guesswork.

An empirical model of this sort treats the *processes* that generate the outcomes under study as if they occurred in a "black box." All that is considered explicitly is the observed association between variables. The object of the modeling is to find patterns in the data. There are many different ways of looking for a statistical pattern: regressions may be linear, exponential, quadratic; one may try to fit the data with Fourier series or polynomials; the data may be rescaled; key factors may be sought among the data variables or among various functions of various combinations of the data variables; ad infinitum. The only way to know how well the modeled description conforms to the actual pattern, and which descriptions conform better than others, is to get lots of data and see.

The more complex the relationships, or the more numerous the variables, or the greater the range of values for the variables, the more data are required for a given level of confidence. Owing to the problematical features of the living world, described in the previous sections, large scale empirical modeling of ecological systems requires unimaginable (and unavailable) masses of data to be of any generality. To date, demonstrated success in ecological modeling has been achieved only by studying specific, restricted systems. For example, Wiegert and his co-workers, in order to develop a model predicting the time course of populations of the very few species inhabiting certain hot springs in Yellowstone National Park, have spent many field seasons gathering data on those species in those springs.[38]

An analytical model replaces the "black box" with a system of causal mechanisms. Each of the causal mechanisms that are thought important is represented by a formula (or law), and the computer just does the bookkeeping. The application of this kind of model to broad ecological problems may at first look appealing, for if these were to be modeled empirically, more data would be required than anyone can get. However, the reliability of any analytical model depends on the security of the scientific foundations of the formulas used to describe the component processes, and in ecology secure laws would require knowledge which no one has.

The water quality model developed by WRE makes some pretense of being an analytical model. Two "theoretical bases" are claimed: the "Law of Conservation of Mass" and the "Kinetic Principle." [39] Both claims are unimpressive when examined closely.

The "law" of conservation of mass turns out to be the catechism that matter can neither be created nor destroyed (under conditions prevailing over most of the earth's surface). This special knowledge is corollary to the response a sleight-of-hand coin trick will evoke from a child of normal intelligence: if something is not where you saw it last, you look for it somewhere else. I am not complaining that the "law" is false; only that I can see room for doubt as to whether it will tell us anything we don't already know.

The "kinetic principle" turns out to be an assertion of the applicability to ecological interaction of the physical-chemical law of mass action. Roughly speaking, this gives rise to equations in which the rate of an interaction between two constituents is proportional to the amounts present. That this should hold true, even approximately, in biological interactions is an assumption, not a "law."

It is true that equations embodying such an assumption are frequently *used* in ecology; they can be found in any introductory text. Equations of this sort—associated with the names Gauss, Volterra, Lotka, and Verhulst—have been employed in developing the theories of competition and predator-prey interactions. However, these theories are essentially speculative, asking merely such questions as, "If such and such a simple equation describes, say, competition between two species, then for what starting conditions and values of parameters will there be a stable equilibrium, or perhaps a cyclic solution?" This kind of speculation is good fun, and some of the results have been genuinely enlightening, but it is altogether something different to claim that these equations describe any real situation except some single-celled organisms in rigorously controlled laboratory environments. The equations found necessary to describe even such simple systems as flour beetles living in tanks of flour at constant temperature and humidity are vastly different, and vastly more complicated.[40] Descriptions of, say, predation under field conditions are more complicated yet.[41,42]

However shaky the grounds for its choice, the "kinetic principle" dictates the general form of the equations used in the model to represent interractions between living constituents. There were only six constituents so treated, each an idealized caricature of a broad category of organisms, namely: algae, microscopic animals that feed on algae, bottom dwelling animals that feed on organic debris, and three fish groups classified according to their respective diets and temperature preferences. The spatial structure of the lake appeared in the model as a series of horizontal "slices", each slice corresponding to a given depth range. Vertical movement of materials and organisms from one slice to the next was modeled in a common sense way, but no provision was made for there being any local differences or movement within a slice. That is to say, the lateral dimensions of the lake were ignored.

Three features then, attract our attention in an assessment of the credibility of the WRE model: the dubious form of the equations, the aggregation of diverse species into a small number of functional categories, and the compression of spatial differences into the vertical dimension alone.

Some details of the equations representing biological interactions are presented in Box 1. In brief, there is no easy way to justify the general forms of the equations used to represent biological inter-actions in the WRE model, for on the face of it, their reality does not seem very likely. One particular property of the equations, the consequences of which can be understood in advance, is that the model does not include any mechanism to represent drastic mortality under severe environmental conditions. This seems an inappropriate omission from a model that was intended to predict the possible occurrence of ecosystem dysfunction.

The model is totally unsuited to lumping species together in func-tional groups, such as "Algae." Undesirable water conditions such as massive algal blooms and eutrophication induced fish kills are associated only with certain kinds of algae, which otherwise are rare or absent. The presence of these algae in water of poor quality and their general absence from water of better quality are manifestations of individual species differences, including relative palatability of the algae to organisms that normally graze them, phosphorus require-ments and tolerances, silica requirements, pH tolerances, responses to various algal and bacterial toxins, and the capacity for such tricks as rapid absorption of phosphorus (which is then *stored* for later use).[47]

Not only do various species of algae respond differently to critical environmental variables, they in turn affect these variables differ-ently, both in direct ways, such as the production of specific toxins, and as side effects of metabolic activity, which can alter pH, turbidity,

BOX 1. MODELING OF SPECIES BEHAVIOR IN LAKECO

Let us see precisely how biological interactions were represented in the core equations of the WRE model. The rate of change of biomass of species 1, where species 2 feeds upon it is given as

$$\frac{dA_1}{dt} = (\mu_1 - R_1 - S_1 - M_1) A_1 - \mu_2 A_2 F_{2,1} - P_1 \qquad (9\text{--}1)$$

Here A_1 and A_2 are the biomass of species 1 and 2 respectively; μ_1 and μ_2 are their specific gross growth rates; R_1, S_1, and M_1 describe the depletion of the biomass of species 1 by respiration, settling, and intrinsic mortality, respectively; $F_{2,1}$ is the "biomass conversion factor" for the consumption of species 1 by species 2, and P_1 is a compound term describing physical transport processes (advection, diffusion, inflow, and outflow).

The coefficients S_1, M_1 and $F_{2,1}$ are constants in the model. The settling loss, S, applied only to algae and thus suffered no other form of intrinsic mortality. It certainly is not the case that what M and F portray —per capita mortality rates, and what ecologists call trophic efficiency— are established constants. Biological literature provides individual measurements of these parameters for some species under some conditions and they are by no means constant; nor would we on first principles expect them to be.[43] For example, we surely would expect mortality rates to increase as conditions deteriorate.

The temperature dependence of the specific reaction rates μ_1, μ_2, and R was represented by a familiar rule of thumb from physiology:

$$\mu_T = \mu_{20} \, \Theta^{T-20} \qquad (9\text{--}2)$$

where μ_T is the temperature corrected coefficient, μ_{20} is the value of the coefficient at the reference temperature ($20°C$), T is the temperature in degrees centigrade, and Θ is the temperature coefficient. A value of 1.047 was used for all Θ, meaning that reaction rates double at $15°C$ intervals. It seems reasonable that gross growth and respiration might be corrected in this manner (at least for single-species equations), though the exact choice of a value for Θ is not certain, and one wonders why other biological functions, such as the death rates, were not also corrected for temperature.

Specific gross growth rates, μ_1 and μ_2, were also adjusted for the abundance of resources in the manner of Monod kinetics; the general form of the adjustment being:

$$\mu_a = \mu \left(\frac{x}{K_x + x}\right) \qquad (9\text{--}3)$$

where μ_a is the adjusted coefficient, μ is the value of the growth rate in the presence of a superabundance of resources (i.e., the value of μ_a at saturation), x is the concentration of the resource, and K_x is the concentration of resource at which μ_a is one-half μ (called the "half-saturation constant"). Saturation factors of the form (x/K_x+x) were strung together in various combinations, depending on the number of resources that the modelers wanted to take into account for each biological constituent. In the Tocks simulation, the biological constituents were: "Algae, Zooplankton, Fish 1, Fish 2, Fish 3, and Benthos."

The *algae* were represented as responding to light intensity (L), and concentrations of carbon dioxide (C), nitrate (N), and phosphate (P), as resources. Thus the full equation for the gross growth rate of the algae was:

$$\mu_A = \mu_{A,20} \Theta^{T-20} (\frac{L}{K_L+L}) (\frac{C}{K_C+C}) (\frac{N}{K_N+N}) (\frac{P}{K_P+P}) \qquad (9\text{--}4)$$

The zooplankton were modeled as responding to the concentration of algae (A):

$$\mu_z = \mu_{z,20} \Theta^{T-20} (\frac{A}{K_A+A})$$

The growth rate of *fish 1* was modeled as responding to the concentration of zooplankton; *fish 2*, responding to zooplankton; *fish 3*, responding to benthos; and *benthos*, responding to sediment. Some ecological detail was added for the fish group in that their growth was stopped whenever conditions were outside that group's range for temperature or oxygen tolerance.

There is a nonnegligible literature in agreement with the claim that Monod kinetics of the form of equation (3) are adequate descriptions of the growth of phytoplankton when limited by a single factor, but the claim that the saturation effects of several factors are multiplicative, as in equation (4), is unsubstantiated.[44] Moreover, while many simple equations for population growth do a tolerable job of modeling both the initial rapid growth of an uncrowded population and the slower growth that accompanies crowding,[45] these equations are opaque with respect to the crashes, oscillations, or equilibria that in real populations follow the phase of sigmoid population growth.[46]

In the model of equation (3), gross growth saturates at a constant positive rate in the presence of an excess of nutrients (or other potentially limiting factors), and declines to zero as the critical factor is exhausted. No level or combination of critical factors in the Monod terms can make a

> *negative* contribution to population growth (i.e., can cause population decline) nor can the stoppage of growth described for the fish. The population can diminish under the influence of the same sources of attrition that were operating during the period of population growth (the constant per capita mortality and the removals due to predation), but the model makes no provision for any group's really getting clobbered by environmental deterioration.
>
> So we find no a priori justification for the equations except as very rough—and questionable—guesses.

oxygen content, and assorted nutrient concentrations. The interactions may be quite complicated, as in phosphorus metabolism: all algae can absorb and release phosphate, and, in addition, at least some algae can excrete organic phosphorus compounds which can combine with other compounds in the water to create a colloidal phosphorus component.[48] There are interconversions between particulate and dissolved organic and inorganic phosphorus in water, mediated in part by free enzymes released by some organism(s).[49] Even what we commonly suppose to be strictly physical phenomena, such as diffusion of certain gases at the water surface, may be affected by compounds of biological origin.[50] In short, the dramatic change of character in a body of water undergoing eutrophication is a process in which dramatic species differences play a critical role. An analytical model of lake eutrophication that does not include the effects of these differences is immediately suspect.

There remains the matter of spatial representation. Treating the lake as a series of horizontal slices, where lateral differences within a slice can be ignored, is equivalent to assuming instantaneous and perfect mixing within each slice. This assumes, for example, that any nutrient input from a point source is immediately diluted over the entire length and breadth of the lake.

Let us remind ourselves that the intended reservoir will be 37 miles long and about two-thirds of a mile wide; that there will be a major backwater where the present valley has a Y-shaped configuration; and that the preponderance of the nutrient input will enter the lake from the upstream inlet and a small number of local sources, such as sewage treatment plant outfalls or streams draining areas with a heavy nutrient burden.

The rates of biological uptake of nutrients are very fast—particularly for phosphorus, which is likely to be the key nutrient in determining water quality.[51] For example, a stand of the plant Callitriche can reduce the phosphorus concentration in the water from 2.05 to .01 mg/1 in one hour.[52] A good portion of the phosphorus absorbed by phytoplankton gets sequestered in the lake sediments in a short time.[53] The only common circumstances under which phosphorus is released from sediments in significant amounts is when the lower water layers are so depleted of oxygen as to present a chemically reducing environment. In shallow bodies of water, this would tend to occur as a consequence of the rapid deposition of organic detritus associated with high rates of algal production, so in this manner eutrophication can be an interestingly self-aggravating condition. These properties of phosphorus mobilization in lake systems, combined with the expected geometry of phosphorus input, make it certain that quite severe local manifestations of eutrophication would appear long before the lake as a whole were so afflicted.[j] More bothersome from the modeling point of view is the likelihood that these local problems could erupt under a total nutrient budget that would result in perfectly acceptable water conditions if the input were evenly distributed over the lake. This kind of eutrophication would be undetectable by the present sort of one-dimensional model.

By now the reader may be wondering why the WRE model, if it is as improbable a conglomeration of wishful thinking and misrepresentation as I have made it out to be, did not generate projections that were immediately recognizable as nonsense. Answering this question will illuminate the manner in which the coefficients (i.e. the various constants in the equations) were actually arrived at.

The modelers had at their disposal two main sources of data: published accounts of the course of eutrophication and recovery in Lake Washington, near Seattle; and the results of some experiments carried out previously (for quite different purposes) in four two-acre ponds near the proposed dam site.[54] The biological component of the model involved a full 57 coefficients. Justification of the form of the model, and establishment of appropriate values for the coefficients, clearly could not be accomplished on the basis of casual experiments in little ponds. So, to keep the model from behaving outrageously, the limited data were used *twice.*

First, the data were used to make some heroic assumptions about the initial values for the coefficients—as if the model, indeed, were of the analytic sort. Next, during the course of a series of trial runs of the model, the coefficients were subjected to ad hoc readjustments to make the output look more plausible. The contemporary euphe-

---

[j]On a larger scale, this phenomenon is known to occur in Lake Erie, where the western basin is considerably more eutrophic than the eastern basin, and in some portions of Lake Michigan, such as off Green Bay.

misms for this kind of tinkering are "model calibration" or "tuning." What this actually accomplishes is the removal of a potentially useful means of checking the soundness of the model. If, on the basis of independently arrived at coefficients, a model generates crazy predictions, this should alert a circumspect modeler to the possibility that the basic form of the model is incorrect.[k] If instead the modelers juggle coefficients until the output looks right, the model loses its analytical character.

It is no great surprise that the output *can* be made to look right. With so great a number of coefficients decoupled from independent verification, the "model" becomes nothing more than a clumsy curve-fitting device—it could just as well be fitted to the record of the last eleven months' Dow Jones averages or the incidence of miscarriages in China. Thus the fact of a decent fit between model output and the data used to "calibrate" it in no way validates the model as a predictive device. Worse yet, the fact of such tampering with the coefficients makes it impossible to use the test cases in attaching objective confidence limits to the model's predictions: the test cases get swallowed up in adjusting the coefficients. The irony of this is that the model becomes such a tangle that even if it were producing correct predictions we would have no way of knowing it.

Let us, for the moment, forget the model's obvious failings as an analytical model, forget mechanisms, and forget the silly game of attaching ecological names to the mathematical components in the model. It is quite possible, for all the complexity of the underlying biology, that cultural eutrophication, in most cases, is driven by a few simple environmental variables. In fact, we already have every reason to believe that phosphorus load is the major determinant in a lake such as Tocks.[55] Vollenweider's simple empirical model, as described earlier, capitalizes on just this. What if the WRE enterprise blundered into an unnecessarily complicated way of representing a "black box" relationship between phosphorus and eutrophication? If Vollenweider could do it with a sheet of log-log graph paper, a team

[k]The computer's ability to keep track of many simultaneously interacting components of a model permit an application that is probably of greater present importance than ecological prediction; namely, theory testing. One may treat the model itself as a hypothesis, and the test of that hypothesis is the fit of the model's predictions to observed results. If the fit is poor, one then knows that something is wrong with the model: perhaps there are more causal processes importantly involved that were taken into account, perhaps one or more of the formulas representing a causal relation is incorrect, or perhaps the scheme for integrating the effects of the component processes is mistaken. Each of these possibilities can lead to hypotheses which themselves are subject to test, so that with care, much may be learned.

of consulting engineers might well be able to do it with a computer and a lot of money. Only now the "kinetic principle" and "algae" and "coefficients" just appear as decorative flourishes and our appraisal of the reliability of this model, as of Vollenweider's model, rests entirely on how well the output of the model as a whole has conformed to the relevant facts.

Vollenweider's collection of facts from nineteen lakes did not seem the sort of thing we would really want to bet on. The WRE collection of facts from one lake and a few ponds is even less convincing, though the model's predictions might still be correct more often than not— and then again they might not be. Whether they are or not can only be settled by the model's eventual record of successes and failures after a substantial number of independent trials at predicting data that had not already been absorbed in calibration. In the meantime, the computer does not know very much.

V.   HOW NATURAL IS NATURAL?

All sides of the Tocks Island Dam controversy claim to be sensitive to what is "natural." This should not surprise us. Since the Enlightenment, there has existed a fairly continuous Western tradition of identifying the "natural" course as preferable where alternatives exist, though of course there is equal continuity to the notion that life in the state of nature is "nasty, brutish and short."

The unofficial National Park Service plan for a Delaware Water Gap National Recreation Area, *without a dam*, presented in a twelve-page illustrated brochure, uses the words "natural," "naturalness," or "naturalistic" seven times; the title itself reads: "A Natural System Plan for Delaware Water Gap National Recreation Area." The fifteen-page illustrated brochure prepared by the architecture firm, Clarke and Rapuano, and commissioned by the Corps of Engineers, "Tocks Island Dam: A Plan for Its Architecture and Development," uses these words nine times. These words have no special technical meanings: scientists use them no differently from laymen. But the Park Service and the architects do not mean quite the same thing, and other partners to the controversy use still other meanings.

There may be a constituency of hard core conservationists who really think that a "natural" landscape is one that is literally virgin. One consultant's description of the Tocks Island regional setting evokes this meaning (we don't know if it was intended): " . . . the reservoir site, recreation area, and surrounding study area encompass beautiful and unspoiled lands which appear to have been overlooked by development that has occurred around them, and which remain virtually in their natural state."[56]

Of course, the area is far from untouched. In all probability, the area was commercially logged in the early seventeenth century and has been very much under the hand of man ever since. In addition to continued timber operations and replanting with coniferous trees after the hardwoods were removed (or died of disease), there have been coal mines, iron mines, and extensive clearing of land for farms, which were later abandoned. The National Park Service's survey of the area, in fact, lamented past mismanagement of the forests and its effect on the present-day second growth.[57] Nor have human influences been confined to the exploitation of resources. The National Park Service identified a grand total of 32 "historically significant" structures that it planned to remove from the area that would be inundated by the dam.[58] These were to be relocated to sites within the recreation area including "a restored village, an early farm complex, a community grouping and an interpretive motor trail."

So, generally, if the meaning of the "natural system" argument refers to preservation of virgin territory, it has no basis in fact in the Tocks case. But that doesn't necessarily stop such usage. For example, the language of the decision of the DRBC, in 1968, to include "the preservation of Sunfish Pond in its natural state" among the "environmental standards" of its comprehensive plan suggests a token gesture of appeasement to a demand that portions of the landscape be held inviolate.

The primary concern of the Park Service in the Tocks area is recreation, rather than preservation of "wilderness." The Park Service regards fishing, hiking, and sightseeing as appropriate to the area, and these are consistent with treating the landscape as a renewable resource. The Park Service espouses an implicit recreation ideology in which the most worthy activities are those that are "natural" in the setting where they take place. Thus activities and setting are planned jointly.

The Park Service's original 1966 Master Plan for the recreation area designated 42 percent of the acreage as "natural environment," which would receive "little development." The predilection to *manage* the landscape is evident even in the Natural History Survey, where it is noted that the deer and beaver populations will have to be "controlled" in the Tocks area, while the present scarcity of biting insects is taken as an omen that these will not require control. The

preservationist leanings in this report surface in the discussion of
the abundant rattle snakes and copperheads:

> The presence of these snakes in the area should cause no alarm. The
> incidence of snake bite in the area is very low and death from snake bite
> almost zero. However, it would be wise to locate as many of the dens in
> the area as possible. The purpose of this would not be for possible exter-
> mination of the species. They fit in their own ecological niches and are
> very interesting animals that are favorite animals for study by a consider-
> able group of naturalists. It would be wise, however, to locate children's
> camps, hiking trails, and bridle paths at some distance from known den
> areas. . . .[59]

The implication that the annoyance of numerous biting insects
would justify control programs, while literally poisonous snakes are
to be left alone because some people like to look at them, illustrates
that the Park Service is not committed to preservation per se, but
perceives itself as serving a variety of constituencies. Even in the Park
Service's "Natural System Plan" for a recreation area without a dam,
there are plans for *modifying* the river:

> To increase the usefulness of the Delaware River for water sports without
> unduly sacrificing its naturalness, three low level weirs are proposed to
> increase water depth within the existing inner banks yet not preclude the
> use of the riverway for long-distance boating or disturb the fine riffles to
> which fishermen and canoeists are attracted. . . .[60]

In the language of the Park Service the "natural" may be "enhanced"
or "restored" as well as "preserved," and the decisions to enhance,
restore, or preserve depend upon judgments of "highest and best
uses."[61]

The architects' usage of "natural" by contrast seems defensive and
a bit cynical. In places, one senses that they are more concerned that
their product be natural-looking than that it be "natural." In essence
they are trying to argue that the dam will not be an eyesore. For
example:

> In the proposed plan for its architecture and development, Tocks Island
> Dam will serve as a transition buffer between the two landscapes, the
> intent being to make the dam an intrinsic element of the new natural
> scene, just as the farmhouse, barn, silo and other works of man became a
> part of the valley's agricultural scene. This intent will be realized in a
> naturalistic park and through architectural designs that de-emphasize the

purely mechanical functions of the dam structures, bringing them into scale and harmony with the natural setting.[62]

Their plan shows credit-worthy cosmetic intent: transmission lines are placed underground, and stone excavated from the dam site is used to face the powerhouse and visitor center (to "establish a continuity between the structures and the environment").[63] However, that the dam itself will be an "intrinsic element of the natural scene" is a strange claim for a rockpile whose exposed portion, about 80 feet wide and 45 feet high, will stretch straight as an arrow the full 3,000-foot width of the valley floor, with a fenced-in walkway or roadway across the top.

The extreme manifestations of the "natural-looking" as a palliative in the absence of the "natural" are the likes of "wood grain" formica table tops, which fool no one. Perhaps people have a psychological need to see "nature forms," and this need can be satisfied by artificial mimics as well, or almost as well, as by the original objects. Or perhaps the mimics do not really satisfy the basic need, but they serve as soothing reminders of some past pleasures which have been displaced by "progress"; in this sense the mimics may pander to sentimentality. The distinction between the natural and the natural-looking is evident in the way the body of water behind the dam is described by the two camps: those in favor of the Tocks Island Dam speak of a "lake" or even "mountain lake," while the environmentalist groups steadfastly use the word "reservoir."

The insistence on this language is related to a deep moral issue. The despair and fury of the hard core environmentalists is caused by their sensing that people probably *will* enjoy the artificial lake—and artificial grass, and artificial trees, and artificial anything else. The environmental critique of western civilization is not directed simply at cleaning up the litter and making sure there will be fish for the fishermen. In fact, it is a moral indictment of an entire way of life. From this perspective, environmental problems are evidence of moral failures—failures of self-discipline, failures of humility, failures of respect for nature—symptoms of a system that is considered heedlessly exploitative of both men and nature.

In this view then, token "real" parks or artificial surrogates, and patchwork ameliorative programs to clean up one sort of "pollution"[1] or another, are all fraudulent attempts to disguise the fundamental

---

[1]The more archaic usage of the word pollution in reference to moral defilement is a reminder that the remedies to pollution are not necessarily technical.

problem, and are accomplices to the problem to the extent that they divert energy away from basic social change. Consider, for example, Marcuse's assessment:

> ... The issue is not to beautify the ugliness, to conceal the poverty, to deodorize the stench, to deck the prisons, banks and factories with flowers. ... When people are no longer capable of distinguishing between beauty and ugliness, between serenity and cacophony, they no longer understand the essential quality of freedom, of happiness. Insofar as it has become the territory of capital rather than of man, nature serves to strengthen human servitude.[64]

Another clue to the normative, quasi-religious aspect of the "natural system" issue is the way the word "integrity" is used. The stated objective of the Federal Clean Water Act of 1972[65] was to "restore and maintain the chemical, physical and biological integrity of the nation's waters." In the Tocks debate, one of the documents from the United States Department of the Interior Bureau of Sport Fisheries and Wildlife listed ten "recommendations for environmental integrity."[66] Although the document does not define *integrity* explicitly, it is clear that the word is doing double duty, meaning both functional completeness and genuineness or trustworthiness. The functional interpretation is remarkably clear in the language of the House Public Works Committee analysis of the Federal Water Pollution Control Act amendments of 1972, where it is noted that "natural systems" have self-regenerative and self-regulating capacities that may not survive some kinds of disruption. In this sense, the integrity of a natural system is preserved so long as these homeostatic functions persist.

The broader normative sense of environmental integrity, a sense of "oneness" and "wholeness" about nature that reflects mystical attitudes, appears in the Code of Ethics proposed by the Ethics Committee of the Ecological Society of America. (The association is not accidental, as it is a fact of ecology that everything is connected to everything else in a way that is often important to scientific understanding.) The code exhorts the Society to use professional expertise "to find ways to harmonize man's needs, demands, and actions with the maintenance and enhancement of natural and managed systems."[67] How easily a consequentialist concern shades into a value position, without benefit of even a change in vocabulary!

People have tried to calculate the worth of a given natural system in terms of services it can perform, such as the cycling of critical elements, tertiary waste treatment, water retention, timber production, and provision of recreational resources.[68] The ideas behind this sort of accounting are straightforward, but actual analyses, as a rule, do not stand up to close examination. First of all, the basic numbers available (for example, rates of nitrogen fixation per acre of swamp) are not reliable. Second, utility functions are generally arrived at by estimating the cost of performing the same service (such as reducing the same quantity of nitrogen by industrial means) without regard for how much of the natural service really is of any utility, or whether the service might be obtained at lower cost by returning some *developed* plot of land to a functionally natural state. Both these problems, however difficult, are amenable to scientific inquiry.

Of less certain scientific status are the ecological domino theories —claims that apparently minor initial disturbances will propagate themselves through an ecosystem to emerge as literal catastrophes. Things like this do happen: food chain amplification of the effects of some biologically concentrated toxins are a good example. The trouble is that such phenomena, while more or less explicable once they have taken place, are not predictable in advance.[m] No one knows *which* new pollutants or new industrial or agricultural developments will instigate dramatic second and third order effects, and which will have ecological effects limited essentially to the primary perturbation. All we know is that such things have happened, and that they were unwelcome surprises at the time. These kinds of worries are consequential in that they refer to outcomes that are fairly unambiguous in their desirability or undesirability. But as they deal in hypothetical outcomes that are not very predictable, they give rise to decision making problems that hinge not on scientific issues but on risk taking attitudes, so they will become incorporated in arguments for or against preservation of the "natural" that reflect hopes and fears whose origins are in other matters.

We can easily see that a pessimistic view of the unpredictable consequences of ecological intervention, combined with a susceptibility to the mystic unity of ecology, would engender ineffable religious feelings about the value of the natural and the horror at destroying it. In this usage, the meaning of "natural" becomes imbued with a very personal vision of what the world should be like, and purely utilitarian discussion becomes unacceptable.

[m]Actually, ecological processes are so complicated that after the fact explanations may also be confounded. Even phenomena that are known to be recurrent may defy precise explanation—the population cycle of the lemming is a classic example.

VI.   CAN WE SAVE OURSELVES
FROM THE EXPERTS?

The present functioning of ecological expertise is an embarrassment to professional ecologists; but this is merely an irritating contradiction in a self-image shared by a very small interest group. The serious societal issue is whether ecological expertise, as it is currently employed, leads to better or worse decisions, and, more broadly, whether it leaves society better or worse off.

From the standpoint of the truly disinterested decision maker, with no particular scientific background of his own, the effect of ecological expertise on the outcome of the decision process may well appear to be nil. As long as spokesmen who can pass as ecological experts of superficially equivalent credibility are to be found on both sides of nearly any environmental controversy, they cancel. In individual cases, technical expertise of this sort is simply a political resource whose utility to the interested parties depends on the wisdom of the strategy determining its deployment. If all sides have more or less equal access to this resource, and exploit it with about equal intelligence, perhaps no major harm will accrue.

Unfortunately, the ideal of equal access does not often obtain, for technical expertise, like legal expertise, is expensive; and usually, if one party in a political controversy resorts to technical experts, then the other parties must do likewise, for tactical reasons. Where some groups are less able to afford this expenditure, a round of obligatory expertise can have antidemocratic consequences. In the Tocks Island Dam controversy, one can see how the minimal cost of effective participation has been steadily raised. When it was just a matter of one expert's "expert" opinion against anothers, the pro bono efforts of college professors, on the witness stand and in the media, could often equalize things. When concrete analyses began to be issued, a complete counteranalysis was required, entailing tens, perhaps hundreds of highly specialized man-hours, and attendant hardware, supply, and overhead expenses.

This is an especially acute problem with proprietary computer models, for these are so easily shrouded in highly idiosyncratic mummery that any group wishing to "cross-examine" a model's output will need an expert programmer and considerable amounts of machine time just to find out what the model is—assuming they can get their hands on a complete deck or listing. Then they will need recourse to scientists with state of the art status (or at least reputations) to find out in what ways the model does or does not make sense. This is well beyond the capacity of most citizen groups, and it represents more time and money than can routinely be expected as a donation from individuals or private institutions. So the group that can afford the first really messy computer model supporting its position in a given controversy has an edge. Generally, the advantage will lie with project promoters.

What can be done about this? The cheap tactical response is simply to debunk all expertise from a position of nonexpertise in the hopes of neutralizing the expert testimony without incurring a like expense. The danger is that overuse of this tactic, if successful, will ultimately contribute to a political atmosphere hostile to all rational analysis. On the other hand, moderate "pedagogic" employment of the debunking tactic could result in a mood of healthy skepticism among decision makers and the public, but it is difficult to know in advance where the fail-safe point lies.

A more cautious approach would be to build the skepticism into the decision making process. Our legal system embodies one archetype of institutionalized skepticism. Perhaps the rules surrounding the use of expert witnesses in court could be adapted for broader forms of decision making.[n] A reasonably simple checklist of questions could go a long way in helping decision makers, analysts, and interested parties demystify spurious models.

As regards the delay attendant upon the use of technical expertise in an environmental controversy, this is not unmitigated waste, for during this period significant political processes will be underway. This is the time when allies are gained or lost and political momentum maintained or dissipated, as the interested parties persevere in repeating and refining their respective inputs to the various loci of power that effect public decision. This is probably a healthy process.

We recall in this respect now some of the peculiarities of the Tocks controversy, especially as described in the first essay in this volume. We gained the impression that there was a deep level of poorly articulated concerns that involve pervasive value differences, and that this was linked to a tendency for the ostensible objects of debate to function as symbols of the actual tacit concerns. Conceivably, the underlying value positions, which now seem so badly served, are in fact so hazily perceived, even by the individual, that it would be a grave mistake to try to act politically on their promptings in other than an indirect, incremental fashion.

Imagine, for example, holding a national plebiscite on the

[n]A discussion of the traditions relating to the use of expert witnesses is presented by Sive,[69] who incidentally, argues in favor of greater flexibility in the use of expert witnesses in environmental controversy, whereas I am arguing for more strictness. (Politics, bedfellows, and all that.)

question of "economic growth." At the moment, the prevailing level of political consciousness on this issue simply is not prepared for such a confrontation. Not only is there no effective consensus, there are hardly any sensible ideologies—just disjunct attitudes toward the likes of progress, pollution, and wilderness, which, however intensely felt, are not integrated into a meaningfully complete vision of the life styles and types of social organization actually required to satisfy one set of preferences or another. All we find are collections of half-believed slogans—the old ones clearly out of tune with the times and the new ones insecurely held for lack of a palpable tradition within which they could make sense.

When the political alternatives are so unsettlingly nebulous, delaying the decision with the reassuringly familiar public ritual of college professors and engineers contradicting one another provides a salubrious grace period within which support can crystallize around more coherently developed political positions, or within which conventional political forces can reassert themselves. Thus society may benefit even from the employment of ineffectual expertise.

It is tempting, of course, to look for ways to improve the expertise itself. To some extent this will occur inevitably, at a rate commensurate with the progress of the relevant sciences, though with a persistent lag in content. As for talk of quality control within the professions, it is hard to imagine how that can affect the existing incentives for shabby work, or prevent the appearance of official-looking "professional societies" whose functions are purely defensive, while giving a misleading appearance of legitimacy and regulation in exclusive areas of lucrative pseudoscience.

VII. EPILOGUE

Even though environmental issues figured prominently in the pageantry of visible debate in the Tocks controversy, ecological expertise was not instrumental in the decision process. In the one instance of a technical environmental issue that did seem to matter—the likelihood of the eutrophication of a lake—the ecolocical experts simply did not deliver the goods. It seemed that the readily available expertise "on tap," as they say, was not capable of providing a convincing prediction.

The specific matters that are, or might be, effectively attended to by competent ecological experts are necessarily questions of fact that may be far removed from what is really bothering people who participate in the controversy. The underlying concerns of participants are often questions of taste or value, and a conflict over these cannot be resolved simply on the basis of what is true. At best, these will be resolved on the basis of what is fair, and at worst, on the basis of what the decision makers can get away with.

People are worried over the style of life that building or not building the dam portends for themselves; the style of world it will leave for their grandchildren; and the style of decision it implies that "they," as a society, made, compared with the style of decision they prefer to think of themselves as making. Behind all the quasi-scientific frills of environmental debate there are basic questions of what is a good society and what is a good life. Actors in the drama are motivated by usually unexpressed hopes and fears: dreams of a technological city of Oz as opposed to Arcadian longings, desires for a more rational social order versus Orwellian nightmares, entire covert Utopias built around preferred visions of growth or stasis, progress or conservation.

An application of ecological expertise to specific and circum-scribed projects will contribute little to the resolution of these funda-mentally social questions, beyond perhaps clarifying some of the rhetoric. When global scenarios, rather than specific projects, are the *explicit* focus, expert analysis, at least in principle, again comes into its own. Thus the recent Club of Rome efforts may be understood as attempts to confront questions of the technical feasibility of various visions of the future. The sort of question at issue in the Tocks debate was not, for example, whether the shad will continue to migrate up the Delaware; and it certainly was not whether we could design a scientifically managed shad stocking program. Given some possible threat to the shad, decision foundered on the questions of how much we care, and why, and how many of us do and how many of us don't. Before we expect too much from the ecological experts we should try to be certain which questions we want answered.

NOTES

1. Appropriate design specifications are discussed by P.J. Dalley, "Reevalua-tion of fish passage facilities related to Tocks Island Dam and Reservoir," report of the U.S. Department of the Interior, Bureau of Sport Fisheries and Wildlife, June 1971 (memo).

2. Corps of Engineers, *Tocks Island Lake Development: A Comprehensive Evaluation of Environmental Quality. Delaware River Basin, Tocks Island Lake, Pennsylvania, New Jersey and New York; Delaware Water Gap National Recrea-tion Area, DWGNRA, U.S. Department of the Interior, National Park Service; Kittatinny Mountain Project, Sponsor: New Jersey Electric Utilities, Assoc. Agencies FPC and DRBC (Department of the Army, 1971).*

3. T. W. Robbins, M. S. Topping, and E. C. Raney, "Studies of fishes in the Muddy Run pumped storage reservoir and connecting waters, a summary," 1970. Ichthyological Associates, Miscellaneous Report No. 4.

4. Dalley, *op. cit.*

5. Both the Corps and the Fish and Wildlife Service acknowledged the uncertainty, but both were optimistic about the prospects; e.g., Dalley's (*op. cit.*) "Summary and Conclusions" read simply "It is concluded to be feasible to pass American shad and other migratory fish over the Tocks Island Dam and through the reservoir . . ." Conservationists, including some biologists among them, took a dimmer view; e.g., the letter from E.E. MacNamara appended to the Sierra Club response to the Corps' 1971 *Environmental Impact Statement* (published with that statement).

6. W.H. Massman, *Analysis of the River Fisheries*, Bureau of Sport Fisheries and Wildlife, June 1971 (memo).

7. R.M. Jenkins, *Tocks Island Reservoir Fishery Analysis*, Bureau of Sport Fisheries and Wildlife, June 1971 (memo).

8. State of Delaware, Department of Natural Resources and Environmental Control, letter (June 4, 1971) in response to the Corps' 1971 Impact Statement, appended to that Statement.

9. D.W. Slater, W.T. Olds, Jr., W.H. Massman, R.M. Jenkins, P.J. Dalley, G.G. Taylor, *Fish and Wildlife Aspects of Tocks Island Reservoir and Related Developments*, June 1971 (memo).

10. Roy F. Weston, Environmental Scientists and Engineers, *Tocks Island Region Environmental Study*, W.O. 256-03 (April 1970).

11. "An appraisal of the potential for cultural eutrophication of Tocks Island Lake" Jack McCormick and Associates, Devon, Pa, Sept., 1971.

12. "Ecologic Simulation, Tocks Island Lake" D.J. Glanz, G.T. Orlob, and G.K. Young, Water Resources Engineers, Springfield, Virginia, February, 1973.

13. E. Mayr, E.G. Linsley, and R.L. Usinger, *Methods and Principles of Systematic Zoology*, (New York: McGraw-Hill, 1953).

14. C.B. Williams, "The range and pattern of insect abundance." *American Nature* 94: 137–151.

15. A.G. Fischer, "Latitudinal variations in organic diversity," *Evolution* 14:64–81.

16. G.L. Clark, *Elements of Ecology* (New York: John Wiley, 1954).

17. Fischer, *op. cit.*

18. M. Kozhov, "Lake Baikal and Its Life," Dr. W. Junk, The Hague, 1963.

19. H.L. Carson, D.E. Hardy, H.T. Spieth, and W.S. Stone, "The Evolutionary Biology of the Hawaiian Drosophilidae," in *Essays in Evolution and Genetics, in honor of Theodosius Dobzhansky*, M.K. Hecht and W.C. Steere (eds.) (New York: Appleton-Century-Crofts, 1970).

20. R.H. Whittaker, *Communities and Ecosystems* (New York: Macmillan, 1970).

21. N.G. Hairston, "On the Relative Abundance of Species." *Ecology* 50: 1091–1094.

22. C.O. Dirks, "Biological Studies of Maine Moths by Light Trap Methods," *Maine Ag. Exp. Sta. Bull.* (1937): 389.

23. "A Natural History Survey of the Proposed Tocks Island Reservoir

National Recreation Area," National Park Service document (apparently unpublished).

24. C.R. Darwin, *Origin of Species* (London: Murray, 1859).

25. A.J. Nicholson, "The Balance of Animal Populations," *J. Anim. Ecol.* 2(suppl.): 132–178: R.H. MacArthur, "Population Ecology of Some Warblers of Northeastern Coniferous Forests," *Ecology* 39: 599–619; S.A. Levin, "Community Equilibria and Stability, and an Extension of the Competitive Exclusion Principle", *Amer. Natur.* 104:413–423.

26. C.L. Prosser, and F.A. Brown, Jr., *Comparative Animal Physiology* (Philadelphia: Saunders, 1961).

27. For an intriguing example, see B.J. Rathcke, and R.W. Poole, "Coevolutionary Race Continues: Butterfly Larval Adaptation to Plant Trichomes," *Science* 187: 175–176.

28. The implications of this kind of process have been treated by L.B. Slobodkin in several articles: L.B. Slobodkin, "The Strategy of Evolution," *Amer. Natur.* 52: 342–357, and "On the Present Incompleteness of Mathematical Ecology," *Am. Sci.* 53: 347–357.

29. For an introduction to the use of "game" ideas in understanding evolution, see R.C. Lewontin, "Evolution and the Theory of Games," *J. Theoret. Biol.* 1: 382–403.

30. Notorious examples are chlorinated hydrocarbon insecticides and some radioactive fallout constituents. See J.J. Hickey, J.A. Keith, and F.B. Coon, "An Exploration of Pesticides in a Lake Michigan Ecosystem," *J. Appl. Ecol.* 3(suppl.): 141–154; W.C. Hanson, H.E. Plamer, and B.I. Griffin, "Radioactivity in Northern Alaska Eskimos and Their Foods," and D.C. Watson, W.C. Hanson, J.J. Davis, and W.H. Rickard, "Radionuclides in Terrestrial and Freshwater Biota," both in N.J. Wilimovsky and J.N. Wolfe (eds.), *Environment of the Cape Thompson Region, Alaska.* (Oak Ridge, Tenn.: U.S.A.E.C., 1966).

31. This particular account appeared in the *New York Times*, May 10, 1973, p. 63, "The use of DDT upsets nature's balance" and has, in a similar form, been popular on the conference circuit. I have not been able to find first-hand documentation of the entire story. Parts of it concur with the reports reviewed by G.R. Conway, "Ecological Aspects of Pest Control in Malaysia," in M.T. Farvar and J.P. Milton (eds.), *The Careless Technology; Ecology and International Development*, (Garden City, N.Y.: Natural History Press, 1972), a volume which, incidentally, is an excellent compendium of case histories of unintended, and sometimes surprising, results of various technological adventures.

32. M. Kimura, "Natural Selection as the Process of Accumulating Genetic Information in Adaptive Evolution," *Genetical Research* 2: 127–140; R. Levins, "Genetic Consequences of Natural Selection," in T.H. Waterman and H.J. Morowitz (eds.), *Theoretical and Mathematical Biology*, (New York: Blaisdell, 1965).

33. See note 12.

34. Glanz, Orlob, and Young, *op. cit.*, pp. 6–7.

35. Actually, this worry may have more to do with modeling, per se, than we at first suspected, if it turns out that all the filmflam of graphs, equations, and pages of numbers provides a ready camouflage for systematic deception with words.

36. "Report to the Delaware River Basin Commission on Sewage Treatment

Plant Effect on Eutrophication in Tocks Island Reservoir," *Water Resources Engineering*, (November 1, 1972).

37. R.A. Vollenweider, "Scientific Fundamentals of the Eutrophication of Lakes and Flowing Waters, with Particular Reference to Nitrogen and Phosphorus as Factors in Eutrophication," O.E.C.D. document, 1968.

38. R.G. Wiegert, "Simulation Modelling of the Algal-Fly Component of a Thermal Ecosystem: Effects of Spatial Heterogeneity, Time Delays, and Model Coordination," in B.C. Patten (ed.), *Systems Analysis and Simulation in Ecology*, vol. 3 (N.Y.: Academic Press, 1975).

39. Glanz, Orlob, and Young, *op. cit.*, pp. 8–9.

40. D.B. Mertz, "The *Tribolium* Model and the Mathematics of Population Growth," *Ann. Rev. Ecol. Syst.* 3:51–78.

41. C.S. Holling, "The Components of Predation as Revealed by a Study of Small Mammal Predation of the European Pine Sawfly," *Canad. Entomol.* 91: 293–320.

42. ———, "The Functional Response of Invertebrate Predators to Prey Density," *Mem. Entomol. Soc. Can.* 48: 1–85.

43. F.B. Turner, "The Ecological Efficiency of Consumer Populations." *Ecology* 51: 741–742;

J.T. Tanner, "Effects of Population Density on Growth Rates of Animal Populations," *Ecology* 47:733–745;

G. Caughley, "Mortality Patterns in Mammals," *Ecology* 47:906–918;

T. Park, D.B. Mertz, W. Grodzinski, and T. Prus, "Cannibalistic Predation in Populations of Flour Beetles," *Physiol. Zool.* 38:289–321;

P.W. Frank, C.D. Boll, and R.W. Kelly, "Vital Statistics of Laboratory Cultures of *Daphnia pulex* DeGeer as Related to Density." *Physiol. Zool.* 30:287–305.

44. E.D.S. Cormer and A.G. Davies, "Plankton as a Factor in the Nitrogen Phosphorous Cycles in the Sea," *Adv. Mar. Biol.* 9:101–204;

J. Caperon, "Population Growth Response of *Isochrysis Galbana* to Nitrate Variation at Limiting Concentrations," *Ecology* 49:866–872;

J.J. MacIsaac and R.C. Dugdale, *Deep-Sea Res.* 16:415–422;

R.W. Eppley, J.N. Rogers, J.F. McCarthy, "Half-Saturation Constants for Uptake of Nitrate and Ammonium by Marine Phytoplankton," *Limnol. and Oceanogr.* 14:912–920.

45. In fact, there are "too many" equations that will provide a fair fit in these circumstances, and it is seldom that any biological insight is gained from analysing which provides a better fit. See W. Feller, "On the Logistic Law of Growth and Its Empirical Verifications in Biology," *Acta Biotheor.* (A) 5:51–66.

46. A recent exchange concerning the effects of limiting factors on algae illustrates the confusion in inferring levels from rates. See W.J. O'Brien, "Limiting Factors in Phytoplankton Algae: Their Meaning and Measurement," *Science* 178:616–617; and M.G. Kelley, and G.M. Hornberger, "Phytoplankton Algae: Nutrient Concentrations and Growth," *Science* 180:1298–1299.

Attempts to apply analytical mathematics to population models usable beyond the sigmoid phase have largely proved a valley of no return. See P.J.

Wangersky and W.J. Cunningham, "Time Lag in Population Models," *Cold Spring Harbor Symp. Quant. Biol.* 22:329–338; and R.M. May, "Biological Populations with Nonoverlapping Generations: Stable Points, Stable Cycles, and Chaos," *Science* 186:645–647.

It is possible to construct reasonably accurate computer models for this sort of population projection, but the models are complex and their data requirements are monumental. See P.W. Frank, "Prediction of Population Growth Form in *Daphnia pulex* Cultures," *Am. Nat.* 94:358–372.

47. J. Shapiro, "Blue-Green Algae: Why They Become Dominant," *Science* 179:382–384;

T.C. Goldman, "Carbon Dioxide and pH: Effect on Species Succession of Algae," *Science* 182:306–307;

C.L. Schelske and E.F. Stoermer, "Eutrophication, Silica, Depletion and Predicted Changes in Algal Quality in Lake Michigan," *Science* 173:423–424;

P. Kilham, "A Hypothesis Concerning Silica and the Freshwater Planktonic Diatoms," *Limnol. and Oceanogr.* 16:10–18.

M. Lefevre, M.H. Jakob, and M. Nisbet, "Auto-et hétéroantagonisme chez les algues d'eau douce," *Ann. Stat. Centr. Hydrobiol. Appl.* 4:5–198;

M. Lefevre and G. Farrugia, "De l'influence, sur les algues d'eau douce, de produits de décomposition spontanée, des substances organiques d'origine animale et végétable," *Hydrobiol.* 20:49–65;

G.E. Fogg, C. Nalewajko, and W.D. Watt, "Extracellular Products of Phytoplankton Photosynthesis," *Proc. Roy. Soc.* (B) 162:517–534;

P.R. Gorham "Toxic Waterblooms of Blue-green Algae. *Can. Vet. Jour.* 1:235–245;

T. Overbeck, 1962. "Untersuchungen zum Phosphathaushalt von Grünalgen," *Arch Hydrobiol.* 58:162–209.

48. D.R.S. Lean, "Phosphorus Dynamics in Lake Water," *Science* 179:678–680.

49. T. Overbeck, and H.D. Babenzien, "Uber den Nachweis von freien Enzymen im Gewasser." *Arch. Hydrobiol.* 60:107–114; and J.D.H. Strickland and L. Solarzano, "Determination of Monesterase Hydrolysable Phosphate and Phosphorus Esterase Activity in Sea Water," in H. Barnes (ed.) *Some Contemporary Studies in Marine Science* (London: Allen & Unwin, 1966), pp. 665–674.

50. W.F. Libby and R. Berger, "Equilibration of Atmospheric CO_2 with Sea Water: Possible Enzymatic Control of the Rate," *Science* 164:1395–1397.

51. The usual turnover time for phosphorus in lakes is about one week. See G.E. Hutchinson, *A Treatise on Limnology* vol. I. (New York: John Wiley, 1957).

52. J. Schwoerbel and G.C. Tillmanns, "Untersuchungen Über die Stoffwechseldynamik in Fliessgewässern. I. Die Rolle höherer Wasserpflanzen: Callitriche homulata Kutz," *Arch. Hydrobiol.* (28 Suppl.) 5, 2/3:245–288.

53. G.P. Fitzgerald, "Aerobic Lake Muds for the Removal of Phosphorus from Lake Waters." *Limnol. Oceanogr.* 15:550–555;

T. Berman, "Phosphatase Release of Inorganic Phosphorus in Lake Kinneret," *Nature* 224:1213–1232;

C.H. Mortimer, "Chemical Exchanges Between Sediments and Water in the

Great Lakes—Speculations on Probable Regulatory Mechanisms," *Limnol. Oceanogr.* 16:387–404;

C. Serruya, "Lake Kinneret: The Nutrient Chemistry of the Sediments," *Limnol. Oceanogr.* 16:510–521.

54. C.F. Baren, "Limnological Effects of Simulated Pumped-Storage Operations at Yards Creek," Delaware River Basin Commission, December 1971.

55. D.W. Schindler, "Eutrophication and Recovery in Experimental Lakes: Implications for Lake Management," *Science* 184:896–899.

56. R.F. Weston, *"Tocks Island Regional Environmental Study,"* *op. cit.*, p. 22.

57. "A Natural History Survey of the Proposed Tocks Island Reservoir National Recreation Area," National Park Service, *op. cit.*, p. 3–4.

58. Press release from offices of U.S. Representatives Dow, McDade, Rooney, and Thompson, April 1971.

59. National Park Service, *DWGNRA Master Plan*, 1966, p. C-6.

60. "A Natural System Plan for Delaware Water Gap National Recreation Area," N.P.S., p. 6.

61. From a survey of the Master Plan issued by the N.P.S. in 1971 ". . . the scheme is established to preserve and enhance all those resources both natural and cultural, which form the fabric of a pleasant and rewarding outdoor recreation experience as well as restore to their highest and best uses other lands with outstanding natural scenic potential." N.P.S. quoted in "The Keystone Project, Tocks Island Revisited" *Delaware Basin Bulletin* 10 (Sept/Oct. 1971): Published by Water Resources Association of the Delaware River Basin.

62. "Tocks Island Dam: A Plan for Its Architecture and Development," Clarke and Rapuano, Inc., for Corps of Engineers.

63. *Ibid*, p. 14.

64. *Liberation* 17:3–12. "Ecology and Revolution" S. Mansholt, M. Bosquit, E. Morin, and H. Marcuse.

65. *Federal Water Pollution Control Act Amendments of 1972*, Report of the Committee on Public Works, U.S. House of Representatives, H.R. 11896. Page 76 of the record contains a very interesting amplification of the meaning of "integrity" and "natural" in the Committee's usage.

66. W.T. Olds, Jr., "Reevaluation of wildlife resources related to Tocks Island Dam and reservoir, Kittatinny Mountain Project, and Delaware Water Gap National Recreation Area, New Jersey, New York, and Pennsylvania," Department of Interior, Bureau of Sport Fisheries and Wildlife, June 16, 1971.

67. Reported in R.B. Platt, "The issue of professionalism" *Bull. Ecol. Soc. Amer.* 54:2–6.

68. For example, E. Odum and H.T. Odum, "Natural Areas as Necessary Components of Man's Total Environment," *Trans. 37th N. Amer. Wildlife and Natural Resources Conf.*, pp. 178-189.

69. D. Sive, "Securing, Examining and Cross-Examining Expert Witnesses in Environmental Cases," *Michigan Law Review*, 68:1175–1198.

Part 5

Analysis in a New Key

There is a fancy held by some that romance and history have no rightful place in a rigorous work of analysis. The following essay by Frank Sinden on the recreation and transportation planning for the Tocks project should quash such fancies. This essay combines detailed quantitative investigations with the reminiscences of old-timers and the dreams of present-day planners and antiplanners, and what emerges is a picture of the alternatives truly open to those planning a recreation park on the Delaware, or anywhere.

THE FAVORITE SPRING, SUMMER, AND AUTUMN RESORT.

OPEN FROM MAY 1st UNTIL NOVEMBER.

THE KITTATINNY,
DELAWARE WATER GAP, MONROE CO. PENNA.

Chapter 10

A New Park on the Delaware

Frank W. Sinden

I. THE HEYDAY OF THE WATER GAP

From the coming of the railroad in the middle 1800s to the Great Depression of the 1930s, the Delaware Water Gap was a thriving resort. Summer after summer, families from New York and Philadelphia, with their Gladstone bags and wicker baskets, flocked to its hotels and boarding houses. By 1930, just before the precipitous decline, there were twenty hotels in the vicinity of the Water Gap itself and dozens of smaller establishments strung out for miles along the river upstream.

One of the earliest, and ultimately largest, hotels was Kittatinny House, which was situated on the Pennsylvania side just upstream from the Water Gap on a plateau 80 feet above the river and athwart a mountain stream that ran down from a scenic pond called Lake Lenape. At one time the stream ran right through the kitchen, where it was used for cooking and washing. As demand grew, the Kittatinny House was joined by other hotels. On a high ledge just behind it was built the Water Gap House, the plushest of them all. On the river itself, the steamboat, "Kittatinny" churned up and down on a three-mile run within and below the Gap. The more fashionable places were often graced with celebrities—Civil War generals, politicians, and, later, movie stars. The latter were sometimes there on business, actually making movies. By the standards of the day, a great variety of movies could be set against the Water Gap's scenery with sufficient plausibility. Among those made there were hillbilly comedies, Perils of Pauline serials, and even Tom Mix westerns.

The river and adjacent lands north of the Water Gap and west of Kittatinny Ridge, where the Tocks reservoir would be situated, forms a natural province, which the Indians called the "Minisink." In a guidebook[1] published in 1870, Luke Brodhead, whose family owned two of the Water Gap hotels, and whose family name is attached to the largest local creek, describes the Minisink as follows:

> The forty miles of the course of this stream along the base of the mountain from Port Jervis to this place, is unsurpassed in the variety and beauty of the pictures it presents; and taken in connection with the fine character of the carriage roads, the numerous waterfalls adjacent, there is not perhaps a more desirable drive of the same extent along any river in the country.

The Minisink scenery had been valued for generations. In the early days, Durham boats, poled by hand, and rafts of logs coming down on the spring freshets often carried passengers for the pleasure trip. Inns along the bank catered to the raftsmen and their guests. Then, as now, bridges were few: overland travelers were pulled across the river on hand- or current-driven ferries in return for a small toll, and many of the ferrymen's names are still on the map.

In 1860 the beauty of the Minisink inspired an ambitious attempt to establish a steamboat line all the way from Belvidere, just below the Gap, to Port Jervis, 40 miles above. Despite the rocks and shallow water, the project was deemed feasible and a steamboat specially designed for the run was actually built at Easton. Unfortunately, this boat, the "Alfred Thomas," never survived its maiden voyage. As the new steamboat, loaded with dignitaries, plowed up the river to cheering crowds on the banks, the engineer, in his enthusiasm, "ran the pressure of steam up to 125 pounds to the square inch, when it should not have exceeded 80—the consequence of which was the explosion of the boiler."[2] Thirteen people were killed and no further attempts to extend steam navigation to the Minisink were made.

Although the Water Gap in its heyday reached to the social pinnacle, not all its visitors were rich. Nearby villages contained many humble boarding houses, and upriver in the Minisink a number of farmhouses took in guests of modest means. Most visitors came in family groups and returned to the same places year after year.

The railroads, whose advent in the middle 1800s made the Water Gap into a resort, provided not only transportation, but part of the entertainment:

> The Belvidere, Delaware and Flemington Railroad passes for the whole distance, from Trenton to Manunka Chunk, along the bank of the Delaware River, and one's eyes seldom look upon a more enchanting series of landscapes than stretches along this river, in one long and varied line of beauty, from New Hope and the Nockamixon Rocks to the Delaware Water Gap. The road possesses the reputation of admirable management, of which its cleanly and comfortable passenger cars give good evidence.[3]

Trains and vacations soon became inseparable concepts, and resorts and railroads became partners in promoting business. Just as Luke Brodhead was kind enough to give a railroad a plug now and then, as in the passage above, so the railroads were kind enough to run vigorous advertising campaigns promoting the Water Gap. This happy symbiosis endured for many decades.

But the railroads exacted an environmental toll, to which Luke Brodhead was not insensitive, despite the fortune the railroads brought to his family's hotels:

> The railroad, though a great improvement over the old method of reaching the Water Gap by stage-coach, has nevertheless made some innovations upon the primitive beauty of the place, that are not pleasant to contemplate: besides destroying that charming walk once studded with sycamores, free from underbrush and turfed with green, situated between the base of the cliff on which the hotel rests and the river, which the earlier visitors delighted in calling "Love Lane," it has forced the carriage-road so far up the ravine at Rebecca's Bath, as to destroy much of its former beauty, and caused the demolition of many grand old trees, under whose shelter passed the carriage-road of former days.[4]

The automobile, aided by the depression, brought the railroad-resort system to an end in the 1930s. Within a decade most of the big hotels had been destroyed by fire and neglect. Now, 40 years later, after traffic, air pollution, energy shortages, and further innovations upon primitive beauty that are not pleasant to contemplate, the old system is regarded by many people with strong nostalgia. One person whose regard for it goes beyond nostalgia is a man named Tom Taber.

Tom Taber is a peppery gentleman of 75 who has been urging New Jersey railroads to restore passenger service for two decades. He especially wants to see excursion trains running to the recreation areas—to the Jersey shore, to the Water Gap, to the Poconos. Restoration of recreation service, he feels, is a logical first step toward a general revitalization of all passenger service.

Although Tom Taber has never worked for a railroad, he knows every inch of track in the region and most of what has gone on in regional railroading during the last hundred years. He is currently putting some of it down in a history of the Lackawanna Railroad. His office, packed with memorabilia, is right on the platform of the Madison, New Jersey station. When a train pulls in, he glances automatically at the clock. Following is some of what he said recently about the time, not so long ago, when railroads were vigorous enterprises:

"The Lackawanna was ambitious, but couldn't compete in speed with the New York Central and Pennsylvania, because their main line to Buffalo had the worst hills to go over. The Lackawanna had to have something to talk about, so they offered anthracite coal (which was clean) plus scenery in the Poconos. To promote the cleanliness they had a young woman, stage-named Phoebe Snow, who rode the trains in a spotless white dress. Everyone knew the jingles about her:

> When Phoebe Snow sets out to go
> From New York City to Buffalo
> All dressed in white
> She travels right
> Upon the Road of Anthracite.

At one time the name Phoebe Snow was considered as imperishable as Bon Ami, Kodak, and Coca-Cola. The jingles were endless and spawned hundreds of unprintable satires. . . .

"Anthracite didn't produce any real smoke—all you saw was a bluish-white haze above the stack. During World War I, all the anthracite was requisitioned for ships—the submarines looked for smoke in those days—and the anthracite railroads had to switch to soft coal. Phoebe's white dress was promptly replaced by an olive drab uniform. . . .

"In 1949 the Lackawanna established a train through the Water Gap to Buffalo and Chicago named after Phoebe Snow and it ran until the Erie merger in 1960. Then the Erie-oriented management killed it. But when William White came back as chairman in 1963, the first thing he did was to put Phoebe back on the tracks, and she ran until 1966.

"After World War II there was an upsurge of passenger service— improved equipment, speeded-up schedules. The zenith occurred around 1950, but then about five years later the recession in passenger service began to be obvious. Now, of course, the management just doesn't want to fool with passengers. They're not even interested in running the trains they've got to Great Gorge, McAfee, the Poconos, the Shore, etc. But they could. There is ample equipment right now sitting idle, doing nothing, from Friday evening to Monday morning. Why not send it out to those places—*do* something with it? If you suggest it to the management or the State [which subsidizes passenger service] they just huff and puff and vaguely talk about operational details. When you try to pin them down (I speak their language, they can't kid me) they just avoid the issues. The mind! The mentality! Good God, when I was a kid—why every Sunday, every railroad ran excursions all over hell's half-acre. The Jersey Central and Pennsylvania for years and years ran special excursions: Point Pleasant; a dollar a round trip; Atlantic City, $2.50; Philadelphia, $2.50; Baltimore and Washington, $3.00; Scranton and the Poconos, $2.50—*every* weekend. Mauchunk and the Switchback, Lake Hopatcong—all summer long. In the entrance to the Jersey Central Ferry on Liberty Street, there was a board at least fifteen feet long covered with one solid mass of Sunday excursion handbills printed on long narrow strips of cheap paper of various colors. Got a lot of them around here someplace. We called them throwaways. On Saturday noon after work everybody went down to see where the excursions were going. . . .

"You never heard of the Switchback? Oh my, where have you been? Gee, if that were there today it would be a gold mine. It was on the Lehigh up above Allentown. You got in a car, were pulled up to the top of a mountain on an inclined plane, then you did a free flight. Coasted downhill, around curves, here, there, everywhere. Then at the bottom, they grabbed it on a rope and pulled it up to another mountaintop. It was partly thrills and partly scenery. In those small open cars you knew you were moving. On one three-mile stretch especially, it went like a bastard. . .

"The Water Gap was a big attraction. You had a whole string of big resort hotels along the Delaware—in fact a couple of them looked right down on the Water Gap Station. Kittatinny House—a hell of a big place—looked right across the river at the face of the rock. At Stroudsburg Station (and also at Cresco and Mount Pocono) the platform was long, and each hotel and boarding house had a stage backed up there, with the driver hollering out the name of his hotel. Same thing at Atlantic City. . . .

"They could be running trains right now. Getting to Stroudsburg is a cinch—block signals all there, track's in first class shape—no excuse there. But the railroad does nothing on its own initiative. The State orders them to run this train or that train and pays them for it. The State is paying the railroad nine million dollars this year in subsidy. . .Get the State to take some action? Good God, man, did you ever go over to Egypt and try to argue with the Sphinx?"

By the early 1960s when the Delaware Water Gap National Recreation Area (which was to surround the Tocks reservoir) was conceived, a new generation had grown up with no memory of the railroad-resort system. The automobile had brought with it new styles and seemingly new imperatives. The second great heyday of recreation on the Delaware, as planned by the Park Service, was to be very different from the first. Mass beaches and campsite cities were the accepted amenities and automobiles were the accepted means of transportation. Trains were out of the question. Now, ten years later, in the midst of pollution and energy crisis, the new heyday is still on the drawing board and some second thoughts are being expressed. Is Tom Taber behind his time—or ahead of it?

II. A NEW HEYDAY ON THE DRAWING BOARD

A basic tenet of the environmentalists, virtually a cliche, is that we have been brought to our present predicament by compartmental thinking. That is, we have subdivided our problems into small pieces, and then studied the pieces as if they had no relationship to each other. The piecemeal solutions, though possibly optimal within their scope, have often created new problems outside their scope. The new problems have again been attacked in a compartmental fashion, and so forth.

Perhaps this mode of thought is inevitable, since the human mind is finite and requires boundaries and limits in order to operate. Like a flashlight it can only illuminate one spot at a time. At any rate, it is often possible, in retrospect, to see how arbitrary constraints have propagated through the stages of a complicated planning process. Such a propagation is visible, for example, in the planning for transportation of visitors to the Delaware Water Gap National Recreation Area.[a] The original planning, done under the aegis of the Corps of Engineers, is presented in House Document 522,[5] an eleven-volume work covering many aspects of the Tocks Island Dam project as well as other projects in the Delaware River Basin. Comprehensive as this document is, it inevitably has boundaries, and one of these excludes consideration of transportation outside the Park. As we shall see, this exclusion had serious consequences.

[a]The term "National Recreation Area" is used to designate parks designed for intensive use where conservation is subordinate to recreation. In a "National Park" the priorities, in theory at least, are reversed. For simplicity I will use "park" in its ordinary generic meaning to include both, and "the Park" to designate the Delaware Water Gap National Recreation Area.

The primary impetus for undertaking the study presented in House Document 522 was, of course, the bad flood of 1955, which led to consideration of a large main stem dam. But a dam large enough to control bad floods would, among other things, create a lake that could be used for water sport. The planners felt that the recreational value of the lake would be best exploited in the public interest if it were surrounded by a park or "recreation area." Thus the Park evolved as an adjunct to recreation, which in turn was a by-product of flood control.

The detailed planning of recreational facilities was done by the National Park Service and was presented in a "Master Plan"[6] published in 1966. (The general outline of the Plan is also given in House Document 522, Appendix W.) This plan provided for very intensive use. According to the Nathan Report[7] (discussed below), "Attendance estimates anticipate that the project will be the most intensively used Federal recreation facility in the United States." This seemed justified because elaborate demand studies set forth in House Document 522 had concluded that the potential demand for outdoor recreation would exceed any conceivable supply that could be provided by the Park. Thus the capacity of the Park rather than demand appeared to be the limiting factor. Nevertheless, no analysis of capacity in either social or environmental terms was done.

In round figures, the plan provided for 150,000 people at one time and ten million visitor-days per year. This very high capacity was achieved in large part by means of giant beaches, some of which were to accommodate more than 10,000 people (see Fig. 10–1). Wherever the ground along the shore was level enough or could be made level enough by means of "land sculpturing," beaches, picnic areas, and parking lots were planned. Campsites were located in great number (see Fig. 10–2) throughout the Park, and scenic roads were provided so that a great many sightseers could be accommodated simply as auto passengers. The main limiting factors in this planning appear to have been the steepness of terrain and the difficulty of internal road access. Traffic outside the Park and other outside impacts were not considered.

The beaches and picnic areas did tend to concentrate people near the water's edge, though the steeper uplands were still to be densely used. The planners tried to locate the largest concentrations near the existing roads or roadheads, notably near the Route 206 crossing at Milford and around Wallpack Bend, which is accessible by a steep road over Kittatinny Ridge at Millbrook, and at a number of points accessible from the relocated Route 209 in Pennsylvania. Since the Park was long and narrow, every internal point was close to the

Figure 10-1. Beach Scene Showing an Estimated 3,000 People
Some Tocks beaches were, and still are, supposed to hold crowds three or four times this size at a density of one person for every 50 square feet. (The density in the picture is much less than this.)

boundary and could, in principle, be reached by a short transverse access road. This was generally the pattern followed, with little provision internally for longitudinal movement. If attention is focused on the amenities of the Park, and if virtually all movement is imagined to be by automobile, then certainly minimizing internal roads with their inevitable lines of noisy, polluting, pedestrian-menacing cars is a commendable goal. But the effect of this focused attention was to displace the longitudinal movement to the external roads.[8]

Pennsylvania and New Jersey, recognizing that the project would have important effects of many kinds in the surrounding region, co-sponsored an "impact study" by Robert Nathan Associates, which was carried out in 1966, the same year in which the Park Service Master Plan was released. Nathan Associates had access to the

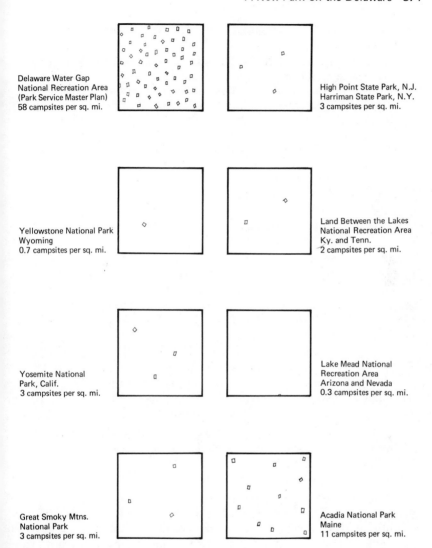

Figure 10-2. Campsites Compared to Total Park Area for Various Large Parks

developing Park Service plans and relied basically on them for the number and distribution of visitors in the Park. Nathan concluded, among other things, that

...present and planned roads within the primary impact area will be unable to handle the anticipated level of traffic to DWGNRA [Delaware Water Gap National Recreation Area]. Although the high-speed expressways will bring vehicles easily to the DWGNRA vicinity, a distributor system from the expressways to Park entrances and between destination areas is lacking. . . . U.S. Route 209 in Pennsylvania will evidence the most severe traffic problems, since it must also serve as the main north-south connector for the Pennsylvania Counties' general traffic. Sustained traffic volumes during summer months will be two to three times the capacity of relocated Route 209 as presently planned. Although destination areas in New Jersey served directly by Route 206 and N.J. 23 will be better able to absorb traffic demands, severe problems will occur on under-capacity roads southwest of 206. While the congestion is not expected to reduce levels of visitation substantially, it will have a deleterious effect on the environment.[9]

In view of this unpleasant news the New Jersey Department of Transportation commissioned the engineering firm of Edwards and Kelcey to make a study of the nearby roads on the New Jersey side and to recommend a specific plan for accommodating the traffic. Edwards and Kelcey, taking the Nathan impact study, the Park Service Master Plan, and the Corps' House Document 522 as given, laid out a dense network of freeways in the nearby parts of Sussex and Warren Counties.[10] They estimated the cost of this network at 680 million dollars (see Fig. 10-3). A highway impact study undertaken by the Pennsylvania Department of Transportation[11] estimated that the relocation and widening of Route 209, which was the main near-region construction occasioned by the project on the Pennsylvania side, would cost 40 million dollars. Added to the New Jersey figure this brought the total near-region highway cost to over 700 million dollars, or more than twice the estimated cost of the Tocks Dam project itself.[b]

The indirect impact of the highways in stimulating growth of the near-region would be much greater than the direct impact of the visitors to the Park. The visitors would create some demand for food, gasoline, and local services, but this would be small compared to the demands of the permanent residents and industries who would flock in on the heels of the new highway construction.[12] Thus the occurrence of an unusual (even freakish) flood appears to have led, by a circuitous route, to the planning of vast and seemingly unrelated development. One may speculate on the possibility that the planning could ultimately come full circle. If the new development stimulated by the highways should occur on the flood plains of Delaware tributaries, as it has in other parts of the basin, then flood damage, which was to be ameliorated by the dam, might in the end be worsened.

[b]In H D 522, Vol. X, p. U-59, the Corps includes $5 million for a minimal replacement of Route 209 that would not increase its capacity.

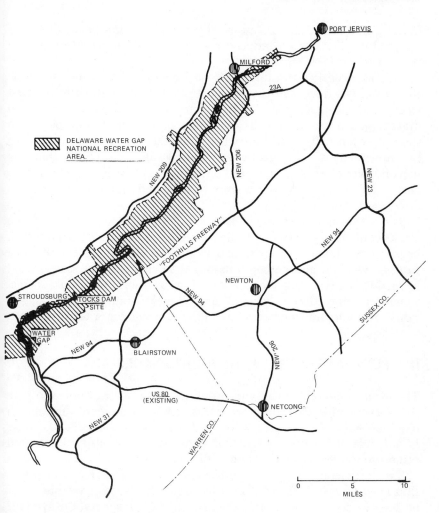

Figure 10-3. Proposed Freeways in Sussex and Warren Counties
The freeways follow virgin rights-of-way leaving the old roads intact. Old roads
are not shown.

The high social and dollar cost of the regional highway network
proposed by Edwards and Kelcey led Governor Cahill of New Jersey
to insist, among other things, that the planned visitor load be
reduced from ten million to four million visitor-days per year. His
Department of Transportation estimated that this would reduce the
cost of the regional highway net from $680 million to $370
million.[13] On the social side, the governor hoped that the reduction
would bring to a manageable level the enormous pressures that would
otherwise engulf the local communities. In response to Governor

Cahill's statement, the Delaware River Basin Commission officially adopted in May 1973 a reduced recreation plan prepared jointly by the Corps and Park Service.

This apparently substantial retreat, however, was more ostensible than real. The new plan turned out to be nearly identical to the first stage of the original plan. A Park Service official who had helped draft it said privately that he expected the full ten million people to show up eventually, and that when they did, the original plan would be implemented. He further saw no reason to suppose that the demand would stop at ten million. The Corps of Engineers, for its part, did not rush to revise its claimed recreation benefits downward.[14]

There the matter stood in late 1973. In 1974 and 1975, as the Tocks controversy developed, the possibliity of a park without a dam began to be taken seriously, and as a result, planning for the area took a new turn and perceptions began to change. This story is told in section V. The next two sections disgress briefly to discuss recreational transportation in general and to make some specific suggestions for public transportation to and within the Water Gap Park.

III. PUTTING THINGS IN THE RIGHT PLACES

The environmental, social, and economic costs of transportation are so overwhelming that they are necessarily a prime consideration in planning for outdoor recreation. As we saw in the case of Tocks Island, just the economic cost of highways alone easily dominated other economic costs associated with the project.

Two efficiency questions with respect to recreational transportation need to be addressed: (1) How should facilities of various types be located so as to minimize the amount of transportation needed? (2) How can the transportation that *is* needed be made efficient in energy use, pollution, social impact, safety, and economic cost? In the days of Luke Brodhead, before the automobile and the population explosion, these questions would have seemed less urgent. In those days the trip itself was part of the pleasure, and the need to minimize it would probably not have seemed pressing. Under modern conditions, improving efficiency may be the only reasonable way to restore the trip to its former civilized status.

The first efficiency question takes us back to Square One. In a region totally planned from scratch, recreational facilities (along with others) could be laid out in an efficient fashion with dense facilities like swimming pools and zoos close in and more expansive facilities like parks for canoeing, camping, hiking, etc. farther out. If the location of facilities and the supply of transportation were governed by perfectly competitive markets, then, in theory at least, efficiency of location would be guaranteed by the invisible hand. In fact, since neither is governed by anything like a perfect market, we are able to observe the highly inefficient location of things across the landscape. We must, therefore, consciously consider locational efficiency in planning new facilities.

Even in a real region, such as that surrounding New York, where the possibilities of rearrangement are limited, many questions about efficiency of location can be raised. With respect to Tocks Island one may ask, for example, if it is efficient to provide massive swimming facilities so far from the metropolitan centers, if similar facilities can be provided at various lakes, ponds, and reservoirs that are closer in. Reservoirs in scenic locations, completely surrounded by barbed wire, stand unused in northern New Jersey. Natural ocean beaches occur on the doorstep of New York, and will be augmented by Gateway National Recreation Area. Swimming at a crowded beach (50 square feet per person is the density planned for Tocks beaches) is an essentially urban activity that does not require the unique features of the Delaware Valley. In contrast to mass swimming, dispersed activities, such as hiking, canoeing, and camping are not so easily provided closer to the urban centers.

A complication of the locational problem concerns human diversity and social class. Whom would the Tocks beaches serve? The urban poor, or the suburban middle class? Some proponents of the dam have argued that they will serve the urban poor. If this is the case, then the question should not be: "Given Tocks, what is the benefit to the urban poor?" but rather, "Given the urban poor, how much recreation benefit can you buy for them with the fraction of the Tocks budget properly allocable to recreation?"

This budget would buy a lot of neighborhood parks and swimming pools. Since it is reported by those who run day camps that poor children more often than rich children do not know how to swim and fear the water, it is not clear that occasional five dollar trips to Tocks beaches (the minimum transportation cost from the major cities) would be better for poor children than frequent short trips to a neighborhood pool or pond. The significance of location is a complex matter.

The location of the Tocks dam, hence of the surrounding park, was chosen for flood control rather than recreation. One may therefore ask whether, in the absence of flood control, this site would be chosen for recreation at all if transportation costs were fully considered. The answer is probably yes, but not as the site of a giant swimming pool. The upper Delaware River is one of the last large, free-flowing rivers in the East. The stretch to be included in the Park, the old Minisink, contains wooded islands and gentle riffles that make it ideally suited for interesting but nonexpert canoeing. The flat, relatively high flood plain provides much usable land for camping and long distance bicycle trails. It is bounded on both sides by steep wooded slopes, which, on the Pennsylvania side especially, are cut by a number of rocky creek gorges containing beautiful waterfalls. On the New Jersey side, the Appalachian Trail runs along the top of the Kittatinny Ridge, 1,200 feet above the river, and provides many scenic views. Several clear ponds, each with its own miniature watershed lie on top of the Ridge. Flatbrook Valley, joining the Delaware at Wallpack Bend, has great natural beauty and antique charm, as well as a good trout stream. The area contains several unspoiled old villages and farms of some historical interest as well as important archaeological sites. These assets led the conservationists to support the creation of the Park while opposing the reservoir. They argued, in fact, that the recreational value of the site was greater without the reservoir than with it.

The Minisink as it is offers some unique opportunities. One possibility is to build miles of scenic bicycle trails on the flood plain, where they would be free of steep grades and away from cars. Bicycling is an ideal activity for a public park because it is quiet, clean, and accessible to almost everyone, young and old. Laid out with imagination, bicycle paths through the Minisink flatlands could be very beautiful, passing variously under the lines of old trees on the river bank, across open fields, through the woods around ravine heads, past waterfalls and historical sites, across the river by ferry and so forth. The Park is big enough to allow for leisurely trips of more than a day.

If the Park offered uncrowded, rural recreation natural to its setting (such as 40-mile bicycle or canoe trips) and not available closer to the cities, then it would appear to be reasonably efficient with respect to location—that is, it would appear not be unduly wasteful of transportation. On the other hand, if the Park were noisy and overcrowded, so as to offer little respite from the urban hassle, or if the activities it provided could just as well be offered closer to the cities, then its use of transportation resources could well be questioned.

The second efficiency question concerns the nature of the transportation itself. The planners of the Water Gap Park assumed that virtually all visitors would come by car. This assumption was made at the outset and was carried through all stages of planning without serious question. At one point the authors of the Nathan Report did make a wistful, passing remark about buses, but they were clearly resigned to the automobile: "Although public bus lines may (and probably should) serve the recreation area from metropolitan centers and neighboring communities, expected increases in rates of automobile ownership will sustain the dominance of automobile travel to the area."[15]

It is hardly necessary to dwell at length on the problems created by automobiles. It is well known that they use more energy, make more pollution, pre-empt more land, and kill more people per passenger mile than trains or buses. But important as these differences are, what is most important in the long run is the profoundly wasteful and destructive pattern of development that has almost always occurred in every new territory invaded by the automobile. Technical invention can make cars safer and more efficient, but only social invention (which is much harder) can change the kind of development that seems to follow merely from the existence of private capsules capable of scurrying arbitrarily over the landscape.

Is it really necessary to accept the consequences of massive auto travel to and within the Park as the planners assumed, or can we do better? Can public transportation with its well known drawbacks be adapted to the conditions of our time? Can a workable symbiosis with the automobile be devised? The idea of public transportation in National Parks is being increasingly discussed and even experimented with. Experimental public systems are planned or operating in Yosemite, Grand Canyon, Mesa Verde, and elsewhere. In some cases severe auto congestion has virtually forced the Park Service to act. When the highway between Anchorage and Fairbanks was improved, the spur road to Mt. McKinley became jammed with cars. As a stopgap measure, leased school buses were brought in to carry passengers over the rugged 85-mile route. The magazine *Audubon* commented on this operation as follows:

> One logical result of the prohibition of motorized sightseeing at Mount McKinley has been a marked increase in the number of hikers and backpackers. For them the free public transportation is a special boon. They can board or leave the buses as they please anywhere along the park road. A survey conducted last summer among the bus passengers revealed that 90 per cent of the respondents favored the use of mass transit within the park.
>
> At first the new regulations received considerable static from local Alaskans, businessmen, editorial writers, and congressional representatives. But by the end of the season in 1972, most of the critics (as well as the

tourists) had been converted to the new stytem. Those who hadn't would have been won over by witnessing the scene at summer's end when the park road was reopened to all traffic for ten days before being closed for the winter. On Labor Day weekend, cars were clocked through the Savage River checking station at the rate of one every three minutes. Their occupants pockmarked the roadside with trash and beverage bottles. Wildlife fled. A pall of dust hung over the road's route. It was a brief, grim reminder of what might have been.[16]

IV. PUBLIC TRANSPORTATION IN THE NEW PARK

The long, narrow shape of the Water Gap Park lends itself ideally to internal public transportation. All that is needed in principle is a single, longitudinal link. Because the Park is narrow, every point would lie within a mile or two of such a link. Access from outside could be along radial routes converging on hubs at the two ends of the Park, as shown schematically in Figure 10-4. An important feature of this general pattern is that it imposes no burden on the near region along the flanks of the Park. It is precisely in this region that the Edwards and Kelcey Plan was concentrated, and in which the large secondary impacts predicted by the Nathan Report would occur.

Even small numbers of visitors would support a frequent schedule on the internal link. Fifty-passenger vehicles on a five-minute headway carry 600 passengers per hour. Over a four-hour entering period this service would carry 2,400 visitors from each end into the Park, for a total of 4,800 visitors in one day. Under the original Park Service Plan the Park was to accommodate about 150,000 visitors on a peak day; under the reduced plan about 40,000. This is clearly far more than is needed to support the five-minute service postulated above, even if many people are accommodated in mass facilities such as picnic areas and swimming beaches near the Park entrances. If the Park is designed for more moderate numbers of people engaged only in dispersed activities such as hiking, bicycling, canoeing, etc., then demand for the public transportation link would be correspondingly less. But even in this case the demand would support a very frequent schedule on a single link.

In the absence of a reservoir, the service could be provided by buses running on existing roads. Since roads run along both sides of the river and up Flatbrook Valley, it would be possible to subdivide the link into two or three parallel routes. Although this would, in a sense, be a convenience for visitors, it is not, I believe, the kind of convenience the Park should provide. Within reason, people should

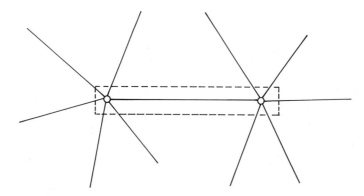

Figure 10-4. Conceptual Network for Public Transportation

be encouraged to walk, cycle, or paddle to where they are going. A single route not only minimizes the intrusion of motorized transport but also makes for simplicity: there is no worry about which bus goes where. A single route does necessarily run along one side of the river and not the other, but simple ferries of the kind that existed in colonial times could easily provide access to the opposite shore. In many places the ferries could be driven by the current, as they once were.

The internal route could run along either the New Jersey or the Pennsylvania side of the river. On the Pennsylvania side, plans for moving Route 209 (which would be inundated by the Tocks reservoir) are advanced and land is being acquired for the new right-of-way. In the absence of a reservoir, the old 209 could be used exclusively for the internal transportation link.[c] This would leave the New Jersey side with its scenic Old Mine Road and Flatbrook Valley entirely free of motorized traffic (except possibly for emergency vehicles) and available for walk-in camping and bicycling on autoless roads.

In the motorless part of the Park, all movement would necessarily be slow. But slowness has a special esthetic value. It allows the world to expand again to its original size. I know from experience that England seen from a five mph canal boat is a huge country. Similarly,

[c]It should be noted, however, that if no reservoir is built, then the option of leaving Route 209 where it is remains open. In view of the inevitable environmental cost of the new 209, this option should not be dismissed lightly. Nevertheless, the advantage to the Park of removing the noise, fumes, and unsightliness of the present heavy truck traffic on 209 is very great. The noise is continuous and audible throughout the section of the valley where 209 is close to the river.

the old Minisink, seen only from a canoe or a bicycle and never from a car, could be perceived in its true dimensions with the details of nature in sharp focus.

If a reservoir is built, then in order to provide the internal link, some new stretches of road would have to be built to replace inundated roads. The internal link would probably have to be on the New Jersey side. Ferries, with special landings to accommodate the varying water level, would have to be motorized; otherwise the public transportation link could be similar to that described above. The Park Service Master Plan includes a number of boat launching ramps for people who bring their own boats on trailers. Although heavy motor boats cannot easily be carried by public transportation, they could be offered for rent. A rental system would be advantageous anyway in that it would facilitate control of the number, type, and safety of boats used on the reservoir.

Buses for the internal link should be designed so that they do not insulate the passenger from the outdoors as the high, sealed-up, air conditioned highway buses do. They should be low, open, and quiet, with an expansive view in all directions. Speed should be moderate—probably not over 35 mph. Since the necessary range is small, this would appear to be an ideal situation for the battery-pack bus, with charging stations at the two ends of the Park.[17] (At the end of a run the spent battery-pack is slid out of the bus and replaced by a recharged pack. The operation takes only a few seconds.) Provision should be made for carrying camping gear and bicycles. Hang-up racks of the kind used on European trains can carry bicycles with little wasted space. Trucks or trailers with suitable racks could bring canoes back upstream, as they now do.

If the external transportation is public and is provided by buses, then the same buses could be used both inside and outside the Park. A bus from outside arriving at one end of the Park could make one or more trips on the internal link before returning along its external route. This would simpler and cheaper then having two separate sets of vehicles, and it would eliminate the need to transfer at the end of the Park. It would, however, entail some compromise in bus design: inside the Park the bus should be primarily quiet and odorless; outside it should be primarily fast and comfortable. These conditions are not entirely compatible.

The attractiveness, hence feasibility, of a public transportation system depends significantly on its details. Appendix B to this essay presents one way of filling in the details of the general arrangement described in the preceding paragraph. The purpose of this exercise is not to suggest specific details for a real system, but merely to demonstrate (I hope convincingly) that at least one system exists that does the job insofar as the circumstances under which it would operate can be predicted. Appendix B takes account of the analysis of external public transportation set forth both below and in Appendix A.

A. External Public Transportation

The 680-million-dollar freeway network designed by Edwards and Kelcey for Sussex and Warren Counties (Fig. 10–3) is a dispersion device whose function is to spread the cars over the countryside so that they do not jam up in one place. A network for public transportation should have just the opposite sort of geometry. It should consist of a few routes converging at hubs, as in the network of Figure 10–4.

In Appendix A to this essay, a network of real roads conforming to the general pattern of Figure 10–4 is considered. It is shown that the density of demand on the main radial routes would be more than adequate to support very frequent schedules, which are essential in overcoming the inherent inconvenience of public systems relative to the automobile. Headways should be not more than five or ten minutes so that visitors can reasonably ignore the precise timetable.

By far the heaviest traffic would fall on the easterly spokes to New York and the southerly spokes to Philadelphia. An obvious candidate for the link to New York is the main line of the Erie-Lackawanna Railroad, which runs from Hoboken through the Water Gap to Stroudsburg and beyond, and which until recent years has carried regular passenger service. At present it carries commuter traffic as far as Dover, which is about halfway between Hoboken and the Water Gap, but the rest of the line is used only for freight. As pointed out by Tom Taber, service to the Water Gap Park with its heavy weekend peak would nicely complement the weekday commuter service. A number of improvements in the line are planned. At the outer end, electrification may be extended a few more miles out to Netcong and at the inner end rearrangements are planned that will allow Erie-Lackawanna trains to go directly under the river to Penn Station in New York. Another Erie-Lackawanna line presently carries a few trains from Hoboken to Port Jervis at the northern end of the Water Gap Park, but the route is circuitous and under current schedules the trip takes a little over two hours. Rail service from other directions does not appear to be feasible without extensive track changes. Buses, on the other hand, could operate in any direction using existing highways.

Since many people would have to drive their cars to reach the train or bus line, parking lots would have to be provided at the stations. These lots may be thought of as replacing those otherwise needed inside the Park: without public transportation, visitors' cars must be stored in the Park; with it, they can be stored in scattered outlying lots. Some of the outlying lots, moreover, would not need to be new; they could be existing lots used by commuters during the week. Furthermore, some Park visitors from urban areas would be able to get to the station without driving. For these reasons, the total new parking area needed with a public system would be less than the total parking area needed inside the Park if all visitors travelled by car.[d]

The nuisance of transferring from car to bus or train is the major inconvenience that needs to be overcome by a public system. Several factors can relieve it. Sufficiently short headway can prevent the tedium of waiting; well located routes and stations can eliminate the need for anyone to go out of his way to get to a station (how this can be done is shown in Appendix A); safe, convenient walkways, carts to handle luggage, clear direction signs, etc. can reduce the physical nuisance; attractive design of structures and landscape, and clean vehicles, can counter the image of decrepitude associated with public transportation. Such seemingly minor amenities deserve very careful attention.

Only very limited parking should be provided at the Park, so that motorists who choose to drive all the way run a high risk of being turned away. An exception should be made for people whose driver's licenses show residence in one of the neighboring counties, and who therefore could not reasonably be expected to use the public lines. According to the estimates made in Appendix A, neighboring county people would make up about 10 percent of all visitors. A special parking lot could be provided for them.

A single, flat, per-car fee covering both parking and round trip transportation on the public line for all of the car's occupants could be charged at the entrance to the station parking lot. In addition to being simple, such a fee would create an incentive to double up on the use of cars. A reasonable structure for the fee would be $F = F_o + cD$, where F_o is the fee at the Park (distance $D = 0$) and c is a per-mile surcharge. The pecuniary incentive to drive all the way to the Park is small when c is small. To make the incentive negative, c should be less than the per-mile cost of driving—i.e. it should be less than

[d]The Park Service Master Plan includes parking for 33,000 cars. This would require about 330 acres. Under the reduced plan parking requirements would be about one-third of this.

about 12¢ per mile. It could well be much less than this, possibly even zero. It would be desirable, of course, for the public system to be self-supporting. Once c is chosen, the requirement of self-support puts a lower bound on F_o. Since in theory public transportation has great economies of scale relative to the automobile, even a self-supporting fee should seem moderate to an automobilist.

Unfortunately, the theoretical economies of scale of public transportation are not all realized in real markets. An important theoretical economy, for example, is in labor: one driver of a 40-passenger bus substitutes for about fifteen auto drivers. But this tremendous labor saving does not get counted in cost comparisons, because auto drivers do not count the value of their driving labor as part of the cost of driving. (Why is this? If driving is so much fun, why isn't the bus driver eager to drive for nothing?) At any rate, when the value of the auto driver's labor is omitted and that of the bus driver is included, the costs of bus and auto transport are comparable at three or four cents per passenger mile. (This assumes three people per car, which is twice the national average, but possibly reasonable for recreational trips.) The bus's economy in physical quantities is offset by the driver's wages. In effect, the bus substitutes paid labor for fuel, steel, concrete, and a lot of unpaid labor. This trade-off would appear to be socially and environmentally good, but our attitudes, habits, and imperfect markets are such that it is a hard trade-off to realize.

The Nathan Report found the secondary impacts of auto travel and the new highways it would entail to be large. The highway builders, seeing these impacts as good, tried to reinforce them. Edwards and Kelcey state this goal explicitly in their report: "In many instances, the alignment of a new road was located far from communities and existing routes generally heading for the same destination, to open up new areas for development."[18] To those who are concerned about the automobile and skeptical of conventional development based on it, this is a dismaying statement. But public transportation can also open up new territory, as the trolley-car builders of the early 1900s well knew. If we substitute public transportation to the Water Gap Park for the freeway network, will the accelerating effect on development be any less?

Since the public transportation system is concentrated (e.g., it does not extend to the flanks of the Park at all), its effects would not impinge on as large a territory as those of the highways. Nevertheless, a densely operated commuter line such as the Erie-Lackawanna might well accelerate the creeping suburban strip beyond Dover and Netcong toward the Water Gap. Whether such development would be "bad," however, is not clear. Dense housing clustered within walking distance of the stations might well relieve some of the pressure for further sprawl.

A bus service operated primarily on weekends, with its main movement toward the Park in the morning and away in the evening, would hardly provide a very attractive schedule for would-be commuters. Moreover, its destinations, as seen by the commuter, would be somewhat limited and designed for far-end auto connection. Thus it would appear that public transportation to the Water Gap Park would stimulate relatively little secondary development, at least of the sprawly kind. Highways, on the other hand, are there twenty-four hours a day, ready to be used for any purpose. They therefore tend to stimulate development of all kinds, often in a pattern that is inefficient with respect to location.

We are all aware of the difficulty public transportation has had in competing with cars. Nevertheless, times are changing. The need for public transportation is gradually seeping into the public consciousness. In those situations where the conditions are right for it—as they seem to be in the case of the Water Gap Park—public systems should be set up, with meticulous attention to those details that can overcome the crucial nuisances, and with the strong incentives (a high probability of being turned away if you drive to the Park) that are probably needed at this early stage to wean people away from their cars.

V. A PARK WITHOUT A DAM

Within the water resources establishment, there are two diametrically opposed views of recreation on reservoirs. The older view, held almost unanimously by private and municipal water companies, is that reservoirs should be sealed off from public use. Thus, the map of northern New Jersey is dotted with small and not-so-small reservoirs, often in scenic locations, that are entirely encircled by chain link fence. According to the adherents of this view, the costs incurred because of pollution of the water by swimmers, damage to the watershed by picnickers, removal of trash, insurance against liability, etc. cannot be recovered at a level of admission charge that anyone will pay. Companies that have tried recreation, it is asserted, have had to give it up and close the gates. The argument is invariably reinforced by startling statistics on per capita trash quantities or on the fraction of swimmers that can be expected to urinate under water. A statistic of the latter variety is faithfully reproduced in the comprehensive consultants' report of 1975.[e]

The opposite view, held by the Corps of Engineers, is that reservoirs should be "multipurpose" and that one of the purposes should be recreation. The more swimmers and tramplers of the watershed, the better. As planned, Tocks conforms to this view to an extreme degree, since it provides for more people per acre and more acres than almost any comparable project.

The two views appear to be absolutely contradictory. If it is true that private companies can make no net profit by opening their reservoirs to recreation, then it should be impossible for the Corps to claim a net benefit for recreation. Yet the Corps does claim such a benefit in large amounts.

It is curious that the conflict between the two views never seriously entered the Tocks controversy. To be sure, the opponents did suggest the recreation alternative of opening up the many closed-off reservoirs closer to population centers than Tocks. But the suggestion was never taken seriously, and the consultants, in discussing it, merely repeated the arguments, noted above, that they heard from the reservoirs' owners. Nowhere did they attempt either to refute these arguments or to apply them to the Tocks reservoir itself. The discussion of the Tocks reservoir occurred in another part of the report and was based on arguments received from other sources.

Only one person confronted the issue squarely, and that was Walter Lucking, president of the Hackensack Water Company. Lucking was appointed in 1974 by Governor Byrne to the ad hoc "Citizens' Advisory Board," whose function was to monitor the developing consultants' study and then to make recommendations about it to the governor. In accordance with his adherence to the first view, Lucking supported the construction of the Tocks reservoir, but recommended that it be entirely closed to the public. Presumably this was to be accomplished by means of the usual chain link fence, which in this case would have to be 80 miles long. As far as I know, this suggestion had never been made before, despite the fact that it would have solved the problems of regional impact and traffic in a single stroke.

The adherents of the heavy use view within the Corps and Park Service were apparently unfazed by the strong criticism of their original plan that had come from many quarters between 1970 and 1975. In 1974 they engaged the consulting firm of Clarke and

[e]URS Madigan-Praeger et al., p. XIII-73, without, of course, any mention of the fraction of fish with similar habits.

Rapuano to update their plans and reconcile differences of detail between the two agencies. A draft report in circulation in mid 1975 showed almost no significant concessions to the critics. There was, for example, no discernible attention paid to Governor Cahill's insistence that the yearly visitor load be reduced from ten million to four million. The original three phases remained, complete with dates:[19]

Phase I	1982	4,000,000 annual visitors
Phase II	1990	7,000,000 annual visitors
Phase III	2000	10,600,000 annual visitors

The "Foothills Freeway," which had set off a storm of protest when first proposed, also still remained, albeit in a shortened version and with a new name: "Kittatinny Highway." In some cases concerns expressed by local citizens were dismissed in a singularly insensitive way. One section, entitled "Detrimental Uses" is here reproduced in its entirety:[20]

> Park oriented uses, such as restaurants, gift shops, motels, service stations and transient campsites, will be generated by TIL-DWGNRA. These kinds of uses already exist in the surrounding land and cannot be considered detrimental. There would be no uses resulting from TIL-DWGNRA that would be detrimental.

Because this work was carried on without public participation and, in fact, out of the public view, it played no significant role in the debate during 1974 and 1975.

Meanwhile another current in the debate that *was* in the public view rapidly gathered momentum. This was the discussion of a park without a dam, or more generally, the future of the valley without a dam. As the possibility of no dam gradually began to seem likely enough to be taken seriously, a number of individuals and groups who had taken no part in the debate over the dam entered the discussion of the park. Their participation, along with a series of events and changed circumstances, led gradually to a changed perception of the issue.

The first written proposal for a park in the Minisink Valley without a dam was the Park Service's brief but lyrical "Natural Systems Plan," which was inadvertently leaked to the public in 1972 (see Essay 3). This plan, however, was too sketchy to make a serious case for a damless park. In late 1973 the Save-the-Delaware-Coalition scraped together enough money to engage the professional consulting firm, Candeub-Fleissig, to prepare a more detailed plan. Two things are especially notable about this effort: First, the consultants and their sponsors recognized the paramount importance of transportation and tried to lay out an efficient system whose adverse impacts both inside and outside the Park would be minimal. They even adopted one or two suggestions from an early draft of this essay. Second, they found that the absence of the dam greatly relieved the problem of accommodating large numbers of people without crowding.

The reasons were both spatial and temporal: The absence of the dam made available 10,000 acres of eminently usable flat land — almost the only flat land in the valley. Moreover, the activities appropriate to a park without a dam—bicycling, canoeing, hiking, camping, etc.—can be pursued much of the year, particularly in the spring and the fall when the weather is usually at its best. The reservoir plan, by contrast, depended heavily on swimming, which is confined by temperature and drawdowns to the three summer months. Both the extra space and the temporal spreading of activity were helpful in reducing crowding.

By the summer of 1974, with both the Park Service's "Natural Systems Plan" and the Save-the-Delaware-Coalition's "Concept Plan for the Delaware River Park" in the public arena, discussions of a damless park had penetrated to official circles. Stimulated by a conversation with Commissioner Bardin and encouraged by Assistant Secretary of the Interior, Nathaniel Reed, a small group within the Park Service directed by David Kimball began work on a park without Tocks. Concentrating first on transportation, they laid out alternative routes for internal public transit, and specified roughly where entrances and nodes of concentrated activities should be. After some study they concluded that the annual visitor load should be two million or less. This is much more in keeping with normal densities for rural parks than the extreme figures that had been planned for the reservoir-based park.

On some other aspects, Kimball's group soon found valuable support in the Appalachian Mountain Club (AMC). Well versed in the practical lore of trail construction and maintenance, and enthusiastic about a damless park, the AMC undertook a detailed survey of the valley's soils, vegetation, drainage, etc. in close cooperation with Kimball's group. Weekend after weekend in early 1975, AMC volunteers explored the dozens of ecologically fragile creek ravines along both sides of the valley and took copious notes on what they found. As a result, the AMC's recommendations had the most solid foundation in data of any yet made.

Until about 1974 public discourse had focussed mainly on outdoor recreation as conventionally understood: physical activity in the open—swimming, hiking, setting a picnic table, building a fire, launching a boat, and so forth. But in the meantime another issue in the controversy, which suggested a rather different tone for the park and which added another dimension to "recreation," had been gaining prominence. This was the issue of historic and archaeological sites.

Since most of these are on the flood plain, the only question for the Tocks Island Dam planners had been how to salvage material or information from the most important ones before they were flooded. But if no dam were built, then the settings as well as the buildings and artifacts could be preserved, and in many cases the settings were of prime importance. If the landscape remained intact, it became possible to imagine a far more coherent and vivid picture of history being presented to the visitor. Thus history had much more potential as an element in a river-based park than in a reservoir-based park. Even more importantly, the archaelogical sites could be examined by scientists in a far more orderly manner. And some that would otherwise have to be hastily dug for salvage could be preserved for the future.

In February 1974 the historic issue was raised high in public consciousness by an action of the Corps of Engineers. For some time the Corps had been wrangling in the courts with a group of young squatters who were using empty land and buildings that had been acquired by the government. Having failed with orthodox methods of eviction, the Corps finally moved in with bulldozers. At dawn of Ash Wednesday, armed U.S. Marshalls appeared without warning, ordered the squatters (including young women with babies) out into the cold, and pushed the houses down before their eyes. Thereafter for the next two or three days the Corps demolished houses systematically, including many of historical value. One building whose destruction especially roused the ire of local citizens was the Everett House, which was said to have been in mint condition. Finally, when the Corps began to dismantle the Zion church, an 1850s building which was on the National Register of Historic Places, a group of citizens went into court and won an injunction against any further destruction of historic buildings.

This incident set off a flurry of angry organizing. A series of bus tours brought the matter to the attention of local officials, congressmen, and the press and public. Many participants on these tours were especially receptive because they were gearing up for the bicentennial and were already in a state of raised historic consciousness. The

Daughters of the American Revolution, who had not previously been involved in Tocks, found the energy to get 5,000 signatures on a petition urging Governor Byrne to preserve the valley.

The grievances of the activists went beyond the destruction of historically valuable buildings. The Park Service was accused of allowing important stone buildings, which could not be moved from the flood plain, to fall into decay, while moving worthless wooden buildings into inaccurately restored villages, and of neglecting to carry out legally mandated surveys. The Park Service pleaded lack of funds.

One spot that seemed destined for controversy was the town of Milford, Pa., whose location at the Route 206 crossing guaranteed its status as a park gateway whether the dam was built or not. Despite the growing line of tourist establishments along the highways, Milford retained, especially in its back streets, the old-fashioned air of a small town of 1900. It also contained, on a high hillside over-looking the valley, an elaborate estate called "Grey Towers" (complete with sweeping lawns, romantic grape arbors, terraces, reflecting pools, and a forbidding main house straight out of Sherlock Holmes), which had been the home of Gifford Pinchot, first head of the U.S. Forest Service and former governor of Pennsylvania. In Dave Kimball's view, Milford was on the thin edge and could go either way: it could become a garish tourist trap or it could be preserved as one of the valley's main historic centers.

Just north of Milford was "Arisbe," the rambling and eccentric wooden house of the American philosopher C.S. Peirce. Acquired by the Park Service in the late 1960s, this house was brought into the DWGNRA by means of a small boundary adjustment. Enthusiastic members of the Peirce Society had worked out detailed room-by-room plans for an intellectual museum explaining Peirce's wide-ranging thought, but by late 1975 no money had been found for restoration. So long as the reservoir seemed inevitable, the Peirce Society took little interest in the project. Dominated by mass beaches, it seemed to have no particular relationship to "Arisbe." But when the possibility of a park based on history emerged, they quickly extended their enthusiasm to it.

At a public hearing held by the Park Service in March 1975, interest in the historical possibilities surfaced in yet another sector. Mr. Robert Brooks, a descendent of the Lenni Lenape Indians who had once inhabited the valley, argued eloquently that a colony of Lenni Lenapes should be allowed to return and establish a cultural center. He ended his plea with a sonorous Indian language prayer full of whooshes and whistles. This was a timely reminder to the white Park

Service and white audience that history did not begin with the colonists.

Indeed, the soil of the Delaware flood plain above the Water Gap contained an almost unbroken archaeological record of human activity dating back to 10,000 BC or almost to the last Ice Age. According the archaeologist Russell Handsman,[f] this flood plain was one of the few spots in the region where the record had not been jumbled by construction. So far, the main disturbance of the deep soil had come from archaeologists themselves, who were doing salvage work in anticipation of the dam. With no dam in the offing, much less digging would have been done, and at a more deliberate rate and more closely coordinated with digs outside the area to be flooded. In the years between 1970 and 1975, Handsman observed, a fundamental change of outlook had occurred in the profession of archaeology. There had developed a new concern with preserving sites for future generations, when more refined techniques might be able to glean better information. In the absence of a dam threat, then, only a small, carefully selected set of sites would be opened. Also, thought could be given to stabilizing one or two of them for in situ public display.

Having brought together so many disparate groups by means of the historical theme, the activists began in 1975 to urge Congress to change the status of the park from a National Recreation Area to a National Historical Park. Although Park Service officials believed that the area would not satisfy existing criteria for a National Historical Park, they pointed out that Congress could do anything it liked. Whatever the official designation turned out to be, it appeared certain in late 1975 that history and archaeology would be a major element in any park without a dam, or a major issue if the controversy over the dam continued. Hardly visible in the original Tocks planning, the subject received thorough and sensitive treatment in the 1975 consultants' study.

From the beginning of the Tocks controversy, the value of the Minisink Valley's historic and prehistoric remains was dutifully mentioned in every report, but never as if it were important enough to make a difference. As early as 1966 there even appeared a book entitled "Before the Waters," which contained photographs of the houses, scenes, and people that were to be replaced by the Tocks reservoir. But the author, Elizabeth Menzies, believed the dam was inevitable. For her, the book was not a part of the politics of opposition; she only wished to record the sad passing of a place and a time.

[f]Private communication.

The convergent circumstances that brought history to prominence as an issue were mainly these: first, the gradual acceptance of the park without a dam as a credible possibility, which attracted the attention of such diverse groups as the Peirce Society, the Appalachian Mountain Club, the Lenni Lenape Indians, and the D.A.R.; second, the coming bicentennial, which heightened the general interest in history; third, the Corps' 1974 demolitions of historic buildings, which set off an angry reaction resulting in new grass roots organizing and publicizing; and finally, what is sometimes called the "crisis in archaeology"—the rapid destruction of the archaeological record all across the country because of development —which had brought archaeologists to the view that conserving as many sites as possible was a matter of utmost urgency.

The convergence of these circumstances was not entirely coincidental, however, because to a large extent they were simply separate manifestations of the change in public attitude toward the natural and human heritage that had occurred between 1965 and 1975. If the "environment" is taken to include culture as well as nature, then the historical issue was as much an environmental issue as any other.

APPENDIX A.
THE PATTERN AND VOLUME OF PARK TRAFFIC

The potential benefits of public transportation can be realized only if the traffic along each route is sufficiently intense. If the traffic is thin, then either the vehicles must be small so that there is little economy of scale, or else service must be infrequent so that the value of the transportation to its users is low. In order to increase the traffic density on each route, parallel routes can be spread widely apart so that each serves a large traffic generating area. But if the routes are too widely separated, then the distance users must travel to get to the public route becomes inconveniently long and again the value of the service is low. Neither the distance between routes nor the distance between vehicles along a route must be too great. Or, stated more simply, the number of vehicles per square mile must not be too low. On the other hand, the size of the vehicles must be sufficiently large if economies of scale are to be realized. These contrary constraints can be met only if the traffic generated per square mile per hour in the area served is sufficiently high.

This appendix examines whether the conditions for economical public transportation are met for the Water Gap Park. The answer appears to be yes for most of the people living within 50 or 60 miles of the Park even if the number of visitors is considerably less than the four million currently planned for. The analysis is based on a bus system using existing roads. The link between New York and the Water Gap, which is by far the heaviest, could be provided by the Erie-Lackawanna Railroad, but for simplicity this possibility is not recognized explicitly. The general results are the same whether this link is provided by bus or train.

The model for the analysis is the following. Let $p(x)$ be the population density at position x, and let $f(r)$ be the annual visits per capita for people living at distance r from the nearest end of the Park. Then $f(r) \cdot p(x)$ is the absolute number of visits generated per square mile per year at position x. Imagine that each visitor drives from his home to the nearest end of the Park by the best route, and consider at every point on every road the intensity T of the traffic so generated. Let $N(T)$ be the set of points on the road network at which the traffic density of Park visitors is greater than T. If T_o is the minimum traffic density that can support public transportation, then in principle public transportation could be provided on the sub network $N(T_o)$.

What does the subnetwork $N(T_o)$ look like? Since the traffic is most intense near the hubs at the ends of the Park, $N(T_o)$ will contain stretches of the radial approach roads if it contains anything at all. But it may also contain branches and subbranches from these roads. In the terminology of Graph Theory, $N(T_o)$ comprises two connected trees rooted at the hubs.

The traffic density T_o is actually realized on the public transportation system only if each visitor transfers from his car to the public system as soon as he finds himself on the subnetwork $N(T_o)$. (This assumption is implicit in the assertion that public transportation can be supported on $N(T_o)$.) On the other hand it is not necessary to assume that anyone goes out of his way to take the public system. It is assumed that everyone starts out to drive by the most direct route and transfers only if and when he comes to a station.

Since stations cannot be distributed continuously along the branches of $N(T_o)$, some visitors may have to drive some distance along $N(T_o)$ before coming to a station. The necessary discreteness of stations reduces the realized traffic density on the public system somewhat below T_o in some places. A full-fledged optimization of design would have to take station spacing into account, but this level of refinement need not concern us here.

Determination of the Network $N(T_o)$

The traffic density varies not only spatially but temporally: with season, day of the week, and weather. However, there is no particular reason to suppose that temporal variations influence the shape of the spatial distribution. We assume, then, that the temporal and spatial effects are multiplicative. According to the spatial model outlined above, the absolute number of visitors generated per square mile per year at position x is given by $f(r)p(x)$. We assume that the number of visitors so generated on day t is given by the multiplicative formula $s(t)f(r)p(x)$, where $s(t)$ is the fraction of the yearly visits that occurs on day t.

We will consider the three factors in the formula separately. Population distribution $p(x)$ is straightforward. The agglomerations around Philadelphia and New York dominate the region over-whelmingly. The visitation rate f as a function of distance r is difficult to determine, though some data for other recreation projects have been collected. Generally these data have been fitted to an exponential decay function of the form $f(r) = Ae^{-ar}$. On the basis of some existing sets of data,[a] we assume a to be such that f falls off by a factor of ten in 50 miles. Fortunately the distribution of population is such that the results are not very sensitive to a. The routes to New York and Philadelphia are dominant in any case.

By examination of road maps we determined the routes that would carry the heaviest Park traffic, i.e., the routes that would be included in the network $N(T_o)$. Like a tributary in a river system, each route has a well defined territory or "shed" from which it draws its traffic. Given the existing roads, the region divided itself naturally into about fifteen major "traffic sheds" generating widely varying amounts of traffic. How many of these traffic sheds are included in $N(T_o)$ depends on the overall level of traffic, hence on $s(t)$, and also on the choice of T_o.

A rough figure for T_o, the traffic required to support public transportation, is 1,000 visitors per day. This is sufficient to maintain a ten-minute headway over an arrival period of three and one-third hours with full 50-passenger vehicles. If the total visitor load is 10,000 visitors in one day, then according to our estimates only two routes have enough traffic to support a public system, but these two

[a]The sources are the following:

1. Lewis and Clark Lake: Jack L. Knetsch and Marion Clawson, "Economics of Outdoor Recreation," Baltimore: Johns Hopkins Press, p. 65.
2. Kerr Reservoir: Knetsch and Clawson, p. 71.
3. Swanson Lake: Knetsch and Clawson, p. 69.
4. Palisades Park: Nathan, p. 63, note 4.
5. Tocks: Nathan, p. 66, Table 2.

The data are too sparse, scattered, and subject to special effects to support much precision, but decay by a factor of ten in 50 miles is reasonably consistent with most of the data.

routes together carry 50 percent of the visitors. If, on the other hand, the total visitor load is 50,000 visitors, then eleven of the fifteen routes have enough traffic for a public system, and these eleven routes carry 95 percent of the visitors. To appreciate the amount of transportation needed to get people out to the Water Gap Park, it may be noted that the 40,000 visits on a peak Sunday envisioned under the reduced reservoir based plan is more than the entire Erie-Lackawanna daily commuting load.

On any one route, the traffic density falls off with distance from the Park. With only two important exceptions, however, most of the traffic is generated near the outer ends of the routes so that the vehicles need not run with only a few passengers over long stretches. The two exceptions are Route 611 and the Northeast Extension of the Pennsylvania Turnpike. The former has a peak at about 20 miles because of Easton-Phillipsburg and the latter at about 30 miles because of Bethlehem-Allentown. A few special buses might serve these areas.

The distribution of visits over time—represented in our formula by $s(t)$—depends strongly on the kind of recreation offered. Using figures given in the Nathan Report,[21] we estimated the loads for various types of days, and found the variation to be considerable. The Nathan figures, of course, assume a reservoir and the correspondingly short summer season based largely on swimming. The best weather, however, usually occurs in the fall and the spring, when the reservoir would be too cold for swimming or unattractive because of drawdown. A park without a reservoir would offer a much longer recreational season (bicycling, canoeing, hiking, and camping can be pursued during much of the year) and therefore a more uniform demand for transportation. Thus it is difficult to estimate the temporal pattern of demand with any precision without taking account of the recreational facilities.

The temporal pattern is most favorable to public transportation, of course, when it is most uniform and predictable (with the exception that weekend recreational peaks dovetail nicely with weekday commuting peaks). The most important unpredictable element in recreational demand is the weather. This does not figure so much, of course, in business traffic. How is this unpredictable demand to be handled economically? If service is maintained regardless of the weather, then much gasoline, oil, labor, and other resources will be wasted. It was, after all, partly to avoid such waste that public transportation was suggested in the first place. If service is cut back on rainy days, then physical resources can certainly be saved although drivers' wages could present a problem.

A reasonable way to meet this problem, I believe, is to offer a fixed seasonal salary in return for which a driver agrees to be available at specified times. The salary should be set so that when divided by the expected time worked (in the probabilistic sense of "expected") the quotient is a reasonable hourly wage. Under this arrangement the uncertainty is shared between the drivers and the management: the drivers have no financial uncertainty but they do have some uncertainty about their free time. The management has some financial uncertainty, since in sunny years there may be a surplus of fare revenue over expenses, and in rainy years a deficit. In accordance with standard business practice, some margin could be included in the fare to compensate for the risk.

In sum, the volume and pattern of traffic to the Water Gap Park appears to be more than adequate to support public transportation.

APPENDIX B
DETAILS OF A SPECIFIC PUBLIC TRANSPORTATION SYSTEM

This appendix sketches in details for one of the general arrangements discussed in the text. The attractiveness of any public transportation system for the Water Gap Park will depend strongly on the smoothness of the transfer between car and public vehicle. This appendix concentrates, therefore, especially on the details of this transfer.

The general arrangement considered is the following (see Fig. 10B–1). Each of several outlying parking lots is connected to the Park by a nonstop bus route. This is possible because most potential visitors live 50 miles or so away from the Park (see Appendix A). Each route enters the Park at one of the two ends and continues along an internal longitudinal road (all buses would use the same two-way road) to the far end of the Park, making half a dozen or so stops at main centers along the way. These centers would typically have picnicking, swimming, camping, canoe and bicycle rentals, trailheads, historical villages, etc. within close range. At the far end of the Park some buses would be stored until the evening exodus, while others would continue to shuttle back and forth along the internal road, serving local passengers.

This would be the general pattern. The actual geography dictates some exceptions, particularly the following two. (1) About five of the bus routes would begin most naturally in city centers, which many people could reach by public transportation. These termini would need special designs suitable to their urban settings. (2) About four of the bus routes (including two or three of those in (1)) should,

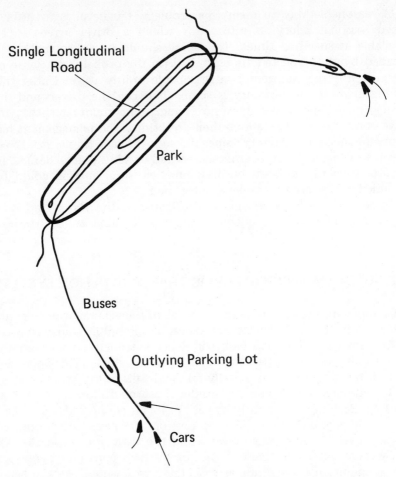

Figure 10B-1. Typical Bus Routes, Showing Superposition of Routes on Internal Road.

Buses carry local passengers inside Park.

if possible, be replaced by the main line of the Erie-Lackawanna Railroad.

Numbers

We will assume 45,000 day visits at one time. This is approxi-mately the peak load currently assumed in the Park Service-Corps of Engineers (PS-CE) plan. The dam opponents, in their alternative plan with no reservoir, assume the same yearly load as PS-CE, but because their plan has a less pronounced seasonal peak, the maximum daily load is less than 45,000.

The 45,000 visitors fall naturally into fourteen or fifteen traffic sheds of about 3,000 visitors each (see Appendix A). A parking lot to serve 3,000 visitors would need to hold about 1,000 cars. Buses carrying 45 passengers each, leaving from such a lot over a four-hour busy period, would on the average be spaced 3.6 minutes apart. (This, of course, is very approximate: some departures would have to be scheduled throughout the day, and during the peak the rate might be higher). Since the time required to load a bus would probably be longer than the time between departures, two or three buses would be at various stages of loading at any one time. There would be no wait for a bus to arrive; the wait to physical departure would be no more than the bus loading time.

1. **Separation of Pedestrian from Vehicular Traffic.** Figure 10B–2 shows a general parking lot arrangement that separates auto, bus and foot traffic. People with gear could back into a parking space so that their trunks or tailgates would open directly onto the walkway.

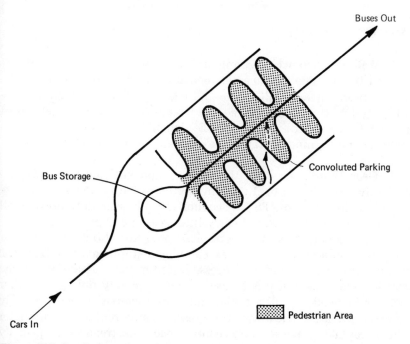

Figure 10B-2. Parking Lot, Showing General Arrangement to Separate Auto, Foot, and Bus Traffic

MORNING

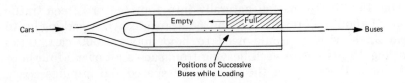

So that positions of successive buses are not too close together, lot should be
filled first on one side, then the other.

EVENING

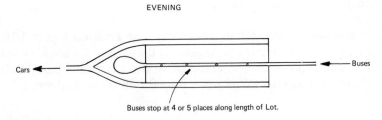

Buses stop at 4 or 5 places along length of Lot.

Figure 10B-3.   Morning and Evening Parking Lot Operation

   2. Walking Distance.   Examination of a scaled version of this lot
showed the average distance between auto and bus to be about 90 ft.
in the morning and 125 ft. in the evening. This is probably considerably less than the distance one would have to walk to get out of
a typical parking lot in the PS-CE plan. (The asymmetry between
morning and evening operations is explained in Figure 10B-3.)

   3. Gear Handling.   Both the prodam and antidam plans provide
primarily for day use. Even the extraordinarily dense campsite
"cities" planned by the PS-CE account for only a small fraction of all
visitors. Most visitors would carry little gear—perhaps a lunch, a fishing rod, or a bathing suit. Nevertheless, provision should be made for
carrying bulkier things such as camping equipment and bicycles.
Storage for this should be accessible from the outside of public
vehicles. One possibility is to use trailers. Probably only every other
bus would need to pull a trailer. Boats and canoes should probably
be taken privately. However, the present canoe rental system, under
which rental agencies carry canoes back upstream on specially
designed trucks, seems to be perfectly satisfactory. There is presently

little incentive to take your own canoe. In any case, under every plan, canoeists and boaters are a small fraction of all visitors.

4. Bus Stops in Park. Each route has enough traffic to justify its own set of stops (e.g., platform and shelter) inside the park. The stops for different routes could be clustered together at main centers, but they need not be. The routes can be thought of as independent operations that are simply superimposed. On the interior road, the effect of the superposition is to create total traffic of one bus every 20 seconds or so.[a] This is not very heavy traffic by ordinary standards. Buses running shuttle service during the middle of the day, and perhaps all buses, could probably afford to drop off passengers at any station on request. This would constitute the only real interaction between routes.

5. Information. To use the New York subway system efficiently one must be privy to a great many arcane facts. To hardened New Yorkers, knowing these facts has a certain one-up value, but to visitors, the need to know them is a considerable nuisance. For the Water Gap Park system, whose purpose, after all, is pleasure, I believe that simplicity is important. Many visitors will use the system only occasionally. For going out to the Park, the only information necessary would be the location of the nearest parking lot. Since this would be near home, on a prominent road, its location would soon be common knowledge. Coming home, it would only be necessary to locate a station with the right label on it. Since all stations lie along the same road, that should not be difficult. One could take a shuttle bus if necessary.

6. Overall Size of Operation. It is important to appreciate what it means to move 45,000 people out to Tocks and back. This is an enormous operation, whether it is done with automobiles or public vehicles. The entire Erie-Lackawanna commuter rail system, with all its various tentacles reaching into northeastern New Jersey, moves only 38,000 people each way on a typical day. If each bus in the system we are considering made only one round trip in a day, then about 1,000 buses would be needed. This number can be reduced to the extent that demand peaks can be flattened so that some buses can make more than one round trip. For example, campers going out in the evening or coming back in the morning would help. Costs

---

[a]During the PM busy period, 20 seconds between southbound buses (ten routes), 40 seconds between northbound buses (five routes).

could be reduced somewhat if idle buses could be used for commuter service on weekdays.[b] About one-fourth of the buses could be eliminated by using the main line of the Erie-Lackawanna. There is an ideal spot for a cross-platform transfer near the Water Gap. Of course, many train passengers might choose to stay in the Water Gap area and not take a shuttle bus.

The cost of this large public transporation system needs to be compared not to zero, but to the cost of the automobile alternative (15,000 cars). The highway costs alone are at least in the hundreds of millions (depending on what you include and whose figures you believe), but in addition there are the considerable environmental and social costs, including the degradation of the park, the impact on the surrounding region, and the inevitable extra loss of life and limb.

NOTES

1. L.W. Brodhead, *Delaware Water Gap, Its Scenery, Its Legends and Early History* (Philadelphia: Sherman and Co., 1870). p. 252.

2. *Ibid.*, p. 268.

3. *Ibid.*, p. 272.

4. *Ibid.*, p. 25.

5. *Delaware River Basin*, House Document 522, 87th Congress, 2nd Session, 1962.

6. *Master Plan*, Delaware Water Gap National Recreation Area, National Park Service, 1966.

7. *Potential Impact of the DWGNRA on its Surrounding Communities*, Washington, D.C.: Robert R. Nathan Associates, February 1966.

8. *Ibid.*, p. 171.

9. *Ibid.*, p. 9.

10. Edwards and Kelcey, *Approach Roads Study, Tocks Island Region*, New Jersey Department of Transportation, April 1969, Parts I and II.

11. *Highway Impact Study, DWGNRA*, Bureau of Advance Planning, Pennsylvania Department of Highways, December 1966.

12. Nathan, *loc. cit.* p. 124 and p. 159.

13. William T. Cahill, Governor of New Jersey, *Statement Concerning the Tocks Island Dam*, September 13, 1972.

14. Letter dated August 1, 1973, from Worth D. Phillips, Corps of Engineers, to Harold Lockwood, acknowledging that the Corps had not found time to revise the recreation benefit downward.

15. Nathan, *loc. cit.*, p. 69.

16. *Audubon*, July 1973, p. 108.

[b]This is complicated, though, because some costs (e.g., most maintenance) are related to mileage rather than time. These are not helped by augmenting use.

17. For a brief survey of electric bus technology, see Hoffman, "Electric Bus Designs for Urban Transportation," *Transportation Research* 6(1972):49.

18. Edwards & Kelcey, *loc. cit.*, Part II, p. 10.

19. Conceptual Development Plan, p. 62.

20. *Ibid.*, p. 29. (TIL-DWGNRA is the "Tocks Island Lake-Delaware Water Gap National Recreation Area.")

21. Nathan, *loc. cit.*, Table 1, p. 63.

Afterword

Both in New Jersey and in the U.S. Congress, the current debate is over whether it is better to defer the Tocks Island Dam or to deauthorize it. A third course—building the dam now—is not in favor. We draw this book to a close with selections from a list of options New Jersey, in particular, was judged to have available, in an artful report submitted to the governor by his Environmental Commissioner.[a] The Commissioner's list will remind the reader of the multiplicity of substantive questions related to the future of the Tocks Island region still to be resolved. The readers who started our book *here* may assume that essentially all the technical issues raised within the list of options below are discussed in more detail in some essay of this volume.

Alternative Courses That the Governor Could Support

Option 1. Support early construction of the project as now designed without any conditions.

Option 2. The same as 1, but on condition that the project not include the park. It would become a water supply and flood control project surrounded by an undeveloped environmental preserve having very low levels of visitation.

---

[a]These points were contained in a discussion paper given to the governor by David Bardin on the day before the DRBC meeting in July 1975 in which the fate of the Tocks Island Dam was, for the time, decided.

Option 3. Support early construction of the project subject to a set of preconditions which can, in fact, be fulfilled. The preconditions would include:

a. The consent of the Basin states to a formal, legally binding entitlement for New Jersey to withdraw an extra 300 mgd from the Delaware for export to the northeast part of the state.
b. Creation of a New Jersey mechanism for paying for the water supply and for exploiting it.
c. Reform of federal land acquisition procedures.
d. The completion of a design for the park acceptable to New Jersey, which includes overnight family camping facilities and a comprehensive program to limit visitation to the level necessary to control adverse impacts in the park and in the surrounding region.
e. Federal assistance to the state and local governments for land use planning and impact relief.
f. Provision of a temporary fish ladder to allow shad to migrate during the construction period.

Option 4. Support construction of the project, but only after fulfillment of a set of preconditions that will be very difficult to meet. The preconditions could include, in addition to those listed under Option 3, the following:

a. The federal government funds Corps of Engineers construction of the intrastate transmission facilities necessary for New Jersey to divert water from the Delaware.
b. The federal government funds 90 percent of the costs of the highway improvements required by visitor traffic connected with the DWGNRA.
c. New York State commits itself to the construction of facilities for tertiary treatment at Port Jervis and the facilities necessary to treat runoff and other nonpoint pollution sources in the upper basin to the levels required to maintain the Tocks Island reservoir in a noneutrophic condition.
d. The federal government funds construction of public transit to the project area from New York and Philadelphia metropolitan areas (including Camden, Trenton, and Newark).
e. Aeration system to be installed in the reservoir to maintain 5 ppm of dissolved oxygen for the sake of fish at the cost of the electric utilities or the federal government.

Option 5. Support the dam project in concept and continued authority for its construction, but build it at a later (specified or uncertain) date sometime near or after the year 2000. During the interim period, land acquisition would be completed, and a river-based park would be put into full operation with a two million visitor per year capacity. Either allow pumped storage to be judged on its own or insist on its delay.

Option 6. Deauthorize the dam project but acquire the remainder of the land and continue with the park.

Option 7. Deauthorize the entire project: the dam, the park, and the pumped-storage project.

Option 8. Same as 7 but directing the Corps of Engineers to get on with the search for alternatives.

Select List of Technical and Economic Studies
on the
Tocks Island Dam Project

Candeub-Fleissig, "Park Concept Plan Based on a Free-Flowing Delaware" sponsored by Save-The-Delaware-Coalition. This plan is intended to demonstrate that the unflooded river and flood plain have at least as much recreational value as the reservoir. It does not propose a wilderness park.

Clarke and Rapuano, Inc., *Conceptual Master Plan for Tocks Island Lake and Delaware Water Gap National Recreation Area,* November 1973. Commissioned by the U.S. Army Corps of Engineers, Philadelphia District and the U.S. National Park Service.

Delaware River Basin Electric Utilities Group, *Master Siting Study:* Delaware River Basin as Related to the Tocks Island Reservoir Project," November 1971. The Delaware River Basin Commission Staff study calculated projected water demands for the Basin in a completely different and much more comprehensible way than had the U.S. Army Corps of Engineers in 1961. The study focused on cooling requirements for power plants, maintenance of water quality in the estuary, and out-of-Basin shipments of water to northern New Jersey as comprising the main future call on Delaware water.

Delaware River Basin Electric Utilities Group, *Master Siting Study: Major Electric Generating Projects, Delaware River Basin, 1972–1986.* Report to the Delaware River Basin Commission, December 1971. Delaware River Basin Commission rules of practice and procedure require that an application for approval of an electric generating project with a design capacity of 100,000 kw or more shall include a "Master Siting Study."

Delaware River Basin Electric Utilities Group, *Master Siting Study: Major Electric Generating Projects, Delaware River Basin, 1974–1988*, May 1974.

M. Disko Associates, *New Jersey Water Supply: Alternatives to Tocks Island Reservoir*, prepared for Environmental Defense Fund, October 1973. This study investigated alternative water supply sources for northern New Jersey, notably one employing the concept of high flow skimming of Delaware River water.

Edwards and Kelcey Inc., "Approach Roads Study, Tocks Island Region;" Part I, April 1969; Part II, March 1971. The Edwards and Kelcey study done for the New Jersey Department of Transportation estimated the cost of the road network that would be required in the impact region to service the expected ten million annual visitors to the Delaware Water Gap National Recreation Area.

G.A. Englesson and R.H. Anderson, United Engineers (Raytheon), "The Impact of Consumptive Use of Water on the Salinity Distribution in the Delaware Estuary," June 1974. Prepared for the Delaware River Basin Electric Utilities Group.

Environmental Defense Fund, *Flood Control and the Delaware River*, April 1973. This study investigated flood control alternatives to the Tocks dam and reservoir.

S. Freeman, E. Mills, and D. Kinsman, "Water Supply and the Tocks Island Dam," (unpublished mimeo, undated).

S. Freeman and W. Schmid, "Supplement to 'Water Supply and the Tocks Island Dam' " (unpublished mimeo, undated).

J. McCormick and Associates, *An Appraisal of the Potential for Cultural Eutrophication of Tocks Island Lake*, September 1971. Under prodding by the Council on Environmental Quality, the U.S. Army Corps of Engineers commissioned this study by an independent consultant group. The study concluded that there *might* be a problem of eutrophication.

R. Nathan Associates, "Potential Impact of the DWGNRA on its Surrounding Communities," February 1966. This study, commissioned by the old New Jersey Department of Conservation and Development, foresaw relatively slight direct impact on the Tocks region, except for jammed roads, but a potentially significant secondary impact from developments impelled by the new roads that the Delaware Water Gap National Recreation Area would require.

M. Pirnie Engineers and Albright and Friel, Inc., *Report on the Utilization of the Waters of the Delaware River Basin,* September 1950, prepared for Incodel.

Save-the-Delaware-Coalition, "Papers in Support of a Free-Flowing Delaware River," October 1973. This report is a compendium of studies, mostly written independently of each other by concerned individuals, on various aspects of the project. It offers alternatives for each of the four purposes: water supply, flood control, power, and recreation.

E. Snyder and A.C. Pastowski, Department of Planning, Conservation, and Economic Development, Sussex County, "DWGNRA Impact on Sussex County," October 1973.

Tippetts-Abbett-McCarthy-Stratton, *Water Resources Study for Power Systems* March 1972, sponsored by the Delaware River Basin Utilities Group.

U.S. Comptroller General, General Accounting Office, "Review of Tocks Island Reservoir Project," Report to U.S. Senate, October 1969. Some members of the Senate Subcommittee on Public Works became concerned in 1969 that the U.S. Army Corps of Engineers was manipulating its benefit cost analysis to make the Tocks project look better than it actually was. The ensuing study by the General Accounting Office did find certain problems in the analysis that tended to diminish the benefit-to-cost ratio.

U.S. Army Corps of Engineers, *Delaware River Basin Report,* House Document 522, Aug. 16, 1962 (in 11 volumes). This report set forth a comprehensive plan for the development of water resources in the Delaware Basin. It was adopted in its entirety by the Delaware River Basin Commission in 1962 and thus has become the comprehensive planning instrument for Basin water resources. The report included the first and still most complete benefit-cost analysis of the Tocks project, which was by far the largest component in the overall plan.

U.S. Army Corps of Engineers, *Environmental Impact Statement on Tocks Island Lake*; draft statement, February 3, 1971; final statement, October 1, 1971. The initial Corps' Impact Statement was but seven pages in length, and in the eyes of many environmentalists, an insulting and arrogant pro-forma compliance with the National Environmental Protection Act. In the aftermath of strong public objection and objection also from the Council on Environmental Quality, the Corps produced a much longer and more complete Impact Statement in the fall of 1971. Appended to the statement were a series of public and agency criticisms of the first impact statement and of the project in general.

U.S. Army Corps of Engineers, *Tocks Island Lake Development: A Comprehensive Evaluation of Environmental Quality, 1971.* An environmental impact analysis of the three components associated with the Tocks project: the dam and reservoir; the Delaware Water Gap National Recreation Area; and the Kittatinny Mountain pumped-storage project.

U.S. Army Corps of Engineers, *Supplemental Data Report and Supplemental Information to the Final Environmental Impact Statement, Tocks Island Lake Project, 1974.*

U.S. Army Corps of Engineers, North Atlantic Division, *Northeastern United States Water Supply (NEWS) Study.* Since 1965, the North Atlantic Division of the U.S. Army Corps of Engineers has been conducting a series of studies (mostly undertaken by contractors of the Corps) on northeastern United States present and long range water needs.

U.S. National Park Service, "DWGNRA Master Plan," 1966; and "Review of DWGRNA," September 1971. These studies sketched the basic plan for the recreational area. This plan of course centered on the reservoir as its chief feature. In this respect it was in direct conflict with the "natural systems plan" described below.

U.S. National Park Service, "A Natural Systems Plan for the DWGNRA," 1971 (anonymous author). This memorandum sketched a plan for the Delaware Water Gap National Recreation Area based on the river rather than the reservoir; it thus provided a recreation alternative were the dam not to be built. It was commissioned by the Assistant Secretary of Interior for National Parks, Outdoor Recreation, and Sports Fishery, a strong dam opponent.

Wapora, Inc., *Tocks Island Lake, Techniques for Water Quality*

Management, 1973. Commissioned by the U.S. Army Corps of Engineers to investigate how to *manage* eutrophication of the Tocks lake if it should occur.

Water Resources Engineers, *LAKECO: A Model of a Reservoir*, December 1972 and *Ecologic Simulation—Tocks Island Lake*, February 1973. The first report describes a mathematical model whose purpose is to predict eutrophication of lakes and reservoirs. It adjoins simple biological equations to an existing temperature stratification model. The second report applies the model, under a contract with the U.S. Army Corps of Engineers, to the Tocks reservoir. The report concludes that with sufficient phosphorous removal the reservoir would not eutrophy.

R.F. Weston, *Tocks Island Region Environmental Study*, April 1970. This report, prepared for the Delaware River Basin Commission, discusses alternative regional sewage systems including very elaborate ones.

URS/Madigan-Praeger, Inc. and Conklin and Rossant, *Tocks Island Lake Project and Alternatives*, July 1975. This was an unprecedented $1.5 million study authorized by Congress and directed by the Corps of Engineers. The study was supposed to be, and in some measure was, the prelude to a definitive decision by the Delaware River Basin Commission on the Tocks project.

Index

About the Contributors

David Bradford, currently on leave as Deputy Assistant Secretary for Tax Policy, Department of Treasury, is Associate Professor of Economics, Princeton University.

Robert Cleary is Assistant Professor of Civil Engineering, Princeton University.

Harold Feiveson is Assistant Professor, the Woodrow Wilson School of Public and International Affairs, Princeton University.

Daniel Goodman is Assistant Professor of Population Biology, Scripps Institution of Oceanography.

Allan Krass is Professor of Physics, Hampshire College.

Michael Reich is a graduate student in Politics, Yale University.

Thomas Schrader is a staff analyst at the U.S. Environmental Protection Agency.

Frank Sinden is a research mathematician at the Bell Telephone Laboratories and Visiting Senior Research Scientist at the Center for Environmental Studies, Princeton University.

Robert Socolow is Associate Professor of Aerospace and Mechanical Sciences, Princeton University.

The Center for Environmental Studies at Princeton University was founded in 1970, and the program of study leading to this book was one of its first undertakings. All of the authors at one time or another were associated with the Center.

DATE DUE	
MAR 17 1981	FEB 04 1994
C T JUN 1998	
ROOM USE	
JAN 4 1994	
RESERVE ROOM	
MAR 1995	
C T MAR 24 1995	

MP 728